Paul B. Kidd is a Sydney-based author, Radio 2UE broadcaster, freelance *60 Minutes* researching producer and photo-journalist who specialises in Australian true crime, fishing, humour and adventure. His articles, interviews and photographs have appeared in most Australian major outdoors and men's publications and in numerous magazines and websites worldwide.

Paul B. Kidd is a recognised authority on Australian serial killers and other criminals who have been sentenced to life imprisonment, never to be released. The author of 14 books on Australian true crime and fishing, he lives in Sydney's eastern suburbs.

More true crime titles by Paul B. Kidd

Never to be Released: Australia's Most Vicious Murderers
Never to be Released: Volume 2
Never to be Released: Volume 3
Never to be Released: Volume 4
The Knick Knack Man: Inside the Mind of Australia's Most
    Deranged Serial Killer
Shallow Graves – The Concealments of Killers
Til Death Us Do Part: Australian Marriages that Ended in Murder
Australian Crime File
Australian Crime File Volume 2
Celluoid Serial Killers: The History of Serial Killers in the Movies
The Mutilator and Australia's Other Signature Serial Killers

Australia's SERIAL KILLERS

PAUL B. KIDD

PAN
Pan Macmillan Australia

First published 2000 in Macmillan by Pan Macmillan Australia Pty Ltd
This revised edition published in 2011 by Pan Macmillan Australia Pty Ltd
1 Market Street, Sydney

National Library of Australia
Cataloguing-in-Publication data:

Kidd, Paul B. (Paul Benjamin), 1945–.
Australia's serial killers – the definitive history of
serial multicide in Australia.

ISBN 978 1 7426 1144 0.

1. Serial murders – Australia – History. 2. Serial murders
– Australia – Case studies. 3. Serial murderers –
Australia – Case studies. I. Title.

364.15230994

Typeset in 11/13.5 pt Caslon 540 by Post Pre-press Group
Printed by IVE

*In loving memory of the victims of serial murder in Australia,
from their families, friends and loved ones.*

Contents

Foreword

by Professor Paul Wilson
from the first edition of *Australia's Serial Killers*

Over the last 20 years, public interest in serial murder has increased dramatically, coinciding with a heightened interest in both popular and professional writings dealing with such crimes.

Australians undoubtedly have an appetite for evil and the macabre, as shown by the success of recent films and books like *The Bone Collector* and *Summer of Sam*. We are fascinated with villains, violence and horror. Why? Probably because they are exciting, sometimes sexually titillating and also because they bring to the foreground those dark and mysterious forces that occupy our nightmares and subconscious mind.

Perhaps the most popular and widespread depiction of serial murder among the general public is Thomas Harris's classic *The Silence of the Lambs*. The book and film not only portrayed the serial murdering character of Hannibal Lecter, but also that of several FBI profilers, and it was perhaps this movie that also brought the latter into the spotlight.

I'm interested in these films and books for the same reasons. But as a forensic psychologist and criminologist, the area of serial murder and criminal profiling has allowed me to examine the motives of those that kill and kill again. Having exposure to these offenders has also prepared me for those occasions when I have been asked to provide profiles of unknown offenders in an attempt to assist law enforcement, or defence lawyers concerned that their clients may have been unjustly charged.

In these times, with technology increasing at an extraordinary rate, we are finding that although our knowledge of the serial murder phenomenon is better than it was previously, we still have a long way to go – a way, I should add, that will be made easier by the concerted effort of authors and researchers in their attempts to summarise case studies, theories and inferences into logical volumes.

And, I would suggest, these books must not be written only for academic and professional audiences, but also for a general audience.

For this reason, I am delighted to be asked to provide the foreword for Paul B. Kidd's book, *Australia's Serial Killers – The Definitive History of Serial Multicide in Australia*. Serial murder is a phenomenon that has, in some way, touched just about every country around the globe – and here in Australia we are no exception. This book comes at an interesting time, when tertiary institutions such as Bond University are beginning to look seriously at serial murder and related crimes and the techniques that can be used to detect those who commit such offences.

Thankfully, serial murder is not a common occurrence in Australia. However, a number of cases – such as the backpacker murders – have proved to be not only resource-intensive but a great challenge to law enforcement agencies. When faced with the prospect of investigating a serial crime, these agencies are often forced to think laterally and draw on new methods in an attempt to reduce public panic and to catch the offender or offenders. This is the point at which psychological profiling may be called upon, and there is no doubt that serial murder is the crime with which this technique is most often associated.

Psychological profiling, as well as forensic techniques like DNA testing, are essential methods for modern-day investigators of serial crime. As Paul correctly states in his book, serial murderers are by nature difficult criminals to apprehend. Some of his case studies show that the perpetrators may change their modus operandi, or method of operation, in a deliberate attempt to throw investigators off their trail. Or they may commit their crimes in such a way that it becomes almost impossible to find behavioural patterns used to link related crimes. As a result, their crimes may go unconnected and uninvestigated for extended periods of time.

It is widely accepted that the United States has approximately 75 per cent of the world's serial murderers, though these figures are difficult to confirm. One thing we do know is that relatively few serial murders occur in Australia, although no-one has yet calculated whether, on a population basis, we have a higher or lower rate of offences than in other developed countries.

Australia's Serial Killers represents the first fully comprehensive survey ever published on Australian serial murderers, and documents their crimes and cases in detail. Paul has spent the last 10 years researching serial murder in Australia, and the material contained within this work is the most comprehensive documentation we have to date. In addition to Paul's previously published *Never to be Released* series, this book, with its vivid descriptions of the crimes and offenders, contributes significantly to the public record of major crimes.

I would once again like to commend Paul on this work. *Australia's Serial Killers* contributes a great deal to the understanding of serial murder in this country and the enormous fear and public concern that this type of crime generates. It is a necessary and useful addition to every Australian true crime enthusiast's library.

On a related topic, it is pleasing to see that criminal profiling is increasingly becoming a major source of attention in the popular media. This is important, as profiling is one of the tools that offers great promise to the investigation of not only murder, but all forms of violent and serial crime. It will be interesting to watch over the coming years how this exposure will affect the professional development of profiling and serial crime investigation. Hopefully, with books like this, we should see greater acceptance and use of this valuable investigative tool.

Professor Paul Wilson
Dean, Humanities & Social Sciences
Bond University, Queensland
30 April 2000

Introduction

In the early 1960s, it seemed as though serial murder was following me around. When I left my home town of Perth in March 1963 to live in Sydney, Perth was under siege by the then unknown serial killer Eric Edgar Cooke, and a month before I left I could well have become one of Cookie's victims.

In the early hours of the morning of 16 February 1963, I was walking past our neighbours' house on my way home at the precise time that Cooke was murdering Lucy Madrill in their backyard, just 100 metres away from our front door. Given that Cooke had previously murdered three complete strangers at random, I considered myself to be very lucky that he hadn't killed me also.

I first became aware of the Mutilator murders when I moved to Sydney in March 1963. William MacDonald was arrested and charged shortly after I arrived. I followed his September 1963 trial closely and, like almost everyone else, I was surprised when the jury found him to be sane. I reckoned that the Mutilator was crazy for sure. Little did I realise then that 37 years later, I would actually get to meet MacDonald and that I would become the only friend he has ever had.

These experiences in the early 1960s had piqued my interest in serial murder in Australia. And in the 16 years that it has taken to research, write and then revise *Australia's Serial Killers*, I have come to realise that very little is known about Australia's serial murderers, both here and throughout the world. The 1999 edition of Michael Newton's *The Encyclopedia of Serial Killers* listed just one Australian serial killer – Ivan Milat. The other recognised world authority on these murderers, *The Encyclopedia of Serial Killers* by Brian Lane and Wilfred Gregg, which claims to be 'the most comprehensive file on the world's serial murderers ever published', lists only 11 of these criminals in our history.

Each of these respected publications is a long way off the mark. A general knowledge of Australia's dark history of serial murder is left wanting because, until now, no-one has ever done a comprehensive study of our cases of serial murder. This is undoubtedly because 'serial killer' is a modern-day term that has gathered momentum only in recent years. Research indicates that the first time the term 'serial killer' was used in popular literature was in the 1981 Thomas Harris novel *Red Dragon*, which went on to become the movie *Manhunter*. Curiously, the term does not appear to have been used in a movie until the serial-killer thriller *Cop* six years later.

But what gave the world its first real insight into the minds of these killers and the people who hunt them was the 1991 screen adaptation of the Thomas Harris novel *The Silence of the Lambs*. It is my belief that this movie had such an extraordinary impact on movie-goers that it deep-etched the term 'serial killer' into our vernacular forever.

Even so, serial murder has been going on for as long as humans have been on this planet. The term 'serial killer' was first coined in the mid-1970s by American FBI agent and murderer profiler Robert Ressler. Until then, serial killers were known as 'repeat offenders', 'spree killers', 'thrill killers', or 'mass murderers' and their crimes were referred to as 'stranger killings'.

Ressler was attending a week of international crime lectures at Bramshill, the British police academy. At one point, the lecturer was discussing what the British police called 'crimes in series' as in a series of rapes, burglaries, arsons and murders that had been carried out by the one person. This reminded Ressler of the serials he saw as a kid on Saturday afternoons at the movies where a cliff-hanging ending would lure him back the following week to see the next episode.

To Ressler, the terms 'serial killer' and 'serial murder' sounded a lot better than 'series' and were an appropriate way of characterising the distinctly episodic activities of those who murder repeatedly. Ressler began to use the term 'serial killer' at his lectures at the FBI training centre's Behavioural Sciences Unit at Quantico, Virginia. The rest is history.

The development of the term 'serial killer' – which excludes killing in times of war and the repeated killings of hired hitmen – also brought about a distinct definition between 'mass murder', 'spree killings' or 'thrill killings', and 'serial murder'. Mass murder usually takes place at the one spot, such as a shopping mall, university, school or a busy thoroughfare. The perpetrator would lie in wait for his victims and then kill as many as possible before he is either killed by police, captured alive, or would turn the weapon on himself, which is most often the case. An example of mass murder is the case of gun fanatic and frustrated soldier Julian Knight, the Hoddle Street murderer who killed seven people and wounded 19 others when he opened fire on motorists and pedestrians at Clifton Hill in suburban Melbourne in August 1987.

In spree or thrill killings, the perpetrator seeks out and kills his victims as he moves about from one place to the next over a period of hours, or sometimes days, until he is either killed, captured or takes his own life. Sometimes the spree killer's victims are known to him, like the case of unemployed labourer Malcolm George Baker, who killed five members of his family and a complete stranger at three different locations over a one-and-a-half-hour period on the New South Wales Central Coast in October 1992.

On other occasions, the spree killer's victims have been strangers, such as the case of drifters Andrew 'Rambo' Norrie and Scott Thompson who, for no apparent reason, dressed in army camouflage greens and loaded up with rifles and ammunition, went on a killing spree in lower Queensland in 1986 that left two people dead and two families terrorised.

Following on from Robert Ressler's creation of the terms 'serial killer' and 'serial murder', Colin Wilson and Donald Seaman, in *The Serial Killers: A Study in the Psychology of Violence* (1992), state that FBI analysts define a serial killer 'as a murderer who is involved in three or more separate events, with an emotional cooling-off period between each homicide'.

But it is respected American criminologist Eric W. Hickey who defines serial murder best in his 1997 university paper 'Serial Murderers and their Victims' by stating that 'the definition of serial murder should include all offenders, male or female, who kill three or more victims over days, weeks, months or years. This cooling-off period is the critical factor that separates the serial killer from the mass and spree killers.'

And, in accordance with these international definitions, each case of serial murder in this book involves at least three victims, and their murders were committed over a period of time – some days, others weeks or months, and yet others years apart. But there are some exceptions to the rule. In the original edition of this book, in 2000, I included the case of Barry Gordon Hadlow who, while he killed 'only' two innocent children, committed the crimes in such an identical fashion and so many years apart there is little doubt that had he not been detected he would have most certainly killed again and again until he was finally brought to justice. Added to the Hadlow exception in this, the revised and updated edition of *Australia's Serial Killers*, are two new cases: those of Mark Mala Valera and Peter Norris Dupas. The reasons for their inclusion are explained in the relevant chapters.

While true-life serial killers are now an inescapable part of our culture, perhaps even more so is the *fictional* serial murderer made popular by such novelists as Thomas Harris, Patricia Cornwell, James Patterson and Michael Connelly, who have a tendency to glamorise, and in some cases almost make us empathise with, their serial killers.

However, we must never lose sight of the reality and the enormity of the crimes committed by the beasts in this book. Because these murderers fall under the label of serial killers doesn't make them anything less than the cold-blooded murderers they are; murderers who have brought untold grief and misery to the families and loved ones of their victims. There are no 'career serial killers' such as the fictitious Hannibal Lecter, John Doe of *Seven*, Connelly's Dollmaker, or a Bone Collector among this lot. Oh no! None of the psychopaths you will read about in this book shaved every hair off their body and wore condoms to avoid DNA detection. Nor did they taunt police with cryptic letters suggesting where the next killing might take place and what type of innocent member of the public would be the victim.

And none of Australia's serial killers is a psychiatrist, detective, journalist, or other alleged intellectual genius as one finds in bestselling novels. This is the real world. Among the serial killers in this book are a grandmother, a soldier, a pie salesman, a housewife, a road worker, a babysitter, a truck driver, a mail sorter and a tourist.

Australia's serial killers are seemingly everyday folks like you and me who, for whatever reason, resorted to multicide by numbers. And rather than plot and scheme their next murder as they do in novels, they blundered from one victim to the next, in most cases leaving glaring clues until they were eventually brought to justice by their own ineptitude or by police diligence.

The real world of serial murder is as barbaric and gut-wrenching as any novel. And in bringing these shocking cases to you I haven't attempted to conceal the horrors that the perpetrators inflicted on the men, women, children and babies that they preyed upon.

It would be very lax of me if I did not mention the enormous contribution to this book by two of my colleagues, crime reporters Steve Warnock and Steve Barrett. With the exception of William 'the Mutilator' MacDonald, it was impossible for me to interview any of the living serial killers in this book because of the strict regulations enforced by the various corrective services throughout the country. So, where possible, I did the next best thing.

Steve Warnock had spoken with the Lonely Hearts Killer, Rodney Francis Cameron, in jail a few years back and his chilling interview is at the end of chapter 16. Steve Barrett was crime reporter with Sydney's Channel 9 at the time of the 'granny killings' in the early 1990s and was granted an interview with their perpetrator, John Wayne Glover, after he had been sentenced to six terms of life imprisonment. That interview is recorded at the end of chapter 22.

I am also very proud of the contribution to this book of two of Australia's leading academics in the world of serial murder, serial-killer profiler and forensic psychiatrist Dr Rod Milton and criminologist Professor Paul Wilson. During the writing of this book, Dr Milton has been an invaluable source of psychological information on serial killers, particularly those in recent years.

And I believe that Professor Wilson's enormous input into the general knowledge of crime in Australia made it impossible for me to ask anyone else to write the foreword. This book would not be complete without their contributions.

Paul B. Kidd,
Sydney, June 2006

CHAPTER 1

The Cannibal Convict

Alexander Pearce
Tasmania, 1822–23

The story of Australia's first recorded serial killer, Alexander Pearce, is a sad and pitiful one. Pearce was an ordinary man whose only crimes, until he was transported to Australia, were theft and drunkenness. His story is one of extraordinary survival; even so, there is no escaping the fact that it is a horrific story of serial murder and cannibalism.

Pearce's own account of the ordeal leaves readers with the impression that it was not he who instigated and committed the horrendous murders, but fellow absconder Robert Greenhill. However, as Pearce was the sole survivor, no-one will ever know whether there was any truth to his story.

After reading the following pages the reader may conclude that Alexander Pearce became a man who had to kill or be killed, a desperate man driven to ravaging human flesh from starvation, a survivor who proved to be the strongest among them because he was the only one to walk out of the forest alive. And considering the circumstances surrounding his survival, it is debatable that his actions could be labelled as serial murder at all. It is what Pearce did after his *second* escape from prison that has labelled him a monster and earned him the dubious honour of being Australia's first serial killer.

Alexander Pearce was born in the county of Fermanagh in the north of Ireland in 1793. A short-statured, blue-eyed, pock-marked Irishman, at the age of 26 Pearce was tried and convicted of stealing six pairs of shoes at the Lent 1819 sessions of the County Armagh Assizes, and sentenced to be transported to Van Diemen's Land on board the *Castle Forbes* for seven years' penal servitude.

Pearce arrived in Hobart Town (now Hobart), Tasmania, in

1820. He was flogged on numerous occasions for absconding from work gangs and getting raucously drunk in taverns. Within two years, Pearce's days as a trusted convict came to an abrupt halt when he was caught for forging and uttering, and absconding into the woods for two months. The court decided that he was incorrigible and he was sent to the newly established penal settlement at Macquarie Harbour, Tasmania, to serve the remaining five years of his sentence.

Macquarie Harbour, an inlet 32 kilometres deep on the south-western Tasmanian coast, was aptly nicknamed 'The Western Hell' by the convicts, and the headlands leading into the harbour itself were named 'Hell's Gates' (so named to this day). The convict settlement was established on Sarah Island, a four-hectare island situated in the middle of the bay.

As the inlet was surrounded by virtually impenetrable woodlands, escape from the settlement was deemed impossible, and yet to ensure the convicts didn't plan on making any such attempts they were flogged regularly as a small reminder of what would happen to them should they get caught.

Escape by sea was thought to be even more difficult. The entrance to Macquarie Harbour is a mere 100 metres wide, but considered unnavigable by small boats as the deadly rips and back currents brought about by the shallow bottom and the bottleneck made attempts to pass through it suicidal at the very least.

The convicts at Macquarie Harbour were kept busy harvesting the rugged Huon pine trees that grew in abundance to the south-east of Sarah Island. Work gangs escorted by armed troopers rowed daily to the mainland in small boats to cut down the huge trees and prepare the timber for sale to the burgeoning local boat-building industry.

Alexander Pearce arrived at Macquarie Harbour in August 1822, and it didn't take him long to realise that he had made a grave error in misbehaving in the large open-plan penal camp environment of Hobart Town. In comparison, Macquarie Harbour was a hell on earth; it offered no relief from the cruelty and misery handed down by the guards.

Less than a month after his arrival, Pearce heard of an escape plan made by fellow convicts and asked to be included. On 28

September, Pearce and convicts Alexander Dalton, Thomas Bodenham, William Kennerly, Matthew Travers, William Brown and John Mathers overpowered their guards and forcibly seized two boats at the timber-cutting site at Kelly's Basin in Macquarie Harbour.

The seven men rowed the two boats to the nearby coal works and met up with Robert Greenhill who had arranged stolen provisions – 10 pounds of flour and six pounds of beef – from the residential huts of the local employees.

The escapees then scuttled one of the boats, proceeded downriver, and took to the land that afternoon. Their intention was to walk all the way to Hobart Town. The journey was sheer madness considering that they had no idea the town was a distance of 110 miles through some of the most rugged and uncharted wilderness areas in the world and without so much as a compass to guide them.

The rain was relentless during the first several days of the journey and it was bitterly cold, making it impossible to light a fire. Soon their clothes were soaked and torn to shreds and their food supplies were consumed.

On the eighth morning, the sun came out and the escapees woke to find that three of their companions – Dalton, Kennerly and Brown – were missing. They concluded that they had left them with the intention of going back to face their punishment at Macquarie Harbour rather than press on in the impossible conditions.

After ten days, the five remaining men were exhausted with hunger and fatigue. Without food supplies they had no choice but to boil up their kangaroo-skin jackets and eat what they could of them.

On the eleventh night, they consulted with each other about the best thing to do for their preservation. They all knew that there was no other choice: one must die or they would all die. They must sacrifice one to keep the others alive.

That night, on 9 October 1822, five desperately hungry men in the Tasmanian wilderness huddled around a campfire and agreed to murder and cannibalism. After the fateful decision was made they nervously drew lots to decide which man would die first. It was Bodenham who drew the short straw and he accepted his fate without question.

The unfortunate Bodenham was granted a few minutes to make his peace with his maker and then the tough young convict Greenhill killed him with a single blow of the axe to the back of the head. He was cut up, cooked over the open fire, and eaten.

The men continued to eat the flesh for as long as it lasted, which was seven more days. Their progress through the scrub was extremely slow; they were impeded at every step by intertwining roots and heavy brush, which restricted their passage to a maximum of about four miles a day. The four remaining men reached a small valley, and they drew lots again to see who would be sacrificed. It fell to the fate of John Mathers.

But Mathers would have no part in it and when Greenhill snuck up behind him with the axe and swung it to kill him, Mathers warded off the blow and wrestled the axe from Greenhill's grasp.

Although the weather had improved, it did little to boost the spirits of the group, and they were in terrible condition. The attempt on Mathers's life had widened the division between them and they paired off for safety – Pearce with Mathers on the opposite side of the campfire to Greenhill and Travers – the idea being that one would sleep while his partner kept an eye on the other pair.

During the night, while Mathers was asleep, Greenhill crept over and killed him with a single blow from the axe. Mathers's remains kept them going for days.

The fourth day after Mathers's death, Travers was bitten by a snake. His leg swelled enormously and he could no longer carry on. He begged them to leave him to die in peace, but Greenhill told him that he was a loyal friend and that he would remain with him in the hope that he would survive. Pearce and Greenhill remained with Travers for five days, and on the sixth day, when he lapsed into a deep sleep, Greenhill killed him with a single blow from the axe and the two men ate Travers's remains for the next couple of days.

Pearce and Greenhill had lost their boots, and what little clothing they had on their bodies was in tatters. They were covered in scratches and sores, but somehow the men made it to the top of the next mountain and couldn't believe their eyes when they saw vast plains stretching below them.

The escapees believed that they were on the verge of a settled district and that food and warm clothing wasn't far away. Their hopes were further boosted when they saw smoke rising in the distance, but when they arrived at the spot they found it to be an Aboriginal settlement with about 50 natives gathered about.

Knowing that they were timid folk and frightened of white men, Pearce and Greenhill yelled and screamed enough to create the impression that they were a party of at least a dozen men and the natives fled, leaving their cooking pots with fresh kangaroo stewing in it. The two men devoured what they could and, carrying as much food as their weak bodies would allow, they pressed on.

The following morning, they had to accept the realisation that they were hopelessly lost. The disappointment of not reaching civilisation for the many weeks they had travelled was bitter and it caused enormous tension between the two men.

Over the ensuing days, together they raided more Aboriginal camps, filling themselves with kangaroo meat and taking as much food as they could carry. But as the food supplies again grew scarce and the hunger pains took over, each man eyed the other, knowing where his next meal had to come from if he were to survive.

The fact that Greenhill had possession of the axe and literally guarded it with his life kept Pearce on razor's edge. Pearce claimed that he awoke one night to see the shadowy figure of Greenhill creeping towards him with the axe raised high above his head. Feigning a nightmare, Pearce sat bolt upright and Greenhill sank back into the darkness. From then on, Pearce never shut his eyes for a second.

Pretending to be unaware of Greenhill's motives, Pearce made certain that his travelling companion lapsed into a false sense of security and, at the first opportunity – when Greenhill fell asleep – Pearce slipped the axe out from his grasp and killed him with several determined blows to the skull.

The grim job done, Pearce settled down to feast on his deceased adversary and built up his strength over the next four days. When it was time to move on, he took a thigh and an arm, which sustained him for another four days.

A week after he had murdered Greenhill, Pearce's fortunes

seemed to change. He miraculously captured two ducks with his bare hands and ate them raw. He then came across a flock of sheep in the bush, a sure sign that he had reached civilisation. He eventually cornered a lamb, killed it with his hands, and fed on its flesh.

As he was eating, a dog barked behind him and he turned around to find a cocked musket pointed at his head. What a sight the semi-naked and barefoot little Irishman with the heavy beard must have been to the shepherd, Tom Triffet, who had bailed him up! When Pearce told Triffet that he had escaped from the new convict settlement of Macquarie Harbour on the other side of Tasmania and had made it to the outskirts of Hobart Town on foot, the man lowered his gun in disbelief and took Pearce to his hut where he nursed him back to health.

One the eleventh night, after Pearce had fully regained his stamina, there was a knock on the door of his hut. It was two escaped convicts named Ralph Churton and William Davis who had turned bushrangers. When they discovered that Pearce had also escaped, they had little trouble in persuading him to join them. Pearce left a note of thanks to his benefactor and took off with the two men to their hide-out deep in the woods where they kept a small arsenal in two huts and a flock of 180 stolen sheep – enough provisions to feed an army.

Within six weeks Pearce and his fellow convicts found themselves surrounded by a party of armed troopers from the 48th Regiment with the specific job of rounding up bushrangers. They tried to make a run for it, but it was useless: Pearce and Churton were captured immediately. When Davis offered resistance he was wounded in the ensuing shoot-out and captured.

Alexander Pearce had been on the run for 113 days when he was taken into Hobart Town in irons on Saturday, 11 January 1823. Retribution for the bushrangers Churton and Davis was swift and they were tried and hanged seven weeks later.

Curiously, although he was caught in the company of the two bushrangers, Pearce was not tried for bushranging. Instead, he was taken back to Macquarie Harbour where he arrived to a hero's welcome and, incredibly, even though he had readily told the authorities of the murders and cannibalism, he was only flogged, sentenced to a term of solitary confinement, restricted to wear heavy irons, and kept under close surveillance.

Of all of the accounts of Alexander Pearce's escape and recapture, none are clear as to why he was returned to Macquarie Harbour when his escape and survival could only have been encouraging to other convicts, why he didn't receive additional years in prison on top of his original sentence, or why he wasn't given a more severe punishment – if not indeed hanged – for his crimes. The most commonly accepted theory is that the authorities simply didn't believe Pearce's outrageous confession. They thought that he was protecting his fellow escapees who were still living in the bush and would turn up at any time. Pearce had produced absolutely no evidence to substantiate his account, so it would be difficult to sentence a man to hang on the strength of the story alone.

In the wake of his ordeal and his new celebrity status within the prison, it is quite feasible that Alexander Pearce could have easily lived out the remainder of his sentence at Macquarie Harbour and set free to return to Ireland or start a new life in Hobart Town. But that was not to be the case. Nine months after his re-incarceration, Pearce escaped with Thomas Cox, a young former farm labourer from Shropshire, England, who was transported for life in 1819 and hero-worshipped Pearce.

Who persuaded whom to escape has never been truly established and Pearce steadfastly maintained that Cox was the instigator. But in view of Pearce's track record, the reader can only assume that it was Pearce who convinced the besotted Cox to abscond with him for ulterior motives.

Five days after their escape, the crew of the schooner *Waterloo*, passing down Macquarie Harbour, saw a figure waving vigorously from the shore. They rowed towards the figure in a dory and immediately recognised the man as Alexander Pearce, the escapee.

Pearce informed them that Cox had drowned when they had tried to swim a river. Pearce was searched and, to the horror of his captors, a raw piece of meat, clearly that of a human being, was found in his pocket. In his other pockets were found items of 'normal' food that would have sustained Pearce for days, eliminating the possibility of his eating human flesh out of starvation.

Pearce led his captors to the mutilated body of Cox in nearby scrub. When asked by Lieutenant Cuthbertson if he had murdered the man, Pearce replied: 'Yes, and I am willing to die for it.'

At his trial back in Hobart Town for the murder of Thomas Cox, Pearce claimed that when they arrived at a river that had to be crossed he discovered, to his annoyance, that Cox couldn't swim and a violent argument followed during which Pearce picked up an axe and killed Cox with it. With the dead body at his feet, the urge to eat human flesh came over Pearce and he immediately reverted to cannibalism.

'I ate part of him that night and cut up the greater part of his flesh in order to take it with me,' he told the court.

But Pearce, guilt-ridden, could not proceed and signalled the passing schooner. The court heard that Pearce was tortured by an over-burdened conscience and was also half demented.

Pearce was found guilty of murder and sentenced to hang. On the eve of his hanging, he confessed to Father Philip Connolly that he was weary of life and that he wanted to die for the misfortunes that had fallen upon him and the atrocities that he himself had committed.

On the morning of 19 July 1824 at Hobart Town Gaol, the little Irishman with the pock-marked face was hanged by the neck until he was dead. Before he was hanged, Coxswain Smith of Macquarie Harbour asked him to account for his actions and Alexander Pearce answered: 'No man can tell what he will do when driven by hunger.'

AUTHOR'S NOTE: After his death, Alexander Pearce's head was separated from his body, and 30 years later it mysteriously turned up in a huge collection of skulls owned by American Dr Samuel Morton, who had a fascination in the science of phrenology (based on the now discredited theory that bumps on the exterior of the human skull reflected the character of the subject). From there Pearce's skull, minus the teeth and lower jaw, found its way to the Museum of the University of Pennsylvania where it is currently on exhibition to the general public.

CHAPTER 2

The Berrima Axe Murderer

John Lynch
New South Wales, 1840–41

Situated in the southern highlands of New South Wales, about an hour-and-a-half drive from Sydney along the old Hume Highway, the village of Berrima, population 300, is a welcome sight for the many tourists and interstate travellers who choose to stop for a relaxing short break before resuming their journey.

Steeped in history, there are many places to visit in the picturesque village, including numerous arts and crafts shops, a museum, and the old courthouse. Visitors can also enjoy a refreshing cup of tea and delicious country-style scones in Berrima's charming cafes, or a cold beer at Australia's oldest hotel, The Surveyor General, if the journey allows the time.

In the heart of the village is Berrima Gaol, today a minimum-security prison that is home to many long-term prisoners who are no longer considered a risk to the public. Berrima is the last step of their incarceration on their way back into mainstream society. At the entrance to Berrima Gaol there is an arts and crafts shop that specialises in selling items made by the prisoners.

But the laid-back country village of Berrima was once a thriving business centre. And it was here that the most prolific serial killer in Australia's history roamed almost 150 years before the term 'serial killer' ever existed, murdering at will until he was finally brought to justice, tried at the Berrima Courthouse, and put to death on the gallows in Berrima Gaol.

The extraordinary story of the unfolding of the Berrima axe murders and the ultimate capture of John Lynch, convict, bushranger and serial killer, began on the morning of 19 February 1841. Drover Hugh Tinney, on his way to Sydney with a team of bullocks, stopped near the Ironstone Bridge just outside Berrima and noticed a dingo fossicking around a pile of brushes and trying to get at whatever was concealed beneath.

The local police were summoned, and closer inspection revealed the body of a man whose skull had been pulverised at the back, suggesting that he had been bashed to death with a heavy, blunt instrument, most likely an axe or a tomahawk. The man was lying on his back with a smile on his face, indicating that he had been in good humour as he was attacked from behind and had no idea of what hit him.

From items found on his person by the police, the man was identified to be a local farmhand named Kearns Landregan, who was last seen in the company of a farmer named Dunleavy. The pair had dinner two nights earlier at the Woolpack Inn at Nattai, not far from where Landregan's body was discovered.

The trail led to a nearby farm once owned by the Mulligan family but now owned by a John Dunleavy, who had allegedly bought the property from the family for £700 before Mr and Mrs Mulligan and their teenage son and daughter mysteriously packed up and left town without telling a soul.

The barmaid from the Woolpack Inn identified the mysterious farmer Dunleavy as a local whose real name was John Lynch. With other irrefutable evidence gathered by police, on 21 February 1841, John Lynch was charged with the murder of Kearns Landregan. But even in the light of the overwhelming evidence against him, Lynch steadfastly maintained his innocence in the belief that he would be exonerated and freed.

On 21 March 1842, Lynch appeared before the Chief Justice of New South Wales, Sir James Dowling, at Berrima Courthouse. After all of the damning evidence was heard, it took the jury only an hour to find him guilty of murder.

After the verdict was handed down, the court heard that Lynch was also incriminated in the murder-disappearances of at least another eight people in the district with whom he was seen, or known to have been associated, at the time they went missing.

The court also heard that Lynch had narrowly escaped the gallows in 1835 when, as an active bushranger, he had been incriminated in a murder committed in the district but, miraculously, had come out of it unscathed even though he had admitted his guilt.

That was not to be the case this time. Sir James Dowling had no hesitation in sentencing Lynch to death by hanging. But before passing sentence, Justice Dowling said: 'John Lynch, the trade in blood which has so long marked your career is at last terminated, not by any sense of remorse, or the sating of any appetite for slaughter on your part, but by the energy of a few zealous spirits, roused into activity by the frightful picture of atrocity which the last tragic passage of your worthless life exhibits.

'It is now credibly believed, if not actually ascertained, that no less than eight other individuals have fallen by your hands. How many more have been violently ushered into the next world remains undiscovered, save it in the dark pages of your memory.

'By your own confession it is admitted that as late as 1835 justice was invoked on your head for a wilful murder committed in this immediate neighbourhood. Your unlucky escape on that occasion has, it would seem, whetted your tigrine relish for human gore, but at length you have fallen into toils from which you cannot escape.'

John Lynch stood unmoved in the dock, a smirk of defiant indifference on his face as the judge announced: 'You are sentenced to be hanged by the neck until you are dead.' Not even the harsh words from the judge and the death sentence could dampen the optimistic Lynch's belief that he would be reprieved and eventually set free.

Lynch steadfastly clung to the story that he was innocent. But it was to no avail, and only after every avenue of appeal was exhausted, on the eve of his execution, did he confess to his crimes. In his confession, Lynch said that he believed that he had gone about his robbing and killing under the watchful eye of God and with His divine approval.

John Lynch called the Reverend Mr Summer and police magistrates to his cell to witness his full confession. It was a confession that rocked the fledgling colony of New South Wales to its foundations and ensured John Lynch's place in the annals of Australian crime forever.

A diminutive but solidly built man of just five-foot-three with a rugged complexion and brown hair, John Lynch was aged just 19 when he was sentenced to deportation for stealing offences in County Cavan, Ireland, where he was born. He arrived in Australia in 1832 on the convict ship *Dunregon Castle*. After working as a convict labourer at numerous farms in the area he joined a renegade gang and became a bushranger, robbing and stealing about the countryside and selling his ill-gotten gain around the district.

Lynch's close shave with the hangman in 1835 was over the murder of Thomas Smythe shortly after Smythe had given evidence against Lynch's bushranger gang. Lynch and two other bushrangers were tried for the murder, and even though he had admitted to taking part in killing Smythe, the jury chose not to believe him. He was set free while the other two bushrangers were found guilty and hanged.

One of Lynch's customers for the stolen property was a farmer, Mulligan, and in his confession Lynch maintained that it was a dispute over the price of some of these items with Mulligan at his farmhouse that started him on his career as a multiple murderer.

Lynch approached Mulligan for payment for stolen goods that he was holding for him, but Mulligan was prepared to pay only about a quarter of what Lynch was asking. A bitter argument ensued, and Lynch stormed off swearing revenge.

He went to a farm at nearby Oldbury where he had once worked for the owner, a Mr T.B. Humphrey. He stole an eight-bullock team and drove them off. 'I'd broken them myself,' Lynch said in his confession. 'I took them because I wanted to start out again honest. I intended taking the bullocks to Sydney and selling them.'

But it didn't take long for Lynch to forget about his 'honest new start' and lapse back to his thieving ways. 'At Razorback Mountain,' Lynch said, 'I met a cove named Ireland and fell in with him.'

Ireland was travelling with an Aboriginal boy. Together they were driving a full bullock team and its load of wheat, bacon and other produce to Sydney in a delivery for its owner, a Mr Thomas Cowper, who was unknown to Lynch.

'It seemed to me,' said Lynch in his confession, 'that it would pay me better to kill Ireland and take possession of the dray and its load of saleable produce than to drive Mr Humphrey's bullocks to Sydney.'

Ireland took quite a liking to the diminutive Irishman Lynch, and when they pulled up for the night he prepared him dinner and finished off the evening with one of Ireland's cigars. All the while Lynch was plotting how to murder Ireland and his young helper and make off with their wares.

According to Lynch's confession, it was at this time as he lay awake beneath the Southern Cross that he consulted God and sought His approval for what he was about to do. Lynch didn't make it clear whether or not God actually gave His blessing to the forthcoming massacre, but, seeing as he had at least consulted God in the first place, he said this was as good as getting the go-ahead and that the good Lord would look after him.

The following morning Lynch asked the boy to help him round up his bullocks. The lad was only too happy to oblige. As the boy walked ahead in the scrub and well away from the camp, Lynch crept up behind him and, with a tomahawk he produced from inside his jacket, he smashed in the back of the lad's head. 'All it needed to kill him,' Lynch said, 'was just one tap with the tomahawk. He dropped like a log of wood.'

Lynch returned to the camp to find Ireland preparing breakfast and, rather than murder the unsuspecting farmhand immediately, he explained that the boy had run off looking for the bullocks and they should eat without him.

When breakfast was cooked and Ireland was about to serve it up, Lynch distracted his attention by pointing to the scrub. Ireland turned his back to look and Lynch cracked his head open with the tomahawk. As the man lay dead at his feet, Lynch wolfed down a hearty meal before dragging both bodies to a cleft between two rocks and covering them with brush and stones.

Lynch pointed the stolen (Humphrey's) team of bullocks and dray in the direction of Berrima and set them loose, anticipating that someone would round them up and return them to the Oldbury farm and nothing would come of it. He then took possession of Ireland's team with the farm produce.

With the good Lord looking over his shoulder, Lynch could see no hurry in continuing his journey and remained at the camp for two more days. On the second day he was joined by two men named Lagge and Lee who were in charge of a team of horses.

Lynch said he thoroughly enjoyed the company of the two men and they ate, drank and sang songs well into the night. The men even performed an Irish jig for Lynch's entertainment. It was for these reasons that Lynch didn't attack the men with his tomahawk and steal their possessions as they slept.

The following morning, unaware of their narrow escape from death, Lagge and Lee invited Lynch to travel behind them for company, an offer which he readily accepted. As they approached Liverpool on the outskirts of southern Sydney, Lynch said that he nearly died of shock when a man cantered his horse alongside him and the dray and asked him what he was doing driving his team. It was Thomas Cowper, the owner of the rig for which Lynch had murdered Ireland and the boy.

As quick as a flash Lynch smiled at the man and replied: 'I'm glad I've seen you. I was just wondering whether I'd knock into you. The fact is that your man Ireland was taken ill back there and begged me to take the load to Sydney for you. He said I'd probably meet you somewhere along the way.'

Lynch explained that he had left the boy to look after Ireland overnight at the camp and that they were probably slowly making their way back home. Cowper expressed his gratitude to Lynch for having taken the load of perishables on ahead towards Sydney.

Thomas Cowper's gratitude deepened when Lynch was only too happy to continue to Sydney with the dray and its load while Cowper went back to search for Ireland. Silently thanking the Lord for looking after him through the close shave, Lynch arranged to meet Cowper in Sydney in a few days' time and drove the bullocks on ahead until he caught up with Lagge and Lee. The men parted company at the junction of Liverpool Road and Dog Trap Road, as Lagge and Lee turned in the opposite direction and headed towards Parramatta.

Now that he was no longer travelling in tandem, Lynch made good progress, and by driving all day and night he reached Sydney two days before his scheduled time to meet Cowper. He realised that he had no time to lose, as Cowper would come looking for him when he could not locate his missing employees and most likely call the troopers.

Lynch employed the services of a drunk to sell the produce so that he could not be incriminated at a later date, and if questioned by police, he could stick to his story about Ireland being taken ill and the produce being stolen from the back of the dray while it was unattended.

After pocketing the cash from the sale of the farm produce, Lynch headed south out of town along the Illawarra Road towards the Berrima Road. Once again, he was presented with yet another incident that astonished him, which further convinced him that the Lord was on his side.

'As I neared the George's River, I saw Chief Constable McAlister of Campbelltown and, fearing he'd recognise me, I turned into a cross track leading towards the Berrima Road,' Lynch said in his confession. 'This close shave frightened the living daylights out of me and I decided that I would get rid of Cowper's team at the first opportunity, as it could only eventually get me into trouble.'

As Lynch approached Razorback Mountain, where he had killed Ireland and the boy, he met the Frazers, a hard-working father-and-son pair who were making their way towards Berrima in a team owned by a Mr G. Bawten.

Lynch took an immediate fancy to the team and, from the minute he was in the Frazers' company, he was plotting their deaths and the disposal of Cowper's team. He would claim the Frazers' team as his own.

He travelled with the Frazers to a campsite at the Bargo Brush where two married couples were already camped. 'We all had supper,' Lynch said, 'then I crawled under my dray with the intention of sleeping. No sooner had I got there than I saw a trooper ride into the camp. He asked Frazer if he had seen the dray I had stolen from Cowper and Frazer shook his head and said he didn't know nothing about it.

'The trooper didn't see me under the dray,' Lynch said, 'and, much to my surprise, he rode off.'

Lynch said that his escape was nothing short of a miracle, and if the Cowper dray had been painted bright pink it couldn't have stood out any more. But even though it was under the trooper's nose, he didn't notice it. And Lynch had the good fortune to be concealed beneath it when the trooper arrived. It was almost too good to be true.

Yet again the Lord had intervened and saved Lynch from apprehension. He believed that he was invincible and could go on killing as he desired. Lynch claimed to have consulted with the Lord, who told him that in the light of his narrow escape the Frazers had to be killed and Lynch must take possession of their team.

As part of his murderous plan, during the night Lynch set his bullock team free and in the morning he and the Frazers woke to find that the bullocks had scattered far and wide. 'My team appears to have strayed,' Lynch told the Frazers in the morning. 'I'll have to go home and fetch another one. Meanwhile, I'd better hide the dray. Could you give me a hand?'

The unsuspecting Frazers were only too happy to assist John Lynch, unwittingly, in his scheme to murder and rob them. Lynch said that, after the three men had hidden the dray, 'I helped them hitch their horses to their cart and we drove out of Bargo Brush. They agreed to let me travel as near as possible to the place where I was supposed to live.'

With the incriminating Cowper team and dray successfully disposed of, Lynch relaxed and concocted his plan to murder the kindly father and son, and with God to guide him he figured it wouldn't be too hard.

They travelled until dusk, when they reached Cordeaux Flat, and made a camp for the night. 'In the morning, young Frazer and I went in search of the horses,' said Lynch. 'I put on my coat so as to hide the tomahawk. I let the youngster go ahead. Then, when we were in the bush, I thought to myself, there's no difficulty in settling him. So I crept up behind him and hit him with one blow.'

The boy died instantly and Lynch hid the body beneath some wood and returned to the camp with one horse. Mr Frazer inquired as to the whereabouts of his son.

'When I told him he was looking for the other horse,' Lynch said, 'he became agitated, not because he suspected I killed the boy, but because the horses had never strayed before.'

Lynch distracted Frazer by pointing to what he said was his son in the bushes and, when the man turned to look, he hit him 'a nice one on the back of the head and he dropped like a log of wood.'

After thanking the Lord for His assistance in murdering the father and son, Lynch dragged their bodies into the bush and buried them in a shallow bush grave. He hitched their team of horses to the dray and headed towards the Mulligan farm to settle an old score.

As he rode up to the farmhouse, he saw Mrs Mulligan sitting in a rocking chair on the porch. She asked where he got the horses and dray and he replied that they belonged to a man in Sydney. Lynch asked after her husband and son and daughter and Mrs Mulligan told him that they were in the fields, working.

'What do you want?' the woman inquired.

'The £30 your husband owes me,' he replied.

'What £30?' Mrs Mulligan asked.

'You know very well what – for the articles which I got from burglaries and highway robberies I did at the risk of my life and which your old man was supposed to be holding for me,' Lynch said.

'There's only £9 in the house,' Mrs Mulligan replied, giving Lynch the impression that she was fobbing him off until she could talk to her husband.

In his confession Lynch said: 'I was much discouraged by her putting me off but I didn't show it. Being a fair man, I decided to wait until her husband returned and give him the chance to pay me my money, and if he refused then I would see to it that he would get to meet the Almighty.'

Lynch then elected to walk to the Black Horse Hotel at Berrima and buy some rum in the belief that it would get Mulligan in the right frame of mind to pay him the money. On his return he saw Mr and Mrs Mulligan together on the verandah and they greeted him in a friendly manner.

Mrs Mulligan fetched glasses for the rum and they sat on the verandah drinking and chatting. Lynch eventually brought up the matter of the £30 to which Mr Mulligan asked him to be reasonable about the amount. Lynch left the verandah and sat brooding on a log nearby, deep in consultation with the Lord about what he was going to do next. According to Lynch, the Lord gave his blessing to murder them.

After Mr Mulligan had returned to the fields and Mrs Mulligan had disappeared back into the house, Lynch lured their young son Johnny into the woods on the pretext of cutting some wood for his mother. Once out of sight, Lynch killed the boy with a single blow from his axe to the back of his skull, covered his body with brush, and returned to the farmhouse.

'Where's Johnny?' Mrs Mulligan inquired.

'Gone to the paddock with the horses,' Lynch said.

According to Lynch, he knew then that Mrs Mulligan suspected he had murdered her son and she became hysterical and told Lynch to fire his gun to attract attention.

'What's all the urgency?' he asked. 'He's all right. I only saw him a few minutes ago.' But the woman insisted that Lynch shoot his gun to indicate to anyone within earshot that all was not well.

'But if I do, it will alert the police,' Lynch said, as Mr Mulligan approached and asked what was going on. They were both suspicious of Lynch's actions now and, in fright, Mrs Mulligan disappeared back into the house while her husband headed towards the woods in search of his missing son.

He didn't get far. Lynch ran up behind him and, with one swing of the axe, felled him to the ground, stone dead. After dragging his body into the woods, he saw Mrs Mulligan coming towards him, and as she ran into the woods he tripped her up and killed her with a blow to the head from the axe.

Lynch knew that the Mulligans' 14-year-old daughter was in the house. As he entered, he saw her standing in the kitchen in terror, having seen at least one of the murders committed.

'I saw her standing behind a table holding a butcher's knife,' Lynch confessed. 'She was sobbing with fear and trembling violently. I hadn't been prepared for this, so I just stood there staring at her. Then I yelled, "put that knife down!" but she didn't move so I yelled again, "put that knife down!"

'She stiffened, her eyes bulging fearfully from their sockets, with a strange animal noise squealing from her tightly compressed mouth. The lobes of her nostrils were flared and she stood there impotent with terror.

'"Put that knife down," I told her. "I don't want to kill you, but if I let you live you'll only put me away." I then ordered her to get down on her knees and pray as she only had 10 minutes to live.'

Lynch then took the terrified young girl into the bedroom and raped her repeatedly. 'I then brought her back out into the kitchen and tried to comfort her, saying that life was full of trouble and that she'd be better off dead. Then I mercifully distracted her attention and, as she turned away, I struck her with the axe and she fell dead without a murmur.'

Lynch then assembled the Mulligan family's bodies in the bush and set them alight atop a huge pyre of branches and logs. 'They burned like bags of fat,' he said.

From then on, Lynch's confession focussed on his cleverness at getting rid of the Mulligans' possessions and taking over the farm as his own. Every personal item and all of the deceased family's clothing were burned. He then inserted an advertisement in the *Sydney Gazette* stating that Mrs Mulligan had left the family home without her husband's consent and that he, John Mulligan, wouldn't be responsible for her debts. It gave the impression that the Mulligans had broken up and it would come as no surprise that under these circumstances the farm had been sold. Next, Lynch, again under the name of John Mulligan, wrote to all his creditors telling them that he had sold the farm to a John Dunleavy for £700 and Dunleavy had taken responsibility for any outstanding debts. He forged a deed of assignment stating that John Mulligan had signed over the farm and all its affects to John Dunleavy.

With all in order Lynch became squire Dunleavy and, considering that he was very well known throughout the district and still moved about freely (though this time under the name of John Dunleavy) without anyone becoming in the least bit suspicious about the name change, Lynch probably couldn't be blamed for thinking that God truly was looking after him.

Lynch even hired a couple, Terence and Clara Barnett, to run the farm for him while he took the produce to the markets. The bodies of the four Mulligans he had murdered hadn't been discovered and no-one seemed to be looking too hard for them.

For the next six months Lynch lived a charmed existence and had it not been for making the diabolical mistake of murdering the Irishman Kearns Landregan, he could have quite possibly lived out his life on the Mulligan farm and no-one would have been any the wiser. John Dunleavy, aka Lynch, was a good farmer who was loved by his staff and trusted by his creditors and was, from all accounts, a gentle and considerate human being.

The only reason Lynch could give as to why he committed his ninth murder in such a slovenly manner, leaving clues and witnesses all over the district, was that he was absolutely convinced that he was under the protection of a supreme being and therefore beyond capture. The normally thorough Lynch hadn't even gone to the trouble to prepare an alibi for the Landregan killing.

In his confession Lynch told of the circumstances leading up to the murder of the Irishman. He met Landregan on his way back from Sydney one day and offered him a fencing job on his farm. As they passed Crisp's Inn, Landregan hid himself and explained to Lynch that Crisp had summonsed the Irishman for stealing a bundle of clothes from him and he didn't want to be seen.

'After I heard that I was determined to get rid of him,' said Lynch. It was an amazing motive for murder, considering Lynch's own history of theft and armed robbery. The reader can only assume that, having transformed himself into the respectable farmer John Dunleavy, Lynch now considered that such thieving rabble were best put to death.

After they had dinner together at the Woolpack Inn, which was witnessed by all of the staff and numerous patrons, Lynch drove Landregan to the Ironside Bridge, where they set up camp for the night. As Landregan sat on a log chuckling away to himself at a joke that Lynch had told him, Lynch snuck up behind the unfortunate man and cracked him over the back of the skull with his tomahawk. But the huge Irishman didn't die with the first blow, said Lynch. He just rolled to the ground unconscious with the smile still all over his face. It took a couple more blows to smash in the back of his skull and kill him. Had his body not been found, it is feasible that Lynch's divine luck might have held and the killings would have gone on.

Towards the end of his confession to killing Landregan, Lynch admitted to taking £40 from the dead man's pockets. This threw a completely different light on Lynch's motive for murder. It seemed that it was robbery and greed, after all, that was John Lynch's undoing.

John Lynch was hanged at Berrima Gaol on 22 April 1842. With the gruesome tally of nine victims, he is Australia's most prolific individual serial killer.

CHAPTER 3

The 'Rough on Rats' Murderess

Martha Needle
Melbourne, 1885–94

Few, if any, serial killers in the world have matched the grisly deeds of Martha Needle, who murdered her entire family over a six-year period.

To add to her crimes, when Martha became lonely as a consequence, she found herself a new lover and began killing off *his* family. Had it not been for a bit of good fortune on behalf of her last intended victim, Martha could very well have done away with each member of her lover's family as well.

Martha was born in South Australia on 9 April 1863. In 1880, as a ravishing 17-year-old, she married her childhood sweetheart, 22-year-old carpenter Henry Needle. Two years later, the happy couple moved to Victoria and settled in a house in Cubitt Street in Richmond, a suburb of Melbourne, where Martha gave birth shortly after to their first child, Mabel.

On 28 February 1885, three-year-old Mabel died after suffering from a mysterious two-month illness that reduced her once-healthy little body to skin and bone. Martha Needle was inconsolable over her daughter's death. Outwardly, she lapsed into bottomless fits of depression and cried for hours at a time. In private, she found enormous consolation in the arrival of a cheque for £100 – a sizeable amount in those times – from the insurance company with whom she had taken out a policy against Mabel's life shortly after her birth.

Two more daughters, May and Elsie, were born in quick succession to the passing of Mabel, but despite the joyous occasions it was obvious to many who knew the Needles that their marriage was a disaster. Henry Needle was a brooding, quick-tempered man who didn't think twice about taking his hand to his wife if the occasion suited him. It was 'over-the-back-fence' neighbourhood gossip that Henry beat Martha regularly and didn't allow her to go out and enjoy herself. He treated his wife as his slave, expecting his meals to be prepared on time and the children to be spick-and-span for his inspection when he arrived home from work.

With a sneaking premonition that Henry wasn't going to be around much longer, Martha secretly took out an insurance policy on his life for £200, just in case any mysterious disease should befall him and leave her and her two daughters without a breadwinner.

Incredibly, shortly after the policy was taken out, Henry Needle fell ill and his body rapidly deteriorated, even though his loving wife nursed him and maintained a bedside vigil. Desperate for a way to return her husband to good health, Martha summoned one doctor after the other to his bedside, but each walked from the room baffled as to what the mysterious disease could be and collectively concluded that it was liver failure.

A distraught Martha Needle collapsed when the doctors finally conceded that there was nothing they could do for her husband, but she rallied what little strength she had left to care for him until he drew his final breath on the morning of 4 October 1889.

As there were no suspicious circumstances, the doctors promptly agreed that the cause of Henry's death was 'inflammation of the liver and intestines', and it was written on the death certificate.

Curiously, the grieving widow's attitude towards her late husband changed soon after the funeral. She made no secret of the fact that she wasn't sorry he was dead. After the continual beatings, she realised that she had chosen the wrong man and the marriage wouldn't have survived, anyway.

Now a wealthy widow with the insurance money, Martha Needle turned her talents to running a boarding house from a large residence she rented in Richmond. The business was at first very profitable until Martha grew tired of the daily grind, and in October 1890 she closed up and moved to a nearby cottage with her two children in favour of a more relaxed lifestyle.

And in the unforeseen circumstance that anything should happen to her youngest daughter, four-year-old Elsie, Martha took out an insurance policy for £100 on her life. The ink on the policy was hardly dry when the child came down with a mysterious ailment that soon had her plump, cherubic little body deteriorate into mere skin and bones. Again Martha Needle had to go through the torment of maintaining a bedside vigil beside her daughter as the doctors informed her that the child was dying of an incurable 'wasting disease' and that it was only a matter of time before she, too, would join her sister and father at the cemetery.

On 9 December 1890, frail little Elsie succumbed to the illness and passed away. Neighbours and friends rallied around and pitied the distraught Martha, who had lost her husband and two loving daughters to such a cruel and unrelenting assortment of unusual diseases. Yet somehow Martha dragged herself out of the depths of her grief to check the letterbox every day for the insurance money so that she could start a new life with her one remaining daughter, five-year-old May.

For the following six months, little May and her mother consoled one another over the loss of their family. And just in case the extraordinary run of bad health in the Needle family should continue and anything should happen to May, leaving Martha in need of funds to bury her girl and tide herself financially through the grieving process, Martha took out an insurance policy, this time for the lesser, yet still sizeable, amount of £60.

And the continuation of bad health is exactly what happened. Just six months after the passing of Elsie, May was stricken with a mysterious illness and became bedridden. The child grew thinner and her illness worsened by the day and when the doctors gave her no hope of survival, this time diagnosing the illness as incurable 'tubercular meningitis', the sobbing Martha sat beside her daughter's bedside day and night until she slipped away in the morning hours of 27 August 1891. Incredibly, once again the circumstances were not considered suspicious by the doctors and a post-mortem was not conducted.

Without a family and few friends to speak of, the 29-year-old Martha became lonely. Soon she found company in her employ as a housekeeper for two brothers, Louis and Otto Juncken, who owned and operated a very successful saddle- and whip-making shop in Richmond.

Martha lived with the brothers in the premises above the business and, after rejecting the older Louis's advances towards her, started a relationship with Otto who was many years her junior. Soon the couple were seen at the theatre and dining and dancing together regularly. It was obvious that the young leatherworker had become besotted with the family servant.

As the relationship between Otto and Martha became more intense, the rejected and insanely jealous Louis did his best to discourage it. Just as he was making life difficult for the couple by attempting to bully his younger brother into giving her up, in August 1893, Louis was stricken with a mysterious illness that confined him to bed and weakened his body to the point where he could hardly move.

Casting all family differences aside, the devoted housekeeper Martha turned to her nursing skills and, miraculously, assisted Louis back to health. Otto was amazed at her dedication and for a short time Louis was extremely appreciative of her unfailing help through his illness. From then on the three of them seemed to get along very well.

But when he heard that Otto and Martha planned to wed, soon Louis's jealous rages re-emerged and before long the household fell back to much bickering and backstabbing.

In a desperate attempt to break up the young couple, Louis took Otto to a holiday resort, but returned two weeks later to find Martha in bed, supposedly about to draw her last breath, and a suicide note in the kitchen. *When my body is found*, it read in part, *let me be buried with my children.*

This was enough for the lovesick Otto, who proposed to Martha there and then at her bedside. As he knelt with her frail little hand in his, stroking it gently, he said: 'Promise me you will never try to take your own life. As soon as you are feeling well, I want you to marry me.'

The older and wiser brother, however, could see through the charade and summoned a higher power to adjudicate. He made Otto promise that he would not marry the household servant until their mother had been brought up from Adelaide to give Martha the 'once-over'. If she approved of the union, then he would concede defeat and give them his blessing.

But on 24 April 1894, just when he thought he was on the verge of getting rid of the 'hussy' who had entranced his younger brother, Louis again fell mysteriously ill and was soon bedridden with severe attacks of vomiting and chronic stomach pains.

Again Martha nursed him, but this time he showed no signs of improvement and just when the doctors feared that he would die, a relative by marriage, Mrs Jones, arrived unexpectedly on 30 April and personally took charge of nursing poor Louis back to health.

By 8 May, Louis had fully recovered and was out of bed and his usual argumentative and troublesome self. Considering her job well done, Mrs Jones left him back in the care of the doting Martha, but four days later the vomiting and chronic stomach pains recurred after Louis ate a hearty breakfast Martha had prepared for him. This time there was no recovery.

Louis Juncken struggled with the illness until 15 May and it was only his strong physique and will to live that saw him linger so long. On his death certificate the doctor wrote that he had died of 'inflammation of the stomach and the membranes of the heart'.

Two days later, another brother, Hermann, arrived from Adelaide with Louis's mother and the pair took an instant and intense dislike to the housemaid intending to marry Otto, who happened to be out of town on business at the time. It didn't take long for the arguments to erupt, and when her fiancé returned Martha was surprised to find that he not only sided with his family against her but also suggested that Martha move out immediately and that his mother and Hermann move in with him instead.

The spurned Martha left the Juncken household swearing revenge and left Otto a very uncomplimentary farewell note signed *your cast-off housekeeper*. The now unattached Martha Needle rented a cottage nearby and was surprised to find that one of her first visitors was Hermann Juncken.

Hermann explained that the reason for his visit was that, while he understood that legally there was no way he could stop her and his brother Otto from marrying, he had decided to try and convince her that the union was not a wise one. Otto was so young and it would be in everyone's best interests if she bowed out gracefully and left his family in peace.

While Hermann was putting his case across, Martha was on her absolute best behaviour. He couldn't help but notice what a sweet woman she was and wondered to himself if perhaps he may have misjudged her. When Martha cordially asked him to call again in the not-too-distant future, Hermann readily accepted and it was only a matter of days before he was again knocking on her door on the pretext that he had family business to discuss with her. He was ushered inside and made extremely welcome by the gushing Martha, who had even prepared tea and scones straight from the oven for him. But as soon as Hermann took a mouthful of tea to wash down the scones and homemade strawberry jam, he became so violently ill that Martha had to call for the local Dr Boyd to make an immediate house call. Fortunately, the doctor arrived in time to administer an emetic, and undoubtedly saved Hermann's life.

Puzzled by the mysterious attack, but never for a second suspecting foul play from the angelic Martha, Dr Boyd took Hermann home and put him to bed under the watchful eye of his doting mother. Within three days Hermann was out of bed and knocking on Martha's door to pick up from where they had left off.

This time, when Hermann swallowed the tea the attack of nausea was a dozen times worse than it had been three days earlier, and if Hermann hadn't noticed Dr Boyd's buggy two doors away from the Needle residence as he knocked on Martha's door, there is little doubt that he would have died there and then. It was an extraordinary piece of luck that saved his life and would send Martha Needle to the gallows.

In chronic pain, Hermann staggered to the neighbour's house where Dr Boyd was making a very timely house call and the doctor performed emergency treatment on him which, without a doubt, saved his life. But Dr Boyd wasn't prepared to accept the second attack as another stomach upset. This time, he was convinced that Hermann had been poisoned and sent away samples of his vomit to be analysed. His hunch was right. The samples showed traces of the deadly and fast-acting poison arsenic.

Dr Boyd and Hermann Juncken went to the police, and after they told detectives of the poisoning attempt and the deaths of Louis and Martha Needle's entire family they decided to set a trap for the murderess.

That same afternoon, 28 May 1894, Hermann Juncken again called on Martha Needle for tea and scones and a friendly chat. Only this time, as she handed him his cup of tea, police suddenly appeared and grabbed her as she frantically tried to wrench the cup from Hermann's hand and upset the contents. Realising that the game was up, Martha made a dash for a bottle of chloroform and threatened to swallow it.

'Are you trying to kill yourself?' asked one of the detectives, as he seized the bottle from her hand.

'I would be much more likely to do that than poison anybody else,' Martha replied defiantly.

Martha Needle had been caught in the act as few murderers in history had been caught before. The facts were irrefutable: analysis of the tea destined for Hermann Juncken's stomach would reveal that it contained 10.46 grams of arsenic, enough to kill five grown men.

But where did she get it? A search of the house unearthed a tin of Rough on Rats rodent poison. The label read: *This product induces certain death*. Friends would later recall that over the years there always seemed to be a tin of Rough on Rats in the Needle household.

Charged with the attempted murder of Hermann Juncken, Martha Needle was safely behind bars as the police set about exhuming the bodies of Louis Juncken and Henry, Elsie, and May Needle. In light of the circumstances, it didn't come as a surprise when every one of them showed traces of arsenic.

From information gathered about the circumstances leading up to the deaths of her previous victims, police and forensic experts concluded that Martha Needle had given them drinks laced with just enough Rough on Rats to keep them progressively sick until the doctors declared that they had no hope of survival – thus ruling out the possibility of an autopsy – before she administered the final and fatal dose.

And in the light of these revelations, astonished doctors,

police scientists and the investigating officers could only arrive at the terrible conclusion that, apart from the obvious motive of greed, Martha Needle thoroughly enjoyed watching her victims – which included her three very own daughters – die in excruciating pain. It is little wonder then that to this day Martha Needle is recognised as one of the most ruthless, cold-blooded and calculating female serial killers of all time.

The police considered the circumstances surrounding Louis Juncken's death to provide the most solid evidence and proceeded with charging Martha Needle with his murder. Commencing on 24 September 1894, Martha Needle was tried before Mr Justice Hodges in the Melbourne Criminal Court. The evidence was damning and the result was a foregone conclusion.

The only witness who had a good word for the woman who had murdered her whole family and then tried to kill his was Otto Juncken, who broke down and told the court of Martha collapsing in tears when she visited her children's graves. Poor deluded Otto's explanation for Martha's murderous behaviour was that she sometimes took fits and wasn't aware of what she was doing. And, as if to give the court a demonstration of this, Martha went into a fit in front of the jury and remained in a trance-like state for five hours.

But the farce convinced no-one, especially the judge and jury who returned with a guilty verdict in no time at all. In sentencing her to death, Justice Hodges didn't mince his words: 'Martha Needle, it is not my intention to give you one moment of suspense. If your conscience is not already at work, nothing that I say will have any effect.'

When His Honour announced the words 'you will be hanged by the neck until you are dead', Martha Needle appeared to collapse and, as she was supported by wardresses, she managed a smile and said to them: 'I am alright, thank you. Please let me alone.'

In the month she was in the death cell awaiting her execution, Martha Needle vigorously protested her innocence, but it did her no good. On 22 October 1894, she was led to the gallows in Old Melbourne Gaol to receive her punishment for the murders of five innocent people.

As she mounted the gallows Martha Needle calmly held her head high and refused all offers of religious comfort. She had saved some advice for the hangman as her final words. 'Don't strap me in too tightly,' she said. 'I know that I shall go off easily. In a case like this, you see, the quietest death is the quickest.'

Martha Needle then fell silently to her death.

AUTHOR'S NOTE: The legend of Martha Needle did not end in her execution. She became posthumously infamous in Melbourne, most likely due to her unusual name, Needle, and the brand of toxin that she used – the Rough on Rats rodent poison – rather than her actual crimes, as horrendous as they were.

In 1940, a Melbourne newspaper reported that a group of Melbourne citizens had combined to form a group called the Melbourne Bread and Cheese Club. Their intended headquarters was to be a house in Cubitt Street, Richmond. When they discovered that it was the actual house where Martha Needle had murdered her husband and her daughter Mabel, the members elected to adopt Martha as their 'patron saint'. They commissioned a portrait of her holding a tin of Rough on Rats, which was hung in pride of place in the premises.

In 1993, a Bruce Thomson play about the life and times of Martha Needle, entitled *The Eye of Martha Needle, La Mama*, was performed at the Fringe Arts Festival. Produced by Ariette Taylor, the play focused on Martha Needle's relationship with the three Juncken brothers. The play began in Martha's cell in the last hour of her life and flashed back in time to such elaborate scenes as a last supper complete with candelabra, silver service, and birds in cages hanging from the ceiling.

The *Age* review of the play in March 1993 read: *On opening night the production opened uncertainly, as the actors negotiated the cramped surroundings. By the end it was running much more smoothly. Jane Longhurst had her moments as the young and spirited title hero, though the performance as a whole was somewhat strained. There were good performances from the men, especially William Gluth as the righteous chaplain and Greg Stone as the near-victim. Rebe Taylor did nicely as the singer-commentator. In the end Martha Needle remains a mysterious and enigmatic figure. We can be sure of one thing, however. She did not wipe out her entire family. For Wednesday night's audience included her great-grandnephew. What he thinks of his infamous forebear may be a story in itself.*

Readers may find it hard to imagine how anyone could refer to Martha Needle as 'the young and spirited title hero'. Obviously the reviewer had no idea of Martha's hideous crimes. Either that, or Martha was portrayed as 'young and spirited' by the playwright. The latter seems to be the obvious answer, though it is doubtful that her victims saw her in such a fashion.

CHAPTER 4

The Baby Farmers

John and Sarah Makin – Sydney, 1892
Frances Knorr – Melbourne, 1893
Alice Mitchell – Perth, 1900–06

At the turn of the twentieth century – as it would be for many years to come – single mothers were frowned upon by society. To have a child out of wedlock, the unfortunate mother would have to bear the brunt of open ridicule and social exclusion.

There was hardly an alternative, as contraception was unavailable and abortion clinics were few and far between. Even then, the methods used for termination were so poor that those women fortunate enough to arrange one ran enormously high risks of contracting serious infection, becoming sterile, or even losing their own lives during the procedure.

And so, as babies were kept, the practice of 'baby minding' became a profitable business. Few mothers were willing to have their child adopted out, so they would place the baby in the care of a child-minder who ran a nursery in a large house with hired staff. For a nominal weekly or monthly fee the baby would be looked after and the parent, or parents, could visit their progeny on a regular basis. Once the child had grown to a manageable age, he or she could be introduced as a niece or nephew of a deceased relative and grow up without the attached stigma of being labelled a bastard and the mother a whore.

The vast majority of baby-minding centres throughout Australia were run and assisted by honest and decent women – trained nursing sisters who genuinely loved babies and cared for them as would the natural mother given the time or the means. But to an unscrupulous few, the growth in the area meant the opportunity to cash in on the misfortunes of others. It made it easy for these child-minders to sell babies to childless couples desperate for a baby of their own, take the money and conceal it from the natural mother.

It gave others the opportunity to take the mother's money for care, food and doctor's bills and let the child live in squalor and eventually die an agonising death from starvation, neglect and disease.

To others still, it became the opportunity to profit from murder. These serial infant killers became known as 'baby farmers'.

John and Sarah Makin
Sydney, 1892

On 11 October 1892, drainer James Hanoney was digging in the soft earth to clear an underground drain in the backyard of a house in Macdonaldtown, an inner-city suburb of Sydney, when he found the cause for the blockage. It was two bundles of evil-smelling clothing. Baby clothing. He removed the offending material and, to his horror, found the decomposing remains of two babies. He immediately called for the police, who uncovered the putrefying corpses of yet another five infants in various parts of the backyard.

Through tenancy records, detectives traced the abode of the previous tenants of the cottage, 50-year-old John Makin and his wife, 47-year-old Sarah Makin, to a house in nearby Redfern where they uncovered the buried remains of more babies. When police eventually tracked the Makins down to their new family home in nearby Chippendale, they found more dead babies buried in the backyard, bringing the grisly tally to 12.

The entire Makin family of Sarah, John and their four daughters, Florence, 17, Clarice, 16, Blanche, 14, and Daisy, 11, were placed under arrest. John and Sarah Makin were charged with murder.

The Makins' trial was held in the Sydney Supreme Court. The courthouse was packed to overflowing each day and the huge crowds waiting outside were constantly updated by runners with the progress inside the court. The defence told the court that the Makin family were professional child-minders who looked after babies for a weekly fee until the mother came to take the child away, or until they found suitable parents for babies up for adoption. In some cases, the Makins arranged it so that a mother could still visit her baby after a new home and loving parents had been found for the child.

Then the prosecution put the record straight and told the court that, in theory, this was all very well, but this had not been the case with the Makin family at all. The Makins found it easier and much more profitable to murder the babies, continue collecting a weekly contribution from the mother and, at the same time, keep her from seeing her baby by deception.

The first witness was Amber Murray who, as an 18-year-old, had given birth to an illegitimate son, Horace, in March 1892. Unable to care for the child on her own, she offered him up for adoption in an advertisement in the *Sydney Morning Herald* which said, in part, that she was seeking a kind and loving mother to adopt her baby boy. The ad stated that she was prepared to pay a weekly premium for the child's support.

She received a reply from a married couple in the working-class suburb of Redfern, Sydney, who said that they would love to take the child on for a premium of 10 shillings per week.

Amber Murray called in at the address the following day and met John and Sarah Makin and two of their daughters, all of whom fell in love with little Horace on the spot. They said that they had lost a little boy of their own and couldn't wait to take him into their home and give him all of the love and attention that he wanted.

Amber Murray didn't find it unusual that there were five or six other babies in the house, and the Makins explained them away by saying that they were just minding them for friends for a short time. Amber Murray left Horace with the Makins after they had made a deal that she would pay the 10 shillings each week on the proviso that she would be permitted to visit little Horace from time to time. It was agreed. It would be the last time she would ever see baby Horace alive.

John Makin called in each week as regular as clockwork to collect the 10 shillings from Amber Murray, but every time she asked to see her boy she was put off with some excuse or another.

Collecting the premium for Horace one day, John Makin told Amber that the family were moving to Hurstville in the southern suburbs and he would forward her the address after they had settled in, in about six weeks' time. In the meantime, he still called in each week to collect the 10 shillings.

But the Makins didn't move to Sydney's southern suburbs at all. Instead, they took a house in nearby Macdonaldtown and moved in clandestinely in the dead of night. Later, at the trial, daughter Clarice Makin would give damning evidence that when they moved from Redfern to Macdonaldtown there was no sign of little Horace Murray. Although she didn't use the exact words, it was inferred that tiny Horace had already been murdered while John Makin continued collecting his weekly premium.

The Makins did not stay long at the house in Macdonaldtown and, in August, they moved to Chippendale where they were eventually arrested after drainer James Hanoney made his horrifying discovery on 11 October 1892.

Amber Murray and three other grieving mothers identified clothing that had been pawned by Sarah Makin as belonging to their babies. It was clothing that they had brought to the Makins especially to keep their little loved ones warm, and they had left bundles of it with the family.

Another couple testified that they delivered their illegitimate child to the Makins and gave them a considerable 'up-front' payment, also agreeing to pay 10 shillings a week until they had sorted out their affairs and could take back the baby. Within days the baby had died and the grieving parents gave the Makins two pounds towards the funeral, which the family did not attend.

In the witness box, the Makins were damned as their lies were torn to shreds by the prosecution. Time and again when they denied any knowledge of keeping any babies, of murdering babies, or taking weekly premiums from the parents, they were caught up in their own web of deceit until even their own children chose to go against them.

Sixteen-year-old Clarice Makin took the stand and testified against her parents by identifying clothing found on one of the dead babies as clothing she had seen in her mother's possession. Eleven-year-old Daisy Makin testified that only two baby girls accompanied them when they moved from Redfern to Macdonaldtown, inferring that little Horace Murray had been murdered and buried at Redfern.

The verdict was inevitable and the only penalty was death. As Mr Justice Stephen sentenced John and Sarah Makin to death by hanging, he looked at the pair in the dock and, in reference to baby Horace Murray, said: 'You took money from the mother of this child. You beguiled her with promises which you never meant to perform and which you never did perform, having determined on the death of the child. You deceived her as to your address and you endeavoured to make it utterly fruitless that any search should be made and, finally, in order to make detection impossible, as you thought, having bereft it of life, you buried this child in your yard as you would the carcase of a dog . . . No-one who has heard the case but must believe that you were engaged in baby farming in its worst aspect. Three yards of houses in which you lived testify, with that ghastly evidence of these bodies, that you were carrying on this nefarious, this hellish business of destroying the lives of these infants for the sake of gain.'

He then passed the death sentence. John Makin held up his wife as she collapsed in the dock. His Honour promised to pass on to the Executive Council of New South Wales the jury's recommendation for mercy on Sarah Makin.

After two appeals were dismissed, John Makin went bravely to his death on the gallows. Sarah Makin won her reprieve and was sentenced to life imprisonment with hard labour. She was released in 1911 after serving 19 years behind bars and faded into obscurity.

None of the Makin children had a conviction recorded against them.

Frances Knorr
Melbourne, 1893

In September 1893 in the Melbourne suburb of Brunswick, Mr Clay, the new tenant of a house that had been empty for three months, decided to turn the backyard into a vegetable garden. As he began digging, to his horror, just below the surface of the unkempt backyard, he unearthed the decomposing remains of a baby girl. Around the infant's neck was a tightened length of rope.

Police were immediately summoned to the house to examine the find. Neighbours also pointed out to them a house nearby where the previous tenants had also lived, and when they dug around the garden there, police found another two decaying infants, both boys, buried just beneath the surface.

The previous tenants of both addresses, Mr and Mrs Knorr, had recently moved to Sydney and weren't hard to find. They had found a house in Brisbane Street in the inner-city suburb of Surry Hills and were picked up by police within days of the discovery of the three tiny bodies and extradited to Melbourne to face the authorities.

Autopsies revealed that the little girl had died of strangulation and the two tiny boys had been suffocated. Rudolph and Frances Knorr had a lot of questions to answer.

Police learnt that Frances Knorr was born Minnie Thwaites in Chelsea, London, of a highly respected, God-fearing family. An unruly child and promiscuous teenager, she was sent from the family home to do her best in Australia and arrived in Sydney in 1887, aged 19.

She changed her name to Frances and fell in love with Rudolph Knorr, a German waiter whom she met while she was working as a domestic servant. Rudolph was well known to police in both Melbourne and Sydney as a petty criminal.

They married and had a daughter named Gladys. After a series of misadventures in which Rudolph did 18 months in Pentridge for fraud and Frances had an affair with an Edward Thompson with whom she lived for a time until he cast her aside, they reunited and turned to the new industry of child minding for a living.

It wasn't hard to do. Any woman with a child or children of her own who could get away with claiming to be a nurse could take babies in on a long-term, full-time basis. The usual deal was that the mother would make an initial down payment of between five and 20 pounds and then make a smaller monthly payment. In return, the infant would be cared for and the mother would have access to her baby at pre-arranged visiting times.

The trouble with such loose arrangements was that often the mother would turn up to find the child-minder had taken her down payment and gone missing, presumably having sold the baby, and numerous others, to childless couples for an extortionate sum, and set up business again in another suburb or state.

Child minding, or 'baby farming' as it would become known after the scandals of the deaths and sales of babies were made public, was indeed a fatalistic industry. In Victoria in 1893, there were over 60 inquests into the deaths of babies that had been found dead when abandoned or had died through neglect. More than 20 of these cases were treated as murder, but the perpetrators were usually long gone and no-one was charged with a capital offence. Many more infants had gone missing without trace, presumed sold.

Frances Knorr was known at numerous addresses throughout Melbourne during her child-minding career and didn't stay in the one place too long. Many women wanted to have a word with her about their missing babies but were too frightened to report it to the police for fear of being exposed as single mothers.

As they arrived at her house to arrest her, Sydney police found Frances Knorr in bed about to give birth to her second child. After it was born in custody, the Knorrs were taken under armed escort to Melbourne aboard the steamer *Burrumbeet*.

The inquest into the death of one of the baby boys – discovered to be Isaac Marks – found in the backyard in Brunswick was held in Melbourne Morgue in October 1893. The doctor who examined the deceased infant said that a tape that had been drawn around his neck was the width of a sovereign coin, thus limiting the breathing capacity and causing the baby to suffocate.

Among the 33 witnesses called was a 13-year-old nursemaid who had worked for Frances Knorr on and off for several years. Her evidence was damning. She recalled Frances Knorr borrowing a spade from a neighbour and then complaining that the front garden was too rocky and that she would have to dig in the back garden instead.

The jury heard evidence that Frances Knorr had so many dealings with unwed mothers who were reluctant to come forward, swapping babies and farming babies out to other child-minding centres at reduced rates, that she found it almost impossible to keep a track of what was going on. She had even pretended that her own baby, Gladys, belonged to another mother and that she was minding it for her.

After the inquest was held into the deaths of the bodies found in the backyards of two of her previous lodgings, Frances Knorr was committed for trial on three counts of murder. But even in the face of the indisputable evidence, she steadfastly denied murdering the babies or having anything to do with their burial.

At her trial the prosecution was swift to play its trump card and produced a letter that Frances Knorr had written from her cell in Old Melbourne Gaol to the lover who had cast her aside, Edward Thompson, asking him to fabricate certain evidence on her behalf. The letter was given to police by Edward Thompson's mother.

It was also a crude attempt by Frances Knorr to incriminate Eddie Thompson and have authorities believe that he was in some way responsible for the deaths and burials of the children. Frances Knorr wrote to Thompson urging him to pay a particular man and a woman money to say falsely that they had buried the child they had together, who had died of consumption. She said in the letter that the woman would confirm this in court and clear them both of any wrongdoing.

Thompson denied knowledge of any such involvement and the police believed him. When this ploy failed, Frances Knorr dramatically changed her evidence in the middle of the trial. She admitted to burying the babies in the backyard and that they had died of natural causes. This was a total contradiction to the evidence extracted in the autopsies, which proved that they had definitely been murdered.

At the end of her five-day trial, Frances Knorr was found guilty and sentenced to death by hanging. As she sat back in the dock sobbing at the sentence, she turned to Edward Thompson who was sitting in the court and screamed: 'God forgive you for your sins, Ted! God help my poor mother! God help my poor babies.'

In the days leading up to her hanging, Frances Knorr embraced God and finally confessed to her sins of murder. 'Placed as I am now within a few hours of my death, I express a strong desire that this statement be made public with the hope that my fall will not only be a warning to others but also act as a deterrent to those who are perhaps carrying on the same practice. I now desire to state that upon the two charges known in evidence as Number 1 and Number 2 babies, I confess to be guilty.'

Although the Melbourne hangman, Thomas Jones, appointed to hang Frances Knorr had a record of sending 15 men to their deaths on the gallows, he wasn't too keen on the prospect of hanging his first woman, who also happened to be the first woman to be hanged in Victoria in 30 years, so he took to the bottle. Two days before Frances Knorr's execution date, Tom Jones committed suicide by cutting his own throat while in a drunken stupor.

But the hanging was still scheduled to go ahead with a new hangman despite the desperate pleas of hundreds of Melbourne citizens for a reprieve on the grounds that it was inhuman to hang a woman who was also a mother.

From the Sunday night on the eve of her hanging until 10 o'clock the following morning, Monday, 15 January 1894, a crowd of 200 protesters gathered outside Old Melbourne Gaol and sang hymns and petitioned for a last-minute reprieve. But the government stood its ground and the execution would go ahead.

As the execution party reached the scaffold to await the arrival of the condemned woman, they heard hymns being sung from her cell in a strong yet plaintive voice. Frances Knorr had been singing hymns since dawn and continued to do so as she walked the few paces from her cell to the scaffold unaided, had her hands and feet tied, and the noose placed around her neck.

She stopped singing only in the last few seconds to say in an unbroken voice: 'Yes. The Lord is with me. I do not fear what men may do to me, for I have peace, perfect peace.'

Then Frances Knorr, killer of defenceless babies entrusted to her care, dropped the two-and-a-half metres to her instantaneous death.

After Frances Knorr was hanged, authorities assessed that, given the period of time that she was in the child-minding business and the amount of women who clandestinely came forward later and told police that they had given her their babies, she could have murdered as many as 13 of the unfortunate infants.

Alice Mitchell
Perth, 1900–06

It was the illegitimate birth of a baby girl, Ethel, in 1906 to Elizabeth Booth at the House of Mercy in Perth, Western Australia, that ultimately led to the exposure of serial infant killer Alice Mitchell.

Once she had taken babies into her care and received the mother's money, Alice Mitchell left the infants to wallow in squalor unfit even for farm animals. Eventually, 37 babies left in her charge died, either due to Alice's negligence or outright murder.

The House of Mercy in Highgate Hill, Perth, was run by Catholic nuns as a refuge for unmarried mothers. The rules of the house were strict, and three months to the day after Elizabeth Booth had given birth to the bouncing, healthy little Ethel she was bid farewell by the kindly nuns and sent out into the world to fare for herself and her infant.

As she had no intention of adopting Ethel out, and the father had fled, the only alternative left to Elizabeth Booth was to work to provide for them both. But seeing as she had little education and had only ever really worked as a house servant to wealthy families – who would not accept a mother *and* child on the payroll – Elizabeth had no choice but to find alternative accommodation for her baby and try and visit her as often as her working hours would allow.

The baby lodgings that were recommended to her were just around the corner from the House of Mercy at 24 Edward Street, East Perth. It was run by a friendly, plumpish, middle-aged nursing sister named Alice Mitchell, who showed the new mother around some parts of the premises.

Feeling it was safe to leave her baby with nurse Mitchell, the two women agreed on a price of five shillings a week, five shillings for vaccinations and an additional five shillings for every doctor's visit, which would always be carried out by the same medical practitioner, Dr Officer.

Three days later, the mother called in to see her baby and was told that Dr Officer had examined the infant and that she was in excellent health. The accounts were settled and Elizabeth Booth left for her new job as a housemaid content in the knowledge that her beloved daughter was in the best possible hands and that she could drop in and see her whenever time allowed.

Forty-four days later, baby Ethel was dead. The innocent infant became another victim of what would become the most infamous case of baby farming in the country. And if it wasn't for Alice Mitchell's greed and then Elizabeth Booth's determination to find out what happened to her child, there is little doubt that the practice would have continued for a lot longer and many more babies would have died.

The chain of events that led to Alice Mitchell's downfall started when another mother fell behind in her payments, and Alice Mitchell summoned the police to call in the debt. The police constable was unsure about what to do in such a civil matter, so he called in his boss, Sergeant Patrick O'Halloran, who visited Alice Mitchell at her boarding house and demanded to be shown around.

What the sergeant saw appalled him. In his official report of the inspection he said of one baby: 'The child was in an appalling condition. Pus was coming from its eyes, it was fly-specked, extremely wasted and giving off an offensive odour.'

Sergeant O'Halloran returned with a government medical officer who, also appalled at the filthy conditions behind the closed doors – never seen by the mothers themselves – pronounced that the child that Sergeant O'Halloran had commented on in his report was close to death. It was Elizabeth Booth's baby daughter. The infant died two days later.

Heartbroken over the death of her once-healthy baby, Elizabeth Booth went to the police and told them that she suspected foul play.

Interviewed about her arrangement with Alice Mitchell, Elizabeth Booth said that she usually called in late at night after she had finished her work. Each time she was put off from seeing her child on the excuse that the bub was asleep and could not be disturbed. After weeks of being put off she finally demanded to see her child and was shocked at the sight. The baby was a crying bag of bones and was covered in sores from head to foot. It was the last time that she would see little Ethel alive.

Armed with information taken from the inspection of the

premises and the death of Elizabeth Booth's baby, police began a full investigation into the child-minding practices of Alice Mitchell. The discoveries would shock the nation and once and for all bring a close to uncontrolled child minding.

Since 1900 Alice Mitchell had run a number of baby-lodging establishments in Perth and had moved from one address to the next as things got too hot for her. Adult boarders in her establishments told police of rooms full of babies lying on the floor in their own excrement and piles of used, unwashed napkins riddled with maggots left in the corner. The stench from the rooms was unbearable and flies laid their eggs in the weeping sores on the children's faces and bodies. The babies were allowed to crawl out into the backyard where fowls were kept, immerse themselves in the mud, and eat the chicken droppings that littered the yard.

As the investigation progressed, it was revealed that over the six years that she had been in business, 37 infants had died at the hands of Alice Mitchell, yet not a word of it had reached the ears of the police. And investigators had little doubt that the death toll was a lot higher, but no further records could be found among the squalor.

What amazed police the most was how on earth 37 babies could have been buried by their grieving mothers without the authorities becoming aware of it. It was law that a coroner's certificate be issued before any burial could proceed and the police notified. Yet not one such certificate had ever been issued following the deaths of the babies in the care of Alice Mitchell.

To the astonishment of police and Health Department officials, it was discovered that the undertakers did not know such documentation was required. And it wasn't just an isolated incident with the one funeral director. The four main Perth funeral directors all claimed that they were unaware that coroner's certificates were required and had carried out 37 funerals – ironically, some at the government's expense – for babies from the establishments of Alice Mitchell without the inkling of a suspicion that all might not be in order.

In a complete whitewash of the most prolific case of the serial murder of babies in the world, Dr Officer, who was the only doctor to service the babies in Alice Mitchell's charge, claimed that he had never noticed anything irregular about the conditions at Alice Mitchell's establishments.

Further, a Miss Lenihan, the council Health Department inspector who was in charge of such establishments in the area and whose job it was to do regular and thorough check-ups on the babies and their conditions, said that she heard about the odd death from time to time but it wasn't anything worth reporting to her superiors. And in spite of the huge amount of evidence to the contrary, Miss Lenihan maintained that Alice Mitchell's establishments were always found to be in satisfactory condition.

On 12 March 1907, at a coroner's inquest, a three-man jury found that 'the child Ethel Booth died from wilful starvation and culpable negligence by Alice Mitchell'. The coroner, Mr Cowan, said that the case was 'the most revolting ever dealt with. It is loathsome, disgusting, filthy and monstrous'.

Alice Mitchell was arrested and charged with the wilful murder of Ethel Booth. During her trial it was revealed that there were a number of people in high places who were negligent in their duties. It left a nation wondering how so many could overlook the blatant fact that the cold-blooded murder of babies was being carried out under their very noses, and no-one was prepared to do a thing about it for fear of incriminating themselves.

The lady inspector of health, her superiors, the doctor, the undertakers and many more people in prominent positions were paraded before the court and reprimanded in the sternest possible way.

But without the bodies, the evidence, witnesses to actual murder, people willing to talk, the result was always going to be a good one for the serial murderess of babies. Alice Mitchell escaped the charge of wilful murder. Instead, she was found guilty of the manslaughter of little Ethel Booth and was sentenced to five years' hard labour. The case so appalled the nation that it was the catalyst for the tightening of the laws governing the regulation of baby-minding clinics across Australia.

CHAPTER 5

The Windsor Murderer

Frederick Bailey Deeming
England and Melbourne, 1891–92

Frederick Bailey Deeming was one of the most despised serial killers in Australia. While investigating the murder of Deeming's wife in Melbourne, police inquiries led detectives to England, where it was discovered that he had committed other incomprehensible murders.

Deeming was so loathed for his horrific crimes that on his execution day a crowd of 12,000 citizens gathered outside Old Melbourne Gaol and when it was announced that Deeming was dead they let out an uproarious cheer.

The outrageous story of Frederick Deeming's crimes first came to light on 3 March 1892 when police were called to investigate a vile smell coming from an unoccupied house at No. 57 Andrew Street in the Melbourne suburb of Windsor.

Inside, beneath a hearthstone of the fireplace and embedded in cement, uniformed police unearthed the decomposing body of a young woman aged about 30. A post-mortem revealed that her throat had been cut and she had been dead for about three months. There was no sign of blood anywhere in the house.

The two detectives assigned to the case, detective sergeants William Considine and Henry Cawsey, immediately set about checking out the previous tenant of the cottage, who had vacated the premises a few weeks earlier. The letting agent told them that the premises had been let to a man named Druin and local tradespeople came forward with a solid description of the missing man.

An ironmonger who had delivered some cement, a broom, a trowel, a closet pan, and a spade to Mr Druin a few weeks earlier described him as being in his mid-thirties, of medium height, slight build and fair-haired, with a fair, reddish beard and a large distinctive moustache. The ironmonger also couldn't help but notice that the flamboyant Mr Druin wore a lot of jewellery and spoke loudly with a Lancashire accent.

Tracing a torn luggage ticket they found in the house, Considine and Cawsey learned that Mr Druin, travelling under the name of Albert Williams, had arrived in Melbourne from the United Kingdom on 9 December 1891 on the passenger vessel *Kaiser Wilhelm II* with his young wife, Emily. When questioned by detectives, other people who had taken that voyage had no trouble recollecting the loud, boasting, oafish behaviour of Mr Williams, who bored anyone who would listen to his obviously fictitious adventures to every corner of the globe. He also repeatedly offended the ship's crew by accusing them of stealing his valuables. The passengers and crew were very pleased to see the back end of Mr Williams.

Suspecting that the putrefying corpse in the house in Windsor was that of Emily Williams, the two detectives issued a nationwide alert for Albert Williams, and a description, including his unusual characteristics, was wired to every police station in the country. They figured that, should Mr Williams alias Druin maintain his described persona, he shouldn't prove to be all that hard to find. They figured correctly.

In the meantime, the circumstances surrounding the death of Emily Williams had caught the public's interest in Victoria. As a curious crowd of onlookers gathered to watch her coffin being lowered into a pauper's grave a week after the discovery of her body, an observant employee of a coastal shipping company reported to police that he'd seen a man who answered to the missing Williams' description boarding a vessel that sailed from Melbourne to Perth on 23 January. The flamboyant character had travelled under the name of Baron Swanston.

The baron wasn't hard to find. In the small mining settlement of Southern Cross, situated in the goldfields 400 kilometres east of Perth, he had taken a job as the engineer in charge of machinery at the Fraser Gold Mine. The baron's city clothes, jewellery, large distinctive moustache and English accent stood out like a bushfire on the horizon, and the day after the remains of Emily Williams were laid to rest, a trooper wired the detectives in Melbourne to tell them that the man they were looking for was safely under lock and key in the Southern Cross Gaol in which he looked terribly out of place among the usual collection of drunken miners.

Williams, aka Baron Swanston, was arrested at about 1 p.m. on 14 March 1892, and said as he was handcuffed: 'I shall say nothing. I am innocent. I have never been to Windsor to the best of my knowledge. I do not know where it is.' He then added: 'My name is not Williams.' The arresting trooper, P.C. Williams, replied, 'I can't help that,' as he loaded him into the wagon to take him to jail.

By the time the arrest of Albert Williams alias Mr Druin alias Baron Swanston reached the people of Victoria via the blazing headlines WINDSOR MURDERER ARRESTED, detectives Considine and Cawsey knew him by yet another name – only this time it was his correct name: Frederick Bailey Deeming.

They had discovered that Deeming had first arrived in Sydney from England in 1881. In 1885 he was operating a gas-fitting shop in Sydney and lived with his English wife Marie and their two baby daughters in a house they had bought in the inner-Sydney suburb of Petersham.

Those who knew Deeming at the time said that when his gas-fitting shop mysteriously burned to the ground and the insurance money fell short of covering his bills, he resorted to petty theft, which included raiding his clients' gutterings of lead and selling it as scrap. He was besieged by irate customers every time it rained. They also said that Deeming was an expert at drawing unwanted attention to himself, and because of this he did a short sentence in jail after mouthing off in a pub that he had given false evidence at the bankruptcy court.

The people who remembered the Deemings recalled his wife as being physically nothing like the description of the Emily Williams found dead at the house in Windsor. In fact, she was different in every way: older, shorter, and with a much darker complexion. It would appear that there had been two Mrs Deemings. But where was the original one, the mother of the children?

With Deeming locked up safely in Southern Cross awaiting

extradition back to Melbourne to face a murder charge, the detectives set about trying to locate the missing Mrs Deeming and the children. The only lead they had to go on was a crumpled up invitation to a dinner given by Albert Williams at the Commercial Hotel, Rainhill, a village situated 14 kilometres east of Liverpool in England.

Believing now that an Albert Williams may actually exist, detectives Considine and Cawsey sent a telegram to the Lancashire police asking them to investigate the dinner and, if at all possible, locate Mr Williams and ask him if he could throw any light on Frederick Deeming's missing family.

Local police's inquiries led them to the Rainhill newsagency, which was owned and operated by a Mrs Mather who turned out to be the mother of the dead Emily Williams-Deeming found under the fireplace in the house in Melbourne. She collapsed when told of the death of her daughter. After she recovered from the horrible news, Mrs Mather explained that she also ran a letting agency in the village and her daughter had met Mr Williams, whose description matched that of Deeming, when he arrived in the village in late October 1891 and rented a local house named Dineham Villa for his employer, a Colonel Brooks, who was arriving from India shortly after. The colonel never turned up.

While waiting for his employer to arrive, the free-spending Williams lived at the local Commercial Hotel and held court at the bar each night where he told tales of his adventures around the world.

Emily Mathers fell for him and they were married in the village on 22 September 1891. Williams threw a lavish reception before departing for London with his bride to catch the *Kaiser Wilhelm II* to Australia where they intended to spend their honeymoon. Williams left a trail of unpaid bills in both Rainhill and London in his wake.

But there was talk among the Rainhill locals of a woman and children living at Dineham Villa. A neighbour spoke of talking to a boy and a girl one afternoon after they had asked if they could have some of his strawberries. Before he could find out anything about the children they were called inside by a woman who abruptly closed the door and pulled the curtains. There had also been brief sightings of the woman and children by other neighbours. Now they seemed to have vanished.

Locals informed Liverpool police who broke into Dineham Villa to be confronted with the most pungent smell, which was immediately identifiable to anyone who had ever experienced it before. It was the unmistakable smell of death. The policemen retched as they made their way to the source of the smell and, after they pulled the fireplace apart with crowbars and shovels, they removed the hearthstones to uncover the bodies of a woman and two children, all in advanced stages of decomposition. The corpses were wrapped in oil cloth. The woman lay upon her back, while the two children were laid face-down, one on each side of her.

The continuance of the strong smell from the floor itself prompted a further investigation and police found another two children embedded in the cement. One body was an infant and the other a small girl lying at the woman's feet.

It was a sight that they would never forget. The woman and a nine-year-old girl had been strangled and the others had had their throats cut. Police found a book with the bodies in which the name Deeming had been crossed out and Williams added. This left little doubt in the minds of the police that Deeming and Williams were, in fact, the one person.

Two days later, at the Rainhill inquest into their deaths, the coroner surmised that the nine-year-old girl had woken from her sleep as the murderer was silently going about his business and had been strangled to keep her quiet. Also at the inquest, two very distressed men from Liverpool came forward and identified the woman, formerly Marie James, and the children as being the wife and family of their brother Frederick Deeming, who had brought them back with him to England a few months earlier.

They explained to police that their brother was a cockney, born in London on 30 July 1853. As a young man he travelled as a ship's purser and his travels took him to many parts of the world. He had married Marie James of Birkenhead, England, in 1881. Their two girls, Bertha and Mary, were born in Sydney. In the mid-1880s the Deeming family spent some time in South Africa and their third child, a boy named Sydney, was born at sea.

Deeming and his family returned to England in 1890 and their fourth child, Leala, was born at Birkenhead. After a brief stay with his brothers, Deeming and his family had disappeared, obviously to nearby Rainhill where it seemed that Deeming kept them under wraps at Dineham Villa while he played the eligible bachelor in the town.

It seemed that he then met Emily Mather and, having no further use for his wife and four young children, he cold-bloodedly murdered them all and concealed their bodies under the fireplace. He married Emily and took his bride with him to Australia where it appeared that he soon murdered her as well.

The discovery of the five bodies was made on 16 March 1892, just two weeks after the body of Emily 'Williams' had been found in identical circumstances in the house in Melbourne. Frederick Bailey Deeming had a lot of explaining to do. He was to be taken under armed escort to Perth to face an extradition hearing so that he could be taken back to Victoria and tried for the Windsor murder.

Deeming left Southern Cross Gaol in the charge of three armed constables for the five-day domestic passenger train trip to Perth, which stopped overnight in different towns. On the train journey Deeming fainted twice and could not sleep or eat. A strict watch was kept over the prisoner day and night and the handcuffs were never taken off him.

Upon arrival in York on the last night of their journey, the train was met by a crowd who had heard that the man who had slaughtered his entire family and a second wife was being taken to Perth and was passing through their little town. The platform was packed with onlookers and as Deeming stepped from the train under close guard he was aware of the intensity with which the crowd was scrutinising him. Fearing an upheaval against him that the police would not be able to control, Deeming raised his chained arms and brazenly said to them: 'Ladies and gentlemen, you need not look at me. I am not guilty, but I have been victimised.' When the train moved off he smiled at the glaring crowd.

The awaiting crowd at Perth was so large that, instead of alighting at Perth Central railway station, Deeming was taken off at the nearby Lord Street Crossing and placed in a waiting van before being transported to the Waterside Lockup. At the lockup an inventory was taken of a trunk full of Deeming's possessions that police had confiscated. Its pitiful contents were, in part, one silver case with *Emily* engraved on the outside which contained one pair of gloves; one double-photo frame containing two photos: one of Deeming and a little girl about six years old, and the other of a family group of Deeming, wife Marie James and their three children; a pocket book containing a small timetable of trains to and from Rainhill and St Helen's Junction; one small battle axe a foot long with a very sharp silver blade about three inches wide; one master mason's apron with *F.B.D.* stamped on it; and a book of common prayer with *December 26th 1889. Emily* written on the leaf of the cover.

On 24 March 1892, Deeming's extradition hearing took place in the Perth Police Court. Deeming appeared haggard and thin, and during the proceedings he held frequent conferences with his counsel. Detective Sergeant Cawsey, who had sailed all the way from Melbourne to personally escort Deeming back to trial, waited patiently as Deeming's counsel, Richard Haynes QC, desperately fought the extradition order on the grounds that there was no way his client would get a fair trial in Melbourne – as the angry mob that had formed outside the Perth court already indicated.

The extradition order was finally granted and Deeming was placed in the custody of Detective Sergeant Cawsey. At 11 a.m. on 27 March 1892, Deeming, Cawsey, three armed police officers and two reporters boarded the train at Midland Junction on the outskirts of Perth for the arduous 560-kilometre overnight rail trip to Albany in southern Western Australia to rendezvous with the SS *Ballarat*, which was going back to Melbourne.

On arrival at the train's first stop for coal and water at York, 100 kilometres out of Perth, there was a huge angry crowd to greet them. The word had spread all the way down the train line by telegraph that the despised child-and-wife killer was passing through, and the curious and vindictive all gathered to have a look and voice their opinions.

Many women were in the crowd and they shouted collectively: 'Lynch him!' 'Drag him out!' and 'Pull him to pieces with bullocks!' The shutters on Deeming's compartment were put up to conceal him but the crowd surged forward and pushed upon the carriage until it almost rocked, and one person in the mob broke a window. For fear of being lynched by the angry mob, the terrified Deeming jumped from one side of the compartment to the other and begged the police to shield him.

At the next stop, at the small country town of Beverley, when the waiting angry mob found out that Deeming was smuggled into a room in the railway station they gathered near the door of the room and, at one stage, threatened to bash the door down and drag the prisoner away to an unknown fate.

After secreting the nervous Deeming back to the safety of the train and it got underway, Deeming took a fit and began to struggle and kick so violently that it took four men to hold him down for the full half-hour duration of the spasms. Still in the handcuffs, Deeming's wrists were badly battered and swollen when the fit subsided but, plead as he may, they stayed on even when Deeming had two similar fits a short time after.

To avoid any scuffles with the irate citizens of Albany, where Deeming was due to arrive the following day, the train was stopped at a crossing about 50 metres from Albany Prison and the drawn and weary Deeming was transferred to the care of the prison governor, Mr McGovern, without the slightest fuss.

Once inside the prison Deeming cheered up immediately, in no time his bravado returned and he was back to protesting his innocence to anyone who would listen, and joined in games of draughts with his keepers. He was given a medical checkup which showed that, apart from a lot of anxiety and fear, he was in perfect health.

The plan was that Deeming and his escorts would stay at the jail that night and at five o'clock the next morning Detective Cawsey, Detective Smyth of Albany, and the trooper who had arrested Deeming at Southern Cross, Constable Williams, would escort Deeming on the SS *Ballarat* to Adelaide. From there they would take a train to Melbourne. Deeming would be alternately handcuffed to the three policemen for the entire journey.

Although under hourly surveillance in his cell all through the night to prevent him from doing any harm to himself, in the morning Deeming's minders were astonished to find that their prisoner was missing his most distinctive feature – his large moustache.

Ever since he came before the public as a notorious criminal, Deeming's moustache had been one of the chief signs by which he had been tracked, and the police were startled to find it gone. A quiet, sarcastic smile broke over Deeming's face when he noticed the consternation of the police. The loss of his long moustache had exposed to view a wide, ugly mouth and brought Deeming's bold chin into greater prominence. It was agreed by his keepers that he had made an excellent job of removing the moustache, considering the absolute lack of tools.

In the prisoner's clothes they found a piece of bottle glass a little bigger than a shilling, and in the cell they also found the neck of a medicine bottle. The smaller piece of glass had been broken off the bottle and used as a razor. But to their astonishment, they discovered that about three-quarters of the hairs in the moustache had been plucked out by the roots. Deeming must have suffered the intense agony of pulling out his moustache without uttering the slightest sound or moving his body. The glass had been used chiefly to cut the hair above the corners of his mouth. It was concluded that no-one had helped Deeming and that he had picked up the neck of the bottle in the exercise yard.

The move by Deeming concerned Detective Cawsey as it made the murderer look a completely different person, but he also knew that it could clinch the case against him.

Such was the hostility towards Frederick Deeming right across the nation that when the SS *Ballarat* dropped anchor at Larges Bay in South Australia two days later, Detective Cawsey and his team were told that there was a large and aggressive crowd waiting at the Port Adelaide wharf to harass their prisoner. They quickly decided that it was far safer to continue the voyage to Melbourne rather than risk their passenger being abducted and lynched on the train journey from Adelaide to Melbourne.

When the sea journey resumed, Deeming became moody and at last he seemed to fully understand the nation's hatred against him. 'They might wait until I'm found guilty,' he complained. 'Many innocent men have been hanged. I'm not afraid to die. If I have to die I'll die like a man, but first I'll make sure of some revelations that will astonish the world.'

At 9 a.m. on 2 April 1892, the *Ballarat* anchored in Port Phillip Bay and Deeming was whisked away to the Police Court. He was formally charged with the murder of Emily Williams. When asked his name he refused to answer and was charged as Albert Williams.

The trial of Frederick Bailey Deeming began in Melbourne on 2 May 1892, with the accused being charged in the name of Albert O. Williams. His defence was that he was not guilty on the grounds of insanity. But, although Deeming had been examined by six doctors – as many as six times by some – not one of them could unequivocally say that he was insane.

The trial took four days and the evidence against Deeming was damning. Doctors suggested that he suffered from epileptic fits. He was certainly infected with venereal disease and this may have impaired his mind, for he was moody and loquacious and fantasised about his past. He claimed that his dead mother had told him to kill Emily Mather and that he sometimes had been overwhelmed by the irresistible impulse to slaughter the current lady in his life.

Dr Shields, a prison doctor, said of the accused: 'I have frequently conversed with him but cannot believe anything he says.' On the subject of whether Deeming knew the difference between right and wrong, Dr Shields said: 'That stealing, for example, was a matter of conscience. Murder was also permissible in certain circumstances.' He told the court that Deeming had admitted that several times he had gone out with a revolver searching for women who had given him VD, intending to kill them. Deeming believed in the extermination of such women.

And then, as the trial reached its conclusion, came the moment the packed public gallery had all been waiting for. Against strong advice from his counsel, Deeming took to the stand to speak on his own behalf. At last the public would get to hear from the man who had cold-bloodedly murdered two of his wives and slaughtered four of his young children the same way a slaughterman at an abattoir would kill a sheep for the table. Now they could judge for themselves whether or not the man capable of crimes that surely only a madman could commit was indeed insane.

They were not to be disappointed. Deeming made an imposing sight as he spoke, often closing his eyes and rocking from side to side. He used no notes and held onto the rail in front of him. He said in part: 'I don't think there has ever been a man brought into court that has ever been prejudged more than I have been. Before I arrived in the colony my photographs were distributed about the city of Melbourne, in paper shops, in jewellers' shops, and it is from these photographs I have been identified. I will ask the jury themselves if it would be possible to go and pick out 200 people in Melbourne who would not execute me without the option of a trial.'

Deeming then went on to deny that his wife Emily was actually dead. 'And my only comfort is in knowing that I have not done it and that the woman is not dead. And that alone will comfort me, let the end be what it may.'

But any sympathy he may have squeezed out of the jury was quickly dissolved as his ego took over and he began to boast of his conquests: 'It is not giving up this life I fear – not the slightest. I have gone through the world, and after the dangers I have faced I am not afraid to give up my life. I have been on the Zambezi among the blackfellows and have been battered about the head and gone among bears and gone into lion's caves and brought them out alive, as it has been stated in the papers, and now they are alive in the hands of a man in England.'

In the end the entire courtroom saw not a madman but a sane man who was so insatiably wrapped up in his own importance and ego that it overwhelmed him. They were watching a man who was indeed capable of the most ghastly crimes without so much as batting an eyelid. Deeming condemned everyone and everything, and after an hour of diatribe he stopped speaking and, as he looked about the stunned courtroom, he instantly realised that he was a doomed man.

It took the jury 40 minutes to find Frederick Bailey Deeming both sane and guilty of the murder of his second wife, Emily. Turning to the judge, Deeming said: 'I hope in passing sentence your honour will make it as short as possible. I have been here for four days and I have been here since 10 o'clock this morning and it is time I was released from it.'

The judge said: 'It is not my intention to say one word beyond passing upon you the sentence of the law.' His Honour then sentenced Frederick Bailey Deeming to be hanged by the neck until he was dead.

Before dawn, on the cold, grey and sunless Monday of 23 May 1892, a huge crowd began to gather out the front of Old Melbourne Gaol to be the first to hear the joyous news that Frederick Deeming had been hanged. Inside the jail, the convicted man watched as the minutes ticked by to 10 a.m., the time of his execution. As it neared the time, arguably the most despised killer in Australia handed the jail chaplain, Reverend Scott, a letter. It read in part: *I die a fully penitent sinner and a Christian and I still tell you, as I always have, that I did not intend to kill my poor Emily. I can only look upon my execution as a murder. Still death will be a relief to me.*

During the time that Deeming was praying while waiting to be executed, it was stated that he appealed for forgiveness for having murdered his family without warning.

At 10 a.m. the sheriff and the jail officials of the execution party entered Deeming's cell and walked him the three paces to the trapdoor where he stood while they gave him a stiff drink of brandy. His arms were pinioned and a white cap had been drawn over his head, leaving his face uncovered. Deeming's face was blanched and he quivered. He looked around the men before him as if searching for a friendly face. There had been talk of a speech on the scaffold but now it was obvious that Deeming could not have spoken had he wanted to.

The hangman, Unthank, who went by the name of Jones and hid his features with a large, false white beard, was waiting with his black-bearded assistant in a cell near the scaffold. He stepped forward, placed the noose over Deeming's neck and pulled it tight.

The sheriff asked: 'Albert Williams, do you have anything to say before you die?' Deeming made a strange gurgling noise so incoherent that it was understood by some to mean no and by others 'Lord, receive my Spirit'.

The hangman drew the white cap over the culprit's face, adjusted the noose and stepped back beside his assistant. For a second or two Deeming stood unsupported on the trap. He swayed from side to side, probably only half-conscious of what was happening. Just as the prayer for the dead was ending, the trap suddenly sprang open. Deeming fell just over two metres and died instantly. His neck dislocated, his body hung suspended but perfectly motionless.

The first of the 45 witnesses to Deeming's hanging filed out through the prison gates and announced to the huge crowd that had gathered that the despised Frederick Bailey Deeming, killer of women and children, was dead.

The crowd let out a huge cheer that could be heard for miles around.

CHAPTER 6

The Murderous Mistress

Martha Rendell
Perth, 1907–09

Martha Rendell has gone down in history as being among the most sadistic serial child killers the world has ever known alongside more notorious monsters such as New York's Albert Fish who murdered, cooked and ate a child and sent her parents a note telling them what their daughter tasted like, and England's 'Moors Murderers' Ian Brady and Myra Hindley who recorded their victims begging for mercy as they raped and tortured them before ending their lives.

Martha Rendell was found guilty of murdering her lover's three young children for no apparent reason other than that she delighted in watching them suffer over a long period of time and eventually die in horrifying agony.

The man who brought her to justice, Detective Inspector Harry Mann, one of Australia's finest criminologists of his time and, later, chief of the Western Australian Criminal Investigations Bureau, described Martha Rendell as 'a woman completely without emotion who delighted in seeing her victims writhe in agony and from it somehow derived a form of sexual satisfaction'.

The story of the Rendell serial murders began in South Australia in 1906 when a carpenter who worked for the railways, Thomas Nicholls Morris, moved his family of wife and five children to the Perth suburb of Subiaco at the behest of his wife. Mrs Morris wanted her husband as far away as she could get him from the woman with whom he had been having a passionate affair, the tall, voluptuous 35-year-old brunette wife of a neighbour and mother of two, Martha Rendell.

At first it appeared to be a good move and the Morris family, now rid of the disruptive mistress, settled easily into their new surroundings. Western Australia was in the middle of a boom due to the discovery of vast gold deposits in Kalgoorlie and Coolgardie, and Tom Morris had no trouble finding work and providing comfortably for his family.

But the family's peaceful life didn't last long. Within a few months Martha Rendell turned up in Perth, after having abandoned her husband and children in Adelaide, determined to get her lover back. Soon the happy Morris household was torn apart by blazing rows which finally concluded with Tom Morris ordering his wife from the house and telling her to never set foot in it again while he remained there with the children.

Shortly after, in February 1907, Tom Morris moved into a rented weatherboard house in East Perth with his five children and Martha Rendell as his 'wife'. The children were warned under the threat of a severe beating to call her 'Mother' and the neighbours knew her as 'Mrs Morris'.

The Morris children, Olive, Annie, Arthur, William and George, ranged in age from five to 18 and the two eldest teenagers, William and George, had left school and worked in full-time jobs. This left the evil Martha Rendell lots of time to prey on the youngsters.

Except for the besotted Tom Morris, there was not a soul who had a good word for Martha, least of all the Morris children. She was a hateful person. Her loud verbal abuse and physical beatings of the two younger Morris children, five-year-old Olive and seven-year-old Annie, was the talk of the neighbours who were at a loss to understand what the charming and mild-mannered Tom Morris saw in his brash, loud-mouthed and overbearing 'wife'.

Before Martha Rendell had arrived back on the scene and destroyed the Morris family's blissful existence, all of the children were rosy-cheeked and in glowing health. Under the guidance of their new mother they became noticeably pale and scrawny, as if the food they were being given had no nourishment. On top of their poor condition the children were dished out regular beatings. Little Annie was thrashed so hard one day that she couldn't walk, the excuse for the beating being that the child refused to obey Martha Rendell because she was not her mother.

In the winter of 1907 both of the little girls complained continually of colds and sore throats. Eventually, the children were sick all of the time and the sore throats became so painful that Tom Morris insisted on calling in Dr Cuthbert, the local doctor, who prescribed frequent painting of the infected areas inside the children's throats with a prescribed medicine and a medicinal brush. The regular throat-paintings were conducted by Martha Rendell behind closed doors, and when neighbours heard the screams of pain coming from inside the house Rendell explained them away by saying that the children were simply being 'spoiled brats' who didn't like getting their throats painted because it felt ticklish.

Martha Rendell delighted most in tormenting little Annie Morris, the child who had defied her because she wasn't her real mother. From the accounts of the neighbours who had peeked through the windows, the sadistic Rendell rocked back and forth in her chair beside the little girl's bed and watched her pale little body waste away, racked and tormented by her incessant barking coughs. Only the noise of her laughter blocked out the continual moans uttered by the dying girl.

When the little girl complained that her whole body was in agony as if it were on fire and tried to get out of bed but couldn't raise the energy, Martha Rendell called for her older brother George to come and see how 'funny' his little sister looked. George was so horrified that he had to turn away, but Martha forced him to watch as she painted Annie's throat with the long brush, which the little girl tried to rip out of her mouth.

Poor little Annie Morris was saved from more intense suffering when she finally died in agony on the morning of 28 July 1907. Dr Cuthbert conceded that he was mystified as to the circumstances surrounding the little girl's death. But seeing as there was no need to suspect foul play, especially from a woman who Dr Cuthbert believed to be Annie's real mother because he had never been told otherwise, no autopsy was requested. He issued a death certificate stating that the child had died of diphtheria, a serious infectious disease that attacks the membranes of the throat and releases a toxin that damages the heart and nervous system.

As little Annie Morris was being laid to rest, the evil Martha Rendell was plotting an equally horrible fate for her younger sister, Olive. To protect her from the horrible disease that killed her sister, she insisted on painting Olive's throat with the same brown-coloured 'medication', much to the child's protests that the substance was burning her throat and that the pain was unbearable.

At the insistence of the family, Dr Cuthbert was called in to look at Olive and, again, he was puzzled at the symptoms, concluding that they were the same as the 'diphtheria' that had killed her sister. After consultation with another doctor who was called in to check the child over, he agreed with Olive's 'mother' that the throat-swabbing seemed to be the only way to cure the illness, and that it must continue.

Five-year-old Olive Morris died in agony on 16 October 1907, and a death certificate was issued without the hint of suspicion of foul play.

In the winter of 1908, almost a year after the death of Olive Morris, 14-year-old Arthur was stricken with the same mysterious sore throat and Martha Rendell set about curing him by painting his throat the way the doctor had recommended and the same as she had done for his sisters. Neighbours once again had to get used to the regular blood-curdling screams of pain that came from the Morrises' house each evening as the boy protested in agony to the regular throat-paintings.

Again Dr Cuthbert was called in and again he left the house shaking his head in concern after viewing and examining the emaciated and pain-racked body of the once fit and healthy teenager. Yet, once again, he had prescribed the throat-paintings as the only way to cure the lad.

On 8 October 1908, Martha Rendell claimed her third victim when Arthur eventually died in agony. Martha had maintained a bedside vigil up until his passing, regularly painting his inflamed throat with the 'medication'.

This time Dr Cuthbert, and other doctors he had consulted during the children's illnesses, wanted to perform an autopsy. They had to seek permission from the boy's mother, and the brazen Martha Rendell, posing as the grief-stricken natural mother of the victim, not only gave her permission but, to their astonishment, asked if she could attend the autopsy. The doctors had little choice but to allow her.

The grim-faced murderess stood by as the doctors sliced open the remains of young Arthur Morris and examined his organs in an attempt to find out what had killed him.

Her gamble about being uncovered as a ruthless child-killer paid off. Maybe it was the stern, unemotional presence of the deceased's 'mother' at the autopsy that made the doctors overlook the obvious. But whatever it was, we shall never know what allowed the doctors to conclude that there was no reason why they shouldn't issue a death certificate stating that the child had died from diphtheria. If they had have done their jobs properly and analysed a swab of Arthur Morris's inflamed throat, they would have most certainly arrived at a different conclusion: murder.

Arthur Morris was laid to rest beside his two sisters at Karrakatta Cemetery, situated between Perth and the port of Fremantle. Instead of grieving for the loss of her three stepchildren, Martha Rendell was plotting how quickly she would dispatch George, one of the two remaining teenage boys who was still living at home with his stepmother, his brother William and his father.

Martha didn't wait very long. One night, about six months after the death of his brother Arthur, George felt a burning sensation in his throat as he took a sip from a cup of tea prepared for him by his stepmother. It was nothing to worry about, Martha told him, as she produced a bottle of the brown-coloured medication and suggested he have his throat painted immediately to avoid the same fate as his siblings. She would 'nip it in the bud' right away, she said.

But in light of what had happened to his sisters and brother and the agony he had seen them go through – which seemed to make Martha Rendell gloat rather than worry – the older and wiser George fled from the house and sought sanctuary with his real mother who lived in a suburb not far away. The neighbours noticed George's absence when he did not return after a few weeks and, seeing as his father didn't know of his son's whereabouts and in view of the strange occurrences that had taken place in the house since the Morris family had moved in two years earlier, the suspicious neighbours called the police.

Detective Inspector Harry Mann, a young investigator who displayed Sherlock Holmes tendencies even at this early stage in his career, was put in charge of the inquiry and, along with his assistant, Detective Aubrey Lamond, they set about methodically interviewing the neighbours. During the early days of the investigation it was decided not to let Mr and 'Mrs' Morris know that they were under scrutiny in case something went wrong and they decided to flee or destroy evidence.

Every one of the neighbours had the same story to tell. The Morrises were the gossip of the entire neighbourhood. The neighbours repeatedly told the detectives of the agonising screams in the Morris household that could be heard many houses away. They told of the repeated excuse by their mother of the throat-paintings, how the three once-healthy and athletic children's state had rapidly deteriorated when the throat-paintings started, and how they had ultimately died.

One neighbour told of how, when the screams had become too much for her curiosity, she had peeked through the window on several occasions to see a child screaming and writhing in agony in bed while her mother rocked back and forth in a chair, smiling as she looked on.

After interviewing young George Morris at his real mother's house, Detective Inspector Mann was convinced that he had a major murder investigation on his hands. There was an obvious connection between the children's deaths and the painting of their throats. But what was it?

In secret, so as not to alert the press or the suspected murderers (at this stage, Tom Morris was as much a suspect as his de-facto wife), Detective Inspector Mann had the bodies of the three children exhumed and the State's leading medical authorities were called in to re-examine them. And this time they were told to pay special attention to their throats.

Mann's hunch paid off. Martha Rendell had been painting the children's throats with spirits of salts – diluted hydrochloric acid – a strong, colourless acid formed when hydrogen-chloride gas dissociates in water. Although readily available as a cleansing compound, hydrochloric acid was mainly used in industrial and laboratory processes.

It was little wonder that the Morris children had died in such agony. It seemed apparent that Martha Rendell had disguised the hydrochloric acid to look like the doctor's prescribed medicine by adding some brown colouring.

Martha Rendell and Tom Morris were hauled in for questioning. Neighbours, and the doctors who had attended the ailing Morris children at their home, were shocked to hear that Rendell wasn't their real mother, and at last it all added up. It appeared to be a case of the stepmother getting rid of the unwanted stepchildren because she was jealous of her lover's feelings towards them. But they pondered as to how someone could go about it so cruelly.

Although she claimed to be innocent, the evidence against Martha Rendell was overwhelming and a conviction was inevitable. And while the obviously heavily dominated Tom Morris vehemently protested his innocence, detectives couldn't believe that under the circumstances he knew nothing of what was going on. They were both charged with murder.

Mr Justice McMillan presided over the seven-day trial held in Perth in September 1909, and it was proved beyond any doubt that Martha Rendell was a sadistic monster whose sole motivation in watching and hearing her victims die in intense pain was for sexual perversion, though what sort of sexual perversion was never made clear to the court. It was made apparent that Rendell first laced the children's drinks with small amounts of the hydrochloric acid, and when they complained of a sore throat she began painting their throats with more of the same on the doctor's instructions.

Martha Rendell's only defence was a complete denial of the charges, claiming that she was acting on the doctor's orders and had only painted the children's throats with the medicine that was prescribed for them. She said that the large tin of spirits of salts found in the house was used only for normal household cleaning duties.

The jury chose not to believe her shallow defence and Martha Rendell remained emotionless in the dock as she was sentenced to death by hanging.

Thomas Morris was portrayed by his defence counsel, Mr

J.W. Clydesdale and Mr F.J. Shaw, as a besotted oaf who was totally dominated by his mistress. He would do anything she commanded and lived in dread and fear of incurring her wrath. He was exonerated of all charges and set free.

Despite the enormity of her crimes, there was a large group who lobbied against the hanging of Martha Rendell. Only two women had been previously executed in Western Australia and it was considered 'barbaric' by the many politicians, clergy and other notable public figures who campaigned heavily against her execution. But it was to no avail, and her hanging was scheduled for the morning of 6 October 1909 at Fremantle Prison.

On the eve of her execution, Thomas Morris broke down while visiting the woman who had led his life down the path of destruction, and pledged his love for her as he said his final goodbye.

Martha Rendell maintained to the last that she was innocent, saying before she went to the gallows: 'If I had done it, I would confess. I pray for those who have sworn my life away.'

Martha Rendell, the last woman to be hanged in Western Australia, went to her death without a murmur and was buried in an unmarked grave in Fremantle Cemetery.

AUTHOR'S NOTE: In a bizarre twist of irony, the last man to be hanged in Western Australia, serial killer Eric Edgar Cooke who was executed in Fremantle Prison on 26 October 1964, was buried in the same unmarked pauper's grave on top of the remains of Martha Rendell.

CHAPTER 7

The Schoolgirl Strangler

Arnold Karl Sodeman
Melbourne, 1930–35

What would drive a mild-mannered, loving husband and doting father to strangle four young girls aged between six and 16 years over a five-year period? This is what Melburnians pondered on 1 June 1936 as the trapdoor to the gallows opened at Melbourne's Pentridge Gaol and serial schoolgirl killer, Arnold Karl Sodeman, dropped to his death.

There were few tears among the large crowd gathered outside the prison as the despised Sodeman was hanged, but the lengthy debates at his trial as to whether or not he was sane when he committed his horrific crimes cast a long shadow of doubt in the minds of many.

There was no doubt that 36-year-old Sodeman had committed the despicable murders – he had admitted to them – but his trial soon became embroiled in controversy and bitter legal argument about his sanity. And if family history alone could have saved the child murderer, then Arnold Sodeman would have most likely spent the rest of his days in an asylum rather than face the hangman's noose.

Doctors told the court at his trial that Sodeman suffered from a 'disorder of the mind aggravated by the toxic effect of alcohol'. The court also heard that his mother suffered from bouts of amnesia and both his grandfather and father had died in mental institutions. Given the nature of the crimes and the split personality of the man who had committed them, it certainly seemed as though there were grounds for him to be judged insane. But the court believed otherwise.

The following notice appeared in the *Sydney Morning Herald* on the morning of 2 June 1936:

ARNOLD SODEMAN
Executed in Melbourne

MELBOURNE: Monday. Arnold Karl Sodeman, 36, labourer, of Leongatha, was hanged today at Pentridge Gaol. He had been convicted of the murder of June Rushmer, aged 6½, at Leongatha on December 1, 1935 and was sentenced to death.

Sodeman made no statement. He had had no visitors except his solicitor since he was admitted to the gaol, but his constant companion in the gaol was Edward Cornelius, who had been sentenced to death for the murder of the Rev. Harold Laceby Cecil at St Saviour's Vicarage. The two condemned men played draughts last night. Sodeman ate breakfast this morning and seemed unconcerned as he went to the scaffold. Officials and newspaper representatives were the only persons present at the execution.

Only after his death could Arnold Sodeman justify his supporters' belief that he was insane at the time of his crimes. An autopsy revealed that he suffered from a brain condition known as leptomeningitis, which severely inflamed the brain tissues when alcohol was administered into the body, thus rendering the consumer uncontrollable.

Just days before he was hanged Sodeman himself acknowledged his condition when under the influence of alcohol in a letter he wrote to his distraught wife, which read in part: *I have tried and tried, as you know, to give up drink altogether, to be brave, my only regrets and sorrow are for all those who have suffered through my maniacal madness.*

Born in Victoria in 1900, at the age of 18 Arnold Sodeman was sent to a reformatory for 12 months for forging and uttering. He wasn't out long before he was in trouble with the police once again, this time for holding up and wounding the stationmaster at Surrey Hills station for which he received three years' hard labour in prison. Sodeman showed his indignation over the sentence by escaping, for which he was rewarded with another year's hard labour. He was released in 1922.

It seemed that young Arnold was destined to live a life of crime which, to some in those dark days at the beginning of the Great Depression, seemed the only alternative to dying of starvation at the end of a dole or soup-kitchen queue. Then things changed for the better for the troubled young man when he met and married his 'doll' as he lovingly called his adoring wife and they soon had a baby daughter, Joan.

Now with a family to look after and something to live for, Arnold Sodeman and his wife and daughter roamed rural Victoria from town to town in search of work and accommodation. The devoted couple never separated. It was a situation typical of so many young couples in those horrible times of enormous unemployment. And in the tradition of the great Australian spirit, the family was made as welcome as possible by their fellow Aussies who weren't so down on their luck. Wherever they went people liked the quietly spoken, ruggedly handsome young labourer and his wife, with their darling daughter tugging at their heels.

On the Saturday afternoon of 9 November 1930, Arnold Sodeman, dressed in overalls, shirtsleeves and a wide-brimmed felt hat, approached 12-year-old Mena Griffiths as she was playing with her sisters in Fawkner Park in South Yarra and asked her if she would like to go on a message. The little girl accepted and left her sisters to go with the nice man.

He stopped and brought Mena a bag of fish and chips at nearby St Kilda and then persuaded her to accompany him to a deserted house in Wheatley Road, Ormond, almost 10 kilometres away. Once inside the house, Arnold Sodeman strangled the lass so strongly with his bare hands that his thumb imprints could be clearly seen on the dead girl's neck days later. Once Mena was dead, Sodeman ripped off her pants and used them to tie her ankles together and her hands behind her back. The remainder of the panties were forced down the little girl's throat as a gag. The police found it most unusual that the killer would do this *after* the girl was already dead. This strange manoeuvre would become the serial killer's calling card.

Mercifully, Mena Griffiths hadn't been sexually assaulted. Even so, every known sex offender in Melbourne was hauled in and questioned. One of the men, Robert McMahon, had just been released from Pentridge Gaol after serving six years for rape and, because he was of similar appearance to Arnold Sodeman, he was mistakenly identified by Mena's sisters as the man who took her away on that Saturday afternoon.

But Robert McMahon couldn't have committed the shocking murder as he was in Leeton in western New South Wales at the time and had a stack of witnesses to prove it. Yet there was no convincing the police, and it wasn't until concrete proof of McMahon's alibi was established the evening before he was to be charged that he was allowed to go free.

Just on dusk on a Friday nine weeks later, Arnold Sodeman met up with 16-year-old Hazel Adeline Wilson as she walked out of her home at Melton Avenue, Ormond on her way to meet a friend and then go on to a school dance. The following afternoon her body was discovered by her brother Frank on a vacant lot in nearby Oakleigh Road. It was unmistakably the work of Mena Griffiths's killer. The girl's hands had been tied behind her back with the blue belt she had been wearing over her floral dress, a stocking had been forced down her throat, and her panties had been torn into strips to hold the stocking in place and tie her ankles together.

An autopsy revealed that Hazel Wilson had been tied up after she had been strangled, and that there was no sign of sexual molestation. Although Hazel Wilson's body was discovered less than two kilometres from where Mena Griffiths was murdered, police could not establish a connection between the two girls and hence there was no apparent motive for the killings. They had to conclude that there was a madman wandering the streets. A madman who persuaded young girls to accompany him and then strangled them, seemingly without them putting up any resistance. A madman who didn't sexually assault his victims and would tie them up *after* he had killed them.

Police were baffled and tried to piece together the jigsaw as they hauled in every known male with a criminal record in the area and every known sex offender, child-molester, and sexual deviate in Melbourne. Their extensive inquiries resulted in nothing. Not a single lead. Soon all avenues were exhausted and there were no more leads to pursue, no further suspects to interview, and no more bodies. It was as if the 'Schoolgirl Strangler' had vanished. Perhaps he had died or been killed. Maybe he was in prison.

For almost four years and two months there was a void in the Schoolgirl Strangler serial murders and then, when the names of the two murdered girls were all but forgotten by the press and public, to the horror of Melburnians another body turned up. The Schoolgirl Strangler was back in the headlines.

On New Year's Day 1935, at the seaside resort of Inverloch in South Gippsland, a number of families had gathered for a giant family picnic to welcome the New Year. In the afternoon, one of the gathering, 12-year-old Ethel Belshaw, vanished as she waited for friends outside a nearby icecream shop. Ethel was there one minute and gone the next.

The following day her body was found in bushland not far from the icecream shop. She had been strangled and then gagged and bound with items of her own apparel in a manner identical to the strangler's previous victims. The nightmare had begun all over again.

The biggest manhunt in Victoria's history was launched, and anyone who was in the area at the time of Ethel Belshaw's disappearance or was even remotely associated with the area – any friends or associates of the families at the picnic or anyone who had a police record of any description – was hauled in for questioning. The police were so desperate to solve the case and get an irate public off their backs that they arrested and questioned the 18-year-old brother of one of Ethel's friends who happened to be with them when Ethel bought her icecream. He was released soon after.

One of the men questioned was roadworker Arnold Sodeman, the mild-mannered family man and devoted father of a little girl. He falsely explained his whereabouts at the time of the killing and his alibi wasn't followed up. It was a let-off that police would deeply regret and that would cause anguish for the loved ones of yet another little girl. It was also a mistake that would put the Victorian police force under intense scrutiny.

It was almost a year later, on 1 December 1935, when 6-year-old June Rushmer disappeared while walking home from a nearby park in Leongatha. Her body was found the following day less than two kilometres from her home.

June Rushmer was undoubtedly the fourth victim of the Schoolgirl Strangler. She had been bound and gagged in an identical fashion to the other girls, but this time a man who could possibly be the Schoolgirl Strangler had been spotted riding away from the crime scene on a bicycle. However, the sighting led nowhere and again police found themselves under intense pressure to find the serial killer before he struck again.

But it wasn't the police who would finally bring the Schoolgirl Strangler to justice – it was Sodeman himself and the swift action of a citizen. A short time after the murder of June Rushmer, Sodeman and the members of the road gang with whom he was working were discussing the killing during their morning tea break. For a laugh, one of his co-workers said jokingly to Sodeman: 'Wasn't it you I saw riding your pushbike near there that day, Arnold?'

'No you bloody well didn't!' Sodeman exploded uncharacteristically, and strode off leaving his workmates bewildered. They had never seen this side of their quiet mate and it was enough for one of them to ring the police and tell them of the experience.

Detectives rushed to the scene and Sodeman was arrested and taken into custody. It didn't take him long to confess to the murder of June Rushmer and explain how the killing took place.

He had left home on the Sunday night to cycle back to the road-workers' camp after the weekend. He had given little June a lift on the crossbar of his bike and put her off to walk the remaining distance to her home. As he watched her walk away, something came over him and he pursued her on foot. She became frightened and ran into the bush. When he caught up with her, he grabbed her around the throat from behind and, as she screamed and tried to get away, he strangled her as he had done with the others and then bound and gagged her as she lay limp in his hands.

At first, the public reaction to Arnold Sodeman's confession was shock. He was hardly the monster the public had imagined to be the Schoolgirl Strangler. His family and friends were in disbelief that such a man could commit these crimes. It was exceedingly out of his character. But his workmates knew differently. Arnold Sodeman's angry outburst at that fateful morning tea had exposed another side to the vicious killer. Lurking beneath that placid exterior was a beast capable of the most unspeakable acts.

There would be little sympathy for Arnold Karl Sodeman, the infamous Schoolgirl Strangler. After he had told in detail the killing of June Rushmer, he methodically described the killings of Mena Griffiths, Hazel Wilson and Ethel Belshaw.

Sodeman couldn't explain why he murdered the girls, only saying that an uncontrollable urge to kill came over him and, once he had started on the assault, it was impossible to stop. He explained that he killed the girls without first tying them up by attacking them from the back and his strong labourer's hands asphyxiated them before they could offer any effective resistance. He then tied up his victims and gagged them to make it look like the work of a ritual or sex offender to throw police off his scent. Never at any time had he been tempted to tamper with the girls sexually.

After being found guilty before Justice Gavan Duffy in the Melbourne Criminal Court in February 1936, Sodeman's solicitors, who had an unfailing belief that their client was insane, took their appeals firstly to the Australian High Court and then to the Privy Council in London, England. But on 28 May 1936, the last door slammed shut behind them when the Privy Council informed the Victorian Government that the original verdict must stand. Sane or insane, Arnold Sodeman would go to the gallows for his crimes.

Leading up to his execution, support grew from sections of the community who believed Sodeman to be insane, and a group calling themselves 'Justice for Sodeman' picketed whenever and wherever they could in an effort to stop him from paying the ultimate punishment for his shocking crimes. But Sodeman himself seemed resolved that he should pay the penalty.

Four days after the Privy Council handed down its decision

to execute Sodeman, he went to the gallows. Shortly before he was hanged, he told a policeman: 'I am ashamed of everything I have done. But at the time, I just feel, dully, that I must do what I am doing.'

And so it was done. The Schoolgirl Strangler dropped to his death on the scaffold at Pentridge Gaol, Melbourne, on the chilly Monday morning of 1 June 1936.

CHAPTER 8

The Swaggie Killer

Albert Andrew Moss
New South Wales, 1938–39

In Australia in the late 1920s and 1930s, countless numbers of unemployed men, victims of the crippling Depression, roamed the country on foot in search of any kind of work and a feed. These homeless men were known as swagmen or 'swaggies'. They carried their worldly possessions, rolled up, in their 'swag' or 'bluey' upon their backs. They would make camp along the lush inland rivers and creeks, boil the billy over the open fire, roast a rabbit given to them by a sympathetic farmer, and roll out the swag and sleep beneath the Southern Cross.

One famous Australian expression – 'and thank your mother for the rabbits' – originated from the swaggies in these times. Swaggies travelled from one homestead to another looking for work, and if there was none to give him, the farmer and his wife felt so bad that they were unable to help out a fellow Australian who was down on his luck that they sent the children to the door to give him a pair of trapped rabbits to eat so he wouldn't go hungry. In return, the grateful swaggie would tell the child to 'thank your mother for the rabbits'.

Albert Moss was a swagman and, like so many of the other nomads, no-one would have missed him if he hadn't been seen in months (as was often the case) or even years. That was the way of the bush in those harsh economic times – if someone wasn't seen for a long time, no-one went looking for them, presuming that they would turn up somewhere along the way. It was the perfect situation for a madman to prey upon his own unfortunate kind. A madman like Albert Andrew Moss.

Unlike the other swaggies, who wouldn't resort to a life of crime as a riskier but more profitable lifestyle, Albert Moss was a born criminal, a thief, conman, opportunist, rapist and, ultimately, a brutal serial murderer. Albert Andrew Moss was born in Narromine in outback New South Wales in 1885. A large and powerfully built man, he had no friends, an extensive criminal record and a reputation for arrogance and violence. Moss was well known among the swaggie fraternity and hence he was welcome at very few campfires, even in those times when it was considered an insult to refuse another down-and-outer a feed or warmth by your fire.

By the time he was 17, Albert Moss had been convicted of stealing, and from then on he preferred to get a living from theft and false pretences rather than turning his hand to an honest day's work. He was a regular visitor at various prisons, first serving three months and then six months for stealing. Though he had no schooling and boasted that he was illiterate, Moss picked up some semblance of an education in prison, enough to enable him to carry out forgery and uttering for which he received his next jail term of 12 months.

During this longer incarceration and the numerous smaller sentences that followed, Moss learned to hate jail and the hard labour that went with it as much as he despised any form of physical work on the outside. And so, to avoid imprisonment he invented his own method of escape. His plan was simple and extremely effective. Each time he was apprehended by police on a wide variety of offences that over the years included sheep-stealing, house-breaking and entering, shop-lifting and the attempted rape and assault of a schoolgirl, he would act like a madman by aggressively resisting arrest, frothing at the mouth and gagging on his own tongue as if in a manic suicide attempt. Fearing that he may die of madness, rather than put him in jail police remanded him to medical observation in the serene environment of a mental home or an asylum until his case could be heard.

In court 'Mad Mossy', as he became known, always put on a display for those present in the courtroom and, in doing so, beat the system every time. Moss turned the court into a three-ringed circus, throwing himself violently about, screaming loudly as he tried to bash his head against the wall repeatedly and menacingly threatening police and the magistrate. On most occasions he was sent off to a short stay in a comfortable mental asylum rather than the harsh confines of a prison.

But the insanity ploy didn't always run according to plan. At the hearing for the attempted rape and assault of a schoolgirl in 1926, Moss overdid it slightly when he tried to rip off his own clothes and shocked the magistrate with an exhibition of obscenity worthy of a man completely off his rocker. Moss was so convincing with this performance that he got what he wanted and that was to be certified insane, but he was detained for seven years, until 1933, before he could convince the authorities that he was sane enough to be released.

In the end, between 1911 and 1938, his incredible list of convictions, which must have been some sort of world record for a madman's comings and goings in a court of law, consisted of 14 certifications of insanity, each of which required Moss to be confined in various asylums in New South Wales. Moss escaped two institutions on three separate occasions.

In between his court appearances and visits to mental asylums, Moss always returned to the bush where he was sure of a feed by either stealing livestock or bullying another swaggie into surrendering his camp and tucker or be bashed.

After one of his escapes from an asylum Moss voluntarily returned to the Darlinghurst Reception House and begged to be taken back because he was hungry and broke and he could 'feel one of his attacks coming on'. Not only was he taken back with open arms, but after his worldly possessions were redeemed from the local pawnshop, he was certified sane and sent back out into mainstream society – indicating yet again that Moss was either the world's best conman or that the psychiatrists of the day must have been the biggest fools in the history of medicine.

In another well-known term of the day, it was recognised that Mad Mossy 'had more form than Phar Lap' and his extraordinary record certainly confirmed that. But outside of his record, Albert Moss was committing much more sinister crimes – atrocities such as murder.

Albert Moss's career as a murderer officially started in December 1938, when he killed his first victim, William Henry

Bartley, 41. But it was later widely believed that he had started killing much earlier than that, shortly after Moss was released from Parramatta Asylum around January 1933, following a seven-year incarceration.

William Bartley wasn't a swaggie but a travelling leather worker from the Sydney suburb of Lidcombe. He had found the going tough in the big smoke and opted to the bush on a brand new bicycle, intending to turn an honest quid around the rural districts by plying his trade and camping wherever nightfall found him. Bill Bartley was as good and honest a bloke as you would ever find in the Aussie outback.

And he was in luck. He picked up two days' work from a Narromine stockman named Carpenter, who ordered a special custom-made leather rope and supplied the leather.

On 9 December 1938 Bill Bartley set up camp at Mack's Reserve not far from Albert Moss's camp on the banks of the beautiful Macquarie River and, seeking shelter from the intense summer sun beneath a huge gum tree, he set about his task. Carpenter would later recall that as he delivered the leather to Bartley, he noticed the swaggie neighbour Moss hanging around the camp and talking to the leather worker.

When Carpenter returned two days later to collect his rope and pay Bartley he found that there was no sign of either of the men and, even though he waited well into the night, no-one returned.

Moss was sighted riding a bicycle identical to Bill Bartley's several days later by swaggie John Neville, who had also been camped at Mack's Reserve. Moss explained that the bike had been given to him by a young bloke who had just discovered that he had won a big prize in a Sydney lottery and was in such a hurry to get back to Sydney to claim his prize that he had also given his new friend Moss all of his gear, including his clothes.

Moss couldn't believe his luck when, a few days later, a gold prospector, Irishman Timothy O'Shea, 50, drove into the reserve in his sulky and two horses, set up camp and invited Moss over for a drink, obviously uninformed of the big man's evil reputation. But Moss was aware that O'Shea was reputed to carry a lot of money, as it was rumoured that on his extensive travels throughout the outback he sold his gold for cash and carried it on his person. Tim O'Shea's mistake of camping near Albert Moss would prove to be fatal.

That night, Timothy O'Shea disappeared and later several other swaggies camping nearby would report seeing a big blazing fire at his campsite. A few days later, it was again the observant John Neville who saw Albert Moss driving around in what looked remarkably like O'Shea's sulky, with one horse pulling it and another trailing behind on a rope. When approached by Neville, Moss explained that he had become really pally with the gold prospector. He said that O'Shea had left for Western Australia in a hurry to link up with a couple of mates who had struck it rich, and he had asked Moss to look after his things until he got back.

Although he didn't believe a word of it, and in fear of Moss and of what he was obviously capable, John Neville agreed to join Moss in a bottle of wine and listened as the drunken Moss told him tales that connected him with the attacks and murders of swaggies in his travels. Moss became belligerent as he told the terrified Neville of the demise of another swaggie named Jack Stewart who was viciously murdered at nearby Gilgandra, inferring that it was he himself who had committed the crime.

When Neville tried to sneak away Moss grabbed him and kicked him in the chest, knocking the wind out of him. With murder in his eyes, Moss rushed at the smaller Neville and would have surely killed him had Neville not reached for the empty wine bottle, smashed it over Moss's head, and made good his escape.

The following morning Moss was gone from the reserve and showed up at nearby Narromine soon after, buying drinks at the bar from a large wad of notes in his pocket. Moss stayed in Narromine until after Christmas, then found his way back to Mack's Reserve in search of new victims.

Again Moss was fortunate to camp near another swaggie in possession of worldly goods – even if they were only his swag, an old horse, and a battered sulky as transport. Moss's mark was 68-year-old pensioner Thomas Robinson, who was very well known and respected throughout the district. Robinson was openly critical of Moss and made no bones about warning people to be wary of him as he told them of Moss's dark past.

Conscious that Moss was camping nearby, Robinson took off in his sulky. Moss followed him for 10 days before eventually catching up with him on the night of 21 January at a lonely camping spot known as Brummagen Creek. That night the reserve was the scene of a huge fire, which started at Thomas Robinson's campsite and spread to become so large that it caused enormous damage to the bush and nearby properties. When the local farmers looked for the culprits the following day, the reserve was empty.

The next time Albert Moss was sighted it was at nearby Dubbo six weeks later. Only this time Moss's means of transport, Robinson's horse and sulky, was recognised immediately by none other than the stockman Carpenter, a good friend of Thomas Robinson and who had commissioned the leather rope from Bill Bartley before Bartley had also disappeared.

Moss insisted that the horse and sulky was his, but Carpenter would not be denied. He called the police, claiming that his friend Robinson had been done away with and that Moss had stolen his transport.

In inquiring into the whereabouts of the missing Robinson, police quickly learned that a good number of men had gone missing over the years and among them were two men, Timothy O'Shea and Bill Bartley, last seen with Albert Moss who had mysteriously acquired their possessions. But without any bodies the authorities had little evidence to prove that murder had been committed.

Police pulled together every resource they could find, which included the services of the NSW police force's leading blacktracker, Alec Wiley, and piece by piece they gathered the evidence that would eventually put Albert Moss where he belonged – behind bars forever.

Police quickly discovered that Moss had sold Bill Bartley's bicycle and Tim O'Shea's possessions, and the few swaggies they interviewed who had been in Moss's company recalled him speaking of the difficulty of destroying all of the evidence of a murdered man. In particular, they recalled that he mentioned teeth would never burn.

With Moss safely behind bars in Dubbo, charged with the

theft of Robinson's horse and sulky, an army of police examined every camp reserve that Moss may have stayed at within a hundred miles and paid particular attention to sifting the ashes of the fires. At Mack's Reserve, some bloodstained clothing was found, and human teeth and tunic buttons were uncovered in the ashes of a fire. In the bushes nearby they found a bag containing Tim O'Shea's reading glasses.

When told that the sale of O'Shea's possessions had been traced back to him, that they had found some of O'Shea's remains, and that the case against him was almost watertight, Albert Moss confessed to the murder of the Irish gold prospector.

When taken to Brummagen Creek and questioned about the suspected murder of Thomas Robinson, Moss bunged on his insanity act, leaping about like a wallaby, eating grass and imitating a crow by flapping his arms. But the police knew all about Moss and his antics and his charade went begging.

Moss eventually confessed to killing Robinson, claiming that he had thrown the body down a disused mine shaft. But after finding more human teeth in a campfire at Brummagen Creek, police were convinced that the old man had been killed and burnt the same as Timothy O'Shea.

Albert Moss was charged with the murders of Bartley (whose remains were never found), Robinson and O'Shea but was only convicted of the latter two. In court he went through the old insanity routine, only this time they were ahead of him and revealed that his frothing at the mouth was helped along by a bar of soap.

On 26 September 1939, Albert Andrew Moss was convicted of murder and sentenced to death by hanging. Incredibly, Moss managed to convince the best psychiatrists in the state that he wasn't the full quid and the death sentence was commuted to life imprisonment.

Albert Moss made many confessions while in prison, the most consistent being that he had killed 13 swaggies in all, but it would have been impossible to trace them back to him due to their nomadic lives. Over a period of years he confessed the additional swaggie murders to the man who had played a major role in tracking him down, Superintendent M.F. Calman, and spent many hours in Long Bay Jail with the NSW Government's consulting psychiatrist, Dr John McGeorge, who said: 'Of all the hundreds of killers I have examined professionally, Moss was the most brutal and most cunning. When I told him how lucky he was to get a reprieve from hanging, he said: "You don't know how lucky, Doc. There was 13 of them I killed."'

This was a confession that he would repeat time and again, sometimes shaking his head and wondering out loud if it may not have been 14. But confess as he would, he never once revealed any of the supposed dead men's identities or where their remains were buried.

Albert Andrew Moss, the infamous Swaggie Killer, died in Long Bay Penitentiary Hospital on 24 January 1958 after a long illness.

CHAPTER 9

The Brownout Strangler

Edward Joseph Leonski
Melbourne, 1942

In the late 1930s and early 1940s, the population of Melbourne had been increased greatly by the influx of overseas servicemen, mainly from the United States, and the many refugees who had fled the horrors of war-torn Europe to find a sanctuary in sunny Australia.

And so, in 1942, when three women were savagely strangled to death in the space of 16 days, the finger of suspicion was pointed at the newcomers. Yes, Melbourne had had its stranglings before, but they were always isolated incidents – a domestic argument or the like – and usually solved by police in no time.

But the 1942 stranglings were different. This was the work of a serial killer who lured women into dark places and then throttled the last breath out of them. It was as if Jack the Ripper were reincarnated and on the loose in Melbourne. Women feared to go out at nights without a male escort and when at home they kept their doors bolted and drapes drawn.

A zealous press seized upon the serial killings and dubbed the murderer 'the Brownout Strangler' as he had carried out his killings under cover of the 'brownout', the partial blackout ordered for wartime security.

It was the likes of which Australia had never seen before. Detectives surmised that the killer was most likely one of the many thousands of newcomers from foreign shores. And if that were the case, then it was highly unlikely that the serial killer had the opportunity to get to know all of his victims before he killed them. He would be snatching them off the streets at random and murdering them wherever he saw fit. It was little wonder that Melbourne had gone to ground.

The first of the stranglings that would put Melbourne under siege occurred late on the evening of 2 May 1942. Forty-year-old domestic servant Ivy McLeod became the Brownout Strangler's first victim as she waited for a tram in the clammy autumn cold. Her bruised and battered body was found the following morning in a doorway in Victoria Avenue, East Melbourne, by a horrified passerby.

Ivy McLeod's skull had been fractured, her body was extensively bruised and her clothes had been ripped from her body as if by a person in an uncontrollable rage. If it weren't for the fact that she had been strangled, the injuries could have been the work of a wild beast that had leapt out at her from the shadows. To add to the mystery, the woman hadn't been sexually molested, which ruled out a sexual predator.

Police could find no motive for the murder of Ivy McLeod. She had few friends and fewer enemies. There was nothing to indicate a domestic dispute and puzzled detectives were left to ponder the reasons for such a senseless and barbaric killing. The only lead they had to go on was that an American soldier was seen in the vicinity of the crime. Given that Melbourne was host to thousands of GIs at the time, it was noted but led nowhere.

Detectives were almost certain that they had a serial killer on their hands when, almost a week later, on 8 May, another body turned up savaged in an identical fashion. Melbourne stenographer and 31-year-old mother of two Pauline Thompson was found in a doorway in her own street – Spring Street, Melbourne – not far from her apartment. Mrs Thompson was the wife of a police constable who had been transferred from Melbourne to rural Bendigo, and she lived in the Spring Street apartment with their two children, aged four and seven.

There was little doubt that Pauline Thompson was the victim of the Brownout Strangler, a killer with very powerful, perhaps unnaturally strong, hands. Her face had been badly battered and her clothes had been savagely ripped from her body as if by a monster with elongated claws and fangs. The unfortunate woman's neck was severely bruised from the immense pressure that had been exerted on either side, causing her death. A post-mortem examination revealed that she hadn't been sexually molested.

Again police inquiries led nowhere. All of the squeaky-clean friends and acquaintances of the Thompsons were eliminated as suspects almost immediately, and there was nothing untoward in the family's routine to suggest that it could be a revenge killing or a crime of passion.

The only lead that police had to go on was that on the evening of her death, after she had seen her husband off to Bendigo at Spencer Street Station, Mrs Thompson was seen talking to a couple of American servicemen. This wasn't considered unusual by the people who knew her, as she sang at concerts for the entertainment of Australian and overseas troops in their camps. Police checked it out anyway, but came up with nothing.

Later that month, at 7.30 on the rainy evening of 28 May 1942, the Brownout Strangler struck again in the same vicious and senseless manner when he strangled 40-year-old librarian Gladys Hosking as she made her way home from the Melbourne University's Chemistry Department. The following day, her body was found in Royal Park, covered in yellow clay, not far from an American army camp. Gladys Hosking's clothes had been ripped from her body and she had been asphyxiated by the same pair of muscular hands that had killed the previous two women. She hadn't been sexually assaulted.

To friends and acquaintances, Gladys Hosking was the pillar of respectability. She was reserved, had few, if any, male friends, lived for her work at the university, and dedicated most of her spare time to an amateur theatrical group. There wasn't a possibility in the world that she could have been solicited in a bar or the likes. Detectives surmised that the woman would have been lured to her death as she walked along the street or had been attacked by surprise.

The death of Gladys Hosking confirmed what the police already knew – that the serial killer chose his victims as the mood to kill came over him, and the killings weren't premeditated, due to a lover's tiff or a secret affair. The killer did not get to know the victim beforehand, through a prearranged date or engagement, and plan her murder. The Brownout Strangler was a spontaneous madman who could turn from an ordinary man into a murderer in the blink of an eye as the opportunity to kill presented itself.

It was the killing of Gladys Hosking that was the undoing of the Brownout Strangler. On the night of the murder, the sentry of the nearby army camp was surprised when an American soldier, his uniform covered in yellow mud and clay, came staggering through the sentry gates. Flashing the torch up and down the soldier, the Australian sentry asked how he got in such a condition and, after explaining that he was horribly drunk and had slipped in the mud on his way back to camp, the soldier was allowed to pass.

So when the police arrived at the army camp the following day to ask if anyone had seen anything unusual the previous evening, the sentry told of his encounter with the supposedly drunken, mud-covered soldier, and the entire camp was put on parade for the possible identification of the soldier in a line-up.

In the meantime, police had been making excellent headway on the case. A woman had come forward and told them that she had met a nice young American serviceman and had invited him back to her apartment for tea. When she returned to the lounge room from the kitchen with a pot of tea and scones she was shocked to find the young man sitting in his chair in nothing but his singlet and socks. She immediately expressed her disapproval and told the young man to get dressed and leave, otherwise she would call the police. His demeanour changed instantly. He reacted violently and said: 'I'll strangle you. I'll take your voice from you.'

The woman opened the window and, standing by it, she repeated her threat to call for the police. The man's attitude calmed immediately and he said: 'Please don't do that. I didn't mean any harm. I only wanted your voice.' With that he quietly put on his clothes and left.

There was no doubt in the woman's mind that she had come horribly close to becoming the Brownout Strangler's fourth victim, and she gave the police a perfect description of the man who said that his name was Eddie. She described a large, unusual, reddish birthmark on his body that, ironically, she would never have seen had he not removed most of his clothing.

The perfect scenario in the army camp line-up would be that the sentry would identify the soldier covered in mud from the night before and then further examination of the man would reveal that he had a birthmark, as described by the woman who had the confrontation with him. With this information in mind, police went to the line-up convinced that they were at last about to meet up with the elusive Brownout Strangler who had so needlessly claimed the lives of three perfectly innocent women.

All of the soldiers from the camp near Royal Park, where Gladys Hosking's body was found, were put on parade. Accompanied by Melbourne detectives, the Australian sentry slowly strolled passed each soldier, stopping every so often to scrutinise this face and that in the hope that he would recognise the man that he had encountered in the beam of his torch the night before.

As the sentry was doing his inspection, soldiers of the US Provost Corps, the American army's toughest policemen, were rifling every tent in search of a mud-caked or newly washed uniform or the like in an attempt to expose some incriminating evidence.

The sentry stopped at Private First-Class Edward Joseph Leonski, looked him up and down and walked ahead, only to stop a few paces on, turn around and come back. As he did so, Leonski turned to the soldier beside him and said: 'This looks like the end of the line.' It was. If there was any shadow of doubt in the sentry's mind it was dispelled in those few paces past the big Texan, and he turned on his heel and identified Leonski as the soldier who had returned to camp covered in mud the evening before.

With the exception of one of the soldiers in the line-up, Eddie Leonski's tent-mate, all the men were mystified as to why they were called out. Leonski's tent-mate had more than a better idea that Leonski was the Brownout Strangler and would have eventually gone to the police with what he knew – or so he would later claim.

After each of the first two murders, the soldier had seen his tent-mate in a remorseful state of depression, tortured by fits of crying and severe agitation. He had even confessed that he was the killer, saying: 'I killed! I killed! I'm a Dr Jekyll and Mr Hyde.'

Leonski also carried two newspaper clippings in his pocket about the murders and had said to his tent-mate: 'Everybody is wondering about these murders. I'm not wondering. I know.' In the time that the soldier had shared a tent with Leonski he had grown to like him enormously and considered him to be a true friend. It was because of this loyalty they shared between them that he had never informed on Leonski. If he had, it most certainly would have saved the life of the innocent librarian Gladys Hosking.

When Edward Leonski was confronted with the overwhelming evidence of Gladys Hosking's death, he broke down and confessed and also admitted to the murders of Ivy McLeod and Pauline Thompson.

But the young soldier was hardly the image of the beast that the detectives had imagined was responsible for such ghastly, senseless murders. Twenty-four-year old Edward Joseph Leonski was the epitome of the all-American soldier. He was a tall, powerfully built, good looking and happy-go-lucky Texan-born kid who grew up in New York. And with his blond GI-style crewcut, spit-polished shoes and knife-edge-creased trousers, he could have modelled on one of those posters that read, *Uncle Sam Wants You!*

But being a soldier was about the last thing that Eddie Leonski wanted in life. His ambition was to be a strong man in the circus, and he worked out day and night and became a competitive weight-lifter to help him achieve his ambition. While drunk, one of Eddie's tricks was to lift a man onto the bar with one hand. Another was to walk on his hands for up to half an hour at a time.

He was regarded as an odd individual, yet pleasant enough and harmless. But he was also recognised as a man to be avoided like the plague when he was drunk. As a youth in San Antonio, Texas, he had been charged with, and eventually acquitted of, raping a young girl. His father had been a chronic alcoholic who bashed his wife and family and eventually dropped dead in front of them after succumbing to a week-long bender. His mother, who was a professional female weight-lifter, remarried another alcoholic who wasn't much better. Leonski had one brother who spent his life in and out of mental institutions and another who had been in jail. A third was a hopeless delinquent.

But Eddie was different. His smooth voice, his round baby

face and bright blue eyes, his spruce grooming, the crease in his trousers, and the gloss on his thick fair hair all endeared him to women, whether they were strangers or his own devoted mother and sister. And young Eddie had an infectious grin that spread from ear to ear, just like the famous comedian of the day, Joe E. Brown.

Running away to the circus must have seemed like a wonderful alternative to young Eddie Leonski who, curiously enough, considering his hopeless home life, was an honours student at college and showed a genuine interest in the arts and music. But he was never given the opportunity to express himself.

While working in a grocery store in New York and training in the gym at night, Leonski was conscripted into the US army and he didn't take to it too kindly, particularly when he was shipped overseas to Melbourne, Australia, shortly after he got out of boot camp. At the news of his overseas posting, he reacted by breaking down in tears.

Eddie Leonski was just 24 when his signal's battalion unit was sent to Melbourne. He proved to be a handful, alternating between fits of deep, dark depression and drinking binges that saw him become aggressive and obstreperous. It was during these binges that his army buddies learned to give him a very wide berth.

But the detectives wanted to know why a young man like Eddie Leonski would strangle innocent women with his giant, muscle-bound hands, which looked as though they could crush house bricks. 'I like singing,' was the only explanation he could offer. 'I like to sing softly and I like women with soft voices. That's why I choked those ladies. It was to get their voices.'

Edward Leonski then explained to puzzled detectives how he murdered the three women. He'd had a few drinks, but was not drunk, when he met Ivy McLeod while she was walking down the street to her tram stop and he asked if he could walk with her. She agreed, and after they had walked a short distance, he stepped into a darkened doorway, grabbed her by the throat for no apparent reason, and started squeezing until she fell to the ground dead. As she fell she hit her head heavily, and he fell on top of her and started ripping her clothes off. Her belt wouldn't rip and he became hostile, tearing and pulling at it in a frenzy.

At least this explained to the detectives why it appeared as if Ivy McLeod had been attacked by a wild animal. But why did he kill her? What was his reason? Leonski couldn't explain why. He had no reason.

He said he heard footsteps coming and he ran away, leaving the woman dead where she lay. Back at the army base, when he took stock of himself, he knew that he had killed a woman and he became afraid and repentant. He went to sleep that night, hoping that it was just a bad dream and that it would all be gone in the morning. But it hadn't. When he read about it in the papers it was as if he were reading about another person's crimes, not his.

Eddie Leonski was also sober when he met Pauline Thompson as she was sitting in a café. He complimented her on her beautiful speaking voice and commented that she would probably be a good singer, to which she explained that she sang at concerts for servicemen.

'Would you sing for me?' he asked as he paid the bill and they left the café. 'She sang just for me,' Leonski said in his statement to police. 'She sang in my ear as we approached a dark doorway. Her voice was sweet and soft and I could feel myself going mad about it. I reached for her and grabbed her and choked her. I told her that I just wanted her voice. My heart was pounding a mile a minute.'

With that the GI set upon Mrs Thompson and strangled her until she fell dead at his feet. Then, in a frenzy, he ripped and tore at her clothes until he heard footsteps coming and fled back to his tent to experience the same traumas he had gone through after the first killing.

On the night of the third murder, Leonski said that he was walking home towards the camp in North Melbourne when he came upon Gladys Hosking sheltering from the rain underneath an umbrella and he asked politely if she wouldn't mind if he shared it. The lady agreed and the pair strolled down the street chatting until the lady reached the guesthouse where she lived and bade him goodnight. Before she was inside the doorway he was upon her. 'She had such a lovely voice,' he said. 'I wanted that voice. So I choked her until she didn't make a sound.'

Leonski dragged Gladys Hosking beneath a fence and ripped what clothing he could from her body. The dead woman was covered in thick mud and so was her killer. He returned to camp where he was confronted by the sentry at the gate. The rest was history.

When the news of Eddie Leonski's confession and subsequent charging reached America, his mother was distraught. 'Oh no. It can't be Eddie!' she protested, to no avail. 'Why, he was always gentle and kind. He has always been the best one in the family. Oh, there's a mistake, somewhere. It just can't be Eddie!' But Eddie it was.

At his trial held in the Melbourne Criminal Court, Edward Leonski pleaded not guilty by means of insanity, but psychiatrists from America and Australia agreed that he was perfectly sane at the time of the stranglings and he quietly accepted the guilty verdict and the sentence of death by hanging.

To his jailers, with whom he played draughts, Leonski was 'just a kid', a gentle, laughing young soldier who, above all else, didn't want to cause any trouble. On one occasion, he gave guards an exhibition of his extraordinary strength by crushing a tin of jam with his bare hands until the seams burst and its sticky contents sprayed everywhere.

In the days leading up to his hanging the happy young man with the giant smile, who, as the Brownout Strangler had terrified Melbourne, spent his time singing quietly to himself in his cell. The night before his execution he sang a popular song of the day – 'It's a lovely day tomorrow, tomorrow is a lovely day' – over and over and was still singing it quietly to himself as he walked to the gallows on the morning of 9 November 1942.

As the American provost marshal put the noose around the young soldier's neck, he said: 'I'm sorry, buddy,' to which Eddie Leonski replied: 'It's okay, pal, carry on.'

Then the trapdoor opened and the all-American GI fell to his death, leaving a nation to ponder why the fresh-faced young man with the infectious smile, who dreamed of running away to be the strong man in a circus, would commit such heinous crimes. We shall never know.

CHAPTER 10

The Thallium Killers

Caroline 'Aunt Thally' Grills – Sydney, 1947–53
Yvonne Gladys Fletcher – Sydney, 1948–52

Like the two Marthas around the turn of the century, Caroline Grills and Yvonne Fletcher's chosen method of dispatching their victims into the next life was poison. But while the murderous Mistress Rendell used hydrochloric acid to dispose of her lover's children and Mrs Needle chose arsenic to do away with her whole family, Mrs Grills and Mrs Fletcher's preference was the relatively new poison of the time – a deadly metallic substance named thallium.

While thallium had been popular in Europe for many years as a rat poison, it didn't show up in Australia until the early 1940s where it proved to be extremely effective in the eradication of the ever-increasing hordes of rodents that invaded the eastern states of Australia leading up to, and throughout, the war years. And seeing as thallium was readily available in New South Wales without the purchaser having to record their name and address on a Poisons Purchase Register, as was necessary in other states, it occurred to Caroline Grills and Yvonne Fletcher that thallium could also be used for getting rid of unwanted humans.

It could be said that no-one in Australia gave thallium as much publicity as Caroline Grills. So much so that, in Sydney's Long Bay Jail in the years after she was caught in the act of attempted murder, the little old grandmother, who sang hymns to herself as she embroidered handkerchiefs and would shoo a fly out of her cell with the back of her hand rather than swat it, was known to the other prisoners as 'Aunt Thally'.

At first, Caroline Grills killed for greed. After that, it was apparent that she killed because she enjoyed it. And her specialty was murdering those around her – her relatives by marriage – who affectionately knew the jovial Caroline as 'Aunt Carrie'.

Born Caroline Mickelson in 1890, she was just 17 years of age when she married Richard William Grills and their happy and loving union produced four sons who, in turn, gave them many grandchildren. Caroline's first association with thallium was around 1947, when the couple lived in a house in Goulburn Street in inner Sydney and the area became infested with large rats. The local council recommended the popular Thall-rat, which could be bought over the counter for a few shillings. When Caroline Grills saw what a devastating effect the poison had on the giant rodents and the other rats that feasted on their dead friends, she wondered if it might have the same effect on a couple of people who were stopping her from getting what she wanted.

That same year Caroline Grills's career as a murderess began when she set about planning the murder of her stepmother, 87-year-old Mrs Christina Louisa Adelaide Mickelson, who had married her widowed, ex-seaman father 11 years earlier.

When Mr Grills passed away in 1945, in his will he had given his new wife, Christina, a life-tenancy in the comfortable family home they had occupied in Sydney's fashionable suburb of Gladesville. The will also stated that when Mrs Mickelson passed on, the house would go to his daughter, Caroline Grills. Anxious to move out of the rat-infested dwelling in Goulburn Street and into the luxury of the family home which she believed was rightly hers – sooner rather than later – Caroline decided to give dear old Christina, who looked as though she might live forever, a little nudge along the road to eternity.

One afternoon, as she was visiting her stepmother at Gladesville, Caroline slipped a healthy dose of Thall-rat in her tea. After convulsing so violently that the family doctor had to be called, the unfortunate woman was ushered to bed and conveniently passed away during the night. Due to Christina Mickelson's ripe old age, suspicious circumstances were not considered, hence no autopsy was held and she was cremated days later. Caroline immediately moved into the family house.

Having had such an effective result with the Thall-rat, Caroline Grills waited for a few months before she applied its toxic ingredients to her next victim, 84-year-old widow Mrs Angelina Thomas.

Although not related to Caroline Grills, Mrs Thomas had formed a lifelong friendship with Caroline's husband, Richard, from the time he had lived with her as a young boy in Leura in the Blue Mountains, west of Sydney. Mrs Thomas made no secret of the fact that when she died, her 'foster son' Richard and his charming wife Caroline would inherit her house. Caroline was also very close to Angelina Thomas. She would often make the long journey from Sydney to the Blue Mountains to visit, and would always take along a freshly baked cake or some other goodies for afternoon tea.

After one of Caroline's visits, on 17 January 1948, Mrs Thomas took a turn for the worse and passed away, leaving her house to her beloved Richard and his wife Caroline.

Having murdered two elderly women for greed and inherited everything she would ever need to live a long and comfortable life without the risk of ever being suspected of murder, at this point it is hard to understand why Caroline Grills went on killing. She lived in a big, comfortable family home in fashionable Gladesville and had a 'weekender' in the picturesque Blue Mountains. Her husband Richard had built up a successful real estate business and she was surrounded by a loving, large, extended family of four sons, their spouses and grandchildren and the many relatives by marriage that had accumulated along the way.

At her trial the only possible reason that the Crown could come up with was that Mrs Grills murdered 'for the thrill she got from watching the effect of the poison and knowing that she alone in the world knew what was causing the symptoms and suffering'.

Caroline Grills's next victim was her husband's brother-in-law, 60-year-old John Lundberg. A healthy and extremely fit ex-seaman, he fell ill and his hair began to fall out while holidaying with Richard and Caroline Grills at Woy Woy on the New South Wales Central Coast. After the doctor had visited and was at a loss as to what the mysterious ailment could be, Caroline took it upon herself to nurse the man back to good health. But his condition deteriorated; he lost his sight, and his mind started to wander before he lapsed into a coma and died on 17 October 1948.

Incredibly, doctors could see nothing unusual about the

circumstances surrounding the death of the healthy and athletic John Lundberg and, as with the situation of Christina Mickelson, no autopsy was carried out and he was cremated almost immediately.

On 15 October 1949, a year after the death of John Lundberg, Caroline Grills's sister-in-law Mrs Mary-Anne Mickelson died after a long illness during which she lost her hair and her sight. Throughout her illness she had been lovingly cared for and spoon-fed by Caroline Grills.

In 1951, Mrs Eveline Lundberg, Caroline Grills's other sister-in-law and the widow of the late John Lundberg, became seriously ill. Her hair started to fall out, she began to lose her vision, she suffered agonising cramps in her legs, and lapsed into fits of depression for which there seemed to be no cure. Caroline Grills went out of her way to call in each day on the bedridden Mrs Lundberg.

Eveline Lundberg's daughter Christine Downey and her tram-driver husband, John, lived opposite Mrs Lundberg in Great Buckingham Street in the inner-Sydney suburb of Redfern. They often got together with Eveline and Caroline Grills for a game of bridge during which Caroline would make the endless cups of tea and serve up some of the home-cooked goodies she always so thoughtfully brought with her.

Eveline Lundberg's illness lingered on until 1952, when she became almost completely blind and had to be admitted to full-time hospital care where, under the watchful eye of the nurses rather than Caroline Grills, she started to make a speedy recovery.

With Eveline Lundberg now safely in hospital and out of her reach, Caroline turned her attentions on the Downeys during their weekly card games and administered to them, as she had done with Eveline Lundberg, just enough thallium to make them ill but not kill them. In no time they both experienced impaired vision and sudden hair loss along with cramps and bouts of nausea.

Incredibly, their suspicions were still not aroused, and it was another event entirely that made them think that caring Aunt Carrie might be a little bit more than just a doting, kindly old relative who kept the tea cups topped up and their tummies filled with sumptuous home-cooked goodies.

The Downeys' suspicions were raised during the arrest and trial in September 1952 of a 30-year-old Sydney housewife-turned-serial-killer, Mrs Yvonne Gladys Fletcher. Gladys Fletcher was the victim of repeated drunken bashings by her second husband, Bertram Henry Fletcher, who on one occasion punched her in the face so savagely that she had to be taken to hospital for a blood transfusion.

In his employment as a rat-catcher for a company in Newtown in Sydney's inner-west, Bertram Fletcher had access to any amount of deadly thallium-based rat poison and there was no shortage of it in the Fletcher household to keep it free of the pesky rodents. What Bertram Fletcher didn't know was that he was providing the ingredients to his own murder.

Family friends became suspicious when Bert Fletcher died on 23 March 1952 in circumstances similar to those of Yvonne Fletcher's first husband, department store cleaner Desmond Butler who, after a long illness, died on 29 July 1948. They notified police who exhumed the body of Fletcher a few months after his death to find traces of thallium in his remains.

Police then exhumed the remains of Des Butler, and even though he had been buried for four years he contained enough traces of thallium to enable police to charge Yvonne Fletcher with double murder. At her trial at the Sydney Central Criminal Court in August 1952, she was convicted and sentenced to life imprisonment.

An appeal against her conviction was rejected by the Court of Criminal Appeal on 14 February 1953. Yvonne Fletcher was released from Long Bay Women's Prison on 11 December 1964 after serving over 12 years behind bars. The last that was publicly heard of Yvonne Gladys Fletcher was in the early 1970s, when John Romeril wrote a play about her, titled *Mrs Thally F*.

But it wasn't the trial or conviction of Yvonne Fletcher that aroused the Downeys' suspicions that they were being poisoned by doting Aunt Carrie. It was the *symptoms* of the deaths of Desmond Butler and Bertram Fletcher. Both victims had suffered long, mysterious illnesses during which time they had lost their vision, their hair had fallen out, they experienced agonising cramps in their arms and legs, had become vague about what was going on around them, and were bedridden until they eventually died in extreme pain.

With these strange coincidences in the deaths of Mary-Anne Mickelson and John Lundberg, the hospitalisation of Eveline Lundberg and now their own recurring sickness after consuming cups of tea and goodies during Aunt Carrie's weekly visits, Christina and John Downey went to the police and told them of their suspicions.

Under police supervision, the Downeys went about their lives as if nothing unusual were going on while detectives set about gathering evidence against the suspected poisoner. Christina and John Downey gathered samples of the food and tea offered by Aunt Carrie. All proved to be negative.

It wasn't until 20 April 1953 that they proved their theory to be correct. The Downeys had brought Christina's mother Eveline, now totally blind, home from hospital and, as she was sitting on the verandah enjoying the sunshine, Caroline Grills called in and made a fuss over her by brewing up fresh tea and serving her some homemade pikelets and strawberry jam that she had lovingly prepared at home and brought with her for the occasion.

As Caroline Grills returned from the kitchen with a cup of tea for the blind old lady, John Downey witnessed her reach into her pocket and sprinkle something into the cup and stir it in with a teaspoon.

While Christina diverted Caroline's attention, John swapped cups of tea and put the contents of the suspect cup into a jar for the government analyst. As expected, analysis of the tea proved that it was laced with thallium as were the tasty morsels that Caroline Grills had brought with her and tried to feed to both John and Christina and Eveline Lundberg. The old poisoner had been caught out.

Caroline Grills was arrested shortly after, and when it was discovered that there were traces of thallium in the pocket of the dress she had been wearing the day she called in on the Downeys, she was charged with the attempted murder of Eveline Lundberg. The bodies of two of her victims that hadn't been cremated, those of Angelina Thomas and Mary-Anne Mickelson, were exhumed and when they were found to contain traces of thallium Caroline

Grills was charged with four counts of murder and three counts of the attempted murders of Eveline Lundberg and John and Christina Downey.

The case against the jovial, tiny (she was just 1.22 metres tall), bespectacled, 63-year-old grandmother first caught the public's attention in August 1953, when the Sydney City coroner, Mr E.J. Forrest, conducted an inquest into the death of Mrs Christina Mickelson and found that there was sufficient evidence that Caroline Grills should be committed for trial. But the Crown instead elected to try her for the much more recent attempt on the life of Mrs Eveline Lundberg. They believed they had a much stronger case due to the relevant evidence from witnesses available for cross-examination in the case.

The trial of Caroline Grills opened to a packed courthouse at Sydney's Central Criminal Court on 7 October 1953 before Mr Justice Brereton, who had earlier ruled that the prosecution could use evidence from all of the other poisoning cases with which Caroline Grills had been charged.

Mrs Grills seemed to find much to be happy about in the confines of the courtroom, and laughed and joked with police and her defence lawyers as the proceedings got under way. It would appear then, as it would all the way through the trial, that she was trying to give off the air that such a happy and harmless old lady couldn't possibly hurt anyone. It was a ploy that would be easily seen through.

The Crown case was represented by Mr C.V. Rooney QC, who stated that Mrs Grills had become 'a practiced and habitual poisoner who had lost all sense of feeling'. Mr Rooney then proceeded to itemise every piece of incriminating evidence against the defendant from the motive of inheriting the Gladesville house and the traces of thallium found in the exhumed remains of Mrs Mary-Anne Mickelson through to the irrevocable proof that she had laced Eveline Lundberg's tea on the afternoon of 20 April 1953.

Caroline Grills's only defence was an indignant denial of the charges against her and a continually smiling 'innocent-little-old-granny' persona to the jury and public gallery. When she was placed in the witness box by her defence counsel, Mr Frank Hidden, she admitted that she had used rat poison that contained thallium over the years but denied ever putting it in anyone's drink, adding coyly as she looked at the jury: 'Why on earth would I want to do such a thing as that?'

Caroline Grills had a flimsy excuse for every situation she was cross-examined about, and in his address to the jury Mr Hidden went to great lengths to point out that Mrs Grills was a kindly housewife whom people always went to in times of trouble and whose main pleasure in life was doing good. He emphatically pointed out that there was an absence of motive in the alleged attempted murder of Mrs Lundberg and that there was no direct link with his client and the poisoning.

'If she has committed these crimes,' Mr Hidden concluded, 'there can be a no more treacherous or violent poisoner in history. All the historic cases of murder and attempted murder are prompted by motives of revenge, lust or gain. In these cases there is no question of revenge, of sexual motive, or of gain.'

In his summing up, Mr Justice Brereton did little to hide his sentiments and told the jury that thallium was a diabolical, inhuman and cowardly weapon which destroyed its victim's faculties, led to blindness and possibly death. Use of poison, he pointed out, displayed no particular smartness or cleverness. It was as easy, he said, to administer poison to a blind woman as it was to steal pennies from a blind man. Mr Brereton drew attention to the number of thallium poisonings in the Grills family circle in recent years and pointed out that it was an irrevocable fact that Mrs Grills was a common factor every time. No other person, living or dead, had a link with all of the victims.

In one of the shortest retirements in the history of a murder trial, the jury was gone a mere 12 minutes before they returned with a decision of guilty to the charge that Caroline Grills administered thallium to her sister-in-law Mrs Eveline Lundberg with the intention of murdering her.

Caroline Grills drummed her fingers on the rail of the dock and her face tightened as she heard the verdict. Asked if she had anything to say, the old woman frowned and simply said: 'I helped to live, not to kill'.

Mr Justice Brereton then said before he announced her

sentence: 'The jury has found you guilty and I agree with its verdict. The evidence disclosed that under the guise of friendship and loving kindness, but with apparently motiveless malignity, you administered poison to Mrs Lundberg, condemning her at least to a life of blindness and possible death. You are hereby sentenced to death.'

There was an audible gasp through the courtroom as the judge passed the ultimate sentence. Her husband, Richard, reached out and touched her on the arm, calling softly, 'Carrie' as Caroline Grills was escorted away by the guards.

In April 1954, Caroline Grills appealed against her conviction in the Full Supreme Court on the grounds that the evidence in the other poisonings that she had been charged with should not have been admissible. It was dismissed unanimously.

Predictably, the death sentence was commuted to life imprisonment and 'Aunt Thally', as she was now fondly known within the confines of Long Bay Jail, devoted the remainder of her life to handing out motherly advice and providing consolation to the many lost souls she would encounter in her new home.

Her long-suffering husband, Richard, visited her every week and took along as many relatives as the visitors' list would allow. From all reports, Aunt Thally was always a tower of strength and never once gave the slightest indication that she was upset by her incarceration and she felt that, even though she had been dealt a bad hand, she still had to make the most of it.

On 6 October 1960, Caroline Grills was rushed to Prince Henry Hospital situated next to Long Bay Jail with peritonitis following the rupturing of a gastric ulcer. She died an hour later.

And Mrs Eveline Lundberg, the kindly lady who, for no apparent reason, had been poisoned by Caroline Grills, and blinded and incapacitated as a result, spent her days sitting in the sun on her daughter's verandah in Great Buckingham Street, Redfern. Towards the end of her tragically shortened life, Mrs Lundberg told a reporter: 'She made my life a Purgatory. But I'm not bitter. What's the use of being like that.' Soon after, she died in a western Sydney nursing home.

CHAPTER 11

The Romanian Maniac

John Balaban
Paris and Adelaide, 1946–53

In the Adelaide suburb of Torrensville on 5 December 1952, Yugoslav street prostitute Zora Kusic was found in her small tin shanty with her chest savagely slashed and her throat slit from ear to ear. Her tiny unkempt abode was awash with blood and it had sprayed all over the walls. The blood-soaked murder weapon, a knife that had been wiped clean of fingerprints, was found nearby.

Zora's mutilated body was found by her de-facto husband, who knew of her occupation, when he returned home from work that evening. Police immediately launched an investigation, the likes of which Adelaide had never seen before, to find her killer.

Police warned Adelaide's residents that there was a psychopathic maniac on the loose and feared that he would most likely strike again. Adelaide's women of the night went to ground as police combed the bars, hotels, clubs, cafés, and underworld haunts that Zora Kusic was known to frequent.

As they pieced together her last movements police whittled the suspects down to one man, a John Balaban whom Zora was seen to leave with arm in arm as they headed in the direction of her home on that fateful evening.

John Balaban was a 29-year-old Romanian immigrant and industrial chemist who had only been in Australia a couple of years at the time of the murder. He had recently married an Adelaide woman, 30-year-old Thelma Joyce Ackland, who had a six-year-old son from a previous marriage.

Balaban wasn't hard to find and he was hauled in. Although he vehemently protested his innocence, he was charged with the murder of Zora Kusic. But even though numerous eye witnesses placed him in the company of the murdered prostitute that evening, after a five-day hearing in the Adelaide Police Court, the Romanian immigrant was allowed to walk from the court a free man.

His release would prove to be fatal for three more unfortunate victims. Police had no way of knowing that John Balaban was a serial killer who had just gotten away with his second murder and his release would give him the opportunity to go on killing.

Late on the evening of 12 April 1953, police rushed to a café in Gouger Street, Adelaide after witnesses had reported that there were blood-curdling screams coming from the top floor of the building and a woman had been thrown off the balcony. They arrived to find a seriously injured waitress, 24-year-old Verna Manie, lying in the street. It would turn out that the woman who lived above the café with the Balaban family had jumped from the balcony when she awoke to find John Balaban attacking her with a hammer.

In the upstairs bed police found the dead body of the proprietor of the café, Thelma Joyce Balaban (formerly Ackland), who had apparently had her head beaten in with the blood-soaked claw hammer that was lying beside the bed. In another bedroom they found the body of Thelma's 66-year-old mother, Mrs Susan Ackland, who also had been savagely beaten about the head and died in hospital several hours later.

And to their horror, in another room they found the body of Balaban's six-year-old stepson, Phillip Cadd. Savagely beaten and covered in blood, the lad was barely alive. He, too, died a few hours later in hospital.

John Balaban was found crouching behind a vehicle at the back of the café. He was charged with the three murders and recharged with the murder of the prostitute Zora Kusic. Every grisly aspect of John Balaban's trial, which started in the Adelaide Criminal Court in July 1953, was reported around the nation by a zealous press and the drama was played out to a packed courthouse every day, all eyes trying to get a look at the beast who had committed such appalling crimes.

The trial was a sensation from start to finish. John Balaban pleaded not guilty to murder on the grounds of insanity and, in his defence, the court was told by Adelaide psychiatrist Dr Harold Southwood that Balaban suffered from a mental disorder in the form of schizophrenia involving delusions and hallucinations.

Balaban then told the court that he had killed his wife, mother-in-law and stepson in the Sunshine Café 'because they deserved to be killed'. He told how, earlier in the evening of the murders, he had bashed a number of people, including a 16-year-old girl on the banks of the Torrens River, for no reason at all. Another victim, 20-year-old John Slattery, was admitted to hospital with serious head injuries after he, too, was savagely bashed by Balaban.

In his unsworn statement from the dock Balaban told a stunned court that he killed the prostitute Zora Kusic: 'I became very disgusted with her. However, she enticed me into the shed. I then took a knife and cut her throat. I did not feel sorry for killing Kusic.'

But the biggest shock of all was yet to come. In the middle of the trial Balaban announced that he was also guilty of another murder, that of a woman named Riva Kwas whom he met on a subway tram in Paris in 1946 and strangled her after he had had sexual intercourse with her. Adelaide police quickly got in touch with the French authorities who confirmed that a woman by that name was indeed murdered in 1946 and that the case was still open.

When Crown Prosecutor R.R. Chamberlain QC addressed the jury in his summing up, he said: 'Surely this case is the most extraordinary ever heard in this court, if not in any court where British justice is administered. John Balaban was cruel, sadistic, pitiless, remorseless, giving way to his own perverted ideas.'

The jury had no hesitation in finding John Balaban both sane and guilty of the murders, and the only consoling words anyone had to say to him came from the judge. 'May God have mercy on your soul' he said, as he sentenced Balaban to death.

John Balaban dropped quietly to his death on the gallows in Adelaide Jail on 26 August 1953.

CHAPTER 12

The Night Caller

Eric Edgar Cooke
Perth, 1959–63

In the history of Australia's serial killers, only a handful have held a city, district or a suburb under siege as they went about their reign of terror.

One killer who achieved this was United States GI Edward 'the Brownout Strangler' Leonski who, in 1942, had the women of Melbourne too terrified to venture out of doors as he throttled three of them over a 16-day period before he was caught and hanged. Another, from June 1961 until his capture in early 1963, William 'the Mutilator' MacDonald had Sydney petrified as citizens wondered whether they would be the next victim to be violently stabbed to death and castrated. Between March 1989 and March 1991, the vicious serial killer John 'the Granny Killer' Glover held the beautiful harbourside Sydney suburb of Mosman under a black cloud of fear as he bludgeoned and strangled little old ladies to death in the streets in broad daylight. And then there was Paul Charles Denyer, who bashed and murdered women in the southern Melbourne district of Frankston between June and July 1993 until he was eventually apprehended and put behind bars for at least 30 years.

But no Australian serial killer has ever had an impact on the population of an Australian city the way that Eric Edgar Cooke had on the residents of Perth for the nine months leading up to his capture in late 1963.

In 1963, the laid-back city of Perth in Western Australia, with its population of almost 500,000, was more like a big country town filled with friendly people who trusted one another. People rarely locked their doors or windows, even if they were out, and they left the keys in their cars.

But the simple and optimistic culture of Perth was about to change. There was suddenly a serial killer in their midst, a psychopath who didn't seem to care who his victims were or how he murdered them. A madman who seemingly picked his victims at random as the urge to kill came upon him.

No-one was safe. A man and a woman were shot at in their car. Two men on two separate occasions were shot at point-blank range as they slept in their beds. Another was shot between the eyes as he opened his front door. A young woman was strangled to death and raped. An 18-year-old babysitter was killed as she studied and listened to music in front of the fire.

Detectives were baffled. The victims weren't even remotely connected. It seemed as though the serial killer could come and go as he pleased and it didn't appear as though he had any intention of stopping his murderous activities.

Then the police got a lucky break, around which they combined all of their skills and patience. It was brilliant police work in the end that caught one of Australia's most elusive and cold-blooded serial killers and led to a confession that would mesmerise and horrify the nation.

The man who would single-handedly turn Perth into one of the most security-conscious cities in Australia was born Eric Edgar Cooke on 25 February 1931 in Victoria Park, a suburb not far from the centre of Perth. Eric was the first Cooke child and was followed by two sisters. He was born with a prominent harelip and a cleft palate, and his father, Vivian, despised his facially deformed son from the minute he set eyes upon him. The harelip was operated on soon after his birth and his cleft palate, which would impair his speech throughout his life, was operated on a few years later. Both operations were only moderately successful and Eric Cooke's parents were told that they would have to learn to live with their son's disabilities.

But while Eric Cooke's mother, Christine, realised her little boy's plight and gave him as much love and affection as she could, Vivian Cooke couldn't adjust and, instead of giving his son the love that he needed to make up for his almost unbearable existence and the constant taunting he received from the kids at school, he beat him regularly and savagely.

Vivian Cooke worked as a fitter and turner in a Perth engineering company. He was an alcoholic, as was his father, and in the family tradition he would spend many long hours in the hotel before going home and taking out his drunken aggression on his family. A big, strong man, he would beat his wife and daughters regularly, but he saved the most ferocious thrashings for Eric, whom he beat viciously with his fists and thick belt.

Eric Cooke grew up a friendless loner, an outcast abandoned by everyone except his beloved mother, who would be rewarded with a violent beating by her drunken husband when she stood up for her son. Yet Eric was a shy but very likeable fellow who would do you a good turn rather than a bad one.

Most people who came to know him as he developed into a man liked 'Cookie'. Even the police, who got to know him after they had arrested him on numerous occasions before he was eventually arrested for murder, took a liking to him.

But inwardly, Eric Edgar Cooke was an extremely violent man who had a deep-seated resentment against the society that had rejected him so badly, seemingly from the minute he was born.

Of all of Australia's serial killers, Eric Edgar Cooke had arguably the strongest motives from a very early age to kill repeatedly and enjoy doing so. It is little wonder that many years later when asked to explain his reasons for hurting and killing so many innocent victims, Eric Cooke simply replied: 'I just wanted to hurt somebody.'

Naturally intelligent, he did surprisingly well at school, considering his circumstances, and his intelligence would play an important role in protecting him time and again from apprehension in his career as a burglar, peeping Tom and multiple murderer.

Eric Cooke left school at the age of 14 and took up a job as a delivery boy. Seeing as his drunken father spent most, if not all, of his wages at the hotel, the Cooke household was constantly short of money and Eric had to donate all of his wages but for a few shillings to the household so his mother could feed and clothe Eric and his sisters. This constant lack of money nurtured the thief in Eric Cooke from an early age and anything left lying about – food, valuables or money – would most likely wind up in young Eric's pocket.

And to avoid his father's constant beatings, as he grew older Eric Cooke spent more time out of the house on his own. He decided to put this time to good use by breaking into houses and flats or peeping through windows and watching women getting undressed and, if he was lucky, engaging in sex.

The pickings were easy, as most homes were usually unlocked, some even when there was no-one at home. Being a small man, Eric Cooke could squeeze easily and silently through windows, or slide through a half-opened door without the occupants having the faintest idea that someone had entered their house.

After a while, Cooke began to enjoy robbing houses while people were at home and silently removing the money from a purse or wallet or the coins from a piggy bank and leaving everything else exactly as he had found it. His diminutive size also allowed Eric Cooke to conceal himself in the tightest places in the event of someone waking up, or coming home unexpectedly, while he was in the middle of a burglary.

By the time he was 18, Eric Cooke was regularly burglarising houses and flats around Perth to subsidise his humble income. And when he couldn't find money or valuables to steal and sell, he destroyed clothing and furniture, and often started small fires in the dwellings.

Caught red-handed one night in the middle of a break and enter, police married his fingerprints to those taken from some recent robberies and fires in the Perth district. Eric Cooke made his first appearance before the courts in May 1949 on two charges of stealing, seven counts of break and enter and four counts of arson.

Upon hearing Cooke's plight and that he had stolen to feed and clothe himself and his family, the judge sentenced him to three years in jail with the recommendation that his sentence be reviewed after three months during which time hopefully Eric Cooke would have seen how horrible it was in jail and mend his ways.

Out of prison in the recommended time and on probation after having convinced authorities that crime was not to be his chosen way of life, Eric Cooke took a job as a factory worker and became involved with religion and a completely new social group through the Methodist Church Youth Group. For the first time in his life Eric Cooke seemed to find acceptance among people, and the sports and summer camps gave him the opportunity to create some friends.

After 18 months in his new way of life, the police knocked on Eric Cooke's door and took him away when they found that his prints matched those on a money box that had been relieved of its contents after the home of a Methodist church official had been broken into. Cooke escaped with a £50 fine after members of the church spoke on his behalf and convinced the judge to give the lad with the troubled past another chance.

In July 1953, Cooke took a job as a truck driver at the West Perth Metropolitan Markets. It was here he met 17-year-old Sarah Lavin who worked as a waitress in the staff canteen, and they started going out together. They were married in November 1953 and settled in suburban Rivervale, not far along the Great Eastern Highway from where he was born in Victoria Park, and raised a family of four boys and three girls.

But while Eric Cooke was working during the day and playing out the role of the perfect family man, he continued to break into other people's homes on Friday and Saturday nights. His respectable and scrupulously honest wife accepted the fact that as a legacy of his abusive family background Eric Cooke still had the desire to venture out on his own at odd times, and from the outset she never questioned where he had been. The few pounds that he stole here and there saw to it that he was well dressed and never without money in his pocket and that his family also never went without.

But the idyllic situation didn't last long. In 1955, after he had crashed a stolen car, Eric Cooke was arrested and charged with theft. An unsympathetic judge sentenced him to two years' hard labour. Released in December 1956 and employed as a truck driver soon after, Eric Cooke donned gloves to do his stealing to eliminate the possibilities of the police collecting evidence through his fingerprints and set about rejuvenating his career as a cat burglar and peeping Tom.

On the night of 29 January 1959, Eric Cooke was casing a block of apartments in the riverside suburb of South Perth when he noticed, through a window, the silhouette of a very shapely young woman lifting the covers and getting into bed. Cooke entered and searched her apartment and, finding no money or valuables, crept into her bedroom on the assumption that she was asleep.

Unfortunately for the woman, Pnena Berkman, an extremely attractive 33-year-old divorcee, she woke up and confronted Cooke in the darkness. After a violent struggle that lasted for minutes, with Cooke getting his face and neck savagely scratched, he managed to stab her to death with numerous blows from a stolen eight-inch diver's knife he carried in his belt for such emergencies.

On 25 January 1960, Eric Cooke was arrested for loitering in a Perth park and sent to Fremantle Prison for a month's hard labour. By this stage Cooke was known to police as a peeping Tom and a sexually perverted 'snowdropper' – a person who steals women's underwear from clothes lines and masturbates into them. But while Cooke may have been known to police as a sexual pervert, he had never been charged with any perversion offences.

Although the residents of Perth didn't know it, police were aware that there was a mini crime-wave going on in their city that had escalated considerably by 1963. More cars than usual were being stolen, dozens of houses had been robbed with very little or no sign of forced entry, peeping Toms were looking in windows and stealing underwear off clothes lines, women were being assaulted in their beds, and several women had been seriously injured by hit-and-run drivers of stolen cars. Little did they know that it was all the work of the one man – Eric Edgar Cooke, the outwardly mild-mannered truck driver and father of seven, who had stepped up his activities dramatically. Soon he would add multiple murder to his list.

At 2 a.m. on Sunday, 27 January 1963, Eric Cooke opened fire on a parked car with a .22 rifle he had stolen from a house earlier in the evening. The bullet passed through the neck of one of the occupants, poultry shop proprietor Nicholas August, and smashed into the wrist of the car's other occupant, barmaid Rowena Reeves.

The couple had been sitting in the car enjoying a beer after leaving the nearby Ocean Beach Hotel when it had closed. Cooke had crept up on the car but had been spotted by the occupants who thought he was a pervert and told him in no uncertain terms to 'piss off'. When he didn't budge August threw an empty beer bottle at Cooke, who retaliated by lifting the rifle and shooting him. August started the car and sped off as Cooke fired another shot that missed.

Thwarted in his attempt at murder, Eric Cooke went looking for more victims. In nearby Broome Street, he found a flat with the door open, entered the bedroom and shot 29-year-old accountant Brian Weir in the head at point-blank range. Incredibly, Weir, who was a lifesaver with the Cottesloe Life Saving Club and superbly fit, survived his ordeal but was left paralysed down one side, blind in one eye, barely able to speak and was restricted to a wheelchair for the rest of his short life.

Having shot Weir, Eric Cooke walked swiftly to his stolen car and fled the scene, driving nowhere in particular but on the lookout for another victim. He wound up in Nedlands, a fashionable suburb along the Stirling Highway not far from Cottesloe, and recognised it as the area where he had burgled many homes. He stopped and went on foot in search of someone – anyone – to kill.

Approaching a boarding house, Eric Cooke found 19-year-old student John Lindsay Sturkey sleeping in a bed on the cool of the verandah and shot him once in the head at point-blank range. The young man died instantly.

Walking quickly from the boarding house, he selected another home at random in a nearby street and rang the doorbell twice. When the lights went on and bleary-eyed, 54-year-old retired grocer George Ormond Walmsley answered his front door, Eric Cooke shot him between the eyes and he fell dead at Eric's feet.

It was 4 a.m. Eric Cooke dumped the stolen car and returned home to his wife and seven children as if nothing had happened, not having to explain his whereabouts as not one member of his family would dare ask where he had been. His two-hour rampage had left two complete strangers dead and another three wounded.

Police didn't have much to work with, only a description of the man from the couple in the car and, as it would turn out, not a very accurate description at that. But they did know one thing: it was the work of the one maniac. The bullets had all come from the same gun.

Eric Cooke struck again almost three weeks later, again in the early hours of the morning, but this time he murdered in such a fashion that police could not connect the killing with the work of the Cottesloe–Nedlands gunman. And they had good reason not to believe it was the same killer. The crimes weren't even remotely alike.

At approximately 2 a.m. on Saturday, 16 February 1963, Eric Cooke was cat-burgling an apartment in West Perth when one of the occupants, 24-year-old social worker Constance Lucy Madrill, woke to find him in her room. Cooke knocked her unconscious and then strangled her to death with a light cord before he removed her nightie and had sex with her still-warm corpse. He then dragged the dead woman's naked body out of the back door of the ground floor apartment, across a rear bitumen lane and into the backyard of a house owned by the parents of Perth television personality Caroline Noble. Then Cooke cradled in the dead woman's arms an empty whisky bottle that he had found in the yard – and that is how the shocked members of the Noble family found Lucy Madrill the following morning.

Across the road, at 35 Richardson Street, 100 metres from where Lucy Madrill's body was found, 17-year-old resident Paul Benjamin Kidd and his friend Ian Pottage found a piece of wire rope that appeared to have human blood on it and could have been thrown away by the killer as he made good his escape. It would turn out not to be the murder weapon and the 'blood' was paint. Kidd also told police that that morning he had walked home from the nearby suburb of Subiaco and had arrived home just after 2 a.m., the time that police estimated the murder of Lucy Madrill was taking place just metres away. When it was discovered months later by police that the killer of Lucy Madrill was also the random gunman from Cottesloe, Kidd counted his lucky stars that he hadn't been murdered as well.

The residents of Perth were horrified. First a crazed gunman and now a sex murderer was roaming their once-safe city. What on earth was going on? It was no longer safe to walk the streets and everyone was a suspect. Women locked their windows and doors and cars were no longer left in driveways with the keys in the ignition. In two-and-a-half weeks Eric Cooke had changed the face of their city forever.

And just when Perth residents were learning to relax a little, almost six months after the murder of Lucy Madrill, Cooke struck fear into them again. On the Saturday night of 10 August 1963, 18-year-old university science student Shirley Martha McLeod was studying and listening to music while babysitting for a family in Dalkeith, not far from where the Nedlands murders occurred, when Eric Cooke shot her dead between the eyes with a bullet from a stolen .22 rifle.

Shirley McLeod was found dead in a lounge chair with her pen still in her hand and her notebook in her lap by the parents of the child she was minding when they arrived home at 2 a.m. At first they thought she was sleeping, but when they looked closer they discovered the horrible truth.

Although the bullet from Shirley McLeod's brain didn't match the bullets taken from the victims of the Cottesloe–Nedlands shootings, police had little doubt that it was the work of the one killer. Their reason for arriving at this conclusion was simple: things like this just didn't happen in Perth. The odds of there being three different killers on the loose ran into the millions to one. And they now believed that whoever committed the Cottesloe-Nedlands shootings and the murder of Shirley McLeod could also help them with their inquiries into the death of Lucy Madrill. For the first time homicide detectives believed that they were now looking for the one man. But that one man wasn't going to be easy to find. They needed a break.

The city's residents were up in arms and demanded to know what was being done to protect them from the monster that prowled their streets and killed as he pleased. In an effort to show that they were prepared to go to any lengths to isolate the killer, police took the extraordinary step of fingerprinting every resident of Dalkeith in an unsuccessful attempt to match someone up with a solitary print that hadn't been accounted for at the scene of Shirley McLeod's murder.

Police said that they would print every male in Perth if they had to. But as it turned out, it wouldn't be necessary. A week later, on the afternoon of 17 August 1963, an elderly couple noticed a rifle secreted beneath a Geraldton wax bush while they were taking a stroll along the banks of the Swan River in suburban Mount Pleasant. Suspecting that it may be connected with the killings, the couple notified the police who carefully uncovered the gun and took it away for a ballistics check before methodically replacing it, only this time it was tied to the bush with strong fishing line. They put the Geraldton wax bush under strict, secret 24-hour surveillance.

While the police waited patiently, a bullet from the rifle fired at the police laboratory proved to match the one taken from Shirley McLeod's skull. At last they were onto their man. Now it was just a case of waiting and hoping that he would turn up.

They waited for two weeks and on Saturday night, 31 August 1963, 32-year-old Eric Edgar Cooke drove slowly to the Geraldton wax bush and had a good look around before he reached underneath and grabbed the rifle butt. The police were instantly upon him and Cooke was handcuffed and taken to the Criminal Investigations Bureau headquarters in Beaufort Street for questioning.

A .22 bullet shell found in Eric Cooke's car matched up with one fired from the rifle. They had their man. Perth could sleep easy at last.

When asked about the murder of Shirley McLeod, Cooke denied any knowledge of it and maintained that he was at home with his wife and family on that night. But his statement would prove to be false. Sarah Cooke, a very loyal but extremely moral woman, refused to give her husband an alibi and told the police the truth – that her husband was out on the night of the murder.

'Why did you do that?' Cooke asked his wife after she had told him to his face that she had signed a statement that virtually sealed his fate.

'Because it is the truth, Eric, and you know it.'

'What do you think I should do now?'

'That's up to you, Eric.'

With that Eric Edgar Cooke confessed his crimes, slowly at first, until the floodgates finally opened and it dawned on police that it was just he, and he alone, who had been the source of the crime-wave. It was during these confessions and subsequent trips with police to the crime scenes that police realised Eric Cooke had the most astonishing memory of anyone they had ever encountered and could recall addresses, what took place, how it happened and what was stolen. What the little man with the speech impediment and the harelip confessed to down to the last detail amazed even the most experienced detectives.

Cooke confessed to the murders of Pnena Berkman, John Sturkey, George Walmsley, Lucy Madrill and Shirley McLeod, and the shootings of Brian Weir, Rowena Reeves and Nicholas August. He confessed to breaking into more than 250 homes in Perth suburbs and stealing money, jewellery, guns and other valuables. Cooke was so good at what he did that a lot of the people he burgled didn't know that they had been robbed at all.

Incredibly, irrespective of how long ago he had committed the offence, Cooke remembered every theft in minute detail and how much he had taken. When he took detectives back to the scenes of the crimes, in many cases the people he had robbed remembered that their money was missing but had no idea how it had gone astray as nothing was amiss and there was no sign of forced entry.

Cooke stole dozens of cars and returned some to the exact spot from where he had stolen them with the owners being none the wiser. Others he had abandoned or crashed. For a joke, one car was returned to its owner's home minus the globe in the internal light. When questioned by police after Cooke's confession, the owner said that he had no idea his car had been taken and hadn't noticed the additional mileage. What he *had* noticed was that the light didn't come on when he opened the door, and, on inspection, he found the globe missing. But while he was extremely puzzled, he didn't even consider calling the police.

Eric Cooke confessed to numerous assaults on women as they slept, most of which had been investigated by police at the time as assaults causing grievous bodily harm by an intruder. He also confessed to hitting a 16-year-old girl over the head with a metal object as she aroused from her sleep while he was searching her bedroom. Until Cooke confessed, the girl had always believed that she had fallen out of bed and hit her head.

Cooke confessed to the unsolved hit-and-runs of seven women while he had driven stolen cars down dimly lit suburban streets late at night. He had singled out his victims and had intentionally knocked them down, in some cases causing horrendous injuries.

Eric Cooke also confessed in extraordinary detail to a murder and a manslaughter in Perth for which two other men were currently serving prison sentences. One was the death of 17-year-old Rosemary Anderson on 10 February 1963 at Shenton Park, who was killed when she was run down by a car allegedly driven by her boyfriend, John Button, after a lovers' quarrel. Button signed a confession and was found guilty of manslaughter and sentenced to 10 years' imprisonment with hard labour. Button vehemently denied his guilt at his trial and said that he was cajoled into signing the confession by police. Cooke's meticulous knowledge of the death of Rosemary Anderson – the fact that he could prove that he was in the vicinity of the hit-and-run exactly when it happened and that there was frontal damage to the stolen car that he had allegedly used – indicated that it could have been he and not John Button who had committed the crime.

Eric Cooke also confessed in intricate detail to the murder of attractive 22-year-old Perth socialite Jillian Brewer who was bashed with a hatchet and stabbed to death with a pair of scissors in her apartment at Cottesloe on 19 December 1959. The coroner had said at the time that he believed the same person who killed Jillian Brewer had killed Pnena Berkman in South Perth in January 1959. Police now had Cooke for the Berkman murder.

But in August 1961, two years before Eric Cooke's arrest and confession, 20-year-old deaf mute and convicted petty thief and child molester Darryl Raymond Beamish had been tried and convicted for the murder of Jillian Brewer and sentenced to death, which was later commuted to life imprisonment. Beamish had confessed to the murder through his interpreter, but pleaded not guilty (again through his interpreter) at his trial with his defence lawyers telling the court that he had been coerced by police into a confession and had little or no idea of what he was signing.

Inexplicably, Eric Cooke retracted his confession to the murders of Rosemary Anderson and Jillian Brewer two days later.

Eric Edgar Cooke went to trial for murder in the Perth Supreme Court on 25 November 1963, and the jury had the choice of finding him guilty of wilful murder or not guilty on the grounds of insanity. The trial lasted three days and the jury took just over an hour to find him guilty. Justice Virtue donned the black headgear and sentenced Eric Cooke to be hanged.

As Cooke waited on death row in Fremantle Prison, John Button and Darryl Beamish's legal representatives applied to the High Court of Australia for leave to appeal against their client's convictions. In September 1964, at a special sitting of the High Court of Australia in Perth, both pleas were rejected on the grounds (among other reasons) that Cooke was a notorious liar and that he had made the confessions in the hope that they would delay his execution.

At 7.50 a.m. on the day he was to be hanged, Eric Cooke, in the presence of the Reverend Ralph Thomas, took the Bible in his hand and said: 'I swear before Almighty God that I killed Anderson and Brewer.' Ten minutes later, at precisely 8 a.m. on 26 October 1964, Eric Edgar Cooke dropped into oblivion through the gallows trapdoor at Fremantle Prison. A lone protester held a candlelight vigil outside the prison gates. Eric Cooke was the last man to be hanged in Western Australia.

Eric Cooke's body was buried in an unmarked pauper's grave at Fremantle Cemetery on top of serial killer Martha Rendell, who was the last woman hanged in Western Australia on 6 October 1909. It seemed that, in death, Western Australia's most notorious male and female serial killers were united.

Brian Weir, the lifesaver who was shot at point-blank range by Cooke at Cottesloe on the morning of 27 January 1963, died on 19 December 1965 as a direct result of the injuries inflicted upon him by Eric Edgar Cooke.

For many years after the Cooke murders Perth mothers warned children who didn't lock their windows and doors that they best do so 'just in case Cookie comes'. It is an expression still used to this day by those who lived through those terrifying times when the little man with the harelip and the speech impediment took out his revenge on society. Such was the effect that one man had on a city.

But if ever there was one shred of sympathy for Eric Edgar Cooke, surely it was from a statement given to a member of Cooke's defence team, Mr Des Heenan, by his mother, Christine, in her son's defence. It read:

Eric did not have a happy childhood. He always felt that the other boys were always laughing at him. He had a lot of operations and was always in and out of hospital. I sent him to a speech therapist but people then did not do as much for children as they do now.

His father would not really accept him. He was an unattractive child. He was a nice little boy, it was just that he wasn't normal like other children and my husband never seemed to be able to accept this. He treated him very badly. He used to beat him up for no reason at all. He just didn't seem to want him. He was beaten with belts, sticks and bare fists.

If you publish this I am going to get into an awful lot of trouble. I have to live in the house with my husband and he is a very cruel man.

The poor thing – I don't know what comes over my boy. When he was young he used to suffer from blackouts and he had a tumour of the brain. I think Mr Ainslie removed it.

When he was a young lad, about 16 or 17, my husband accused him of something. My husband was under the influence of drink. My husband bashed him in the head with his fist and Eric's temple hit a light switch which was on the wall between the kitchen and the dining room. He had to go to hospital. I think there was a fracture or something. I think that is why Dr Ainslie had to operate on him.

Since Eric has been arrested I have been forbidden to go and see him by my husband. He is wallowing in self-pity and drinking himself to death. I am sorry for my boy and I wish there was something I could do. I only think he has done what he did because he wanted to be a big shot. I believe he shot the people in question because he said he couldn't stop himself from shooting, but I do not believe that he admitted to strangling the girl or anything like that. I think he has just wrapped everything up in a neat little parcel for the police and presented it to them. I think he is just wanting to hit back at the world or something. I can't believe that he is a deliberate killer.

A couple of years ago my husband attempted to murder me. He was put on a bond by the Police Court. I was taken to hospital. I had a compound fracture of the ribs and one of them was piercing my lung. I was on the danger list and a detective stayed with me. I wouldn't charge my husband because I was afraid. He works at Sydney Atkinsons in the spare parts section. I have had to work all of my married life because my husband doesn't keep me – ever since the kids were at kindy. I am not leaving him now because I have worked for the home and I don't want to leave him to it. On three occasions I have taken him to court for separations. On the last occasion Charles R. Hopkins got a separation for me. This was about 10 years ago. I have not worried about it since, but I have been beaten up regularly. The police won't interfere.

Eric's home life was one life of horror for one little small boy.

AUTHOR'S NOTE. The complete story of the ordeal of John Button, the young man sentenced to 10 years' imprisonment for the manslaughter of his girlfriend Rosemary Anderson and whose case was not reviewed even after Eric Cooke confessed to committing the crime, can be found in Estelle Blackburn's superbly researched, award-winning *Broken Lives*.

After years of protesting his innocence and seeking an appeal against his conviction, and in light of the case put forward on his behalf in *Broken Lives*, on 17 August 1999, John Button was granted the right to appeal his 1963 conviction of the manslaughter of Rosemary Anderson.

In February 2000, United States pedestrian crash expert and University of Texas lecturer Rusty Haight was flown to Western Australia to conduct tests to see if it was possible that John Button's 1962 Simca could have been the car that killed his girlfriend. The tests proved negative.

'John Button's Simca did not hit and kill Rosemary Anderson', Mr Haight told the *West Australian* newspaper. 'I could see nothing, not even the tiniest indication, that the Simca was the crash vehicle.'

On the other hand, Mr Haight's tests supported Eric Cooke's version of the crash, including his use of a stolen FB Holden to carry out the killing, made during his repeated confessions to the crime.

In June 2000, as a direct result of the story in *Broken Lives* and Estelle Blackburn's efforts on his behalf, Daryl Raymond Beamish, the deaf mute who was convicted of the 1959 murder of Melbourne heiress Jillian Brewer at Cottesloe, Perth, and served 15 years of a life sentence despite Eric Edgar Cooke's detailed confession to the killing, was granted the right to appeal his conviction.

On 25 February 2002 (which would have been Cooke's 70th birthday), John Button's manslaughter conviction of 4 May 1963 was quashed by the WA Court of Criminal Appeal. The Chief Justice of Western Australia, David Malcolm, described it as a miscarriage of justice and said a retrial was unnecessary. And in early April 2005, after his sixth attempt, and again aided by extensive investigative reporting by Estelle Blackburn, the High Court of Western Australia unanimously agreed that Darryl Beamish had not murdered Jillian Brewer in 1959 and said it now believed the 1964 gallows confession of Eric Edgar Cooke.

A relieved Beamish said that he wouldn't sue the government for compensation. 'All I ever wanted was truth and justice,' he told reporters. 'The deaf have many problems being understood by people who can hear. There are always mix-ups. I did not understand what happened at the police station, or at court. I just wanted everyone to know for sure that I did not kill anyone. Now they know.'

Although it hasn't been proved conclusively that he committed them, nor will it ever be, hypothetically the murders of Rosemary Anderson and Jillian Brewer bring Eric Edgar Cooke's grisly tally to eight, making him Australia's most prolific individual serial killer of the 20th century.

CHAPTER 13

The Mutilator

William MacDonald
Sydney, 1960–62

Sydney, the early 1960s. Australia's largest city was under siege. A serial killer was on the loose. A homicidal maniac was luring his victims into dark places, violently stabbing them dozens of times about the head and neck with a long-bladed knife and then mutilating their bodies in the most unimaginable manner.

Investigating police had no trouble in linking the murders to a single unknown psychopath, now dubbed 'the Mutilator'. The warped killer's crimes were easily recognised: his victims were always derelicts, and each had been violently stabbed to death in a public place. And in classic serial killer fashion, their assassin had left his gruesome calling card: all of his victims – all male – had had their genitals removed.

But catching the Mutilator would prove to be no easy task. The fiend was as elusive as he was barbaric. When police finally got their man it was only a freak incident, which became known worldwide as the 'Case of the Walking Corpse', that brought him to justice. But instead of apprehending a monster with bloodlust in his eyes and the disposition of a caged beast, police were astonished to find that the killer was not remotely what they, or the general public, had imagined.

The serial killer who would become known as the Mutilator was born Allan Ginsberg, the middle of three children, in Liverpool, England in 1924. At the age of 19 he joined the army and was transferred to the Lancashire Fusiliers where he was raped in an air-raid shelter by a corporal who threatened him with death if he told anyone.

At first, young private Ginsberg was distressed over the incident, but as time went by he realised that he had enjoyed the physical experience and believed that this was the start of his life as a homosexual – a life that would bring him nothing but misery and humiliation. The rape would be constantly on Allan Ginsberg's mind throughout his life and would play an important part in creating the horrific events ahead of him.

As he grew older, Ginsberg became an active homosexual. His overt homosexuality made his own life difficult in those conservative times, and he was forced to move from job to job when the taunts and ridicule became too much for him to cope with.

Allan Ginsberg also began to worry about his sanity. He consulted a psychiatrist in 1947, complaining that the constant persecution was causing illusions and strange noises in his head. At the psychiatrist's recommendation he spent the next three months in a mental institution, but his health remained unchanged.

Disillusioned and convinced that his surroundings were to blame for his unstable mental condition, Ginsberg changed his name to William MacDonald and emigrated to Canada in 1949 and then to Australia in 1955 where he decided to begin a completely new life.

But, new name or not, old habits die hard, and shortly after his arrival he was charged with indecent assault when he touched a detective on the penis in a public toilet in Adelaide. MacDonald was placed on a two-year good-behaviour bond.

He moved once again, this time to Ballarat, but his life always seemed to be dogged with trouble. While working at a construction site, his peers gave him a hiding for being a 'poofter'. He retaliated by purchasing a knife and slashing the tyres of their bicycles.

Again, in circumstances similar to his earlier life in England, MacDonald held jobs only until the taunts became so strong that he had to move on from one state to another, all the while the urge to kill his tormentors building up inside him. Fact or paranoia, it seemed that no matter where he went, he would be the butt of ridicule and taunts. And the corporal who raped him and made him the source of their amusement was never far from MacDonald's mind.

William MacDonald's career as a murderer – but not yet as the Mutilator – started in Brisbane in 1960 when he befriended

55-year-old Amos Hurst outside the Roma Street railway station. Together they went back to Hurst's hotel room where they sat on the bed drinking beer.

The aging alcoholic Hurst was so drunk that he probably had no idea MacDonald was strangling him until it was too late. Later, MacDonald would claim that he had no intention of murdering Hurst when they went back to his room. Once there, however, the urge to kill him suddenly overpowered MacDonald and he squeezed his hands tightly around Hurst's neck. As he was being strangled, Amos Hurst haemorrhaged, and the blood that poured from his mouth soaked MacDonald's hands and arms. MacDonald punched him in the face and Hurst fell dead to the floor. He then undressed Hurst and put him into bed. He washed the blood from his arms, quietly left the building, and returned to his lodgings in South Brisbane.

Terrified that at any minute there would be a knock on his door from the police, William MacDonald searched the papers every day for the story of the murder of Amos Hurst. But no story appeared. Five days later, when he found Hurst's name in the obituary column, he couldn't believe his eyes. It read that the man had died suddenly of a heart attack. What the papers didn't say was that while Amos Hurst's post-mortem showed that he had died of a heart attack, it also revealed that from the severe bruising on his neck there was a possibility of death by strangulation. But under the circumstances, it could have been bruising from a fight or some other drunken misadventure and the case was closed.

Unaware of his close scrape with retribution, MacDonald went about his new-found career as a murderer with added enthusiasm. He bought a sheath-knife and went looking around the wine bars and sleazy hotels of Brisbane for another easy victim.

In a wine saloon filled with down-and-outs, MacDonald met a man named Bill and, to MacDonald, the more they drank together, the more Bill began to look like the corporal who had raped him all those years before. At closing time the pair took a couple of bottles of sherry to the nearby park for more drinking. MacDonald's urge to kill was strong, but he waited until Bill passed out drunk on the grass. Then, taking the knife from its sheath, he was just about to plunge the blade into his drinking partner's neck when the urge left him. MacDonald sat on the man's chest with the knife raised, but the desire to murder had gone. He put the knife back in its sheath and went home, leaving the world's luckiest wino to sleep it off.

In January 1961, William MacDonald found accommodation in East Sydney and took a job as a letter-sorter with the PMG under the assumed name of Allan Edward Brennan. Before long, he was frequenting the parks and public toilets, which were the meeting places of Sydney's homosexuals.

Soon the voices were back in MacDonald's head urging him to kill, and on the night of Saturday, 3 June 1961, he began his career as the Mutilator when he struck up a conversation with 41-year-old vagrant, an unemployed blacksmith, Alfred Reginald Greenfield as he sat on a bench in Green Park opposite St Vincent's Hospital in the inner-city suburb of Darlinghurst.

MacDonald offered Greenfield a drink from his bottle and lured him to the nearby Domain Baths on the pretext that he had more bottles in his bag. But there was more than beer in the bag. MacDonald had bought a brand new long-bladed knife especially for the occasion.

By day, the Domain Baths was a popular public swimming spot situated on Sydney Harbour. By night, the Domain's environs were the haunt of derelicts. There were many alcoves to conceal the drinkers from the winter chill. MacDonald and Greenfield chatted away as they shared another bottle of beer on the half-hour walk to the Domain where they settled into a secluded corner. The need to kill Alfred Greenfield had by now become overwhelming, but MacDonald controlled his urge until the man had drunk all of the beer and had fallen asleep on the grass. William MacDonald removed the knife from its sheath as he knelt over the sleeping derelict. He brought it down swiftly and buried the blade deep into his victim's neck. He lifted and plunged the knife again and again until Alfred Greenfield lay still. The ferocity of the attack had severed the arteries in Greenfield's neck. Blood sprayed everywhere, but his killer had come prepared: he had brought a light plastic raincoat in his bag and had put it on before he attacked the unsuspecting Greenfield.

William MacDonald removed his victim's trousers and

underpants, lifted the testicles and penis and sliced them off at the scrotum with his knife. He then threw Alfred Greenfield's genitals into the harbour, wrapped his knife in his raincoat, put it in his bag and walked home. He stopped along the way and washed his hands and face under a tap. Nobody seemed to have noticed him as he walked home on that showery, dark night. If they did, they didn't remember him.

There was no way that William MacDonald wouldn't read about this murder in the papers. The following day, it was all over the front pages of the evening press. They called it the work of a maniac and dubbed the killer 'the Mutilator'. The press weren't permitted to print the full extent of Alfred Greenfield's injuries, but the rumours spread like wildfire. The press did say that he had been violently stabbed at least 30 times and certain parts of his anatomy were found in the harbour by police divers who were searching for the murder weapon.

However, the police were at a loss as to why anyone would want to murder a harmless wino, let alone cut off his genitals and throw them in the harbour. They initially believed that they would have the case solved in no time. The mutilation suggested that it could be a murder of passion, perhaps inspired by jealousy, and it seemed likely that if any man or woman could do that to another human being in a fit of jealous rage, then it would only be a matter of time before the woman involved came forward in fear of her own life. But no such thing occurred and although police conducted an extensive investigation, they found nothing.

The NSW Government offered a reward of £1000 for information leading to the arrest of the elusive killer. And, in the Australian way, it didn't take long for the sick jokes about the mysterious Mutilator to emerge: 'They caught the Mutilator at the airport yesterday. He was looking for Ansett's hangars (hangers)' and 'To find that bloke's body parts in the harbour they had to send down four (fore) skin divers' were just a couple that kept Sydney amused.

Two months later and Sydney had all but forgotten about the Mutilator. Police wound down their investigations and the savage murder of Alfred Greenfield became another unsolved crime. But when another derelict turned up dead six months later and the similarities between the murders were unmistakable, police knew there was a serial killer on the loose.

On the morning of 21 November 1961, William MacDonald purchased a knife with a six-inch blade from Mick Simmons sports store in Sydney's Haymarket. He told the man behind the counter that he was going fishing. But the urge to kill was back – and it was stronger than ever.

That night MacDonald was walking down South Dowling Street in East Sydney when he saw 41-year-old Ernest William Cobbin staggering towards him. MacDonald lured Cobbin to nearby Moore Park where they sat in the public toilets and drank beer. Cobbin made no comment when his new friend put on a raincoat from his bag. Ernest Cobbin was sitting on the toilet seat when the first blow from the knife struck him in the throat, severing his jugular vein. The Mutilator had brought the knife up in a sweeping motion, the same way that a fighter delivers an upper-cut, and it had the desired effect. Ernest Cobbin's blood sprayed everywhere, all over the Mutilator's arms, face and raincoat.

Severely wounded and most likely in shock, Cobbin instinctively lifted his arm to defend himself as the Mutilator kept stabbing, repeatedly wounding him on the arms, neck, face and chest. Even when Ernest Cobbin fell stone dead from the toilet seat, the Mutilator kept up the frenzied attack until blood was splattered all over the toilet cubicle.

The Mutilator pulled Ernest Cobbin's pants and underpants down to his knees, lifted his penis and testicles, sliced them off with his knife and put them in a plastic bag he had brought with him. When he had finished, he calmly took off his raincoat, wrapped his knife and the plastic bag in it, put them in his bag and walked out of the toilet. He stopped along the way to wash his hands under a tap. Back at his lodgings, the killer washed the bloody contents of the plastic bag in warm water and put them in a clean plastic bag.

The following day MacDonald wrapped the plastic bag with its grisly contents, the knife, and a brick in newspaper, tied them with string and threw them from the Sydney Harbour Bridge into the deepest part of the harbour. This time there would be no evidence left lying around for the police.

On the Monday morning MacDonald went back to his job of sorting letters under his alias of Allan Brennan as if nothing had happened. Meanwhile, the headlines in the newspapers blazed MUTILATOR STRIKES AGAIN. The police had received a phone call at 5.30 a.m. and a hoarse male voice had said: 'There's a murdered man in the toilet in Moore Park opposite the Bat and Ball Hotel,' and hung up, never to be identified.

The horror that the police confronted was unimaginable. Ernest Cobbin had been stabbed about 50 times. His private parts were missing. They had been sliced off with the expertise of a surgeon. The toilet was awash with blood.

Again, the police couldn't find a clue. There were no fingerprints, not even on the beer bottle. The Mutilator had wiped it clean. No-one had seen a thing. The victim was married with two children. He had been living in the inner-Sydney suburb of Redfern but was living apart from his family at the time of the killing and had apparently taken to the bottle. Outside of his mysterious assailant, Ernie Cobbin didn't have an enemy in the world.

In the minds of Sydney's toughest detectives there was no doubt that if anyone had walked in on the Mutilator as he went about his business they, too, would have been stabbed to death. A madman was on the loose – no-one was safe.

Police staked out public toilets and known derelict haunts. Undercover police disguised as vagrants mixed with the down-and-outs of the many wine bars and hotels that catered for that type of clientele. It all proved fruitless.

Police issued the following warning in the hope that it may flush out the mysterious Mutilator: 'We believe police pressure is forcing this murderer into the open and he could now strike anywhere at any time. We feel that any man who is alone in a lonely street or park for more than 10 minutes could be murdered and mutilated by this maniac. We believe he is a psychopathic homosexual who is killing to satisfy some twisted urge.'

As the months passed, police had to concede that they were no closer to catching the Mutilator than they were when Alfred Greenfield's body was discovered near the Domain Baths. But where and when would he strike again? They could only wait and see.

After he murdered Ernest Cobbin, William MacDonald's rage had subsided and he went about his life as usual. He read every newspaper story about his exploits but had great difficulty in understanding that he was reading about himself. It was as if another person were doing these dreadful things and MacDonald was merely an onlooker. It frightened him.

He joined in with his workmates in discussions about the mysterious Mutilator and listened to their theories of what type of person he might be. MacDonald would secretly get upset when they referred to the mystery murderer as a queer and a sexual deviate. He knew differently. For a time, he thought his workmates suspected him of being the Mutilator, but it was only his own paranoia. The thought of giving himself up to police also crossed his mind, but he had to admit to himself that he enjoyed the killing too much to do anything as silly as that.

As the months went by, the urge to kill again became overwhelming. On the morning of Saturday, 31 March 1962, William MacDonald purchased another long-bladed sheath knife from Mick Simmons sports store. He packed it in his bag with his raincoat and a plastic bag.

It was raining lightly that night and William MacDonald was wearing his raincoat. At 10 p.m., he left the Oxford Hotel in Darlinghurst and followed Frank Gladstone McLean down Bourke Street and past the Darlinghurst police station. MacDonald struck up a conversation with the drunken McLean and suggested that they turn into Bourke Lane and have a drink.

As they rounded the unlit corner, the Mutilator plunged the knife into McLean's throat. Frank McLean was a tall, thin man, well over six feet, and could have made mincemeat of the much smaller MacDonald had he not been so drunk. McLean felt the knife sink deep into this throat and started to resist. The Mutilator stabbed him again in the face and, as McLean fell about trying to protect himself, the Mutilator punched him in the face, forcing him off balance. McLean fell to the ground and the Mutilator was on him. He stabbed McLean about the head, neck, throat, face and chest until he was dead.

Saturated in Frank McLean's blood, the Mutilator dragged the body a few metres further into the lane, lowered his victim's trousers and, in an upward stroke, sliced off Frank McLean's genitals.

For the first time the Mutilator was frightened that he had been caught in the act. He had committed the murder only a few yards from busy Bourke Street. As he put the genitals in his plastic bag, he feared that someone may have seen him. He had heard voices and a baby crying as people walked past the entrance to the laneway. In his paranoia he expected a police car to pull up at any minute. But his luck held.

The Mutilator peeked around the laneway and, satisfied that no-one was coming, wrapped his knife and the plastic bag in the raincoat, put it in his bag and strolled down Bourke Street. He also took the bottle of sweet sherry that he and McLean had been drinking, as it was covered in fingerprints. He passed several people along Bourke Street, but they paid him no attention.

Back at his room, the Mutilator washed the contents of the plastic bag in the sink and put them in a clean plastic bag. In the morning he threw the incriminating evidence off the Sydney Harbour Bridge.

Frank McLean's murder took place as Sydney was still in the grip of Mutilator mania from the previous murder just a few months earlier. And this one had happened within metres of a main thoroughfare. McLean, a war pensioner, had left a Surry Hills hotel earlier in the evening carrying a bottle of wine to walk to his room in Albion Street not far away. He was seen turning into Little Bourke Street at about 10.35 p.m. by three trainee nurses of St Margaret's Hospital nearby. At 10.50 p.m. he was found lying in the gutter by a Mr and Mrs Cornish who believed that the crying of their baby in a pram may have warned the murderer of their approach and, in turn, may have saved their and their baby's lives.

The police were so organised in their hunt for the Mutilator at the time of Frank McLean's death that within minutes there were 30 detectives at the murder scene, but again the Mutilator had fled without a trace.

The murders were unprecedented in Australian history. Police could not recall more violent or sickening crimes. One theory was that the murderer was a deranged surgeon. The removal of Frank McLean's genitals had been done with a scalpel by someone with years of surgical experience, the experts said. Doctors found themselves under investigation.

Police even listened to clairvoyants. The most notorious witch of the time, Kings Cross identity Rosaleen Norton, claimed to be in touch with the Mutilator when she had her daily chats with the Devil. Police investigated, just in case.

A special police task force was set up to track down the killer who was causing them so much embarrassment. Teams of detectives worked around the clock, checking out every possible lead – and there were plenty of possible leads. Police phones ran hot. Houses were raided on the slightest suspicion that the Mutilator might be hiding there. Night shelters and hostels were checked and rechecked. Nothing. Still the Mutilator eluded police.

By now the police dossier on the Mutilator was inches thick and they were prepared to try anything, which included sending the details to Interpol in the hope that the killer might be identified by similar crimes overseas. This led to police investigations of an American soldier who had been charged with the murder of a 13-year-old boy in Germany in an almost identical fashion to the Mutilator murders, and the detaining in Melbourne of a 23-year-old German immigrant on the liner *Patris* who was questioned at Russell Street Police Headquarters in an unrelated incident. Both Interpol leads proved fruitless. The reward for information leading to the arrest of the Mutilator was increased to £5000, a staggering amount in the early 1960s.

On 14 April, Patrick Royan, a young airman, informed police that he had been attacked by the Mutilator in Goulburn Street, not far from where Frank McLean was murdered. Royan said that his attacker scaled a high fence and lunged at him with a long-bladed knife but missed, nicking him only slightly. He said that the mysterious assailant was hissing as he attacked. He was described as tall and solid, of foreign appearance, between 30 and 40 years of age, and wearing a light-coloured suit.

Unfortunately, nothing came of the report as it was discovered that Royan was an alcoholic undergoing psychiatric treatment. He had cut himself and made up the story to get a bit of attention. An unsympathetic judge gave him 18 months in prison.

In the meantime, things were not going quite so well for William MacDonald in his private life. In two totally unrelated incidents, he had a severe falling out with his landlord and was sacked from his mail-sorting job at the PMG in the same week. MacDonald had saved a lot of money over the years and he decided to go into business for himself.

Still using the assumed name of Allan Edward Brennan, he paid £560 for a mixed business in Burwood, an inner-western suburb of Sydney. In his little shop, he made sandwiches and sold a variety of smallgoods. The shop was also an agency for a dry-cleaning company.

MacDonald loved it. He had no landlord standing over him and he didn't have to answer to anyone at work. He lived in the residence above the business and, for the first time in his life, he was left alone. So when the urges to kill came on him again, the Mutilator didn't have to worry about the risk of being caught in the act in a public place. He could bring his victims home and have his way with them.

The urge to murder and mutilate came again, stronger than ever before, and on Saturday night, 2 June 1962, William MacDonald waited outside a wine saloon called the Wine Palace in Pitt Street in the heart of downtown Sydney, looking for a victim. He met 42-year-old Patrick Joseph Hackett, a petty thief and derelict who had been out of jail for only a couple of weeks.

MacDonald took Hackett back to his new residence and they continued drinking until Hackett passed out on the floor. The Mutilator used a knife from his delicatessen to stab the sleeping Hackett. On the first plunge, the long knife went straight through Hackett's neck but, incredibly, Hackett woke up and shielded the next blow with his arm, thus diverting the knife into the Mutilator's other hand, cutting it badly.

With blood pouring from the wound in his hand, the Mutilator unleashed renewed homicidal rage on Hackett. He brought the knife down with both hands and plunged it through Hackett's heart, killing him instantly. The floor was awash with blood. But still the Mutilator maniacally attacked Hackett's body with the knife until he was forced to stop for breath. He sat in the pools of blood beside the body, puffing and panting. Blood had splattered all over the walls and the ceiling and had collected in big puddles on the floor.

The Mutilator bandaged his hand with a dirty dishcloth and set about removing Hackett's genitals. But the knife was now blunt and bent from the ferocity of the attack. Too exhausted to go down to the shop to get another one and covered from head to foot in blood, the Mutilator sat hacking away at Hackett's scrotum with the blunt and bent blade. He stabbed the penis a few times and made some cuts around the testicles before finally giving up and falling asleep on the spot.

In the morning, the Mutilator woke to find himself covered in sticky, drying blood and lying next to his victim. The pools of blood had soaked through the floorboards and threatened to drip onto the counters of his shop. The Mutilator had a bath, cleaned himself up and went to the hospital to have some stitches put in his hand. He told the doctor that he had cut himself in his shop.

It took MacDonald the best part of the day to clean up the mess. The huge pools of blood on the floor couldn't be scrubbed out and he had to tear up the linoleum, break it into bits and throw it out. He also removed all of Hackett's bloodied clothing, leaving only the socks.

MacDonald dragged the dead and naked Hackett underneath his shop and left him there. Every few hours he went back to the body and dragged it a little further into the foundations of the building until it was jammed into a remote corner of the brickwork, almost completely out of view. He left all of his bloodied clothing with the corpse.

MacDonald panicked when he finally sat down and thought about what he had done. He thought that the police would come looking for Hackett. Only a few of the bloodstains had come off the walls and there was blood all over the floorboards. If the police even came to ask him questions, he would be caught out. And then there was the cab driver who had driven them to the shop on the night of the murder. He would remember them.

Overcome with paranoia and terror, William MacDonald packed his bags and caught a train to Brisbane, where he moved into a boarding house, dyed his greying hair black, grew a moustache and assumed the name of Allan MacDonald. Every day he bought the Sydney papers, expecting to read of the murder of Hackett and how police were looking for a man named Brennan in connection with the Mutilator murders.

But as the days turned into weeks and months, there was no mention of any body or any search for the missing Brennan. Mac-Donald was beside himself with worry. Had police found the body and set a trap for him? Would they knock on his door at any minute? The mystery of it all was driving him crazy. However, although he didn't know it, William MacDonald needn't have had a worry in the world. He had been declared dead by police, and no-one was looking for a dead man.

A few days after MacDonald had left for Brisbane, customers wanting to pick up their dry cleaning had become concerned that no-one had opened up the Burwood shop. Neighbours assumed that the nice Mr Brennan had left without telling anyone. After three weeks, a putrefying smell was coming from the vicinity of the empty shop. After a month, the smell was so overwhelming that neighbours called the government Health Department who, in turn, called the police to break in the door. The overwhelming smell in the shop was hideous. It led police to the rotting body of Hackett. The corpse was so badly decomposed that it was impossible to identify. The police bundled it into an ambulance and sent it off to the morgue at nearby Rydalmere Hospital where the body was found to be so putrid the mortician had to carry out the autopsy in a shed on the hospital grounds. The only thing they could determine was that it was a man aged about forty, the same age as the missing Brennan.

At this stage, police assumed it was the body of the missing proprietor, Allan Brennan, who had crawled under his shop for reasons known only to himself and electrocuted himself. Police had no reason to suspect foul play. It looked like an accidental death. The body was buried in a pauper's grave at the Field of Mars Cemetery, Ryde, under the name of Allan Edward Brennan.

The only person who wasn't completely satisfied with the police investigations into the death was the coroner, Mr F.E. Cox, who quizzed the police thoroughly before he handed down his decision. Mr Cox listened as police told him that the body was naked except for a pair of socks and that there was no reason why they should suspect foul play. They said that fingerprints had been taken and they failed to match up with anyone on record. The government medical officer testified that there were no broken bones and that death had occurred at least a fortnight before he examined the body.

What Mr Cox wasn't told was that police overlooked the facts that the singlet found alongside the body had dozens of knife cuts in it and that there were large bloodstains on the floor and on a mattress in the apartment above the shop.

Even without the knowledge of these incredible police oversights, Mr Cox wasn't convinced. He returned an open verdict: 'It seems extraordinary that the body of Mr Brennan should have been found in the position and in the condition in which it was found. According to the evidence, the deceased had neither his trousers on, nor his boots, or shoes, or singlet. He was clad only in his socks, with his coat and trousers alongside him. Nothing was found to indicate to any degree of certainty that the deceased had taken his own life, even if it were his intention to do so. It seems to me an extraordinary thing that the deceased should have gone under the house to commit an act that would result in his death. It could have been that the deceased was the victim of foul play, although the police report said there was nothing to indicate foul play. But I cannot altogether exclude that possibility.'

When his colleagues at the PMG read of the unfortunate demise of their old workmate in the death notices they collected for a wreath and attended the small memorial service conducted by a local funeral director.

In arguably the most extraordinary circumstances in Australian criminal history, William MacDonald, the man who had committed five atrocious murders, was a free man – if only he had known it. And if he had never gone back to Sydney, he may well have remained an unsuspected citizen to this day.

Unaware that he was supposedly dead and buried, MacDonald stayed a short time in Brisbane before flying to New Zealand, still in the belief that the police would be looking for him. But the urge to kill was still with him and it was getting stronger every day. He had to kill again and, for reasons known only to himself, he had to return to Sydney to do so.

Mr Cox's suspicions of a sloppy police investigation became a reality about six months after the supposed death of Allan Brennan when, on 22 April 1963, one of MacDonald's old workmates, John McCarthy, literally collided with the 'dead' Brennan as he was walking down crowded George Street in the heart of Sydney. McCarthy nearly died of shock. As he had no idea that the murdered Hackett had been buried as the missing Brennan, MacDonald was surprised when his old work friend was so stunned to see him.

'You're supposed to be dead,' McCarthy told him.

'What do you mean?' the puzzled MacDonald asked.

'They found your body underneath your shop at Burwood. We went to your funeral service,' McCarthy replied. 'But if you're alive, who was the body under your shop? And why did you run away?'

As it dawned on MacDonald what had happened, he ran away down the street.

That night, he was on a train to Melbourne. John McCarthy went to the police, but they didn't believe him when he told them that he had just had a drink with a dead man. The desk sergeant told him to go home and sleep it off.

The sergeant didn't believe him the following day when McCarthy went back and told them the same story. They said he was crazy and, in desperation, John McCarthy rang the *Daily Mirror* and spoke to renowned crime reporter Joe Morris.

'I listened to the story before interviewing him. He didn't sound crazy to me,' recalled Morris. The *Mirror* ran the story, and the legendary headline, CASE OF THE WALKING CORPSE, came about.

As a direct result of John McCarthy's sighting of the 'dead' man and the intense media interest in the bizarre case, police were forced to re-open the investigation. Closer scrutiny of the clothes found beside the corpse revealed that the number 1262 written in indelible ink on the inside of the coat sleeve was that of a garment supplied to a Patrick Joseph Hackett on his release from Long Bay

Jail on 27 October 1962 after serving a 10-day term for indecent language. An embarrassed police commissioner was forced to exhume the corpse and closer examination revealed the stab wounds and the mutilation to Hackett's penis and testicles. From a much closer examination of what was left of the fingerprints, they discovered that the body was that of the petty thief Hackett and not the mild-mannered shopkeeper Allan Brennan.

After the 'Walking Corpse' headline appeared in papers across the nation, other witnesses came forward, including a man whose business was next door to Brennan's shop. He was certain that he had seen Brennan and another man in the shop on the evening before Brennan disappeared. Police felt sure that at last – if not belatedly – they were onto the Mutilator.

John McCarthy supplied an extremely lifelike identikit of the missing Brennan and it was circulated on the front page of every paper across the nation. Meanwhile, William MacDonald had taken a job on the railways in Melbourne and, even though he had dyed his hair and had a light moustache, there was no mistaking that he was the missing Brennan. His new workmates were onto him in a flash and, as he asked the station-master for his pay for the three days that he had worked, the police swooped on the meek and mild-mannered little man who had brought Australia's biggest city to its knees and took him to Melbourne's Russell Street police station for questioning.

William MacDonald didn't oppose his extradition to Sydney to face murder charges. A crowd had gathered at Sydney airport to greet the two detectives and get the first glimpse of Australia's most grotesque and notorious serial killer. They were to be disappointed. The thin, short, shy MacDonald was nothing like the beast that they imagined was capable of such hideous crimes.

William MacDonald confessed to everything. Charged with four counts of murder, he pleaded not guilty on the grounds of insanity. His trial, held in September 1963, was one of the most sensational the country had ever seen and the public hung onto every word of horror that fell from the Mutilator's mouth. When he testified how he had stabbed one of his victims in the neck 30 times and then removed the man's testicles and penis with the same knife, a woman in the jury fainted. Justice McLennan stopped the proceedings and excused the juror from the rest of the grisly evidence. He then ordered MacDonald to continue.

The gallery listened in awe as the Mutilator told of the killings in great detail. He explained how the blood had sprayed all over his raincoat as he castrated his victims, put their private parts in a plastic bag and took them home. The jury was repulsed when he explained what he did with the genitals when he returned to his lodgings.

It didn't take long to find William MacDonald guilty of four counts of murder. As everyone thought that the Mutilator was crazy, there was yet another sensation when the jury chose not to go with public opinion and found him to have been sane at the time of the murders.

Before passing sentence, Mr Justice McLennan said that it was the most barbaric case of murder and total disregard for human life that had come before him in his many years on the Bench. William MacDonald had shown no signs of remorse and had made it quite clear that, if he were free, he would go on killing as often as the urges came upon him.

William MacDonald was sentenced to prison for life and his papers were marked: 'Likely to offend again.' Shortly after his incarceration, MacDonald bashed another prisoner almost to death with a slops bucket in Long Bay Jail and, as a result, was declared insane by a panel of doctors. MacDonald spent the next 16 years at the Morisset Psychiatric Centre for the criminally insane on the New South Wales Central Coast.

In 1980, William MacDonald was found sane enough to be released back into mainstream prison society and spent many years in the protective custody section of Cessnock Prison, about a four-hour drive north-west of Sydney. He requested to live in this section of the jail because it was quieter and he would not be disturbed by the prison louts. Here he has lived a reclusive existence reading and listening to classical music. He is known as Old Bill.

At the time of writing, William MacDonald had been in maximum security at Long Bay Jail hospital for two years receiving treatment for thrombosis in his legs.

The Mutilator is the second-longest serving prisoner in Australia (child killer Leonard Keith Lawson has been in prison since November 1961) and has spent so much time locked up that he is convinced that freedom would kill him. On a day-trip out of Cessnock Prison to nearby Newcastle, he didn't like what he saw.

In a May 2000 interview with author Paul B. Kidd, Allan Ginsberg aka William MacDonald, Allan Edward Brennan, the Mutilator and Old Bill – one of the most feared serial killers in our nation's history – said without the slightest hint of irony of his visit back into society: 'It's terrible out there. People aren't even safe in their own homes.'

INTERVIEW WITH WILLIAM MACDONALD
by Paul B. Kidd

The information in the preceding story about William 'the Mutilator' MacDonald, and the 'Case of the Walking Corpse', comes mainly from a secret interview with Mac-Donald conducted in his cell at Long Bay Jail by legendary *Daily Mirror* police rounds reporter Joe Morris shortly after MacDonald had been found sane and sentenced to life imprisonment in 1963.

Against all prison regulations, Joe recorded every word of the interview on a hidden tape recorder. Before he died in 1991, Joe gave the interview to me and made me promise that I would one day reveal the whole horrible truth of the Mutilator murders as told from the mouth of the perpetrator.

And it wasn't hard to carry out that promise. I have recorded every grisly detail of the Mutilator's crimes in the chapter exactly as it was told to Joe.

But what of William MacDonald the man? Was the jury right in finding him to be sane at the time of the murders? And if he was, what could possibly have driven him to stab four complete strangers dozens of times and then souvenir their genitalia?

Or did the jury get it wrong? Was William MacDonald really as insane as his crimes would indicate? Joe Morris described him at the time of their interview as being 'off his rocker' and it appeared that he wasn't the only one with that opinion. Declared insane by a panel of doctors shortly after, MacDonald spent the next 16 years at a psychiatric centre on the New South Wales Central Coast.

Curious to know more about William MacDonald and the motives behind his murders, I applied to interview him numerous times over the years only to be rejected each time, mainly on the grounds that he didn't want to have anything to do with me because of the chapter I wrote about him in my 1993 book *Never to be Released*.

But I didn't give up and, eventually, in March 2000, to my elation I received a letter back from him not only granting me a full interview if Corrective Services approved but permission to take pictures of him as well. At last I had the opportunity to put the face to the name of the man who I had come to know so well yet had never met, and for that matter, doubted that I would ever meet.

The approvals for the interview from the various government departments took another two months and, eventually, on Friday, 5 May 2000, my photographer son Ben and I met up with NSW Corrective Services Media Liaison Officer Bob Stapleton at the entrance to Long Bay Jail for our 10 a.m. interview with the Mutilator.

So many thoughts raced through my head as we were cleared by the maximum-security guards and ushered through the foyer at the entrance to the hospital wing and into a small unbarred meeting room, which contained a laminated table and four kitchen chairs. What would the Mutilator look like after almost 40 years behind bars? The picture of the rather good-looking young man with the receding hairline at the time of his arrest and the identikit pictures were stencilled in my memory as they were the only pictures that I had ever seen of him.

What of his disposition? Was accepting my visit just a ploy to get near me so he could unleash an assault upon me for writing his story in *Never to be Released* before the guards overpowered him and took him away?

Would he allow me to ask him the blunt questions from the list that I had painstakingly taken days to prepare? I knew that I couldn't ask him any of the intricate details of the actual murders, because that was a Corrective Services condition of the interview. But I didn't want to talk about that anyway – the gory details have already been described in the chapter.

No, I wanted to find out what sort of a man the Mutilator was, and what made him commit such atrocities, so that I could put together the final pieces of the Mutilator murders jigsaw.

I was about to find out.

When the guard ushered William MacDonald into the room and I took my first look at him, a feeling that I have never experienced before – and doubt that I shall ever experience again – swept over me. It could be best described as a combination of relief that we were finally about to meet, and a sadness over this old man's predicament. But most of all it was as if I were reunited with a long-lost friend or a relative I hadn't seen for many years. The feeling was incredible and shall live with me forever.

William MacDonald extended his hand and I shook it. His handshake was firm, warm and friendly. But it was a handshake that hadn't clasped another person's hand in many years.

'Hello Bill,' I said as I introduced myself. 'I've been looking forward to meeting you for a long time.'

'It's a pleasure to meet you,' he replied graciously in a broad Lancashire accent as he sat down to face me. 'I believe you have some questions you would like to ask me.'

At almost 76, Bill MacDonald looked extremely fit for his age. He wasn't handcuffed or manacled in any way and, apart from a noticeable stoop and a slight shuffle in his walk, he appeared to be in good physical health. His lean, 168 centimetre frame could have been the envy of men many years his junior.

He explained that the dark glasses that he wore

throughout the interview were to protect his eyes, as he suffered from an eye disorder and the fluorescent lights could be damaging. His skin was taut and filled with colour but there was no escaping the fact that he was getting on. What little hair he had left had turned to curly grey candy floss and the white Van Dyke whiskers did little to cover the missing row of front teeth.

As the guard left us, I realised in an instant that I wasn't in any threat of danger and that the little serial killer sitting before me was an articulate, perfectly lucid, candid and well-read gentle old man. He managed a faint smile from time to time as he told us that he loved to read the classics and biographies of the famous people of our times. He listens to classical music, his favourites being the tenors Mario Lanza and Luciano Pavarotti, and Mozart, Chopin and Liszt, and the musicals of Gilbert and Sullivan.

Bill MacDonald would have looked more at home playing a violin or conducting a symphony orchestra than sitting before us in prison greens and telling us of his unfortunate life. The Walkman radio he carries everywhere with him is tuned into an FM classical station. He doesn't have a television in his cell, because he cannot watch colour TV due to his eye condition. The jail hospital does not have a black-and-white set and he cannot afford to buy one.

The $10 a week he gets from the government is spent on a can of Milo and other small grocery luxuries. He never reads newspapers because he can't afford to buy them. He recalls that some years back the guards gave him the papers as a Christmas present.

'I spend almost every waking hour in my cell listening to classical music,' he says. 'I don't associate with anyone else within the prison system. I never have. I have never had a friend in my life. I keep very much to myself. I prefer it that way.'

He went on to tell us that in his 37 years behind bars ours was the third visit he had ever had. The other two were from journalists – Joe Morris in 1963 and *Sydney Morning Herald* writer Greg Bearup in 1995. He had heard from one of his brothers many years ago but tore up the letter and never heard from him again.

Bill MacDonald is a homosexual who has never had sex with a woman – or anyone for that matter – for at least 37 years, has never used a telephone in his life, has never received a Christmas or birthday card or a letter, has never driven a car, has never learned how to play cards or chess and never smoked.

'Why did you murder those men?' I asked, hopeful that I had assessed correctly that he would like to talk about the circumstances surrounding his crimes. 'Is it true, as they said in your defence at your trial, that as you were killing them you saw the face of the fusilier who raped you when you were a teenager and turned you into a homosexual and gave you a life of misery?'

Incredibly, he answered. 'I didn't murder those men,' he said matter-of-factly. 'Physically I did, there's no doubt of that. But it is the other person who lives inside me that actually killed them. As a young boy I was diagnosed as schizophrenic and I still am today. Schizophrenia means split personality and it was my other personality that killed those men as an act of revenge on the soldier who raped me. I then mutilated each one in a manner so that he couldn't rape anyone ever again.

'When I read about the murders in the paper the following day it was as if it was all a dream. I knew that it was me that had done it but it was as if I hadn't done it, if you can follow what I mean. Then I would resume my life as normal until the urge to kill the soldier came over me again and then I'd go on the hunt again.'

'So you were only insane at the time of the murders?' I asked. 'These days we call it diminished responsibility, which is roughly the same as temporary insanity.'

'There is no doubt that I was insane at the time of the murders,' he said. 'As you say, temporarily insane. Or in my case, the other personality had taken over. And even though they found me to be sane at my trial, I knew that I wasn't and these urges to kill kept coming over me. After my trial they took another look at me and realised that I was insane and needed help. That's why I was in Morisset Psychiatric Centre for 16 years.'

'Why do you think you chose derelicts to kill? Do you think it was because they were the easiest targets, or was it the decent side of you saying that if you had to kill and couldn't stop it then at least you were only killing people who would be the least likely to be missed?'

'That's very difficult to answer. The other part of me that committed the murders could possibly answer that, but I can't. I think the second of the answers makes sense though, because I'm not really a bad person.'

'Are you, by nature, a violent man?'

'No. Anything but. I had never committed any violent crime before in my life. I like the passive things in life. But the other person who committed those murders was very violent. But he's gone now.'

'Are you sane now? Would you kill anyone now if you had the opportunity?'

'Yes, I am perfectly sane now. And the thought of killing another human being now would never cross my mind. I don't get the urge to kill anymore. I may still be a schizophrenic, but murder is out of the question. It is not even the slightest consideration.'

'Were you glad when you were eventually caught and it was all over?'

'Yes. Very glad. I hadn't eaten for three days because I had no money to buy food. I think I was glad for a couple of reasons in that all of the anxiety of wondering when I would be caught was over and also that I wouldn't kill any more innocent people. When I bumped into John McCarthy in Pitt Street and fled to Melbourne I knew that they were on to me and that it was only a matter of time. Yes, I was very pleased that it was all over.'

'Do you feel sorry for what you did?'

'Yes, very much so. I feel terribly ashamed. Even though I had no control over it.'

'Apart from the murders, what is the deepest regret in your life?'

'That I couldn't have had a normal life. A wife, children, a family home. If I had my life over, that is what I would wish for.'

'Have you accepted the fact that you will die in prison?'

'Yes. It doesn't worry me at all. I don't want to get out, I'd never survive on the outside. I've been in prison too long. Besides, if I was on the outside, I would live exactly the same existence as I do now, like a hermit. I like my own company and I'm happy with my music and reading. I would love to be able to get the papers every day and some day I might be able to afford a black-and-white TV and a CD player and some discs. But outside of that, there's nothing that I want for on the outside that I don't get in here.'

'Would you like to get out for a day and be driven around and shown the sights of Sydney?'

'Yes. I'd love to see the Opera House. It was just being built when I went to prison. I believe that Joan Sutherland was one of the first to sing there. And I'd love to see how much Sydney has changed. Maybe I will one day.'

He agreed to come outside of the meeting room and have a few pictures taken with me, and after they were done we shook hands firmly and said goodbye.

Our interview and chat had lasted almost two hours and space restrictions don't allow me to write every word of it here. However, during the interview I told Bill in front of my son and Bob Stapleton that I felt an enormous compassion for him and that I admired his forthrightness and honesty.

I decided then that I would be his friend until he died and I told him so. In his curious and matter-of-fact manner he nodded his head and said that he would like that and that it would be something new as he had never had a friend before.

I have been to visit Bill as a friend since the interview and have put a few things in place to make the time that he has left in his life more comfortable. He enjoys our visits and warms up to me more every time we see each other.

I like Bill and, although I cannot ever condone his crimes, I think that life hasn't dealt him a fair hand.

AUTHOR'S NOTE. In 2011, at age 87 and having been behind bars for 48 years, William MacDonald is currently in Long Bay Jail and is by far Australia's longest serving living prisoner. He is both sane and in good health.

The full story of the life and crimes of William MacDonald are in the book *The Mutilator and Australia's Other Signature Serial Killers* by Paul B. Kidd.

CHAPTER 14

The Carbon Copy Killer

Barry Gordon Hadlow
Queensland, 1962–90

Barry Gordon Hadlow is unique among Australia's serial killers in that his two despicable crimes were almost three decades apart yet nearly identical in every aspect: each time his victim was a little girl; each victim had been sexually assaulted before she was murdered; the victims' little bodies were wrapped in a bag and concealed; and each time the killer helped police search for the missing child and offered condolences to the distraught parents.

The fact that Hadlow's crimes were so far apart is not because he was remorseful or repentant during that time and didn't *want* to molest and murder little girls, it was because he *couldn't*. He was in prison for most of the 28-year gap between the murders. It was a situation similar to the case of Rodney Francis Cameron (see chapter 16), who was released from prison to kill again after being sentenced for 'the term of his natural life' for double murder. How was Barry Hadlow ever released to kill again in almost identical fashion, especially after a court-appointed psychiatrist's report at his first conviction read that Hadlow would commit further aggressive sexual offences if he should ever be let free? The cases of Cameron and Hadlow remain among the two greatest parole-board mysteries in Australian criminal history.

When Mrs Eunice Bacon read the news of the 1990 abduction and murder of nine-year-old Stacey-Ann Tracey in Roma, 200 kilometres away from where she lived in Townsville, it brought back a flood of memories, none of them good. There were uncanny similarities to the abduction and murder of her own little girl, five-year-old Sandra Dorothy Bacon, 28 years earlier. The Bacon family followed the Roma case right through until a man was arrested. When Mrs Bacon found out that it was the same man who had murdered her daughter almost three decades before, she wasn't surprised.

'Even before they told us, we knew it was him,' Mrs Bacon said. 'The mongrel even helped in the search for the missing girl, just like he did when he murdered our little Sandra. I couldn't believe it when I found out that he had been living out in Roma as a member of what I suppose you could call a normal community.

'I've cried over the past few weeks and I suppose some of the tears have been for the mother of the little girl in Roma. My Sandra's been gone a long time now and the last thing I wanted was for the whole thing to surface again. I believe he should be locked up forever. But then you've got to ask the question: Who's responsible? He or the people who let him out after he killed Sandra? I really knew what Stacey-Ann's mother was going through. You never forget, but you try. It brought back horrible memories. Why little children? Ours was only five.'

On 24 November 1962 in Townsville, a city and port on the north-eastern coast of Queensland, five-year-old Sandra Dorothy Bacon was brutally murdered. The child had been sexually assaulted before she was strangled and stabbed to death with a hunting knife. Such a thing had never happened before in Townsville's sleepy farming community. The nation's press focused its attention on the town. The murder, the capture of the killer, and the subsequent trial were headline material for months.

The little girl's mother, Eunice Bacon, said that everyone who knew Sandra regarded her as a happy, bright little girl. She came from a working-class family and was the youngest of five children. Her father, Donald, was a wharfie on the Townsville docks. The Bacons lived surrounded by their large family of relatives. Uncles, grandparents, aunts and cousins all lived in the same neighbourhood. It seemed a perfect environment for a little girl to grow up in.

On weekends all the relatives would get together for family roast lunches. It was while her grandparents were preparing lunch one sunny Saturday morning that Sandra disappeared. She was running to fetch her sister when Barry Hadlow, a 21-year-old labourer, called her from the porch of a neighbouring house where he had been renting a room for the past three months. 'I'm looking for my sister,' the little girl replied.

'Well, when you find her, could you give her these?' Hadlow called back, holding some comic books in the air.

Hadlow then lured the barefoot Sandra into his bedroom on the pretext of finding some more comic books for her sister. They were alone in the house. Hadlow grabbed the little girl and started to undress her. He held a hand over her mouth while he sexually assaulted her, but he panicked when she started to scream. Wrapping his hands around her tiny neck, Hadlow attempted to block her windpipe with his thumbs. Although he pressed as hard as he could, he had not killed her. She lay motionless on the bed, but she was still conscious. Hadlow then picked up a hunting knife lying beside the bed and stabbed the little girl through the heart.

Police were called when Sandra did not return for lunch and could not be found at any of her usual spots. When a search party was organised, it seemed as though the whole town came to help. At one stage, there were more than 300 volunteers looking for Sandra.

During the search, Barry Hadlow approached the Bacons with some information. Eunice Bacon recalled: 'He came up to me when we were looking for Sandra, but with everything going on I didn't pay too much attention. I just thought it was nice of him to help out when he didn't know us.'

Hadlow also spoke to David Bacon. 'I can sympathise with you,' he told him. 'Once my brother went missing for four days.' David was impressed with the quietly spoken young man who had tried to console him. Hadlow offered his opinions on Sandra's disappearance. He suggested that she may have fallen in the river and been eaten by sharks, or that she may have been snatched by a childless couple. Hadlow also had a third theory: Sandra had been murdered and her body hidden in the boot of a car. This would turn out to be the horrible truth.

Two days after her disappearance, Sandra's body was found in a sack in the boot of a car parked outside the house where Hadlow lived. Hadlow had fled by then but he had told friends where he was heading. Police picked him up later that day as he waited for a lift to take him up north. He wasn't surprised when he was apprehended, and offered no resistance. 'Where have you been?' he asked police. 'I've been expecting you. Yes, I killed her.'

As he was being driven back to Townsville, Hadlow complained to Detective Sergeant Cliff Smith that his thumbs were still sore from pressing on the girl's throat. Smith later said: 'I don't remember everything but I remember he seemed almost proud of what he'd done. In the car he gave us a demonstration. He showed us how he did it. He did seem a bit proud.'

Back at Townsville police station, Hadlow made a full confession. It read in part: 'I sat on the bed wondering what to do with her. She was out of it, but not dead. She did not look like dying quick enough so I got my bowie knife and stabbed her in the heart to finish her off.' After he had hidden the body in the boot of the car, Hadlow took some neighbourhood kids to the movies.

At Hadlow's trial, the prosecution read to the court a psychiatrist's report, which also advised: 'There is no treatment for Hadlow's condition and further aggressive sexual offences will occur if he is not kept in a place of safety.'

Police told the court that Hadlow's destiny was decided as a youth. The other kids at school always picked on him. At all of the schools that he attended he was the boring, overweight, class dunce and school bully. No-one liked the boy and he was bundled through the education system in the hope that a school somewhere would keep him. Hadlow was charged with his first serious crime at 16 years of age.

Amid angry scenes outside the courthouse, Hadlow pleaded guilty to murdering Sandra Bacon and was sentenced to life imprisonment. As he was driven away to prison, the angry mob spat at the van and chased it down the street, screaming for him to be hanged.

During his first years in prison, Hadlow was always in trouble due to the nature of his crime. Eventually, the other inmates left him alone and he settled down to become a model prisoner and devout Christian.

After serving 20 years in maximum security, Hadlow spent the last two-and-a-half years of his incarceration in the low-security Palen Creek prison farm near the Gold Coast. Soon after his release in 1985, he met and married Leonie Moodie. The new Mrs Hadlow had eight children, including twin six-year-old girls, from a previous marriage.

Hadlow had told his wife of his dark past and she was convinced that they could make a fresh start. The family lived in Toowoomba for a short time before settling in Roma, west of Brisbane. Hadlow obtained a job at the local supermarket as a storeman packer. He would often get drunk and tell bizarre stories of his prison background at the local hotel. Those listening were never sure if he was telling the truth. It was these indiscretions that would lead police to his door.

Mrs Janet Tracey chose to move to Roma from Surfers Paradise to give her two daughters, Stacey-Ann and Elizabeth, aged nine and seven respectively, a better life. Believing that the Gold Coast was becoming too dangerous for her beloved daughters, Mrs Tracey, who had recently remarried, decided the family should leave city life behind them and lead new lives in the safety of a small country town. They had been living in Roma for a month when the older, nine-year-old daughter disappeared.

Stacey-Ann was last seen walking her younger sister Elizabeth to school on the morning of 22 May 1990. After she left her sister, she vanished. When the girl couldn't be found by the afternoon, a team of detectives headed by Inspector Bob Pease flew in from Brisbane 400 kilometres away. At first the detectives feared that the girl had been abducted, but with no evidence to back up this theory they concentrated their efforts on searching the local area.

As he had done 28 years earlier, Barry Hadlow volunteered for the search party. Hadlow informed police that the missing girl had told him that she was unhappy with her home life and that she intended running away from her stepfather. Police became suspicious of Hadlow when locals told them about his stories of the years he had spent in prison. They checked him out and when they discovered the nature of Hadlow's criminal past, detectives kept him under surveillance.

Four days after her disappearance, the body of Stacey-Ann was found dumped in scrub country on the Bungil Creek outside

Roma. She had been partially wrapped in a green plastic garbage bag. An autopsy revealed that she had been subjected to sexual acts before she was murdered. Caught on the dead girl's leg was a torn piece of paper.

Detectives brought Hadlow in for questioning. He vehemently denied any involvement and claimed that police were hassling him because of his prior conviction. They searched his flat and found a piece of paper that matched the paper taken from the dead girl's body. It fitted like a piece from a jigsaw puzzle. It was almost as incriminating as a fingerprint and Hadlow was charged with murder and taken to Brisbane under heavy escort. The day Hadlow was arrested, a huge bunch of flowers arrived at the Roma police station. The card attached read: *To the police of Roma from the parents of Roma. Thanks for a job well done.*

In Brisbane, Hadlow professed his innocence and refused to make a confession, even though the circumstantial evidence against him was overwhelming. He would maintain to the end that the police had framed him because of his previous conviction. Hadlow pleaded not guilty at his trial held in Brisbane in March 1991, where it was alleged that he had lured Stacey-Ann into his car, sexually assaulted her in his family residence, and then driven the partially wrapped body around in the boot of his car while looking for a hiding place.

While Barry Gordon Hadlow sat quietly through his 18-day trial, the jury of eight men and four women heard from 69 witnesses and viewed over 100 exhibits. Even when the jury returned a verdict of guilty after 66 hours of deliberation, the 48-year-old Hadlow remained impassive. But when it was revealed to a stunned court that he had committed a similar crime almost three decades before, the prisoner leapt to his feet.

'My life is at stake!' the enraged Hadlow screamed at the judge.

'Yes, your life is at stake,' the judge replied, 'and as far as I'm concerned, you will spend the rest of that time behind prison bars.'

Throughout the trial the jurors who eventually convicted Hadlow had no idea that he had been given a life sentence 28 years earlier for an almost identical crime. When they heard that

Hadlow had murdered a child in similar circumstances in 1962, several jurors gasped in disbelief at the enormity of his crimes. 'Oh my God,' one of them exclaimed as she buried her head in her hands. Only once the jury had reached its verdict could the court be told of Hadlow's horrendous past.

After his initial outburst at Justice Shepherdson, Hadlow unleashed his venom at the police in general and the arresting officer, Detective Graham Hall, in particular. 'This is the greatest travesty of justice since Christ was crucified on the cross. He was crucified with lies, too,' he snarled. 'You couldn't lie straight in bed, you bastard!' And to the warders present he shrieked: 'They'll get theirs – lying dogs! Their lies will bring them down.'

Justice Shepherdson ordered that Hadlow be pacified, after which, doing little to conceal his contempt, he addressed the prisoner: 'It is quite apparent that a dreadful mistake was made in releasing you from prison in 1985. Your case is a salutary reminder for those members of the community who believe that convicted persons should not be kept in custody. From what I read and see and hear of discussions on the radio and on the TV, some members of the community seem to think that instead of sentencing convicted persons to prison, a better course is to require them to attend some sort of therapy course – perhaps sending them to a specified term of listening to poetry.

'It seems fairly obvious that you must have led prison authorities to believe that you were safe to be released. But I suspect that probably one of your weaknesses is small girls and, despite having given the impression you were a model prisoner, it would be fair to say that as small girls are not in prison, any weakness you had was not going to be exposed.

'I just cannot understand how anyone who had the opportunity of seeing the psychiatric report following the Townsville murder could ever have allowed you to be released in 1985. It is my recommendation that you are never be released from custody.'

As the van drove Hadlow from the court to prison, Stacey-Ann's mother screamed: 'I hope you rot forever in Hell, you evil, evil bastard!'

After Barry Gordon Hadlow was convicted of child murder for the second time, an infuriated nation wanted to know how such a creature was allowed back into society. Speaking on behalf of the Queensland Corrective Services Commission, Mr Roger Pladstow said that Hadlow had met all the criteria required for his parole.

'The law here in Queensland is that someone sentenced to life can apply for parole after 13 years and Hadlow was not released until after 22½ years. Even then, it is mandatory for anyone who is sentenced to life to remain under supervision until his or her death. Hadlow had been visited in Roma by his parole officer the week before he murdered Stacey-Ann.'

It is now horrifically tragic history that the parole officer didn't see something to indicate that Hadlow would strike again.

AUTHOR'S NOTE: **Barry Gordon Hadlow died in custody on 14 July 2007 aged 65.**

CHAPTER 15

The 'Kill Seven' Serial Murders

Archibald Beattie McCafferty
Sydney, 1973

When it was announced on 19 April 1997 that serial killer Archibald 'Mad Dog' Beattie McCafferty was to be released from prison on parole after serving 23 years in New South Wales's toughest jails, it sent a shock wave of outrage throughout the country.

McCafferty's crimes were immeasurable. Over a four-day period in August 1973, a drug-addled McCafferty and his gang of teenage followers murdered three innocent strangers because Archie's dead son had ordered him to do so from the grave.

The delusioned McCafferty believed that if he killed seven people his son would come back to him. There is little doubt that had McCafferty and his gang of disciples, later dubbed 'Australia's Manson Family' not been caught, they would have gone on killing until their grisly target was achieved. To the friends and families of his victims there was no doubt that he deserved to die behind bars, which was the recommendation by court-appointed psychiatrists at his trial in 1974.

But Australians breathed a sigh of relief when a further press release announced that McCafferty was to be deported back to the place of his birth, Scotland. Although Archie McCafferty had lived in Australia most of his life, he had never taken the time to become an Australian citizen. Much to the disgust of Scottish authorities, our prison system had found a loophole to rid itself of one of the most vicious and troublesome killers in our history.

Yet even back in his native Scotland, McCafferty couldn't stay out of trouble and it wasn't long before he was back in the courts for breaking the law.

When Archibald Beattie McCafferty was aged 10 his parents, Archie and Clementine, migrated to Australia from Scotland to leave behind their bleak working-class existence and start a new life. The McCaffertys lived first in Melbourne and then in Bass Hill in Sydney's west.

Archie McCafferty was in trouble with the police from a very young age, and by the time he was 12 and placed in an institution for stealing, he already had a long record. By 18 years of age, Archie had been placed five times in institutions and had been classed as an incorrigible juvenile delinquent. One detective described him as 'the toughest kid I have ever met'. At 24, he had been in and out of jail many times and had a record of 35 convictions that included breaking and entering, theft, larceny, assault, vagrancy, and receiving stolen goods.

However, McCafferty was not considered a violent criminal. His assault charges arose from fist fights with the police, but none of his other crimes involved violence. Yet he was obsessed with ferocity. McCafferty loved movies that overdosed on aggression and brutality. His favourites were *A Clockwork Orange* and *The Godfather*, both of which he saw many times over. His favourite scene from *The Godfather* was the one in which Sonny Corleone was riddled with bullets at the toll gates. Although, at this stage in his life, McCafferty was not violent towards other people, he told a psychiatrist that he enjoyed strangling chickens, dogs and cats to see what it was like.

When Archie McCafferty fell in love and married Janice Redington in April 1972, his family prayed that he would finally settle down. The couple had met at a hotel where Janice worked part-time as a switchboard operator. The marriage was only six weeks old when Janice caught her husband in bed with another woman. She wasn't impressed, but Archie responded so violently it prompted his first visit to a psychiatric hospital.

After discharging himself, McCafferty threw away his sedatives, started drinking heavily and took out all of his aggression on his wife. Although Janice was pregnant, McCafferty would bash her repeatedly when he was drunk, which was most nights. He would press his thumbs against her windpipe and only let go as she was about to lapse into unconsciousness.

When he nearly killed Janice one night, McCafferty readmitted himself into the hospital and told psychiatrists that he wanted to kill his wife and her family. He said he wanted to get the evil thoughts out of his head, but he discharged himself a few days later. There was nothing that the doctors could do to keep him there.

The visits to psychiatric hospitals did nothing to change McCafferty's ways. Afterwards, he was straight back on the drink and his intake of a wide variety of illegal drugs increased. So did his uncontrollable fits of violence. He got a job on a garbage truck at one point, and this seemed to pacify him during the days for a short time. At night, however, his fits worsened.

McCafferty's mother claimed that the birth of his son, Craig Archibald, on 4 February 1973 turned Archie into a different person. Janice McCafferty did not agree. She said that he was still drinking heavily and taking all sorts of drugs. She was too terrified to take the baby in the car for fear that McCafferty would have an accident and kill them all.

Little Craig lived only six weeks. At 3.30 a.m. on Saturday, 17 March 1973, Janice took the baby to bed to feed him. She told the inquest into the baby's death that she dozed off and awoke at 9 a.m.: 'I felt something underneath me in the bed. I jumped straight out of bed and I saw the baby's face and realised something was terribly wrong. There was blood on his face and on my nightie. My bra was still undone. I must have rolled over to my left and rolled onto my baby.'

At the inquest, held on 24 August 1973, the coroner, Mr John Dunn, said that the child had died accidentally when his mother went to sleep on top of him while breast-feeding. He completely exonerated Janice McCafferty, and stated: 'I must say in the interests of the welfare of the young mother, I cannot find anything to be critical of her for what happened.'

Archie McCafferty did not agree. He had left Janice a week after the tragedy and, although he did not attend the inquest into his son's death, he sent a scathing letter to the coroner accusing Janice of murdering their son.

Was the death of his son all that Archie McCafferty needed to tip him over the edge? It was a question on which psychiatrists would sharply disagree. The first eruption occurred a week after Craig's death. The McCaffertys had a few friends over for drinks after the funeral and when most of them had gone Archie started playing a record called 'Nobody's Child' in remembrance of his dead son. An argument started and Janice McCafferty fled. Her husband caught up with her hours later at her parents' house in Blacktown, where he accused her of killing his son. When he took to her with a fence picket, Janice's brother and another man stepped in and gave him a hiding.

The following day, McCafferty turned up at his parents' house at Bass Hill. Badly bruised and covered in blood, he pleaded with his mother for help. She despaired at her confused son's plight and begged him to readmit himself to the hospital.

That day, a family friend drove Archie McCafferty to the Parramatta Psychiatric Centre, where he booked in for treatment. It was his third self-admission in nine months, and the one that prompted hospital staff to ring the police when he checked out a few days later.

At this point, it's worth mentioning McCafferty's passion for tattoos which add to his evil appearance and provide some sort of explanation for his later crimes. Visiting the tattooist was like seeing his therapist. The tattooist knew all of McCafferty's innermost secrets. McCafferty confided in him, sought his advice and admired his opinions. Archie McCafferty is covered in more than 200 tattoos – which doesn't leave much bare skin.

As a consequence, when police had to photograph all of McCafferty's identifying marks, they had to use numerous rolls of film. There were even stars tattooed on his ear lobes. Like many of the others on his body they were etched in Indian ink with sewing needles while filling in the long hours in prison. He hated these 'nick' tattoos and got them covered with 'proper' ones whenever he was out of prison.

McCafferty's body is a walking advertisement of his hatred of the police. One tattoo spread across his shoulders and back reads: *The man who puts another man under lock and key is not born of woman's womb*. Another reads: *Kill and hate cops*.

McCafferty has drawings of two bulldogs on his chest and two sharks on each shoulder. There are eyes tattooed on each of his buttocks and the bottom half of his body is covered in drawings depicting love and sex.

Archie McCafferty had saved a space on his chest for a special tattoo and, after his son's death, he knew what that would be. The day he discharged himself from Parramatta Psychiatric Centre he went to the tattooist and had a memorial to his son etched on that special spot on his chest. It is of a cross-shaped tombstone embedded in a blood-red rose, and inscribed: *In Memory of Craig.*

Several weeks later, McCafferty paid another visit to his tattooist for a second special tattoo. This time he would have the figure 7, his favourite number, etched on the web between the thumb and forefinger, next to the head of a snarling panther. It was one of the few places left on his body that was not already covered with ink. Archie McCafferty chose the number for two reasons. He had decided that seven people must die to avenge his son's death. Plus it was his lucky number – Archie McCafferty did everything in sevens. Curiously, the number seven would recur during McCafferty's rampage of murder.

Janice McCafferty had not seen her husband since her visit at the Psychiatric Centre the day after he had tried to kill her five months before. But on 23 August 1973, the night before the inquest into little Craig's death, two bricks with notes wrapped around them were tossed through the window of her home in Blacktown. The first note read: *You and the rest of your family can go and get fucked because anyone who has anything to do with me is going to die of a bad death. You know who this letter is from so take warning because Bill is the next cab off the rank. Then you go one by one.* It was signed *you know who.* 'Bill' was Bill Riean, Janice's mother's boyfriend.

The second note read: *The only thing in my mind is to kill you, your mother and Bill Riean. This is not a bluff because I'm that dirty on all of you for the death of my son, but I can't let it go at that. I have a matter of a few guns, so I'm going to use them on you all for satisfaction. Beware.* Janice was too frightened to go to the police.

The following night, 24 August, the killings began. McCafferty had chosen the day carefully. It was the first day of the inquest into the death of his son.

A week earlier, Archie McCafferty, along with Carol Ellen

Howes, a 26-year-old woman he was living with, had formed a gang from an odd assortment of teenagers. Archie met Howes and 16-year-old Julie Ann Todd when he was a patient at the Parramatta Psychiatric Centre.

Carol Howes was separated from her husband and was the mother of three children aged from four to seven. In the previous two years, Carol had made three attempts on her own life by taking large doses of sleeping tablets. She told McCafferty that she intended to try to kill herself again and he talked her out of it. This formed a bond between the pair and, before long, they had moved into a flat in the inner-western suburb of Earlwood. Julie Todd had met them both at the Centre while she was being treated for mental disorders. Soon after, McCafferty took her in with them when she had nowhere else to go.

McCafferty was living with Howes and Todd at the time of the murders. They were joined by Michael John 'Mick' Meredith and Richard William 'Dick' Whittington, two 17-year-olds McCafferty had met in a Bankstown tattooist's a few days earlier. Mick and Dick had a couple of rifles. The sixth member of the gang was 17-year-old Donald Richard 'Rick' Webster who McCafferty had met only days earlier through his brother.

Led by McCafferty, the gang chose their first victim on the evening of 24 August 1973. At just over five feet tall, 50-year-old George Anson was an easy mark. The World War II veteran was a newspaper seller outside the Canterbury Hotel and each evening, after work, he would drink at the hotel. That evening, just after closing time, Anson was spotted by the gang as he staggered down the street towards his home. They had been cruising the area in a stolen Volkswagen, looking for someone to beat up and rob. Archie McCafferty was flying high on angel dust, a popular mind-altering drug of the time, not unlike LSD.

Anson offered no resistance. He was far too drunk. The gang dragged Anson into a side street. As McCafferty grabbed the older man around the throat, Anson called out: 'You young cunt!' They were the last words he would ever say. McCafferty went berserk and kicked Anson repeatedly in the head and ribs.

It was then that McCafferty heard the voice for the first time: 'Kill seven. Kill seven. Kill, kill, kill . . .' George Anson was kneeling in the gutter when McCafferty produced the knife and plunged it into his back and neck seven times. McCafferty gave the dying man one final kick in the face before running back to the car.

His young disciples were in awe of the blood-soaked McCafferty. All except Rick Webster. 'Why the fuck did you do that?' Webster asked.

'I stabbed him because he called me a young cunt. Now drive, you fucking idiot!' McCafferty screamed at the terrified teenager. From that instant, McCafferty did not trust Rick Webster. He would have to die.

Archie threw the blood-soaked knife to Julie who hid it under the car seat. So strong was Archie's spell over his gang that not another word was spoken about the killing of George Anson until they got back to the flat.

On the way, the gang went to Hartee's drive-in fast-food bar where they ordered hamburgers while McCafferty cleaned up in the men's room. Archie McCafferty was in the horrors. His son was talking to him from the toilet mirror and beckoning him to go with him. McCafferty reached out to touch him, but he vanished. Again he heard the voice: 'Kill seven. Kill seven. Kill seven . . .'

Back at the flat, Julie washed the blood from the murder weapon and returned it to McCafferty. Only then did he talk about the murder. 'I couldn't help myself,' he told them. 'I couldn't stop. I can't understand why I did it. A voice . . . it was Craig's voice . . . told me to kill, kill, kill.'

Three nights later, on 27 August, McCafferty took his gang to the Leppington cemetery to show them the grave of his son. McCafferty had been there with Carol Howe many times since the funeral. Howe said that they would sit at the grave and Archie would sob and say things like: 'The poor little bloke. He never stood a chance. It's not fair. It's not bloody fair.' On one occasion he had promised his son that he would avenge his death.

It was a cold, bleak night, and sheets of rain soaked the six figures as they stood by the grave for some time. Small patches of fog gave the cemetery an eerier atmosphere than usual. Archie was high on angel dust. Now the voice was coming from the grave. 'Kill seven. Kill seven. Kill seven . . .'

McCafferty and his gang then went to a nearby hotel where

they planned the night's events. All McCafferty wanted to do was get back to the grave – and the voice. He instructed his gang to take him back to the cemetery. Along the way they dropped off Julie Todd and Mick Meredith to hitchhike. The plan was that as soon as a car stopped they would force the driver to the cemetery at gunpoint and the gang would rob him.

Back at the cemetery, McCafferty was spinning out. He could see a bright light over his son's grave and a figure standing just out of the light. McCafferty approached the figure who said: 'Dad. Is that you, Dad?' Archie knew that it was his son. He had come back from the grave.

'Is that you, Craig?' he asked.

'Yes, Dad, it's me,' the voice replied.

'But, Son, it can't be. You're dead.'

'Do you want me to come back to you, Dad?'

'Of course I do. But how can you do that, Son?'

'You've got to do something for me, Dad. Do this thing and I will come back to you. Do you want me to come back to you?'

'Yes. Yes. More than anything in the world. I will do anything to have you back. Anything. Anything you ask.'

'You must kill seven people. As soon as you do, you can have me back. But you must kill seven people. Kill seven. Kill seven. Kill seven . . .'

Moments later, a car pulled into the cemetery and stopped about 150 metres from the graveside. In the car were Julie Todd and Mick Meredith. They were holding 42-year-old Ronald Neil Cox at gunpoint. He was a miner who had just finished his shift at the Oakdale colliery and was on his way home to Villawood in Sydney's western suburbs. Cox had felt sorry for the two kids hitchhiking in the rain and had stopped to give them a lift. It was a fatal mistake. Meredith had held a gun to his head and forced him to drive to the cemetery.

McCafferty left the graveside and ran over to them. Ronald Cox was forced to lie face-down in the mud while McCafferty and Meredith held rifles to the back of his head. Cox begged for his life as the voices urged on the murderous McCafferty: 'Kill seven. Kill seven. Kill seven . . .' The number bounced around in his twisted mind.

McCafferty turned to his gang and said, 'I'll have to knock him. He's seen all of our faces. Mick . . . kill him.'

'What are you saying, Archie?'

'Fuck you! Kill him.'

Again Ronald Cox begged for his life, telling them that he was the father of seven children. Although he had no way of knowing, it was a mistake that sealed his fate. At the mention of the number seven, McCafferty and Meredith each shot Ronald Cox through the back of the head.

As they were leaving to drive to Liverpool, McCafferty looked over at his son's grave. The light was still shining over it and the shadowy figure was laughing loudly. Archie burst out laughing with his son. He later told detectives that his only regret about murdering Ronald Cox was that he wasn't closer to his son's grave so that some of Cox's blood could have dripped onto the plaque.

After the killing of Cox, the gang members returned to the McCafferty unit where they drank beer and watched TV. But McCafferty could still hear the voices telling him to 'kill seven', and he instructed two of his disciples to go and find him another victim. In the early hours of the following morning, 24-year-old driving instructor Evangelos Kollias picked up Julie Todd and Dick Whittington as they hitchhiked along Enmore Road. Once in the car, Whittington produced a .22 rifle from under his coat. They forced Kollias into the back seat and told him to lie on the floor while Julie drove the car back to the flat.

McCafferty then took over. With McCafferty driving, the gang set off for Liverpool on the pretext of looking for a factory to rob. But they knew that McCafferty had murder on his mind. Kollias was told to lie low as they did not want him to see where they were going. Assured that he would come to no harm, Kollias lay on the back floor and fell asleep.

McCafferty's plan was to kill Evangelos Kollias, then drive his car to Blacktown and kill Janice McCafferty, her mother, and her mother's boyfriend. That would make six. The seventh victim was to be one of his own gang – Rick Webster. Archie felt that Webster was going to betray him to the police.

McCafferty told Whittington to kill Kollias. Whittington wasn't sure that he could, but as Kollias woke from his nap in the back of the car Whittington held the sawn-off .22 rifle to his head and pulled the trigger. Evangelos Kollias died instantly.

'Shoot him again,' urged McCafferty. Whittington put another bullet into the dead man's head. They dumped the body in a deserted street nearby.

When he realised that Kollias's car didn't have sufficient petrol to get him to his wife's house, McCafferty abandoned the plan to murder Janice and her family. For that night, at least. He still intended to make them the next three victims. And if Rick Webster hadn't lived up to Archie's suspicions and gone to the police, there is no doubt that Archie would have killed them, as the voice kept insisting.

When detectives arrested him, Archie McCafferty told them: 'I was going to Blacktown to kill three people . . . I was going to go into the house and just start blasting away until they were all dead. They are very lucky people that the car didn't have enough petrol.' Then McCafferty had intended to cut off his wife's head and send it in a box to the chief of the Criminal Investigations Bureau.

When one of the gang members told Rick Webster that he was on McCafferty's hit list, Webster decided to tell the police everything he knew. McCafferty, Whittington and Meredith trailed Webster to the *Sydney Morning Herald* building where he worked as an apprentice compositor. With loaded rifles, they sat in a stolen van out the front of the building ready to kill Webster when he came out.

Inside the building, Webster saw them waiting and had a reporter call police. Detectives arrived at the *Herald*, where Webster told them he was too terrified to leave. When they heard his story about the three murders they called for reinforcements and the area was sealed off. Heavily armed detectives surrounded the vehicle while Detective Sergeant K. Aldridge cautiously approached it and pointed his revolver at Michael Meredith. Other detectives rushed the vehicle and apprehended McCafferty and Whittington. They took possession of two loaded and cocked rifles.

On the way to the police station, McCafferty told police: 'All right, I knocked the bloke at Canterbury. I knocked the bloke at

Leppington. And I knocked the bloke at Merrylands. I knocked all three of them.' He made no less a secret of the fact that he would kill again.

At his sensational committal hearing leading up to his trial in February 1974, McCafferty pleaded not guilty to three counts of murder on the grounds of insanity. His five co-accused – Todd, Howe, Meredith, Whittington and Webster – all pleaded not guilty to the same charges.

The press had labelled the murders as 'thrill killings' and everyone wanted to know about the Charles Manson-like cult figure who had led his followers into an orgy of senseless killings. Archie didn't let them down.

On the fourth morning of the committal hearing in a packed courthouse, McCafferty asked the judge if he could make a statement. Although it was an unusual request, the judge allowed it. McCafferty said: 'Excuse me your worship, before the court starts, for the last four days I've sat here and listened to Mr Bannon criticising me on things that I've done. Now I've been wanting to say this for a long time, and I'm going to say it this morning. Mr Bannon, if you're listening, I'd like to cut your head off.'

It was not so much what McCafferty said that put a chill through the courtroom, it was the cold, methodical manner in which he said it. McCafferty had already murdered three innocent people, and the decapitation of Mr Bannon would put him one closer to his target of seven.

The Mr Bannon in question was a barrister acting for one of McCafferty's five co-accused. Shaken, he proceeded with his case safe in the knowledge that McCafferty was handcuffed and heavily guarded as he glared down from the dock.

Archie McCafferty was also heavily drugged. Before the start of the committal hearings each morning and throughout his subsequent trial at the Central Criminal Court, he was given a heavy dose of tranquillisers to subdue his uncontrollable outbreaks of violence. The dosage was enough to bring a racehorse to its knees, yet in McCafferty's drug-soaked system it barely pacified him.

But the drugs did have some of the desired effects. During the 12-day trial, Archie McCafferty had been alert and attentive. He listened closely to the evidence and made notes. He certainly didn't look like the deranged murderer who had been labelled 'Australia's Charles Manson'. In fact, McCafferty often winked at the court reporters and joked with his co-accused. He fingered the bench in the dock as though it were a keyboard and played tunes for the gallery. When the proceedings became tiresome, he deep-etched his name in the bench with a pen. Archie was having a ball. But without his medicinal straitjacket, the 25-year-old Scotsman was a violent man who could kill without question.

While awaiting trial in Long Bay's remand section, McCafferty had nearly killed another prisoner with his slops bucket. The only way to calm him down was with sedatives. At first, normal doses had no effect. So prison doctors kept increasing the dosage until they took effect. His daily dosage of 1500 milligrams of the potent tranquilliser Largactil was almost four times the normal dose of 400 milligrams. Prison psychiatrists agreed that McCafferty's incredible tolerance to massive doses of tranquillisers was in itself evidence that he was insane.

At the trial, three psychiatrists gave their opinions of McCafferty's mental state. Dr William Metcalf, a Macquarie Street specialist, was called to give evidence on behalf of the defence. He said that, in his opinion, McCafferty was insane at the time of the killings because he did not know that what he was doing was wrong. Dr Metcalf pointed out that McCafferty was mentally ill and his mind was not in tune with reality. He was a paranoid schizophrenic at the time of the killings.

A completely different opinion was given by the prosecution's psychiatric adviser, Dr Oscar Schmalzbach, also a Macquarie Street specialist and consultant psychiatrist to the State Government. Dr Schmalzbach said: 'In my view McCafferty knew at the time that what he was doing was wrong. He may have had an isolated schizophrenic reaction at the time of the second killing but this did not make him a paranoid schizophrenic. Such an illness does not exist one day and disappear another day and come back the third day.'

A third psychiatrist who examined McCafferty after the killings did not give evidence. He took the middle view that McCafferty was insane but he knew what he was doing at the time of the killings.

Although they could not agree on Archie's sanity, the three

psychiatrists were united in the opinion that, no matter what, Archie McCafferty could never again be set free. They all agreed that he was an extreme danger to the community.

It was then McCafferty's turn, and the hushed courtroom was captivated as he told of the voice from the grave and how he had been told that seven must die if he wanted to see his son again. He maintained that he was completely insane at the time of the murders. The press lapped it up and Archie didn't disappoint them. At last he was getting the recognition that he so desperately craved – even if he had to kill three people to get it.

And in true trouper fashion, McCafferty saved the best bit until last: his statement, which he read from the dock. He said, in part: 'I would like to say that at the time of these crimes I was completely insane. The reason why I done this is for the revenge of my son's death. Before this, I had stated to a doctor that I felt like killing people, but up until my son's death I had not killed anyone.

'My son's death was the biggest thing that ever happened to me, because I loved him so much and he meant the world to me, and after his death I just seemed to go to the pack.

'I feel no wrong for what I have done, because at the time that I did it I didn't think it was wrong. I think, if given the chance, I will kill again, for the simple reason that I have to kill seven people and I have only killed three, which means I have four to go. And this is how I feel in my mind, and I just can't say that I am not going to kill anyone else, because in my mind I am.

'The day of my son's inquest at the Coroner's Court happened to be the day that I stabbed Mr Anson. The reason why I killed this man was because I heard my son's voice tell me to do so. The same with the second and third person.

'Each time I went to the graveyard to visit my son's grave a violent streak would come over me and I wanted to be so violent, I wanted to kill people. I kept hearing voices, not only my son's voice but other voices as well, which I don't know whose they are.

'On the Thursday that I was apprehended I had every intention of killing Rick Webster as I heard the voices to tell me to do so, and anyone else that the voices tell me to kill I would kill until I reached the figure seven.'

The jury chose to believe that McCafferty was not insane

and returned a verdict of guilty on all counts. Nobody shed a tear for the remorseless killer as the judge handed down the sentence of three terms of life imprisonment. Even as he was being led from the courtroom McCafferty shouted that he would kill four more to avenge the death of his son.

Mick Meredith and Dick Whittington were found guilty of the murders of Ronald Cox and Evangelos Kollias and each sentenced to 18 years in prison. Richard Webster was found guilty of the manslaughter of Cox and sentenced to four years in prison. Julie Todd was found guilty of murdering Cox and Kollias and sent to prison for 10 years. After serving five years in Silverwater Detention Centre, Julie Ann Todd was released and never came under police attention again.

Carol Howes was found not guilty on all counts. Eight months pregnant with McCafferty's child when the verdict was handed down, Howes made a passionate promise to McCafferty from the dock. 'I'll wait for you, Archie,' she sobbed. 'No matter what, I'll always be waiting for you with our child.' She immediately moved into the Blacktown house of Archie McCafferty's parents to have their grandchild.

While serving his prison sentence, McCafferty proved to be a handful for the authorities and he was shuffled around to the toughest jails in the state. Prison officers and psychiatrists regarded him as extremely dangerous. His one consistent and predominant thought was the killing of four more people. A television crew allowed into the notorious Katingal section of Long Bay Jail interviewed Archie who told a stunned audience that there was nothing that anyone could do to stop him from murdering another four people should he be let out.

Placed on massive doses of tranquillisers to keep him under control, by 1978 Archie had served time in almost every maximum-security prison in the state. He was considered to be a jail 'heavy' and an associate of the hardest criminals in the penal system. In April 1980, warders foiled an escape attempt by Archie at Grafton Jail. He had loosened bricks in his cell before prison officers were tipped off and his escape route was discovered. At the time, prison officers said McCafferty was probably the worst criminal in the state's jails.

Police believe that Archie McCafferty was a member of the secret 'murder squad' behind the walls of Parramatta Jail in 1981. They believe that the group consisting of judge, jury and executioner was responsible for four murders within the prison. In September 1981, McCafferty was charged with the murder of Edward James Lloyd, who was stabbed to death in his cell. McCafferty's co-accused, Kevin Michael Gallagher, was eventually found guilty of the murder. But it was proved that McCafferty was present while the murder took place. Though he strenuously denied the charges, he was found guilty of manslaughter and given a further 14 years.

McCafferty protested vehemently against the sentence, claiming that he had been framed. To prove it, he named those who were responsible to the authorities. Archie McCafferty automatically became an outcast within the system that had been his home for the best part of his life.

In 1981, Archie McCafferty had become the biggest headache within the New South Wales penal system. Now, for his own protection, authorities continued to transfer him from one jail to the next in search of a permanent home. In November 1981, McCafferty was caught red-handed in his cell with 10 foil-wrapped packages of heroin. The judge sentenced him to another three years' imprisonment.

During 1983 and 1984, McCafferty was moved repeatedly between Maitland, Long Bay and Parklea prisons under the unofficial but reprehensible practice called 'Shanghaiing', whereby senior prison staff were able to pass on the responsibility of dealing with difficult prisoners to others.

It was noted in official records that McCafferty suffered fits of mental disturbance during this period and he was said to be 'off his rocker'. After giving further information to authorities about serious criminal conduct by various prison officers within the system, he was eventually moved to the Long Bay Witness Protection Unit in 1987. By then, a price had been placed on his head and he was classified a 'supergrass'.

It was in the Witness Protection Unit that McCafferty was revisited by hallucinations involving his dead son. Prison psychiatrists put it down to inhalation of solvents and petroleum and

McCafferty's extreme depression over the lack of prospects for his future release.

As no parole period had been given, it was clear to Archie McCafferty that he would spend the rest of his life behind bars. But he kept applying for parole. In October 1991, McCafferty's application for parole was heard before Mr Justice Wood. The judge granted him a 20-year non-parole period dating from 30 August 1973. Archie became eligible to apply for release on parole on 29 August 1993.

Over the years, McCafferty's anger subsided until he was considered safe enough to be placed at the Berrima minimum-security prison south of Sydney. But each year when he applied to be released on parole it was rejected.

And so, after bucking the system for years and realising that it would never get him released, Archie McCafferty, serial killer and arguably the most violent prisoner the NSW penal system had ever seen, became a model prisoner and for the last four years of his incarceration was allowed to visit and stay with his family of his brother and his brother's wife and children from Friday nights to Sunday nights without supervision.

This position of trust developed to the stage where Archie was allowed to leave the prison each day, six days a week, on work release until the parole board agreed that he was indeed a changed man who was no longer a danger to society and could be released on parole. The only condition of the parole was that McCafferty would be deported.

When Archie heard about his deportation to Scotland, which he hadn't seen in almost four decades and, even worse, to a hostile community that wanted nothing to do with a vicious serial killer, he did everything within his limited powers to stave off the inevitable. But his pleas fell on deaf ears and, amid protests from the Scottish authorities, he was put on a plane on 1 May 1997 and sent back to his birthplace.

In Scotland, Archie was reunited with Mandy Queen, a woman he had married and then divorced while in jail in New South Wales.

Interviewed by Australian current affairs program *Witness* shortly after his arrival back in Scotland, Archie told presenter Paul Barry: 'I've come out of the system a good person. A changed person. I believe that people change.' He then toasted his freedom with a glass of champagne with Mandy Queen and said: 'This is my first drink since 1973. But now there is no need for alcohol in my life. It is a thing of the past. I don't need it.'

In October 1998, Archie McCafferty was put on two years' probation after threatening to kill police officers. McCafferty threatened the police after a car chase near Edinburgh which followed a drinking session and an argument with Mandy Queen, who complained he had left home with their four-month-old baby.

In the Edinburgh Sheriff Court, McCafferty also pleaded guilty to careless driving, driving with no licence or insurance, failing to provide a breath specimen and breach of the peace. The court did not take into consideration McCafferty's previous convictions because they were considered foreign offences.

Archie McCafferty and Mandy Queen were remarried in a secret ceremony in Scotland in October 1998.

Then, on 21 July 2002, Archibald Beattie McCafferty was arrested in New Zealand for failing to declare his criminal convictions when he arrived in the country. He was believed to be on the first leg of a secret journey back to Australia. Detective Sergeant Stuart Mills of Interpol said they were alerted to McCafferty's presence in New Zealand when his wife followed him there.

McCafferty was voluntarily deported back to Scotland immediately.

AUTHOR'S NOTE: In 2003, McCafferty assaulted a policeman in Portsmouth, Scotland. After a year on the run he was fined 50 pounds and given two months' community service. In April, 2004, McCafferty was again arrested and charged with abduction, assault and breach of the peace following an incident in Roxburghshire, Scotland, where he held off ten police officers in a two hour siege while he held a boy at knife point. McCafferty was arrested and remanded in custody. Somehow, yet again, he escaped a custodial sentence. Then on 11 November, 2008 Archie was sentenced to 200 hours community service in an Edinburgh court after being convicted of driving a stolen car.

CHAPTER 16

The Lonely Hearts Killer

Rodney Francis Cameron
Victoria and New South Wales, 1974–90

How psychopathic serial killer Rodney Cameron was ever released from prison after serving only 16 years for the vicious killings of two people in 1974 – one in New South Wales and the other in Victoria – is one of the great mysteries in the history of homicide in Australia.

At the time of his arrest for the 1974 murders, Cameron told detectives that he 'had to kill three', and it appears that he would have carried out his ghastly promise and no doubt more should he have managed to continue.

After serving just nine years in New South Wales prisons for the first murder, Rodney Cameron was extradited to Victoria in 1983 to face the second murder charge. Described by court-appointed psychiatrists as a 'psychopath not fit to be in society', Cameron was sentenced to 'the term of his natural life' behind bars.

Yet incredibly, just seven years later, in 1990, Rodney Cameron was freed back into mainstream society. Within three months the serial killer had struck again. This time his victim was a lonely woman who had answered his plea for companionship on a Melbourne radio station's match-making program. It would earn Cameron the title of 'the Lonely Hearts Killer'.

Rodney Francis Cameron had an unfortunate childhood. His father died shortly after Rodney's birth in Kew, Victoria, in 1955. While most other people's memories of their childhood are filled with happy events such as birthdays or special occasions, Rodney Cameron's most vivid memory was that of his mother dropping dead in front of him in the family kitchen as she baked a cake in the oven.

With both mother and father deceased, the seven-year-old was adopted out. And even at this early stage in his life he was obviously a very disturbed boy, who frequently attacked little girls at school and landed himself in trouble time and again.

When he was caught for placing cardboard boxes on a railway line and in the way of an oncoming train, the young Rodney Cameron was made to appear in the Children's Court. The court heard from a psychiatrist who, after examining the boy, considered that there was 'no therapy available that would be of use to him' and Cameron was placed in an institution.

Back on the streets at the age of 10, Cameron viciously assaulted a little girl and tried to strangle her. Miraculously, the child survived. Then Cameron's adoptive family rejected him when he jumped on, and tried to strangle, an elderly lady in the street. In his teenage years, he also attempted to throttle a girlfriend.

By the time he was 18, in 1973, Cameron was drinking heavily and taking heroin and morphine. He experimented with the occult, devil worship, and demonology. He rejected people who attempted to show him kindness and returned their compassion with extreme aggression and hostility. He also attempted suicide on numerous occasions. It was at this time that Cameron married his first wife, Brenda, who was five years older than him and already had a young son.

In 1974, Cameron found work as a trainee nurse in the Queen Victoria Nursing Home at Wentworth Falls in the Blue Mountains, west of Sydney. He was befriended by nursing sister Miss Florence Edith Jackson, 49, and was often an invited guest in her home.

Miss Jackson was a kind woman who saw a lot of potential in the intelligent but troubled young man. She went out of her way to be friendly to him and give him some of the kindness and affection he had so obviously missed out on in his earlier life.

On 31 January 1974, 19-year-old Rodney Cameron repaid Edith Jackson's kindness by throttling the last breath out of her at her Katoomba home. Cameron strangled his friend into unconsciousness before raping her and strangling her again until she lay dead at his feet. He left his benefactor lying on her back beside the bed with a towel stuffed down her throat.

Leaving little doubt that it was he who had killed the kindly Miss Jackson, Cameron fled the scene and headed south where, a week later while hitchhiking towards Victoria, he was picked up by 19-year-old bank clerk Francesco Ciliberto. At the first opportunity, Cameron bashed Ciliberto half to death with a boulder, then strangled him with a football sock and threw his body off a cliff at Mallacoota in south-eastern Victoria where it landed on a bridge below. In a bizarre similarity to the murder of Miss Jackson, a shirt had been stuffed down Ciliberto's throat.

After the cold-blooded murder of Francesco Ciliberto, Cameron took the victim's car and headed back north where he was eventually arrested in Queensland on 21 February 1974 after he had abducted a mother and daughter. To the astonishment of arresting detectives, Cameron told them that he 'had to kill three', which gave them the impression that they arrested him just in time as he had every intention of murdering his captives.

At Cameron's first trial for the New South Wales murder of Miss Jackson, a Sydney psychiatrist who had prepared a report at the request of the court put it this way: 'I consider there is more than sufficient evidence to support the diagnosis of a personality disorder of the antisocial type. In his case, I think this takes an extreme form and some observers would certainly call him a psychopathic personality.'

Cameron created history when, for the first time ever in a murder trial in Australia, he pleaded not guilty to murder but guilty to manslaughter on the grounds of diminished responsibility, in that he didn't know what he was doing at the time and was temporarily insane. Although it didn't work for Cameron in this instance, it was the catalyst for such a defence and it has been used many times in Australia since.

Cameron was found guilty of murder and served nine years of a life sentence in New South Wales prisons. When Cameron was released in 1983 he was arrested immediately once again. He was taken back to Victoria by detectives with an extradition order to face the charge of the murder of Francesco Ciliberto.

Diagnosed as an 'extreme psychopath' and a 'psychopath not fit to be in society', Cameron was sentenced to life imprisonment for the brutal murder of Francesco Ciliberto with the recommendation by the judge that he should remain in jail 'for the term of his natural life'.

To the relief of authorities, police, and the friends and families of his two victims, at last it appeared that someone had got it right and the psychopathic killer was where he belonged – behind bars for the rest of his life where he could not harm innocent citizens.

But that was not to be. In what would prove to be a catastrophic blunder which would lead to the death of at least one more innocent person, on 12 March 1990, Cameron was released after a successful November 1989 appeal against the length of his sentence. At the time of the controversial decision, it was said that Cameron was believed to have been fully rehabilitated.

While in jail, Cameron was divorced by his first wife Brenda and had married his life-long friend, Anne. Anne had known Cameron all through his troubled youth but had married someone else. When her marriage fell apart in 1982, she became desperately lonely and lacked self-confidence and was advised by a therapist to talk to an old friend for companionship.

Anne started searching for her old friend Rodney Cameron, and when she found him in a Victorian jail in December 1984 she sent him a Christmas card. Cameron replied. They arranged a visit and Anne travelled to Melbourne by coach to visit him. She told the *Sydney Morning Herald*: 'I was ushered into this room and there he was sitting. It will live in my mind forever. I suddenly realised what I had been missing all my life . . . I realised that I had loved him all that time.'

In 1986, they married in jail. Anne went back to her cousin's house with her witnesses for a quiet celebration. Despite Cameron's later crime, she still has no regrets. 'I knew how I felt,' she told the *Herald*. 'I knew there would never be anyone else. It was just the next logical step.'

Upon his release, Anne and Rodney Cameron seemingly settled down to a quiet domestic life in Sunbury, north-west of Melbourne, where (with the help of forged references) Rodney Cameron got a good job as the live-in manager of a stud farm.

Unfortunately for the luckless Anne, who had pinned all her hopes for a happy future on a double murderer, the happy marriage didn't last very long. On the evening of 26 May 1990 on a lonely hearts program on radio 3AW in Melbourne, Cameron described himself as a teetotaller marine biologist from Castlemaine with a Gemini star sign, who played squash and basketball, had no hang-ups, and was searching for a soulmate 'willing to share his happiness and enjoy a good, quiet life'.

Maria Goeliner, one of the nine lonely women who rang the program expressing an interest in meeting Cameron, was described by those who knew her as a loving, trusting person who was looking for someone with whom she could settle down. Maria was introduced to Cameron through the match-making program and, as it would turn out, she was the unluckiest of the hopeful ladies that rang that evening.

Her niece, Josephine Goeliner, would say later: 'I think she must have been quite lonely. She was looking for happiness, but it didn't seem to go right for her. I think she was looking for someone genuine to share her life with.'

Instead of finding the love and happiness that Maria Goeliner wanted so much in her life, she wound up with a psychopathic serial killer who had just been released from prison after serving 16 years. But she had no way of knowing that.

A few weeks later, on 23 June 1990, at the Sky Rider Motor Inn at Katoomba in the Blue Mountains, not far from where Rodney Cameron had murdered Edith Jackson 16 years earlier, the 44-year-old Melbourne woman was found lying on her back with a handkerchief stuffed in her mouth and a pair of pantyhose wrapped around her neck. There were yellow carnations scattered all over her body.

Maria Goeliner had died of asphyxiation, having choked on her own blood after being repeatedly bashed over the head with a blunt instrument. There was also evidence of strangulation. Again, as in his previous murders, Cameron had made no attempt to conceal the body or to cover his tracks. He wouldn't be hard to find.

The couple had arrived two days earlier. They had paid for two days' accommodation in advance for a double room and requested a 'do not disturb' sign on bungalow number 46. About lunchtime on Friday, 22 June, motel staff had seen Maria Goeliner and Cameron together, which was quite possibly the last time that Maria Goeliner was ever seen alive.

The next morning, the motel manager delivered their ordered breakfast and, when there was no response from inside the room, the manager had left the tray inside the door. Finding the meal untouched, the cleaner investigated and found Maria Goeliner on the floor in the bathroom.

In the room was a note from Cameron to his wife, Anne, which read in part: *Anne, I am sorry. Had I not done what happened, my life would have been destroyed. Love eternally, Rodney.*

A week after the murder, Cameron gave himself up to police at Deniliquin in New South Wales, claiming that a mysterious 'second man' named Frederick Mulner had travelled with Maria and him, and it was Mulner who had committed the murder.

Giving him the benefit of the doubt, police searched electoral rolls, phone books, birth and death registers, police records, and every possible avenue available that might produce the missing Mulner. But the mysterious Frederick Mulner never came to light – that is, of course, if he ever did exist in the first place.

The arresting officers at Deniliquin, Pat English and Steve McGlynn, described Cameron as like no other murderer – or human being for that matter – they had ever met. 'To see him, to hear him, you would say he's a politely spoken, neatly dressed, quiet sort of a guy. To realise what he's capable of doing is quite scary. He really shows no compassion,' they said. 'He is calculating and cunning. We regard him as the most dangerous man you would probably ever meet.'

Cameron's trial, held in the Sydney Central Criminal Court in August 1992, was yet another history-making event in that the Crown was allowed to bring up Cameron's past murders. Instead of being protected from his previous crimes in case they may become prejudiced against the defendant, the jury was given every grim detail about Cameron's horrific past offences.

It was the first time that 'similar fact' evidence had been used in a murder trial in New South Wales this century, the only previous known 'similar fact' case being that of husband-and-wife serial baby killers John and Sarah Makin in Redfern, Sydney, in 1893 (see chapter 4). The Makins were convicted of murdering an infant found buried in the backyard of a house in which they lived. Eventually the Privy Council ruled the evidence, that at least 10 other babies' bodies had been found in yards of other homes the couple had occupied, was 'relevant' and could be used.

The Crown prosecutor, Mr Barry Newport, QC, went to great lengths to explain to the jury how they could treat the knowledge that Cameron was a convicted double murderer: 'It was wrong to say, "Well, that's it. He has killed twice before, therefore he did it this time." But it could be used to exclude the possibility that Frederick Mulner had been the killer. After all, how extraordinary it would be if this mystery [person] should be there and the mystery [person] should kill in a fashion so similar to the way in which the accused had killed twice in the past.'

It took the jury only three hours to find Rodney Francis Cameron guilty of the murder of Maria Goeliner.

In passing the strongest possible sentence of life imprisonment with the recommendation that he is 'never to be released', Justice Newman said that only 'old age or infirmity' would ever stop Cameron from carrying out his 'homicidal desires'.

On 20 April 1993, police charged Cameron with the brutal murder of 79-year-old pensioner Mrs Sarah McKenzie almost two decades earlier. It was a case that had remained open as the perpetrator had not been captured.

Police had reopened the McKenzie murder file after hearing from jail informers that Cameron had been boasting of his past crimes.

On 6 February 1974, Mrs McKenzie had phoned police from her home to report that she had been bashed by a man, but when police arrived the house was locked up and there was no sign of life.

Police returned to the house two days later and broke in to find Mrs McKenzie's body in the hallway with 30 knife wounds to her chest, a knife embedded in her neck and a mattock buried in her skull.

Police had discovered that while on the run after murdering Francesco Ciliberto in 1974, Cameron had been booked for speeding in Ciliberto's car at Nowra in southern New South Wales. The same car had been reported by a highway patrol officer at North Sydney about the same time on the day that Mrs

McKenzie was believed to have been bashed to death. The highway patrol officer had found Cameron asleep in the car on the expressway and had questioned him about being in the area.

Cameron strongly denied the allegations, and three days before the trial was to begin in early 1994 it was no-billed by the NSW Department of Public Prosecutions.

On 3 October 1997, the now 42-year-old Cameron requested through officials at Lithgow Prison to speak to police and in a lengthy, videotaped confession told Northern Region Homicide and North Sydney detectives at North Sydney police station that he did, in fact, kill Mrs McKenzie and supplied them with details only the killer could have known.

Later in 1997, in an exclusive prison interview, recorded below, Cameron confessed to Sydney crime reporter Steve Warnock (and later to police) that he had murdered two women in separate knife attacks in Victoria in 1990, that he murdered a man by bashing his skull in with a brick in South Australia in 1974, and to the strangulation of a woman in New South Wales in the same year.

CONFESSIONS OF A SERIAL KILLER
The 1997 interview with the Lonely Hearts Killer by Steve Warnock

There's nothing striking or unusual about the appearance of Rodney Francis Cameron, not that I was expecting to meet a drooling hunchback dragging his knuckles on the ground.

At 42 years old, Cameron doesn't look physically ravaged by the guilt of terrible crimes. His face, angular in an elfish sort of way, is smooth and unlined; the eyes are bright and Cameron's finely cut light brown hair hasn't faded. He's hardly physically imposing, weighing about 65–70 kilograms and standing about 170 centimetres tall. There's even a half-smile from a distance as you walk towards him, the sort of uncertain smile you might expect from a total stranger who's had little contact with the outside world.

It's the handshake – the first physical contact with

Cameron in the NSW Lithgow Jail's protection wing – that tells you something about this quiet, unassuming man. He has incredible power in his wrists and arms, and the pressure as he pumped my hand made me feel uneasy. If he suddenly snapped and attacked my throat with all the wild strength of a madman, I'd be in deep trouble.

In those few seconds of the handshake, I knew all I wanted to know about life-serving serial murderer Rodney Francis Cameron. Dubbed the 'Lonely Hearts Killer', he was convicted for slaying a woman he met through a radio match-making program and showering her body with carnations.

Just a month earlier, I'd received the letter Cameron had written from his maximum security cell at Lithgow, the sender tag signed neatly in blue biro, *R. Cameron 103384, P.O. Box 666, Lithgow*. Cameron was either under great stress – anguishing over crimes unconfessed – or in the early stages of a coolly calculated plan to convince the world he was Australia's worst serial killer.

Just weeks before I received Cameron's letter, he had shocked police with a confession he'd slaughtered another person, taking his grim tally of victims to four. In a lengthy videotaped interview at North Sydney police station, Cameron claimed he'd murdered an elderly war widow, 79-year-old Sarah McKenzie, at her Milsons Point home in Sydney in 1974.

This confession came four years after the NSW Department of Public Prosecutions threw out the case against Cameron, who was maintaining his innocence. Cameron was, officially, still a three-time killer.

The letter Cameron had written to me was extremely personal, strongly indicating he'd killed four more people – and inviting me to visit him. His letter said in part: *I am sure you know who I am and what I am in jail for. The reason I am writing to you is that I will be soon facing another four murder charges.*

Cameron didn't say much more in the letter, but he pledged that if I could see him, *I will outline each murder.*

He wrote: *I want to put my side across, rather than the police side being published.*

At Lithgow Jail's visitors' section, Cameron was brought through a door into a special glassed unit away from mainstream prisoners. A prison officer beckoned me to come over as Cameron waited patiently by his side.

With a simple 'Nice to meet you', the Lonely Hearts Killer gave my hand those almighty pumps before leading me to a table away from the few other inmates. As we went to sit, a middle-aged woman talking to a heavily tattooed con yelled to Cameron: 'You can't sit down there, you've got to be up here.'

Cameron got out of his seat, stood to his full height, and gave her a stare that all but froze her. She turned away and never gave Cameron another look.

'It's OK, Rodney – she's minding her own business. So how can I help you now I've finally got through to you?' I asked.

'As I told you in my letter, I'm going to confess to another four murders – in different states,' Cameron said quietly. 'I'm prepared to tell the police about these murders, and as each interview with them is finished, I'll give you a copy of the taped confession. I'll get everything to you through a lawyer, who'll contact you soon. If you do get to write anything, I don't want you to quote me as though we are talking face to face, do you understand?'

'What's the problem quoting you, Rodney? I mean, that's what I'm here for, isn't it?'

'I have a daughter out there – she lives near the Blue Mountains – and I want to tell her myself about what I have done before it is told to the media. I don't know how she would react if she was to read it publicly coming from me.'

I struck a deal with Cameron that I wouldn't quote him, but I stressed I wanted to know, and quickly, what he had done. Cameron went straight into it, hardly missing a beat.

'OK, I've got to get this off my chest. There were another four. I killed a man in South Australia back in 1974 and I killed a woman here [in NSW] the same year.'

'How did you kill this man?'

'I did it with a rock – smashed his skull – then buried him. I did the woman differently . . . I strangled her.'

By now Cameron had me wanting to scream because jail rules prohibited me from taking in any writing implements, let alone a tape recorder.

'The other two, Rodney, how did they happen?' I asked.

'They were knifed . . . two women in Victoria in 1990. Yeah, they were different attacks.'

I pushed Cameron for more detail – names, dates, times, how it happened – but he cut me short.

'You'll know more as I tell police. You'll have to wait a bit,' he said. 'But I want you to know why I do these things . . . I didn't have much of a childhood, not in any sense. I was an unhappy child and I had no family upbringing. I didn't have a *start*.'

Cameron has previously claimed that he watched his mother drop dead in their Melbourne home. At age eight, he was a vandal; at 10, he tried to strangle a young girl; and as a teenager, he tried to strangle a woman.

Cameron went on to explain that he was a heavy drug-user in the early 1970s, when grass, acid, morphine and heroin started to take hold.

'When I got older [in his late teens], I started to get into hallucinogenic drugs in Sydney . . . drugs like mescalin and acid – you know, LSD. You know what that stuff can do to you. It can really shake up your head.

'I was also into devil worship; the satanism thing. I was out of control – I didn't know where the hell I was. I know it's no excuse, but I was really out of it when I started all this. I just want this off my chest, get it out into the open. I want someone to understand.'

That was it. An unhappy childhood, drugs, then devil worship led to eight murders. I searched Cameron's face for some sign of remorse – a tear, a tremble of the lip, a sigh or a wipe of the brow. Nothing. He fidgeted a little, then looked me straight in the eye when I couldn't help myself.

'Do you think about these people?' I asked. 'I mean, what you've done?'

'Yeah, all the time,' he responded. 'That's why I wanted to talk to you.'

Cameron said he'd told me enough; that he'd given me sufficient to get me on the phone to a Sydney newspaper. I kept my part of the bargain, and a story – sourced to a 'friend' of Cameron's – told how Cameron was now putting his hand up to another four murders, making him Australia's worst serial killer. Cameron had told this to a friend, who told it to a reporter, who told the newspaper editor.

Cameron's confessions stunned me. To confess to police about murders which may not even be on files anywhere, except perhaps as missing persons, is one thing. To pour out a handful of murder admissions to a total stranger who you had summoned by mail was, for me, difficult to comprehend.

That Cameron could rattle off the slayings without so much as a sniff of remorse – except to suggest that his daughter might be upset if she read it in the papers – left me cold.

Until Cameron began talking about murder I was struggling to put him in the serial killer category. But as he went through each slaughter he had my head racing. He had me. I believed him.

I should have known better – Cameron didn't honour his side of the deal. I never heard from the 'lawyer' who would hand over the tapes as Cameron told all to the cops. And I never received another letter from 'R. Cameron, c/o Lithgow Correctional Centre'.

Shortly after the news broke that Cameron was talking about more killings, I did get a call from the homicide police, with one senior officer suggesting I should've spoken to them before I let New South Wales know Cameron was 'owning up'.

Things soon smoothed over, and I gave the police a copy of the Cameron letter. Police subsequently spoke to Cameron about his allegations, but he squared them off, according to a homicide investigator, by accusing them of having tipped off the newspaper about the story and claiming he had never spoken to a reporter.

Now Cameron wasn't about to say a word to anyone about anything, so what the hell was he up to?

If he wanted to get something off his chest, then the police were more than happy to help him cooperate. If he just wanted to get himself into print as Australia's worst modern-day serial killer – albeit without proof – he did that. And that, perhaps, was what Cameron was really up to.

This notion hasn't escaped some police and Corrective Services department officials, who privately believe Cameron may be on an ego trip.

'When you're in there for life, there's not much to look forward to,' one detective said recently. 'Claim you killed eight people – not three or four – and that makes you the number one. It puts you up on top of the list.'

Even the experts can't be sure whether there's any truth in Cameron's confessions. Sydney forensic psychiatrist Dr Rod Milton says a killer such as Cameron with no chance of release from jail might as well shoot his mouth off about crime.

'They don't have a life,' says Dr Milton, who provided police with accurate profiles of Ivan Milat and 'Granny Killer' John Glover when they were on the loose. 'They are limited people anyway, and it's not surprising they might measure their ego by the extent of their crimes in an effort to compete with one another.'

Queensland criminologist and Dean of Social Sciences at Bond University, Professor Paul Wilson, says it's difficult to judge. 'The point is some murderers love being known as "king of the killers" and that leaves you in two minds – he could be lying and he could be telling the truth.'

Professor Wilson cited serial killer Henry Lee Lucas, who claimed to have killed over 300 people on a murder rampage in the United States 20 years ago. 'Although there were quite a few, police reckoned there were nowhere as many as Lucas claimed,' Professor Wilson says.

He argues that if Cameron was genuine in his claim that

he wanted to set the record straight and clear his conscience, he would cooperate with police. 'Most of these people do not have any guilt whatsoever, so I would be wary of Cameron using guilt as a motivation for making a confession,' Professor Wilson said.

'And, no, I would not have expected a breakdown if he was cracking up with remorse, but I would have expected some verbal signs. The more likely motivation for "confessing" is that he wants to play a game – or he wants to be top dog,' Professor Wilson concluded.

The Lonely Hearts Killer, Rodney Francis Cameron, is in Lithgow maximum-security prison with no possibility of parole.

When this interview took place, Steve Warnock was crime reporter for the Sydney Sun-Herald *newspaper.*

AUTHOR'S NOTE: At the time of publication, it was an accepted fact by police that Rodney Cameron had murdered Mrs Sarah McKenzie in Sydney's Milsons Point in 1974. This brought his grisly tally of victims to four. Cameron had not been charged with any of the other murders he alleged to have committed in the interview with Steve Warnock.

But even if Rodney Cameron *was* charged and found guilty of these four murders, he would be disappointed to know that it would not make him the most prolific individual serial killer in Australia's history. That dubious honour belongs to John Lynch of Berrima, New South Wales in 1841, with a horrifying total of nine victims and whose crimes are covered in chapter 2 in this book.

CHAPTER 17

The Truro Serial Murders

Christopher Robin Worrell and James William Miller
Adelaide, 1976–77

James William Miller is one of Australia's least likely sexual assailants and serial killers of young women. Miller is homosexual. Yet by his own admission, between December 1976 and February 1977 he helped the man he loved, Christopher Robin Worrell, dispose of the bodies of seven young women whom Worrell had sexually assaulted and murdered while Miller waited nearby.

When police detained James Miller for questioning in May 1979, he led them to the buried remains of three of Worrell's victims and, for his part in the crimes, is serving six life sentences for murder in Adelaide's Yatala Prison. But Miller steadfastly denies assisting Worrell in the abduction of the victims or the sexual assaults and murders that followed. He admits, however, that he drove the vehicle that Worrell used to pick up the young women and then left Worrell to murder in private before returning to the vehicle, driving Worrell and the deceased women to the outskirts of Adelaide, and helping to bury their bodies.

The only person who could prove James Miller's innocence is the alleged murderer, 23-year-old Christopher Worrell. But Worrell is dead. James Miller claims he has never had sex with a woman. He is a convicted thief, but has no record of violence. At the time of the murders he was 38 years old.

'I was there at the time and for that I am guilty of an unforgivable felony,' Miller has said from his Adelaide prison cell. 'I fully deserve the life sentences I am currently serving. I am serving out a life sentence for Chris. But I never killed any of those girls. That's the truth.'

Miller has been protesting his innocence of the murders for years, on occasion backing up his pleas with rooftop jail protest strikes, including one in July 1984 that lasted for 43 days. But he has been ignored by authorities and his conviction stands.

South Australian Chief Justice Len King agreed that Miller should be granted another hearing on the grounds that the judge at his trial, Mr Justice Matheson, had instructed the jury to find Miller guilty of murder even though he had pleaded not guilty. The Attorney-General, Chris Sumner, refused to grant a retrial.

Miller maintained: 'They can give me life for knowing about the murders and not reporting them. But they charged me with murder as a payback for not informing on Worrell. It's a load of bullshit. At least one of the jurists at my trials knows the truth. In 1987 he [the jurist] paid a couple of hundred dollars out of his own pocket to help hire a lawyer to petition the Attorney-General for a retrial. If a jurist does this, he must have a fair idea of what really happened.'

Protesting his innocence, Miller said: 'Nobody turns into a cold-blooded murderer overnight or helps commit murder. I'm just an ordinary thief, no killer. I have never been a violent man.'

The Truro Serial Murders are among the most infamous of Australian serial killings. Seven young women disappeared in Adelaide in the 51 days between 23 December 1976 and 12 February 1977.

The skeletal remains of four of the victims were discovered in bush graves over a 12-month period between 1978 and 1979 in the Truro district, 80 kilometres north-east of Adelaide. What was left of the first discovered body was found by a mushroomer, William Thomas, on 25 April 1978 in a remote paddock off Swamp Road.

Mr Thomas said he had seen a leg bone with a shoe attached which he believed to be the leg of a cow. He had thought about the find for five days and returned on Anzac Day with his wife to check. He had turned over the bone and seen skin in good condition and toenails painted with nail polish. After he had found a skull, other bones, a bloodstain on the ground, and items of clothing, he had contacted police.

Swamp Road is so named because it divides a huge flood plain into two flat tree-dotted paddocks. The area's only permanent inhabitants are mosquitos and frogs, and the only sign that humans had ever been in the area is the barbed-wire fence running along the roadside. It is a perfect place to hide a body. You would only come across it by accident.

When the mushroomer reported the find, police searched the area thoroughly and found personal effects that would help them identify the victim. It was Veronica Knight, an 18-year-old Adelaide woman who had been reported missing around Christmas in 1976. There was no reason for them to suspect that there were more bodies in the soggy paddock.

Almost a year later, on 15 April 1979, four young bushwalkers discovered a skeleton in the same paddock about a kilometre up Swamp Road from the spot where Veronica Knight was found. From jewellery and clothing uncovered at the scene, police identified the skeleton as that of Sylvia Pittman, who had gone missing the same time that Veronica Knight had vanished.

Police files revealed that five more young women had disappeared from the inner-Adelaide area during that period. The officer in charge of the inquiry, Detective Superintendent K. Harvey, said that police had always considered the disappearance of each girl as suspicious and their cases had been under constant investigation.

Superintendent Harvey said that about 3000 people were reported missing each year in South Australia and usually all but about fifteen of them were located. When none of the girls who had gone missing in that 1976 to 1977 period turned up, he knew it was more than coincidence.

Now that he had good reason to believe that the girls were the victims of a serial killer, Superintendent Harvey was certain that other bodies would turn up and ordered a search of the paddock by 70 police.

'We don't know what we will find,' he said. 'We will be looking for any clues to the killings of the two girls we have found, but we can't overlook the fact that we may find the bodies of some of these other missing girls.'

Eleven days later, Superintendent Harvey's suspicions were confirmed when the huge search party discovered two more skeletons in the opposite paddock. They were identified as Connie Iordanides and Vicki Howell, two of the missing girls.

The police were baffled. The fact that the bodies had been there for so long left them few clues. The trail was stone cold. They appealed to the public for help.

In May, a woman identifying herself as 'Angela' informed police that she knew of a man who could help them with their investigations. She said that a distraught James Miller had told her about girls being 'done in' in a conversation at a funeral in February 1977. Miller confessed that he and the man whose funeral they were attending, Christopher Worrell, 'had done something terrible'. He also told 'Angela' that 'Chris had to die'.

It was eventually revealed that the clandestine 'Angela' was in fact Amelia, who was Christopher Worrell's girlfriend at the time that he was killed. Miller allegedly told Amelia that the bodies were buried near Blanchetown, and she had not realised that it was near the site where the bodies had been found until she saw a map of the area in a newspaper.

'I only had suspicions, but suspicions are not enough to go to the police. I had no facts. I suspected that it was the truth and I didn't want to go to the police,' she said. Miller had told her that the murdered girls were just 'rags' and not worth much. He had said that one of them even enjoyed it.

'I did the driving and went along to make sure that nothing went wrong,' Miller allegedly told Amelia. 'They had to be done in so they would not point the finger at us.' They were claims that Miller was to strenuously deny when interrogated by police days later.

Amelia continued. Miller had told her: 'If you don't believe me, I will take you to where they are. It was getting worse, lately. It was happening more often. It was perhaps a good thing that Chris died.' He also told Amelia that Worrell had 'done away with two in Western Australia'.

The informant said that she had not come forward with this vital information because she did not want to 'dob' anyone in. Besides, she didn't think there was much point in going to the police since the alleged murderer, Christopher Worrell, was dead. She said that Miller would only be used as a scapegoat.

Miller wasn't hard to find. Destitute, he was running odd jobs for Adelaide's Central Mission in return for a bed and food at a day centre. Eight plain-clothes detectives were put on around-the-clock surveillance of Miller. He was picked up when he tried to make a run for it after realising that he was being followed.

Detained for questioning at Angus Street Police Headquarters on 23 May 1979, the detectives heading the investigation, Detective Sergeant Glen Lawrie and Detective Peter Foster of the Major Crime Squad, knew that if they didn't get a full confession, or if Miller didn't reveal the locations of more bodies, then he could walk out of the police station a free man.

In the first few hours of his interview, Miller denied any knowledge of the girls or the killings, giving vague and false answers about knowing anyone named Amelia, let alone having a conversation with her. There was not one shred of evidence to link Miller to the killings. All the detectives had to go on was the say-so of the witness.

When shown photos of Amelia and Worrell together, Miller suddenly remembered knowing them, and when confronted with Amelia's statement accusing him of murder, Miller said (referring to the $30,000 reward on offer for any information leading to a conviction of the murders): 'Maybe she's short of money,' to which Detective Lawrie replied: 'Do you really believe that? Is that what you want me to tell the court?'

Miller then said: 'No. On second thoughts, maybe she's done what I should do. Can I have a few minutes to think about it?'

A short time later, after being interrogated for six hours, Miller finally said: 'If I can clear this up, will everyone else be left out of it? I suppose I've got nothing else to look forward to whatever way it goes. I guess I'm the one who got mixed up in all of this. Where do you want me to start?'

Miller then continued to make the statement: 'I drove around with Chris and we picked up girls around the city. Chris would talk to the girls and get them into the car and we would take them for a drive and take them to Truro and Chris would rape them and kill them. But you've got to believe that I had nothing to do with the actual killings of those girls.'

A seemingly sympathetic Detective Sergeant Lawrie told Miller that he understood that he was hopelessly in love with

Worrell and that he could see how he would do anything for him. This seemed to give Miller confidence in the detective.

'All right then, there's three more,' Miller said quietly. 'I'll show you.'

Detectives Lawrie and Foster breathed an enormous sigh of relief and, even though it was 10.30 at night, Miller was driven under heavy escort while he directed police to Truro, Port Gawler and the Wingfield dump where he pointed out the locations of the remains of three more girls. Forensic evidence later showed that the last victim, Deborah Lamb, could have been buried alive.

Of course, the police didn't believe that James Miller had taken no part in the murders as it was almost impossible to imagine that seven decent young ladies would get into a car with two total strangers and willingly go to their deaths.

In most cases, the women involved had other plans and a casual liaison would appear to have been the last thing on their minds. Debbie Lamb was engaged to be married, Juliet Mykyta was on her way home, and Connie Jordan was waiting for a friend before heading off to the movies. To the detectives it looked more like Miller had helped his friend abduct the women against their wills and more than likely held the victims as they were raped and murdered.

Back at the police station, after leading the detectives to the last three bodies, Miller then told his horrifying story from the beginning.

James Miller had spent the best part of his 34 years behind bars. Friendless and a loner, Miller came from a family of six kids and had left home at a very early age. At age 11 he was sent to the Magill Reform School and, with no formal education, he resorted to stealing for a living and occasionally worked as an itinerant labourer.

In the following years, Miller was convicted on more than 30 occasions for car theft, numerous forms of larceny, and breaking, entering and stealing. But, as he strenuously pointed out time and again, he had never had a conviction for violence or a sexual offence.

Miller was doing three months, the shortest custodial sentence he had ever received, in Adelaide Jail for breaking into a

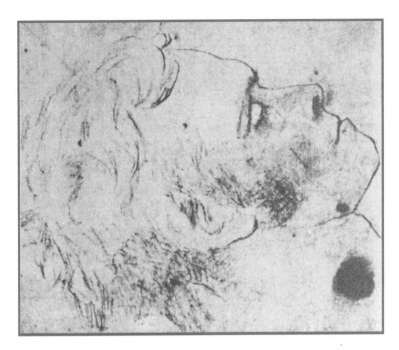

The only known likeness of Australia's first recorded serial killer, Alexander Pearce, is this drawing that was done shortly after he was hanged in Hobart Town in 1824.

The 'Rough on Rats' Murderess, Martha Needle, murdered her entire family and then began killing off her new lover's family before she was finally apprehended in May 1894.

One of the few husband-and-wife serial-killing teams in history, John and Sarah Makin made a living from the reprehensible practice of 'baby farming'. They murdered illegitimate infants left in their charge by trusting mothers who paid them a weekly fee for their children's care. For their crimes, John Makin went to the gallows and Sarah Makin served a 19-year jail term.

Another baby farmer, Frances Knorr, found the practice much more profitable when she collected money for minding infants but didn't have to feed and clothe them because she had already murdered them. Only the second woman to go to the gallows in Victoria, the hangman couldn't cope with the pressure and killed himself on the eve of her execution.

Right: Frederick Bailey Deeming as Baron Swanston. In his dandyish clothes and top hat, it is little wonder that the serial killer stood out 'like a bushfire upon the horizon' among the miners at Southern Cross, Western Australia. He took a position in the township as an engineer at a goldmine.

Inset: This photograph of Frederick Bailey Deeming was taken shortly after he had painstakingly plucked every hair out of his moustache while in the Albany cells to avoid being identified in a future line-up. But it didn't work. In pictures such as this one the moustache was quickly drawn back on by police.

Below: 'I don't think no more of my life than this scrap of paper,' Frederick Deeming points out to the court in this drawing from his 1892 trial. If the jury had any doubt of his guilt, it was soon dispelled when Deeming took the stand and raved for more than an hour, thus ensuring a guilty verdict.

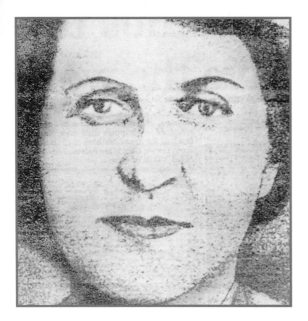

Martha Rendell, who slowly murdered her lover's three young children. Rendell delighted in watching them suffer over a long period of time and eventually die in agony. She became the last woman to be hanged in Western Australia.

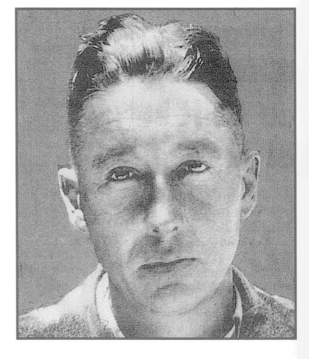

There was no apparent reason why Arnold Sodeman, himself a father of a young daughter, would strangle four girls to death. After he was hanged for his crimes, an autopsy revealed that it could have been the effects of alcohol that drove him to commit his horrific murders.

Albert 'Mad Mossy' Moss, the Swaggie Killer, confessed to killing as many as 13 swagmen, stealing their meagre possessions and burning their bodies. A huge bully of a man, Moss had a criminal record of violence and theft dating back to his teens. He had been in and out of prisons and asylums most of his life. Moss was eventually convicted of three murders and locked away for the remainder of his life.

All the kindly American serviceman really wanted to do was become a strongman in the circus. Instead, Edward Leonski was drafted into the army and shipped to Australia where he strangled three women and wound up at the end of a rope. Leonski went to his death singing.

Right: Caroline Grills specialised in dispatching her victims with the common poison of the time, thallium. The notorious grandmother serial killer did away with her friends and relatives for greed, at first, and then apparently because she enjoyed it. In prison, she was nicknamed 'Aunt Thally'.

Left: Handsome Romanian John Balaban committed his first murder in Paris in 1946, strangling a woman after he had made love to her. In Australia, in 1952, he murdered a prostitute and in 1953 he murdered his new wife, her son and her mother.

Right: During his childhood, Eric Edgar Cooke had to endure a harelip, a speech impediment, school-yard taunts and savage beatings from his father. As a result of this, he took out his revenge on society and became one of the most feared serial killers in Australia's history.

Eric Cooke demonstrates to detectives how he waited with a rifle after he had rung a stranger's doorbell. When his unsuspecting victim answered the door, Cooke murdered him with a single shot between the eyes.

Eric Cooke shows detectives where he claimed he ran down, and killed, Rosemary Anderson, whose fiancée, John Button, was serving 10 years' imprisonment for her manslaughter.

William 'the Mutilator' MacDonald, Australia's most feared serial killer at the time of his arrest in 1963. When he bumped into an old workmate after his supposed death – which led to the famous 'Case of the Walking Corpse' newspaper headline – MacDonald fled to Melbourne, where he was arrested thanks to Australia's first use of identikit pictures.

Above: At first police thought that the multiple wounds to the upper body and the mutilation of the lower body of William MacDonald's first victim, Alan Greenfield, could have been a murder of passion. They soon realised there was a deranged serial killer at large.

Below left: The multiple stab wounds on the neck of the Mutilator's third victim, Frank McLean. McLean's murder took place in a lane just metres from busy Bourke Street in Sydney's Darlinghurst on a Saturday night. Police rushed to the scene only to find that the serial killer had fled.

Below right: The author, Paul B. Kidd, with William 'the Mutilator' MacDonald at Sydney's Long Bay Jail in May 2000. The two men would become friends. MacDonald has been in prison for 43 years. He admits that he is 'institutionalised' and accepts the fact that he will die behind bars.

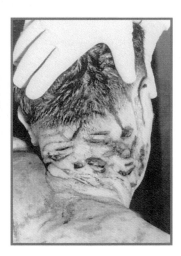

Ben Kidd

Right: In 1962, 21-year-old labourer Barry Gordon Hadlow was convicted of the sexual assault and murder of a five-year-old girl in Townsville, Queensland and sentenced to life imprisonment. Incredibly, Hadlow would be released 23 years later to commit an almost identical killing.

Below: After his release from prison for child murder in 1985, Hadlow (centre) settled in Roma, a few hundred kilometres south of Townsville. Hadlow would often get drunk in the local hotel and tell bizarre stories of his prison background. It was these indiscretions that would lead police to his door once again for child murder.

Right: Barry Gordon Hadlow in 1991 being taken back to prison for a second life term, this time with his papers marked 'never to be released', after being convicted of the sexual assault and murder of a nine-year-old girl in rural Queensland.

Above left: The deranged and drug-addled Archibald Beattie 'Mad Dog' McCafferty after his arrest in 1973. McCafferty and his gang of juvenile cutthroats set about murdering innocent people after McCafferty's son told him from the grave that if he killed seven, he would rise from the dead.

Above right: In 1997, after committing another murder – this time behind bars – and proving to be one of the most difficult criminals the prison system has ever seen, McCafferty was released and immediately deported to his native Scotland, much to the disgust of Scottish authorities.

Inset: The Lonely Hearts Killer, Rodney Francis Cameron, in 1974 at the age of 19. Cameron befriended and murdered a woman in New South Wales and killed a teenager in Victoria who picked him up while he was hitchhiking. Both of Cameron's victims were strangled and an item of their clothing was stuffed down their throats.

Left: Within three months of his release from jail in 1990, the Lonely Hearts Killer had strangled another victim with an item of her clothing. Rodney Cameron has since confessed to another five murders.

Christopher Robin Worrell and James William Miller were the deadliest serial-killing team in Australia's history. While the charismatic Chris Worrell (below) lured young women into the car and sexually assaulted and strangled them, homosexual James Miller (left, centre) drove the vehicle to the Truro district on the outskirts of Adelaide and helped dispose of the bodies. Had Worrell not been accidentally killed, it is likely that many more young women would have been murdered and concealed by the evil pair.

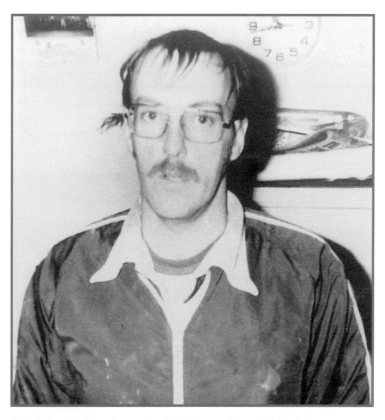

Teenage babysitter Helen Patricia Moore murdered two infants and a seven-year-old boy, and attempted to murder two others, while they were left in her company. Serving a minimum term of 13 years, Moore was eventually released on parole in 1993 to have a child of her own.

The indescribable crimes of serial-killing pederast Michael George Laurance in the mid-1980s shocked the world. His crimes have been likened to the horrors of England's famous Moors Murders in the early 1960s. Laurance's sexual obsessions with young boys eventually led to an overwhelming desire to murder the lads while he was molesting them.

Husband-and-wife serial-killing team David John and Catherine Margaret Birnie abducted young women and took them back to their house where they sexually assaulted and eventually murdered them. They disposed of the victims' bodies in a pine forest on the outskirts of Perth.

The police mug shot of John Wayne Glover, whose crimes were among the most unique of any serial killer in the world – Glover specialised in bashing and strangling elderly ladies to death on public streets in broad daylight.

If pure evil had a face, surely it would be that of Ivan Robert Marko Milat, who murdered seven young backpackers. Police believe that Milat may have killed many more.

As a child, Paul Charles Denyer tortured and killed small animals with his homemade knives. Eventually he preyed on young women, taking their lives by violently strangling and stabbing them.

Mark Mala Valera is led from court to prison, where he will spend the rest of his life. His crimes rate among the most barbaric in Australia's history.

The Salvation Army were of great support for Kathleen Folbigg throughout her trial. After she was found guilty of the serial murders of her four infants, Folbigg became the most hated woman in Australia.

While convicted child-killer Leonard John Fraser was on trial for the murders of four women, one of his alleged victims turned up alive and well.

It was Peter Norris Dupas' ordinary appearance that allowed him to get close enough to his victims to rape and murder them.

Snowtown serial killer Robert Wagner gives the bird as he and his co-accused, Mark Haydon (left) and John Bunting (centre), are taken to court. The number of victims made Snowtown the most prolific case of serial murder in Australian criminal history.

gun shop, when he met Christopher Worrell who was awaiting trial on a rape charge. Worrell was also on a two-year suspended sentence for armed robbery at the time of his arrest.

The homosexual Miller became infatuated with the handsome young man with long dark hair and slim build. They became friends and within a week they were sharing a cell. The 20-year-old Christopher Worrell told Miller that he had never known his real father and his mother remarried when he was six years old. Worrell claimed to have served time in the Royal Australian Air Force.

Worrell was sentenced to four years on the rape charge and an additional two years for breaching his suspended sentence. When Worrell was sentenced, the judge described him as a 'depraved and disgusting human being'. Both Miller and Worrell were transferred to Yatala Prison where, although they no longer shared a cell, they remained inseparable friends until Miller was released after serving his three months.

But it wasn't long before Miller was back at Yatala with his new friend, Chris Worrell. This time he got 18 months for stealing 4000 pairs of sunglasses and offering them for sale in hotels around Adelaide.

Nine months after Miller was released, Worrell was granted early parole and they teamed up on the outside in the house where Miller lived with his married sister and her two little girls. Christopher Worrell was a regular visitor to the Miller household and the two men planned on getting a flat together.

The passive Miller often performed oral sex on Worrell while he read bondage magazines. But Worrell obviously preferred women and, eventually, the sexual side of the relationship diminished and they became more like brothers. Soon they were working together in the same road-labouring gang for the Unley local council. James Miller described these times as the best in his life.

There was nothing that the besotted Miller would not do for his friend Chris Worrell. However, the relationship was often difficult because Worrell was extremely temperamental and moody. He would fly into fits of rage over the slightest thing and it took all of Miller's calming persuasion to quieten him down.

At 23 years of age, Chris Worrell was very good-looking and his natural gift of the gab saw to it that he had no trouble in picking up girls. While Miller drove him around in his old 1969 blue-and-white Valiant, Worrell would solicit girls at bus stops, hotels and railway stations. Miller would drive Worrell and the girl to a remote spot and go for a walk while Worrell had sex with her in the back of the car.

Often Worrell would tie the girls up. When he thought that they would be finished Miller returned to the car and drove them back to town. According to Miller's unsigned statement this happened many times and he had no reason to think that Worrell would start killing the girls.

By December 1976, Worrell and Miller were still working together as labourers for Unley Council and sharing a flat at Ovingham. Every night Miller would drive Worrell to look for girls. In fact, Miller was so devoted to Worrell that he often slept in the car overnight while his friend was in the flat with a new girlfriend.

Miller claimed that on the night of Thursday, 23 December 1976, Worrell told him to drive around the main block of the city shopping centre while he went for a walk. The stores of Adelaide were packed with shoppers buying last-minute Christmas gifts, and there were lots of young women about.

Worrell often went off on his own. This time he was quite a while and Miller had to drive around the block twice before he spotted Worrell and 18-year-old Veronica Knight at the front of the Majestic Hotel. Veronica had accepted the offer of a lift home. She lived at the nearby Salvation Army Hostel in Angas Street and had become separated from her friend while shopping at the City Cross Arcade. On the way to her home, the persuasive young Worrell allegedly talked her into going for a drive with them into the Adelaide foothills.

Miller pulled the car into a side track and Worrell forced the girl into the back seat. Miller went for a walk to allow his friend some privacy and waited for half an hour before returning to the car. Worrell was sitting in the front seat and the girl was lying motionless on the floor in the back. She was fully dressed. Worrell told Miller that he had just raped and murdered the girl. Miller flew into a rage and grabbed Worrell by the shirt.

'You fool, you fucking fool!' he yelled at Worrell. 'Do you want to ruin everything?' While Miller had him by the shirt, Worrell produced a long wooden-handled knife and held it to Miller's throat. He told Miller to let him go or he would kill him as well.

There was no doubt in Miller's mind that Worrell meant it.

Worrell directed Miller to drive through Gawler and towards Truro a few miles further on. They drove down a dirt track called Swamp Road and pulled over next to a wooded area. When Miller refused to help Worrell lift the body from the car, Worrell again threatened him with the knife. They then disposed of the body. 'He asked me to give him a hand to carry her into the bushes,' Miller said. 'Her hands were tied. He always tied them. We got through the fence and dragged her under.'

Together they laid the body on the ground and covered it with branches and leaves. They then drove back to Adelaide. The following day, they reported for work as if nothing had happened. Worrell, who had been in a bad mood ever since the killing, was back to his normal self by the time they arrived at work.

They never discussed the murder. Miller didn't want to raise the subject, as he believed that Worrell would kill him. At no time did Miller contemplate telling the police of the murder. Had he done so, six more young lives would have been saved. Miller's only concern was his friendship with Worrell. In the future, a jury would consider this when they determined whether or not Miller was guilty of murder.

At 9 a.m. on 2 January 1977, Miller dropped Worrell off at the Rundle Mall and agreed to pick him up at the other end. Miller waited for a short time and Worrell returned with 15-year-old Tania Kenny who had just hitchhiked from Victor Harbor on the south coast. Worrell had chatted her up in the street.

They drove to Miller's sister's home on the pretext of picking up some clothes. After checking that no-one was home, Worrell and Tania went into the house while Miller waited in the car. Worrell eventually came out to the car and asked Miller to come inside. From the look on Worrell's face, Miller knew that something was drastically wrong.

In the children's playroom he found Tania's fully clothed

body bound with rope and she was gagged with a piece of sticking plaster. She had been strangled. Miller and Worrell had another violent argument. Again Worrell threatened to kill him if Miller didn't help him hide the body.

After hiding the dead girl in a cupboard, they returned later that night, put the body in the car and drove to Wingfield, to the back of the Dean Rifle Range. Here they buried Tania in a shallow grave they had dug for her body earlier on. Miller maintained that he helped bury the body because he didn't want to get his sister involved.

Once in the car, after the disposal of the body, Miller suggested to Worrell that he should see a doctor to try to find out what made him commit the horrible murders. Worrell told him to mind his own business.

Again, Miller could have stopped the murders there and then simply by going to the police. But he didn't. He later claimed that his attachment to Christopher Worrell, who was the only friend he had ever had, was the one thing that mattered in his life. The killings would continue. And rather than be without his friend, the besotted Miller would allow them to go on.

With the second murder behind them, Miller and Worrell continued to solicit girls every night. Their favourite spots were Adelaide railway station, Rundle Mall, the Mediterranean and Buckingham Arms hotels and hotels in the city. Miller claimed that he never participated in the soliciting of the girls, he was just 'the chauffeur and the mug'.

On 21 January 1977, they met 16-year-old Juliet Mykyta at the Ambassador's Hotel in King William Street. She had just rung her parents to tell them that she was going to be a little late getting home and that they were not to worry. Juliet was a student at Marsden High School and had taken a job in the holidays selling jewellery from a kerbside stall in the city. She was sitting on the steps of the hotel at 9 p.m., waiting for a bus, when Worrell offered her a lift.

Miller drove to one of their usual spots along the secluded Port Wakefield Road and Worrell forced the girl into the back seat while Miller sat in the front, waiting to be told to leave. With Miller in the front seat, Worrell started to tie up the girl. She offered resistance, but Worrell was too strong. Miller said he didn't find anything unusual about Worrell tying up the girl. He had done it to lots of them before, but usually with willing partners. It turned him on. It was his kink.

Miller got out of the car and walked about 50 metres. He heard voices and turned to see the girl falling out of the car to the ground as if she had been kicked in the stomach. Worrell rolled her over with his foot, knelt on her stomach and strangled her with a length of rope.

Miller claimed he grabbed Worrell's arm and tried to drag him off the girl, but Worrell pushed him away and threatened to kill him if he interfered. Miller shook his head and walked away. When he came back, the body was already in the back of the car. Worrell was in a black mood and Miller did as he demanded. He drove the car to Truro, but avoided going near the other body and went instead to a deserted farmhouse on a completely different track away from Swamp Road. From there, they carried the fully clothed body into the thick trees and covered it with foliage. They then drove back to Adelaide.

On 6 February, Miller and Worrell picked up 16-year-old Sylvia Pittman as she waited for a train at Adelaide Station. They drove to the Windang area where Worrell instructed Miller to go for a walk as soon as they arrived. After half an hour, Miller returned to find the girl lying face down on the back seat with a rug over her. She had been strangled with her own pantyhose.

Miller found it impossible to talk to Worrell. As always after a murder, he had lapsed into one of his black moods. Miller didn't say a word and they drove in silence to Truro where they unloaded the body. She was fully clothed and was not tied or gagged. They covered the corpse with leaves and branches and headed back to Adelaide.

The following day, 7 February 1977, Worrell told Miller to pick him up at the GPO at 7 p.m. With Worrell was 26-year-old Vicki Howell. Vicki was older than the others and Miller took a liking to her straightaway. Vicki seemed to have a few worries and mentioned that she was separated from her husband. Miller silently hoped that Worrell wouldn't kill her. She seemed completely at ease.

Worrell even had Miller stop the car so the woman could use the toilet at Nuriootpa. A little further on, Miller stopped the car and, leaving the couple to chat, he went to the bushes to relieve himself. He returned a few minutes later on the pretext that he had forgotten his cigarettes. He was really checking to see if the woman was all right. She was nice. He didn't want Worrell to kill her.

Miller assumed that Vicki would not be murdered and walked away into the bush. Worrell didn't appear to be in one of his moods. When he was satisfied that they had had enough time to talk, Miller returned to the car to find Worrell kneeling on the front seat and leaning into the back. He was covering Vicki Howell's body with the blanket. She had been strangled.

Miller could not control his anger. He cursed and abused Worrell for what he had done. It was not necessary to kill the woman. He could have just talked to her and let her go without fear of reprisal.

After Miller had vented his rage, he went quiet, terrified that Worrell would kill him too. He meekly asked Worrell why he had to kill the girl. Worrell gave no excuse. Instead, he told Miller to drive to Truro. Miller was terrified of Worrell and did as he bade. At Truro, they hid the body under foliage before driving back to Adelaide.

Two days later, on 9 February, Miller and Worrell were cruising in the centre of Adelaide when they spotted 16-year-old Connie Iordanides standing on the footpath laughing and giggling to herself. They did a U-turn, pulled up in front of the woman and asked if she wanted a lift. She accepted and sat in the front between the two men. Connie became frightened when the car headed in the opposite direction. Miller stopped at secluded Wingfield and Worrell forced the screaming girl into the back seat. Miller did nothing to help the girl. He got out and walked away from the car.

When he returned, Connie Iordanides was dead. Worrell had strangled and raped her. She was on the back seat covered with a blanket.

Again Worrell was in a foul mood and Miller was too terrified to say anything. He did as he was instructed and dumped the fully clothed body under bushes at Truro. That night, Miller and Worrell slept in the car at Victoria Park Racecourse.

On 12 February 1977, they committed their fourth murder in a week. In the early hours of Sunday morning, Miller and Worrell were cruising in the vicinity of the pinball arcades at City Bowl and picked up 20-year-old hitchhiker Deborah Lamb. Worrell suggested that they could take her to Port Gawler and the girl allegedly accepted the ride. Once they reached the beach at Port Gawler, Miller left them alone and went for a walk in the scrub. When he returned to the car, Worrell was standing in front of it, pushing sand into a hole with his feet. The girl was nowhere to be seen.

At Miller's trial in February 1980, Dr C.H. Manock, the Director of Forensic Pathology at the Institute of Medical and Veterinary Science, said it was possible that Deborah Lamb had been alive when placed in the grave. 'The sand and shellgrit would have formed an obstruction to the airway and prevented air from entering the air passages,' he said. He added that it was impossible to say this positively because of the advanced state of decomposition of soft tissue when the body was found.

Dr Manock said the pantyhose found wrapped seven times around the mouth and jaw of Deborah Lamb's remains could have caused death by asphyxia. If he chose to, Miller could have saved all of the victims' lives, but he said that he was terrified that Worrell would kill him if he did. Miller maintained that he did not see Deborah's body in the grave. But later he would lead police to it.

Detective Sergeant Lawrie said that towards the end of the interrogation on 23 May 1979, Miller had claimed: 'I know it might sound crazy after all this. I don't hold to murder. I really believe in the death penalty. An eye for an eye. Believe me, I wanted no part of this, it was like a nightmare. Each time we picked up one of those girls, I had no idea of his intentions.'

While returning from Mount Gambier on Saturday, 19 February 1977, Christopher Worrell was killed in a car accident. A female passenger in the car, Deborah Skuse, was also killed. The other passenger, James Miller, escaped with a fractured shoulder.

Miller and Worrell had become friendly with Debbie Skuse

when they first went to visit her boyfriend, whom they had known in jail, only to find that he had walked out on her.

To help Debbie get over the loss they had taken her to Mount Gambier for the weekend, but Worrell had become moody and they decided to return to Adelaide on the Saturday afternoon. Late in the afternoon, Worrell was at the wheel driving recklessly through countryside north of Millicent after drinking several cans of beer.

Debbie begged for him to slow down and a row ensued with Worrell screaming at the distraught girl and telling her to shut up. Then Worrell yelled, 'We've got a blowout!' and the car careered out of control onto the other side of the road and into the oncoming traffic.

In an effort to avoid a head-on collision with a vehicle coming the other way, Worrell careered the old Valiant off the side of the road where it spun over and over, spilling the three occupants out onto the grass. The accident had been witnessed by several bystanders who ran immediately to the scene, but there was little they could do.

Debbie Skuse and Christopher Worrell died instantly. James Miller suffered a shoulder injury and was taken to hospital in shock. It was his worst nightmare come true. The one and only friend he had ever had in the world was dead.

At his funeral, a distraught Miller spoke with Chris Worrell's girlfriend, Amelia – who would later come forward as 'Angela' – and told her that Worrell had had a suspected blood clot on the brain. This prompted Miller to tell Amelia that Worrell had been murdering young girls and that maybe the blood clot had caused him to commit these horrendous crimes.

Although Amelia had been seeing Worrell for only a short time, she had liked him very much and was deeply distressed by his death. Amelia kept her dark secret until the skeletons started turning up almost two years later. Then she told police about what James Miller had told her at the funeral.

After Worrell's death, Miller moved from place to place, sometimes sleeping in abandoned cars and at other times staying at the St Vincent de Paul and the Central Mission day centre. With Worrell dead and Miller living the life of a transient, it is highly likely that the murders would have gone unsolved if Amelia hadn't come forward.

At his trial, Miller pleaded not guilty to seven counts of murder. He sat quietly as the prosecution tore apart his defence. The Crown prosecutor, Mr B.J. Jennings, was merciless in his attack, claiming that Miller and Worrell had 'lived, worked and indeed committed murder together'.

He alleged that it was a joint enterprise that they pick up girls and murder them. 'He referred to the girls as "rags". That was the attitude that led him to throw in his lot with Worrell,' he said. 'No rapist and murderer could have had a more faithful or obliging ally.'

Mr Jennings continued: 'You will never know the truth, but have no doubt that it is a horrible truth that these young women were murdered because they were going to point the finger at the young man who tied them up and sexually abused them. They could also point the finger at the older man who ignored their plight and their terror. If a man assists another by driving him to a place where a girl is going to be raped and killed, then he is guilty of murder.'

It was obvious, Mr Jennings said, that no-one could possibly believe the girls had been willing partners in their own murders and that Worrell had never used any force. This was what Miller would have the court believe. Mr Jennings went on to say that the Crown rejected the claims that Miller had played no part in the sexual prelude to the girls' deaths. He said that three of the victims had been dumped partly clothed. They were Tania Kenny, who was found only in a shirt; Vicki Howell, who was found just in shorts; and Deborah Lamb, who was buried only in pantyhose.

Counsel for the defence, Mr K.P. Duggan, QC, said that there was a tendency to use Miller as a scapegoat: 'He was just waiting for Worrell and there was no joint enterprise as far as he was concerned. Miller had found himself in one of the oldest relationship problems in the world – that of the involvement in the wrongdoing of someone else. He was trapped in a web of circumstance. Although Miller admits that he handled the situation incorrectly, he maintains that he is not a murderer.'

The jury did not agree with the defence and on 12 March

1980 Miller was found guilty of six counts of murder. He was found not guilty of the murder of the first victim, Veronica Knight. The jury agreed that Miller did not know that Worrell intended to murder the girl.

Mr Justice Matheson sentenced Miller to the maximum term of six life sentences. As Miller was led from the court, he snarled at Detective Sergeant Lawrie: 'You filthy liar, Lawrie! You mongrel!'

If anyone in the courtroom had any compassion for Miller, it must have been dispelled in July 1984, when Miller was interviewed in prison after his 43-day hunger strike.

'Chris Worrell was my best friend in the world,' he said. 'If he had lived, maybe 70 would have been killed. And I wouldn't have ever dobbed him in.'

In late 1999, James Miller applied to have a non-parole period set in the hope that one day he may be released. On 8 February 2000, Chief Justice John Doyle of the South Australian Supreme Court granted Miller a non-parole period of 35 years from the date of his arrest.

James Miller died in custody of liver cancer on 21 October, 2008 aged 68.

CHAPTER 18

The Angel of Death

Helen Patricia Moore
Sydney, 1979–80

Helen Patricia Moore was every parent's worst nightmare – a babysitter who murdered the children entrusted to her care. A fresh-faced, 17-year-old cold-blooded murderer who blatantly went on killing those around her until she was eventually caught.

In Sydney's western suburbs, between May 1979 and March 1980, Helen Moore murdered three children and attempted to murder two others committed to her care. One of the survivors was left blind and permanently disabled and died several years later as a direct result of the attempt on his life by his babysitter. In addition to her atrocious crimes, Helen Moore was also charged with the murder of her stepbrother, but the charge was later dropped. Moore would later claim that his alleged cot death was the catalyst for the later killings.

Helen Patricia Moore was born and raised in Sydney's working-class far-western suburbs. At her murder trial her mother, Jesse, told the court that she remembered her little girl as a destructive part-angel, part-nightmare who loved to tear her toys apart and was always a bit distant and weird. Jesse Moore said that at age five Helen was attacked and molested by a pack of boys in the schoolyard, and at six a psychiatric patient ejaculated all over her uniform on a school bus. It was around about this time that she and Helen's natural father divorced.

Her mother also told the court that she had always believed her daughter suffered from a mental problem from an early age and that no-one would believe her. When Helen was aged 13, Jesse Moore took her to a psychiatrist after a particularly vicious fight with her brother where Helen pulled his hair so hard that it almost scalped him. Instead of diagnosing the child, the psychiatrist prescribed Valium for Jesse Moore.

Helen Moore alleged that from the age of eight she was molested by her uncle William McIntosh on a regular basis. His assaults only ended when Moore murdered his daughter, Suzanne, and William McIntosh no longer called at the Moore household. The allegations were vehemently denied by Mr McIntosh.

Helen Moore was aged 17 when her mother remarried. She worked as a clerk at Campbelltown Council and lived at home with her mother, stepfather, and her stepbrothers Peter and Andrew at the new Sydney outer-western Housing Commission suburb of Claymore, situated about as far west as Sydney got in 1979.

The horrors began in March 1979 when Helen Moore's 14-month-old stepbrother, Andrew, died, apparently from cot death. After her arrest for the other murders, Moore was charged with his death, but the charges were later dropped and it was believed that the boy died from a genuine case of cot death.

Helen Moore was deeply distressed by her stepbrother's death as she was extremely fond of the boy. She said later: 'My life started to go wrong when Andrew died. I loved my brother Andrew. I don't know why he was taken away from me but when he was, something happened. Everything in my life went wrong and everything I did went wrong.'

Helen Moore told a psychiatrist, Dr William Barclay, that Andrew's death was so significant in her life that she considered killing other children. 'She thought it wasn't fair that Andrew was dead and that he had lived in a clean house while her cousin Suzanne McIntosh was alive and well in a sloppy house,' the psychiatrist told the court.

But whatever the reason for the cold-blooded murders, something snapped inside teenage Helen Moore's head as she was babysitting 16-month old Suzanne McIntosh on the night of 19 May 1979. She put her hand over the baby's mouth and suffocated her in her sleep. 'She didn't put up much of a struggle,' Moore would later tell the court. Suzanne's passing was put down to cot death.

On 16 January 1980, while babysitting for some neighbours,

Helen Moore attempted to suffocate 12-month-old Nicholas Vaughan in the child's room. Believing he was dead, she returned to the television set and some time later was surprised to hear the baby crying. In panic, she ran to a neighbour for help and the child was rushed to Campbelltown Hospital and lived.

Incredibly, even in the light of all of the unfortunate 'mishaps' while Helen Moore babysat, trusting neighbours still sought out her child-minding services. On 1 February 1980, Helen was babysitting three children at the home of Petene and Roger Crocker when she went into two-year-old Aaron Crocker's room and suffocated him with a pillow until she thought he was dead before returning to the lounge room. Again, the child lived and again Helen Moore panicked when she saw blood running from little Aaron's mouth, and she went to a neighbour for help. After being alerted by a neighbour, Petene and Roger Crocker rushed home to find their boy wearing an oxygen mask and being attended by ambulance officers as they prepared to rush him to hospital.

Little Aaron's caring babysitter visited the infant in hospital. Aaron Crocker was in a coma for weeks, and when he came out of it he was blind and crippled and died several years later.

The father of little Vaughan Nicholson who had miraculously escaped the attack by Helen Moore only two weeks earlier said that when he and his wife heard of what had happened to Aaron Crocker they immediately became suspicious of Helen, yet they couldn't bring themselves to accuse her of murder.

But when two-year-old Rachel Hay, who lived just up the street from the Nicholson family, died a few weeks later, on 24 February 1980, while in the care of the babysitter Helen Moore, the Nicholsons knew there was something 'very, very wrong going on'.

On 31 March 1980, Jesse Moore rushed home from work after she had received a phone call from Helen telling her that her seven-year-old son, Peter, had had a fatal fall down the stairs. In tears, Jesse Moore went to her friends across the road, the Nicholsons, and told them she was going to call the police and tell them of what she suspected: that her daughter was a murderer.

When the police arrived and Helen and Jesse Moore were

being driven to Campbelltown police station, Jesse noticed scratches on her daughter's hands. 'Finally, I knew,' Jesse Moore said later. 'Peter was the only one who died for a reason. He died so Helen could be caught.'

At the police station, Helen Moore confessed to murdering her stepbrother, Peter Moore. She had been left at home to mind the boy while the adults went out for the day. She said that she had come up behind Peter while he was sitting on the lounge watching the morning cartoons on television. He managed to escape her initial assault but she caught him once again and, being a lot bigger and stronger than the boy, she easily pinned him down and pressed her hands over his nose and mouth for about four minutes and suffocated him. She then went upstairs and had a shower before calling an ambulance. The previous day they had spent an enjoyable outing at the zoo together.

Helen Moore then confessed to the other murders and the two attempted murders.

At her trial, held before Mr Justice Roden at the Supreme Court of Parramatta, Sydney, in November 1980, it was not a matter for the court to decide whether or not Helen Patricia Moore was guilty of murder. That had already been established and she had clearly admitted her guilt. It was a case of whether or not Helen Moore was sane at the time of the murders. Her defence lawyers, headed by Mr John Marsden, argued that she could not have been sane at the time of the killings and they backed up their claims with lots of expert opinions.

Psychiatrist Dr Barclay said Helen Moore's schizophrenia went 'far over the borderline and that she did not know what she was doing when she committed the last four offences'. Dr Barclay also suggested that Helen Moore had a mental disorder for which there was significant evidence of a genetic factor. He also suggested that Moore knew what she was doing but did not know that it was wrong.

Another psychiatrist, Dr Greta Goldberg, suggested that the sexual indignities Moore had been subjected to at a young age had left her permanently scarred. Moore had told another psychiatrist that she had been having sexual relations with an older relative since she was eight. Dr Goldberg also emphasised the depressed and alienated background of the accused – Moore's parents had separated; her mother, who had remarried, was prone to rages; and her stepfather was withdrawn. It appeared it had been a lonely, isolated, and struggling existence for the young woman.

Psychologist Michael Taylor also believed that Helen Moore was insane and that she did not know what she was doing or that her actions were wrong.

In summing up the defence's case for insanity, John Marsden suggested to the jury that reasonable men and women would be entitled to find that an 18-year-old woman charged with murdering three children and attempting to murder two others was not guilty on the grounds of insanity. He pointed out that this opinion was obvious – at least to him, anyway. He also pointed out that no normal person could be expected to believe that another normal person could kill three young children by placing their hands over their noses and mouths until they died of suffocation.

The prosecution argued that Helen Moore knew exactly what she was doing and they had their own expert witness, forensic psychiatrist Dr Oscar Schmalzbach, to testify accordingly. Dr Schmalzbach told the court that, in his opinion, the accused was not suffering from a mental disease, she knew exactly what she was doing and that she knew it was wrong.

Justice Roden simplified the arguments to the jury before they retired by pointing out their options: If they were to find Helen Moore not guilty on the grounds of insanity, they had to be completely satisfied that she had been suffering a mental illness that left her unable to know what she was doing and that what she was doing was wrong. But they could also find Helen Moore guilty of manslaughter on the grounds of diminished responsibility and excuse the charge of murder. The law of diminished responsibility, however, does not apply to attempted murder and the decision on those two charges would have to be a plain 'guilty' or 'not guilty' verdict. The third alternative, Justice Roden said, was that of a guilty verdict of murder and attempted murder on all charges.

It took the jury less than two hours to return a verdict of guilty of three counts of murder and two counts of attempted murder. Justice Roden sentenced Helen Patricia Moore to life imprisonment on the murder charges and to 10 years for each count of attempted murder.

In 1992, Helen Moore applied for a sentence review under the Truth in Sentencing legislation introduced in New South Wales in 1989. On 4 September 1992, Justice Loveday handed down a prison term of a minimum of 13 years and nine months with a maximum of 25 years, making her eligible for release on 31 December 1993. The provision of the parole was that she was forbidden to be in the company of any child under the age of 16 without supervision.

Released in 1993 after serving her minimum term but having to remain on parole until the year 2005, Helen Moore complicated the main condition of her parole enormously when, in late March 1995, at the age of 33, she gave birth to a daughter, Lauren. Helen said she had no intention of having anything further to do with the father of her baby who she said was one of her first lovers.

The court, contemplating on what to do in such a difficult situation, ordered that both mother and baby be kept under constant supervision until it was decided, in August 1995, that the baby must never be left alone with the mother at any time during the parole period.

At the time of publication, Helen Patricia Moore and her daughter, Lauren, are living in Australia under 24-hour supervision. Their situation is reviewed regularly, but it is thought that the circumstances will remain until her parole expires in the year 2005. By then, Lauren Moore will be 10.

CHAPTER 19

The Pederast Predator

Michael George Laurance
Griffith, New South Wales, 1984–86

Michael Laurance was one of the rarest forms of serial killers in the world. He was a pederast, a man who derived sexual pleasure from pubescent boys. But while the sexual crimes of pederasts are among the most despicable, history tells us that they very rarely murder their victims.

This characteristic made Michael Laurance unique among Australia's serial killers. Of the five serial killers in our history who exclusively murdered children – Martha Rendell, Arnold Sodeman, Helen Moore and Barry Gordon Hadlow – Michael Laurance was the only one who preyed upon young boys.

So evil were the serial killings of Michael Laurance that in order to draw a comparison we would have to look at the infamous English 'Moors Murders' of Myra Hindley and her lover, sexual sadist Ian Brady, who committed atrocities to children that defy comprehension. In October 1965, police were led to a house in Hattersley, near Manchester, where they discovered the murdered body of 17-year old Edward Evans and two left-luggage tickets that led them to a suitcase at Manchester railway station. The suitcase was found to contain sex and torture books, whips, coshes, photos and two tape recordings.

Some of the photos were pornographic poses of 10-year-old Leslie Ann Downey who had gone missing almost a year earlier. Others were of Hindley posing next to the shallow grave of 12-year-old John Kilbride who had been missing for almost two years. But it was the tapes that reduced hardened police to tears as they listened to little Leslie Ann Downey frantically screaming: 'Don't – please! God help me . . .' as she was sexually assaulted, tortured and eventually strangled by Hindley and Brady.

Myra Hindley and Ian Brady were each sentenced to three terms of life imprisonment without ever the possibility of parole. In 1986, Hindley confessed to the murders of two other children, 12-year-old Keith Bennett and 16-year-old Pauline Reade. And while the almost unbelievable crimes of Hindley and Brady remain among the most despicable of modern time, it was hard to imagine that anything of a similar nature could ever take place again, let alone in rural Australia. But, sadly, it did.

Michael George Laurance was born in Sydney in 1950 and raised in the small country town of Narrabri in the north-west of New South Wales. According to Children's Court records, Laurance claimed that he was brought up by his mother and step-father after his natural father, who was an alcoholic, deserted his family when Laurance was very young.

By his own admission, from the age of 11 Michael Laurance allegedly swapped sexual favours with older men in the district for money and bottles of beer and wine. But he soon discovered that he much preferred young boys and, although the older men were his main source of income, he spent much of his money on younger boys in return for sex. In his teens, he began gathering what would eventually become a huge collection of photographs of naked boys.

At 14, Michael Laurance left school with the reputation of being somewhat dimwitted. He worked as a labourer on farms throughout western New South Wales but spent most of his time scouring the streets, public toilets and community centres in which-ever town he was working in his endless pursuit of young boys willing to accept gifts and cash in exchange for his sexual advances.

At Narrabri in 1973, Laurance was convicted of indecent assault against a boy. And when the mother of another young boy he had been seeing stopped the unhealthy tryst by threatening to go to the police, Laurance tried to commit suicide and ended up in a psychiatric hospital in Orange.

In 1983, Michael Laurance moved to Griffith, a town of 22,000 residents situated in the soil-rich Riverina district in the south-west of New South Wales. Due to its magnificent oranges and grapes, Griffith attracts thousands of itinerant fruit-pickers each year, mainly through the warmer months.

Interestingly, Griffith was also a town with a criminal history. Throughout the 1970s, it was known as the marijuana-growing capital of the southern hemisphere, and Mafia associate Robert 'Aussie Bob' Trimbole emerged as the marijuana king of Australia. Then in July 1977, anti-drug campaigner Donald Mackay went missing, presumed murdered. His body was never found.

The now 33-year-old Michael Laurance moved into the Montana Guest House, a cheap and clean rooming house with quiet but friendly residents in central Griffith. He blended in immediately with the kindly rural folk of the town. But the residents had no way of knowing that the tall, unassuming, red-haired boarder with the country-style sideburns was in fact a sexual predator of the worst possible kind, a sadistic pederast who had had unnatural relationships with more than 150 prepubescent boys since his early teens. Michael Laurance now also fantasised about molesting, torturing, and killing little boys.

The locals admired Laurance's keen interest in junior football, athletics and swimming. But, in fact, he was perving on the young boys as they undressed in the change rooms and becoming aroused while lusting over their almost-naked bodies around the swimming pool.

Laurance told his new-found friends that he was a recovering alcoholic who was driven to drink by the death of his de-facto wife and young son in a head-on car smash. While it was true that he was an alcoholic, the story about the car smash was never confirmed and is extremely unlikely to be true.

Laurance was a regular at the Griffith Alcoholics Anonymous meetings and regularly attended the clinic in his on-going battle with the bottle. He became close friends with the clinic's director who referred him to the Community Youth Support Scheme office. Here, Laurance picked up a job as a part-time cleaner while studying to become an ambulance driver.

Is wasn't long before the staff at the CYSS began complaining that the new part-time cleaner was giving them the creeps. He suffered from dramatic mood swings, wouldn't take orders from anyone, and had become extremely aggressive towards the male members of the staff. Plus they didn't like the way Laurance hung around the young boys in the workshop.

Laurance was pressured into leaving his cleaning job at the CYSS, after which he picked up odd jobs around the town and helped collect furniture for the Smith Family. He befriended one of the Smith Family staff, Maureen Singh, a jovial cooking teacher originally from Yorkshire, and became particularly fond of her teenage son, Andrew, explaining that the boy shared the same name as, and reminded him of, his own son who was allegedly killed in the car accident.

The Singhs lived on the outskirts of Griffith and Michael Laurance visited the house regularly, often staying overnight. They were aware that he had unusual ways but Maureen and her four children trusted him.

In an interview with the *Sydney Morning Herald*, Maureen Singh said: 'He were all right. He used to talk to us. He'd do anything for you; he helped us come and organise the garden, helped us move, he put panelling inside the laundry. He'd do anything for you. You can't tell me he's simple 'cause he's not. He's not psychiatric either, no way.'

In the same interview, Maureen recalled a sinister conversation that meant little at the time but would prove to be significant in light of future events. Laurance told her that he had done a lot of child-minding in the past and to keep any unruly children in line he played a game called 'tie-ups' in which he would firstly tie the children to a chair and see how quickly they could untie themselves, and then he would get them to tie him in a chair and see how quickly he could escape.

Often when Maureen Singh and Andrew visited Laurance at home unannounced, she found him walking around the house with no clothes on. On a fishing trip to nearby Darlington Point, Laurance ran around stark naked and asked Andrew for sex in exchange for money. Laurance made out that it was a joke and Andrew laughed it off.

'He were a good mate of Andrew,' Maureen Singh told the *Herald*. 'He used to treat him real good. But it were a means to his own ends, that's why he was good to us. He were after Andrew.'

In December 1983, Laurance moved into a flat at the rear of 22 Yarrabee Street, near the Griffith Showground. It was a large family house that had been converted into apartments. His landlord, Merv Platt, who lived in the front of the house, described Laurance as a quiet and tidy tenant who paid his rent on time and when he wasn't doing charity work for the Smith Family he was helping his neighbour, the landlord's 82-year-old sister, Aunt Molly, in her garden.

'He was a loner, he ran his own race,' Merv Platt told the *Sydney Morning Herald*. 'But there was nothing in his behaviour which struck me as odd or unusual. He didn't appear to drink. He was just a normal person as far as I knew.'

'Butter wouldn't melt in his mouth,' said Aunt Molly. 'I trusted him. That's how good he was. He acted so naturally. He was neat and clean, courteous and well-spoken, and would often come in for a cup of tea and a chat.'

On Saturday, 29 September 1984, 12-year-old Mark Mott and his 11-year-old mate Ralph Burns disappeared without a trace. The boys had been seen to be having a terrific day together at the Griffith Show with $20 donated by Ralphy's grandfather, 'Bronco' Burns, and $10 that Mark's mum had given her son as spending money. Between the Griffith Show and their homes the boys vanished. Without a single lead to explain their mysterious disappearance, the friends and grief-stricken families of the lads were left to surmise that they had run away together on an adventure and would turn up somewhere along the line.

Although it was of little consolation to their loved ones that Mark Mott and Ralph Burns were much more at home sitting on the bank of a river fishing or participating in adventures than sitting in a classroom, it was all they had to cling to in the hope that one day the door would open and the boys would be back from whatever adventure they had embarked on.

But sadly, that day would never come.

When the boys went missing, there was not one reason for police to suspect that Michael Laurance had anything to do with their disappearance, even when Laurance held them at bay with a rifle one afternoon shortly after the boys had disappeared. The police had arrived to take Laurance away for exposing himself to schoolchildren while clad only in a balaclava. They subdued Laurance, removed his rifle, and took him away after his crude attempt at suicide in which he took an overdose of pills.

After he was released on bail, Laurance was evicted from his flat by Merv Platt and moved into a tiny shack on the edge of an isolated fruit farm at Hanwood, a village about 7 kilometres from Griffith.

Almost 12 months after the boys went missing, Mark Mott's remains were found in the water at nearby Lake Wyangan. Three months later, the skeletal remains of Ralph Burns were found under a nearby bush by a rabbit shooter.

On 21 June 1986, eight-year-old John Purtell disappeared after his team, the Albury Under-8s, of which he was captain, won their game at Griffith. John Purtell was last seen leaving the change rooms after he had showered and dressed. From there he had vanished.

Young John Purtell had come to be in Griffith when his father, Albury brick-laying contractor, Peter Purtell, became friendly with some of the locals while working on a construction site in Griffith in 1986 and arranged for his son's Under-8s team to come across and play the Griffith side. In an ironic coincidence, Michael Laurance was working at the same construction site at the time as an air-conditioning labourer, though he and Peter Purtell had little contact.

When it was discovered that John Purtell was missing, observant bystanders who were in the change rooms that day gave police several eyewitness descriptions of a man who approached John Purtell and offered to wring out his underpants, which the boy trustingly gave him.

An identikit drawing was made up and circulated. The identikit visage had an extraordinary likeness to that of Michael Laurance and after numerous people had pointed the finger at him, police arrived at his door.

Laurance vehemently denied any knowledge of the disappearance of John Purtell and denied being the man in the change rooms at the time in question. Suspicious but unable to prove anything, police had nothing to go on until they called at Laurance's tiny shack again five days later after it was reported that he had made another half-hearted suicide attempt.

Inside the shack, policemen stood in stunned disbelief as Laurance confessed to abducting and murdering John Purtell. He then took them to Purtell's body where he had concealed it beneath a log at Darlington Point, a popular fishing spot on the Murrumbidgee River 30 kilometres from Griffith.

Then out of the blue, Laurance told police, who were still reeling from the first confession: 'Poor little Burnsey and Motty. I killed them, too.' Laurance then had the police take him back to his shack where he showed them a secret compartment in his dining table that was full of albums containing photos of naked boys, newspaper cuttings of missing boys long presumed dead, and other newspaper and magazine articles which showed his sick preoccupation with skeletons and death.

It was then that Michael George Laurance made a full confession. It was a confession of unimaginable horror. He told in graphic detail how he degraded and humiliated his little victims as he sexually abused and eventually murdered them.

On the afternoon of Saturday, 29 September 1984, as Mark Mott and Ralph Burns were making their way home from the Griffith Show down Yarrabee Street, they passed Laurance's residence situated only a few hundred metres from the showground. Laurance spotted them coming and enticed them into his flat by telling them that they could come in and play games.

One of the games was called 'tie-up'. Once the boys were inside, the persuasive Laurance secured them with ropes in such a fashion that they couldn't untie themselves, and then he abused each boy in front of the other.

'We played tie-ups, and when I tied them up I got very sexually excited,' he said. Laurance then told police that he carried Ralph Burns into the bathroom. 'I put Burnsie in the bath and was drowning him, and while I was drowning him I was also playing with his penis,' he told stunned police. 'I held his head under the water and then, when the bubbles stopped and he stopped kicking, I lifted him out of the bathtub, undone the ropes, carried him in and put him in the wardrobe.

'I carried Mark Mott into the shower room and also played with him while I was drowning him. I wanted to stop but I could not, I was so sexually excited. It gave me a thrill watching them die. I got an erection watching them drown in the bathtub.'

That night, Michael Laurance buried Ralph Burns in his

backyard and buried Mark Mott in the backyard of his trusting neighbour, Aunt Molly. Some time later, Laurance dug up the bodies and dumped them at nearby Lake Wyangan where Mark Mott's remains were found in the water almost a year later and the remains of Ralph Burns were found nearby three months later.

On the afternoon of 21 June 1986, as he did every Saturday, Michael Laurance attended the junior football match to watch the Albury Under-8s, captained by John Purtell.

In his confession, Laurance said that after the game he went to the shower block and watched some boys showering and offered to dry out the underpants of two boys. When John Purtell left the shower Laurance allegedly followed him outside and asked him if he would like a hamburger. Purtell went with him and he then drove home to Hanwood on the pretext that he had to feed his cats.

'I just wanted a boy,' Laurance told police. 'Young boys just turn me on. At home I taped his hands in front of him and played with him.'

Laurance said in his confession that he then put the boy in the back of his car and drove to Darlington Point where he played with him again, and when the boy 'started to scream and kick' he taped John Purtell's mouth and nose with 'wide' tape until the lad died of suffocation. He then hid the body beneath a tree trunk and went home and masturbated while thinking about naked little boys.

Laurance's confession was damning and, although he admitted his guilt, at his trial he pleaded not guilty to murder due to a mental condition which diminished his capacity to understand and control his actions. The jury chose to ignore his defence and took only half an hour to find him guilty of murdering the three boys.

In sentencing Michael Laurance, the Chief Justice of Common Law, Justice Slattery, said his 'crimes were such that he should not hold out any hope of ever being released from custody.

'The prisoner carried out these dreadful deeds in a cruel, cold-blooded and unemotional state without any mercy or apparent feeling whatsoever for his young and helpless victims . . . Laurance's claim that he invited Mott and Burns into his flat was unlikely. It is more likely that he met the boys elsewhere, possibly at the Griffith Show, and lured them into his flat for sexual gratification.'

As the judge spoke, Laurance sat emotionless in the dock, as he had been for the duration of the week-long trial.

'After sexually abusing each boy,' Justice Slattery continued, 'Laurance drowned them one at a time in his bathtub after realising his identification and subsequent detection were almost certain. While [Burns] witnessed the bath being run, his last minutes alive must have been appalling. Mott, tied up in the lounge room, would probably have been aware of what happened to his companion and of his own likely fate. They, too, must have been terrible moments for him.'

Of John Purtell, the third murdered boy, the judge said in reference to some cotton found in the boy's throat at the post-mortem: 'The prisoner probably placed a ball of cotton wool in his mouth to stop him screaming. He then taped his mouth and nose, well-knowing that the boy would die. Bound, gagged and taped, the boy subsequently died. It is hard to imagine a more cruel or callous act.

'There is only one sentence for a person who has perpetrated such terrible crimes on young boys and that is life imprisonment, which I now impose. While acknowledging that it was not binding on the executive or parole authorities, nevertheless, having presided over this trial, it is my opinion and my recommendation that the prisoner should never be released into the community.'

At 8.40 a.m. on 16 November 1995, Michael George Laurance was found hanging from the bars of the window in his cell at Lithgow Prison. At a coronial inquest held on 29 April 1996, it was concluded that he committed suicide.

CHAPTER 20

The Moorhouse Street Murders

Catherine and David Birnie
Perth, 1986

The white brick bungalow at No. 3 Moorhouse Street, Willagee on the outskirts of Perth was in poor condition and in bad need of a coat of paint. The unkempt garden was overrun with weeds and dead flowers. It was by far the worst house in the street and its only advantage was that it made the other Housing Commission homes around it look like palaces.

Yet in 1986, this unglamorous dwelling became Australia's very own house of horrors. In the ensuing years, people would slow down and point and whisper as they drove past it. It would become as infamous to Australians as were the chamber of horrors at 213 Oxford Apartments, Milwaukee, to Americans, and London's 10 Rillington Place and 25 Cromwell Street to the British.

It was at 213 Oxford Apartments between 1988 to 1991 that Jeffrey Dahmer, a 28-year-old chocolate factory worker, slaughtered 17 young men, raped and mutilated their corpses and ate their body parts. At 10 Rillington Place in the early 1950s, mild-mannered office clerk and necrophiliac serial killer John Christie murdered his victims, had sex with their corpses and buried their bodies in the backyard, under the floorboards, and in the wall cavities. And at 25 Cromwell Street through the 1970s and 1980s, labourer Fred West and his wife, Rose, raped, tortured and murdered their victims, nine of whom they buried in their own backyard.

The house at 3 Moorhouse Street was the love nest, torture chamber and killing field of Catherine Margaret and David John Birnie who, like the Wests, were a husband-and-wife serial killer team, the rarest form of serial killers in the world. It was here that they committed unimaginable atrocities on their young female victims.

The Birnies weren't particularly fussy about who they preyed upon – as long as they were female. Their victims' ages ranged from 15 to 31. Whenever the Birnies felt the urge to kill they would drive along the highways of Perth and pick up hitch-hikers or other young women in need of a lift.

Their victims never suspected the friendly couple until it was too late. At knifepoint they were taken back to Moorhouse Street, tied up and abused as the Birnies carried out their sexual fantasies. Then they were murdered. The lucky ones were put to sleep with an overdose of sleeping pills and then strangled. The less fortunate victims were either stabbed or bludgeoned to death with a knife or an axe as they sat in their shallow graves in a secluded pine forest outside of Perth. And if their intended fifth victim had not escaped through sheer good fortune and a blunder on Catherine Birnie's part, there is little doubt that the Birnies would have continued their reign of terror in Perth.

On 5 November 1986, Detective Sergeant Paul Ferguson was convinced that there was a serial killer on the loose when 21-year-old Denise Karen Brown was reported missing. It was the fourth disappearance of a woman in the city in 27 days. That type of thing just didn't happen in Perth. Sydney or Melbourne, yes. But not in Perth.

Each of the missing women came from a good home and it was extremely unlikely that any one of them would simply disappear for no reason. Ferguson had eliminated the possibilities of links between the women and investigated the likelihood of secret boyfriends, married lovers, or hidden drug problems that might have caused any of them to disappear. He found nothing. His instinct, drawn from years of experience, told him that there was a serial killer on the loose.

What puzzled Detective Sergeant Ferguson most was that two of the women hadn't completely disappeared – friends and relatives had received letters and telephone calls from them after they had been reported missing. Fifteen-year-old Susannah Candy had posted two letters to her parents, one from Perth and the other from the nearby port of Fremantle, in the first two weeks of her disappearance. Both letters said that she was well and that she would return home soon. And Denise Brown had phoned a girlfriend the day after she had disappeared to tell her that everything was fine. After that, no-one had heard a word. It just didn't add up. Ferguson's gut feeling told him to expect the worst.

He consulted former Criminal Investigations Bureau chief, Bill Neilson, who agreed with his serial killer theory. And if anyone was entitled to an opinion, it would be Neilson, the veteran multiple-homicide investigator, a police officer among the most respected in the state.

Bill Neilson was the officer in charge of the hunt for Perth serial killer Eric Edgar Cooke, the mild-mannered truck driver who had ruthlessly murdered six people, and possibly two others, in the early 1960s to become the most notorious multiple murderer in Western Australia's history (Cooke's story is told in detail in chapter 12). Neilson had brought him to justice and saw Cooke swing at the end of a rope in Fremantle Prison in 1964.

On 10 November, five days after the disappearance of Denise Brown, Detective Sergeant Ferguson and Detective Sergeant Vince Katich were following up leads on Denise's disappearance when they got the breakthrough they were so desperately waiting for. They were told on the two-way radio that a half-naked young woman had just staggered into a small Willagee shopping complex and had been taken to the Palmyra police station.

Thinking that the missing Denise Brown had turned up, Ferguson and Katich sped to the police station. What they found instead was a 16-year-old girl who told them an amazing story. The terrified teenager said that she had been abducted at knife-point the previous evening by a man and a woman who asked her directions as she walked towards her home in fashionable Nedlands.

She was taken to a house in Willagee where the couple ripped off all of her clothing before chaining her to a bed by her hands and feet. The girl said the man repeatedly raped her as the woman watched. The couple spoke of injecting cocaine into the head of the man's penis.

The following morning, after the man had left for work, the woman unchained the girl and forced her to telephone her parents to tell them that she was staying with friends and that she was okay. While she was using the phone the girl was astute enough to note the number.

The woman then left the bedroom to answer the door, presumably to let in a cocaine dealer, and the girl found an open window and escaped. She was able to give police a full description of her attackers, along with their telephone number and address.

When the girl had told detectives Ferguson and Katich of the phone call she was forced to make to her parents, they immediately became suspicious that the couple may be the kidnappers of the two young women who had disappeared and had rung their families under suspicious circumstances.

There was also little doubt in their minds that the fact that the girl was allowed to see the couple's faces and where they lived could mean that she was marked for death once they had finished with her. If this were the case, then it was highly likely that the couple had already killed, perhaps many times.

The girl led the team of armed detectives to the dilapidated white brick house in Moorhouse Street. There was no-one at home. Two detectives hid in a panel van parked in the driveway and apprehended a very tense and nervous Catherine Birnie when she arrived home. She told them where to look for the man. Minutes later, other detectives picked up David Birnie where he worked as a labourer in a spare-parts car yard.

The Birnies vigorously denied the girl's allegations. Instead, they claimed that she had been a willing party and had gone with them to share a bong of marijuana. Birnie admitted to having sex with the girl but maintained that he had not raped her. A search of the house found the girl's bag and a packet of cigarettes she had the commonsense to conceal in the ceiling as proof that she had actually been there, but there was little else to prove the allegation of rape or connect the Birnies with any of the other missing women.

The Birnies were taken to the police station. Knowing that they needed a confession to confirm their suspicions, Ferguson and Katich hoped that under intense questioning one of the Birnies would crack and at least admit to the rape of the young girl. It was her word against theirs.

Ferguson and Katich grilled the Birnies separately. It was David Birnie who eventually cracked. Just after 7 o'clock that evening, Detective Sergeant Katich said half-jokingly in reference to the missing women: 'It's getting dark. Best we take the shovel and dig them up.' To his astonishment, Birnie replied: 'Okay. There's four of them.' The detective couldn't believe his ears.

When told of her lover's confession, Catherine Birnie also broke. They agreed to take the police to the bodies, which were buried not far from the city. It was as though a load had been taken off David Birnie's mind. He spoke freely with the detectives as he directed the convoy of vehicles out of the metropolitan area and towards the State Forest, north of the city.

The convoy moved along Wanneroo Road and through the pine forests. Birnie was so relaxed and chatting in such an easy manner that they were almost at Yanchep before he realised that they had gone too far and instructed them to turn around and go back. Squinting into the darkness, Birnie recognised a track that led off the highway and into the darkness of the Gnangara pine plantation.

About 400 metres into the forest, David Birnie instructed them to stop. He pointed to a mound of sand. 'Dig there,' he said. Within minutes, police had uncovered the corpse of Denise Karen Brown, who had been reported missing only five days earlier.

With a guard placed around the shallow grave, Birnie directed the convoy south to the Glen Eagle Picnic Area on the Albany Highway near Armadale. After travelling for half an hour, Birnie guided police into the forest and along a narrow track. Up an incline, about 40 metres from the track, police uncovered the decomposing body of 22-year-old Mary Frances Neilson who had gone missing on 6 October.

A further kilometre down the track David Birnie pointed out the burial site of 15-year-old Susannah Candy, who hadn't been seen since 19 October. Detective Sergeant Katich was amazed that neither of the Birnies showed any emotion or embarrassment while the bodies were being uncovered. If anything, they appeared to enjoy being the centre of attention as they pointed out the graves to the police.

Then Catherine Birnie said that it was her turn. She wanted to indicate the location of the next grave. She pointed out the burial site of 31-year-old Noelene Patterson who they had kidnapped and murdered on 1 November. Catherine Birnie went to great lengths to explain to the police how much she disliked Noelene from the moment that she and David had abducted her. She was glad that she was dead. As she pointed out the grave, she spat on it. She showed a great deal of pride in being able to find the grave unassisted. It was as if she didn't want David Birnie to get all of the credit.

As they left the burial grounds, David Birnie commented to Katich: 'What a pointless loss of young life.'

There was absolutely no doubt in the big detective's mind that if the young girl hadn't escaped earlier in the day, the killings would have gone on. Psychiatrists attached to the case agreed that Catherine Birnie could not have killed on her own. She just wasn't the type. But the quiet mother of six children was totally obsessed with David Birnie and would do anything for him, including murder. She was even prepared to take her own life for him. When he got too fond of one of their victims, Catherine turned the knife on herself and said that she would rather die by her own hand than see him fall in love with anyone else.

David Birnie was a completely different story. The product of a desperately poor family, he had been in and out of institutions and prison all of his life and was fated to end up in jail for a long time. But no-one could possibly have forecast the magnitude of his crimes.

David John Birnie was born the eldest of six children in the Perth suburb of Subiaco in 1950. His parents, Margaret and John Birnie, had a long history of alcoholism. They did their best for their kids, but times were tough, and for all of their young lives the authorities periodically took the children away from their parents and placed them in government institutions. When David Birnie was 12 years old he was separated from his siblings and grew up in foster homes in suburban Perth.

At the time of the murders David Birnie's mother was living in destitute squalor. Her tiny apartment was overflowing with food scraps, dirty dishes, full ashtrays, and broken furniture. The place was covered in dust and grime. She had given up hope and could not recall seeing her eldest son in years. David Birnie's father died in 1986 after a long illness.

Catherine and David first met as youngsters when their

families lived next door to one another. Catherine's life was also one of doom and despair. Her mother died when she was 10 months old and she was sent to live in South Africa with her father. After two years, she was bundled back to Australia and fostered by her grandparents. A sad little girl who rarely smiled, Catherine had no friends. Other children weren't allowed to play with her, and even before she reached high school her mind was scarred by loneliness. She desperately wanted to be loved. She would find that love in David Birnie later on in her sad life – they became lovers when she was fourteen. But the relationship would drive her to a loneliness and despair that she never thought possible.

Even at this early stage in his life, David already had an extensive record of juvenile offences. The only indication that he might make something of himself was in the early 1960s when he trained as an apprentice jockey. But like most things in David Birnie's life, that didn't last long. Trainer Eric Parnham recalled Birnie as a pale, sickly looking boy who he took on just to give him a job. Birnie was recommended as an apprentice prospect and Parnham went to pick up the boy at his home. The house was a derelict slum surrounded by a pack of dogs. Birnie stayed in the stables for almost a year and showed enough ability to become a good jockey. Parnham eventually sacked him when he was alleged to have bashed and robbed the elderly owner of a boarding house.

Catherine found a friend in Birnie. She would do anything he desired and together they went on a crime rampage that would land them both in jail.

On 11 June 1969, David and Catherine pleaded guilty in the Perth Police Court to 11 charges of breaking, entering and stealing goods worth nearly $3000. The court was told that Catherine was pregnant to another man. They admitted to stealing oxyacetylene equipment and using it to try to crack a safe at the Waverly drive-in theatre. Catherine was placed on probation and Birnie was sent to prison for nine months.

On 9 July 1969, Catherine and David were committed for trial in the Supreme Court on eight further charges of breaking, entering and stealing. They pleaded guilty and Birnie had three years' imprisonment added to his sentence. Catherine was put on probation for a further four years.

On 21 June 1970, Birnie broke out of Karnet Prison in Western Australia and teamed up with Catherine again. When they were apprehended on 10 July they were charged with 53 counts of stealing, receiving, breaking and entering, unlawful entry into premises, and unlawful driving, and use, of motor vehicles. In their possession police found clothing, wigs, bedding, radios, food, books, 100 sticks of gelignite, 120 detonators and three fuses. Catherine admitted that she knew that she had done wrong but said that she loved Birnie so much there was nothing that she wouldn't do for him. She would get her chance to prove this in the years to come.

Birnie was sentenced to two-and-a-half years in prison and Catherine received six months. Out of prison a few months later and away from the evil influence of David Birnie, Catherine went to work as a live-in domestic for a family in Fremantle.

For the first time in her life, the scrawny young woman seemed to have found some happiness. Donald McLaughlan, the son of the family she worked for, fell in love with her and they married on 31 May 1972, Catherine's twenty-first birthday.

Shortly after, she gave birth to the first of their six children. They named the baby boy 'Little Donny' after his father. Seven months later, Donny was killed when he was crushed to death by a car in front of his mother. Psychiatrists would later ponder the significance of this tragedy in the horrors of the future.

In the meantime, the marriage was not a happy one. Catherine pined for David Birnie. No-one was surprised when she bailed out of the marriage. The family had been living in a State Housing Commission home in the working-class suburb of Victoria Park. Catherine had to look after her unemployed husband, their six children and her father and uncle. The place was a pigsty. She took no pride in the kids or the house. There was never money for food. One day she rang her husband and said that she wasn't coming back. She had been seeing David Birnie for two years and was going back to him.

After 13 years apart, Catherine moved in again with David Birnie in Willagee. Although they never married, Catherine changed her name to Birnie by deed poll and became his common law wife.

But the Birnie household was far from normal. David Birnie's sexual appetite was seemingly insatiable. James Birnie, David's younger brother, stayed with the couple for a short time when he was released from prison after serving five months for indecently interfering with his six-year-old niece. He told a reporter: '[The six-year-old] led me on. You don't know what they can be like. When I left prison, I had nowhere to go. I couldn't go back to my mother's place because I had assaulted her and there was a restraining order out against me. I had a couple of fights with Mum and the police chased me off. Mum has alcohol problems. So David and Catherine let me move in. They weren't real happy about it and David kept saying that he was going to kill me to keep me in line.'

James added that David Birnie had few friends, was heavily into kinky sex, and had a big pornographic video collection. 'He has to have sex four or five times a day,' James said of his brother. 'I saw him use a hypodermic of that stuff you have when they're going to put stitches in your leg. It makes you numb. He put the needle in his penis. Then he had sex. David has had many women. He always has someone.'

The killings started in 1986. Together, David and Catherine Birnie had tried everything sexually and they wanted new kicks. They discussed abduction and rape. Birnie turned on his accomplice by telling her that she would achieve incredible orgasms by watching him penetrate another woman who was bound and gagged. Catherine believed him.

Their first opportunity came on 6 October 1986 when 22-year-old student Mary Neilson turned up at the Birnie house to buy some car tyres. She had approached Birnie at his work at the spare-parts yard and he had suggested that she call by his house for a better bargain.

Mary was studying psychology at the University of Western Australia and worked part-time at a suburban delicatessen. She was hoping to take a job as a counsellor with the Community Welfare Department. Her parents were TAFE lecturers and were holidaying in the UK when their daughter disappeared.

Mary was last seen leaving the delicatessen on Monday, 6 October to attend a university lecture. But she never made it.

Her Galant sedan was found six days later in a riverside car park opposite police headquarters. David Birnie had driven it there. It was as if he were leaving a clue.

As Mary Neilson entered the Birnie house, she was seized at knife-point, bound and gagged and chained to the bed. Catherine Birnie watched as her lover repeatedly raped the woman. Catherine asked him questions about what turned him on the most. This way she would know what to do to excite him.

Catherine knew that Mary Neilson would eventually have to die. But it was something that she and Birnie hadn't yet discussed. That night, they took the girl to the Gleneagles National Park where Birnie raped her again then wrapped a nylon cord around her neck and slowly tightened it with a tree branch.

Mary Neilson choked to death at his feet. Birnie then stabbed her through the body and buried her in a shallow grave. He told Catherine that the stab wound would allow any gases to escape as the body decomposed. He had read it somewhere in a book.

The second killing took place a fortnight later when they abducted pretty 15-year-old Susannah Candy as she hitchhiked along the Stirling Highway in Claremont. An outstanding student at the Hollywood High School, Susannah lived at home in Nedlands with her parents, two brothers and a sister. Her father is one of the top ophthalmic surgeons in Western Australia. After her abduction, the Birnies forced her to send letters to her family to assure them that she was all right. But the family feared for her life.

The Birnies had been cruising for hours looking for a victim when they spotted Susannah. Within seconds of entering the car she had a knife at her throat and her hands were bound. She was taken back to the Willagee house where she was gagged, chained to the bed and raped.

After David Birnie had raped the girl, Catherine got into the bed with them. She now knew that this turned her lover on. When they had satiated their lust, Birnie tried to strangle Susannah with the nylon cord, but she became hysterical and went berserk. The Birnies forced sleeping pills down her throat to calm her. Once Susannah was asleep, David put the cord around her neck and told Catherine to prove her undying love for him by murdering the girl. Catherine willingly obliged. She tightened the cord slowly around the young girl's neck until she stopped breathing. David Birnie stood watching beside the bed.

Asked later why she had done it, Catherine Birnie said: 'Because I wanted to see how strong I was within my inner self. I didn't feel a thing. It was like I expected. I was prepared to follow him to the end of the earth and do anything to see that his desires were satisfied. She was a female. Females hurt and destroy males.'

They buried Susannah Candy near the grave of Mary Neilson in the State Forest.

On 1 November, the Birnies spotted 31-year-old Noelene Patterson standing beside her car on the Canning Highway, East Fremantle. She had run out of petrol while on her way home from her job as bar manager at the Nedlands Golf Club.

Noelene lived with her mother in the leafy suburb of Bicton on the shores of the Swan River. She was extremely popular and club members described her as charming and polite. She had been a flight attendant with Ansett Airlines for nine years and had worked as hostess for two years on corporate tycoon Alan Bond's private jet. Noelene had been working at the golf club for about a year when she accepted the Birnies' offer of a lift.

Noelene didn't hesitate to get in the car with the friendly couple. Once inside, she had a knife held to her throat, was tied up and told not to move or she would be stabbed to death. She was taken back to Moorhouse Street where Birnie repeatedly raped her after she was gagged and chained to the bed.

Catherine Birnie hated Noelene Patterson from the minute she set eyes on her. A beautiful, elegant lady, Noelene was everything that Catherine wanted to be. What is more, Birnie was entranced by her. They had originally decided to murder Noelene Patterson that same night but when David Birnie kept putting it off, Catherine became infuriated. She could see that she was losing her man. At one stage, she held a knife to her own heart and threatened to kill herself unless he chose between them.

Birnie kept Noelene prisoner in the house for three days

before Catherine insisted that he kill her. He forced an overdose of sleeping pills down her throat and strangled her, under the watchful eye of Catherine, while Noelene slept. They took her body to the forest and buried it along with the others. Catherine Birnie got great pleasure in throwing sand in the dead woman's face.

On 5 November, they abducted 21-year-old Denise Brown as she was waiting for a bus on Stirling Highway. Denise was a fun-loving girl who worked as a part-time computer operator in Perth and spent much of her spare time at dances and nightclubs. She shared a flat in Nedlands with her boyfriend and another couple. Denise spent her last night at the Coolbellup Hotel with a girlfriend. She accepted a lift from the Birnies outside the Stoned Crow Wine House in Fremantle. A close friend said later: 'She was someone who would do anything to help anyone. She trusted too many people. Perhaps that is why she didn't think twice about taking a lift.'

At knife-point Denise was taken to the house in Willagee, chained to the bed and raped. The following afternoon, she was taken to the Wanneroo pine plantation.

Along the way, the Birnies nearly picked up another victim. After their capture, a 19-year-old student told police how, after finishing university for the day, she was walking along Pinjar Road, Wanneroo, when a car pulled up beside her. There were two people in the front and another slumped in the back seat. Later she recognised the couple as Catherine and David Birnie from photos in newspapers, and realised that the person in the back was probably Denise Brown.

She went on: 'I felt uneasy. I didn't recognise the car. There was a man driving and a woman in the front seat of the car. The man kept looking down, not looking at me and the woman was drinking a can of UDL rum and coke. I thought the fact that she was drinking at that time of day was strange. He didn't look at me the whole time. It was the woman who did all the talking. She asked me if I wanted a lift anywhere. I said, "No, I only live up the road".

'They continued to sit there and I looked into the back seat where I saw a small person with short brown hair lying across the seat. I thought it must have been their son or daughter asleep in the back. The person was in a sleeping position and, from the haircut, looked like a boy but for some reason I got the feeling it was a girl. I told them again I didn't want a lift because walking was good exercise. The man looked up for the first time and gazed at me before looking away again. By this time, more cars had appeared and I started to walk away but they continued to sit in the car. Finally the car started and they did another U-turn and drove up Pinjar Road towards the pine plantation. It wasn't until I saw a really good photo of Catherine Birnie that I realised who they were. Somebody must have been looking after me that day. I don't know what would have happened to me if I had got into that car.'

In the seclusion of the forest, David Birnie raped Denise Brown in the car while the couple waited for darkness. They then dragged the woman from the car and Birnie assaulted her again. In the light of Catherine's torch, Birnie plunged a knife into Denise's neck while he was raping her.

Denise didn't die straight away. Catherine Birnie, still holding the torch, found a bigger knife and urged her lover to stab her again. He didn't need much prompting. He wielded the knife until Denise lay silent at his feet. Convinced that the girl was dead, they dug a shallow grave and laid her body in it.

As they were covering Denise Brown with sand, she sat up in the grave. Birnie grabbed an axe and struck her full force on the skull with it. When the girl sat up again, he turned the axe head around and cracked the girl's skull open, then finished filling the grave.

The brutal murder of Denise Brown had a bad effect on Catherine Birnie. She liked the sex they had with their victims. And she didn't mind the women being strangled and stabbed to death. But after the last murder, she decided that she couldn't go through it again. That is possibly why she left their next victim untied and alone in the bedroom.

She told police later: 'I think I must have come to a decision that, sooner or later, there had to be an end to the rampage. I had reached the stage when I didn't know what to do. I suppose I came to a decision that I was prepared to give her a chance.

'I knew that it was a foregone conclusion that David would kill her, and probably do it that night. I was just fed up with the killings. I thought if something did not happen soon it would simply go on and on and never end.

'Deep and dark in the back of my mind was yet another fear. I had great fear that I would have to look at another killing like that of Denise Brown, the girl he murdered with the axe. I wanted to avoid that at all costs. In the back of my mind I had come to the position where I really did not care if the girl escaped or not. When I found out that the girl had escaped, I felt a twinge of terror run down my spine. I thought to myself: "David will be furious. What shall I tell him?"'

On 12 November 1986, David John Birnie and Catherine Margaret Birnie appeared in Fremantle Magistrates' Court and were charged with four counts of wilful murder. The public were outraged at their crimes and a crowd had gathered outside the court. Police checked the bags of everyone entering the court. The holding cell leading to the courtroom was heavily guarded by police.

David Birnie was led into court handcuffed to a policeman and wearing a faded pair of blue overalls with joggers and socks. The barefoot Catherine Birnie was handcuffed to a policeman and wore a pair of blue denim jeans with a light-brown checked shirt.

They stood emotionless as the charges against them were read out. Neither had legal representation. No plea was entered, bail was officially refused, and the Birnies were remanded in custody. When asked if she wanted to be remanded for eight or 30 days before her next court appearance, Catherine Birnie looked at her lover and said: 'I'll go when he goes.'

On 10 February 1987, a huge crowd gathered outside the Perth Supreme Court. As the Birnies arrived in a prison truck, they called for the reintroduction of the death penalty. 'Hang the bastards!' they shouted, 'String them up!' Under a huge police guard, the couple were led into the holding cells.

Bill Power, the police rounds reporter who covered the Birnies' crimes and trial for the *Perth Daily News* recalls the Birnies' appearance in the Perth Supreme Court as one of the most chilling experiences of his career and remembers it as if it were yesterday.

'There was nothing distinctive about David and Catherine Birnie when they first appeared in court to face multiple murder charges in the serial killings which brought to an end the mystery of young women going missing off Perth streets,' Bill recalled. 'They were a rather nondescript, ordinary looking couple you might find running a petrol station in a country town. David was a weedy little man and Catherine his drab, slightly buxom wife with a very sour face. Both were accompanied by male police officers.

'David Birnie appeared first at the top of the stairs from the holding cell beneath the court and looked totally out of place in the majestic Perth Supreme Court. He was already in the dock glancing around at the massed police, court staff and huge media contingent as Catherine made her way up the stairs to the courtroom.

'The scrawny little serial killer was mesmerising enough but nothing could have prepared me for the moment that Catherine Birnie appeared at the top of the jarrah staircase leading up to the dock where the charges were to be read out to them.

'If you have ever witnessed a wild cat go off, then try and imagine that same hellcat in the confined spaces of a narrow staircase. Catherine Birnie fought against the guarding police officers and refused to allow any of them to touch her as she screamed and spat her words at them until she reached the dock and spotted her beloved David. Only then did she calm down.

'The unusualness of her appearance continued when David Birnie stood before the court to hear the murder charges read against him and Catherine Birnie was allowed to sit on a small wooden bench immediately behind him. As the judge levelled the horrible case against him, Birnie stood motionless with his hands clasped behind his back.

'What I witnessed next I will take to the grave with me,' Bill Power recalled. 'As the heinous charges of abduction, rape, torture and murder were being read out against him, Catherine Birnie bent forward, stretched out her right hand and gently stroked the ball of David Birnie's thumb behind his back. There has probably never before been such a declaration of undying love in the Western Australian Supreme Court dock.'

David Birnie pleaded guilty to four counts of murder and one count of abduction and rape, thereby sparing the families of his victims the agony of a long trial. 'That's the least I could do,' he told a detective. Catherine Birnie had not been required to plead as her barrister was waiting on a psychiatric report to determine her sanity. She was remanded to appear later that month.

'It was all over within a few minutes,' recalled Bill Power. 'And the erstwhile angelic Catherine, who moments before had acted out such a show of dedication, was dragged kicking and screaming and spitting down the wooden staircase to a prison van waiting beside the court. Perhaps she never wanted another man besides David to touch her.'

Mr Justice Wallace sentenced David Birnie to the maximum sentence of life imprisonment with strict security. He added: 'The law is not strong enough to express the community's horror at this sadistic killer who tortured, raped and murdered four women. In my opinion, David John Birnie is such a danger to society that he should never be released from prison.'

David Birnie stood trembling in the dock as the sentence was passed. His bravado returned as he was led to the prison van under tight security. With the angry mob calling for his blood, David Birnie put his hand to his lips and blew them a kiss.

Found sane enough to plead, Catherine Margaret Birnie admitted her part in the murders in the Perth Supreme Court. She stood in the dock, holding hands with David Birnie, the man who had led her down the path of torture, rape and murder. Through the day's hearing they chatted quietly and smiled at each other as the court was told of their 35-day reign of horror.

On occasion, she would stroke and pat his arm. A psychiatrist to the court said that Catherine was totally dependent on Birnie and almost totally vulnerable to his evil influence. He said: 'It is the worst case of personality dependence I have seen in my career.'

On 3 March 1987, Mr Justice Wallace had no hesitation in handing down the same sentence as that imposed on David Birnie. He said: 'In my opinion, you should never be released to be with David Birnie. You should never be allowed to see him again.'

As she was taken from the court, the shabby mother of six took one last look at the man who had influenced her life so strongly and so disastrously.

In prison, David Birnie was repeatedly beaten up. He

attempted suicide later in 1987 and was eventually moved to Fremantle Prison's old death cells for his own protection.

In the years to come, the Birnies would rarely be out of the headlines. In their first four years apart they exchanged 2600 letters but they were denied the right to marry, make personal phone calls to each other, or have contact visits.

In 1990, David Birnie claimed that the denial of these rights imposed 'a punishment over and above that decreed by the law'. He said he and Catherine were suffering physical and mental torture and that denying them contact with each other was an attempt to drive them into mental breakdown and suicide.

In 1992, major crime squad detectives gave David Birnie the rare privilege of a look at the outside world when they drove him around Perth and the suburbs for five hours in the hope that he may confess to other murders that he could have possibly committed. Nothing ever came of it. In 1993, his personal computer was confiscated from his cell in the protection unit at Casuarina Prison when it was found to contain pornographic material.

On 22 January 2000, Catherine Birnie's first husband and the father of her six children, Donald McLaughlan, passed away suddenly in the Western Australian country town of Busselton. He was aged 59. Catherine Birnie made an application to the Ministry of Justice to attend her former husband's funeral. It was refused. Commenting on the decision, the West Australian Premier, Mr Richard Court, said: 'As far as I am concerned, the Birnies have forfeited any rights for those types of privileges.'

According to West Australian law, David and Catherine Birnie will be eligible to apply for parole 20 years after their sentencing – in 2007. But it seems that there is little likelihood that any parole board would go against Mr Justice Wallace's recommendation that they die behind bars.

In January 2000, the acting West Australian Attorney General, Mr Kevin Prince, said that while the Birnies can be considered for parole in 2007, he believed that they would never be released unless they became too frail or senile.

At 4.30 a.m. on 2 October 2005, 55-year-old David Birnie was found hanged in his maximum security cell at Perth's Casuarina Prison. There were no suspicious circumstances.

CHAPTER 21

The Kimberley Killer

Josef Schwab
Northern Territory and Western Australia, 1987

Over a five-day period in June 1987 in the Northern Territory and north Western Australia, 23-year-old German tourist turned serial killer Josef Schwab robbed and murdered five holiday-makers at random, stripped their bodies of their clothing and set fire to their vehicles.

Whether Schwab was insane at the time – which, judging by his actions would easily have been the case – will never be known. A few days after the senseless killings, he was shot dead through the heart in a shoot-out with police marksmen.

Josef Schwab came from the small village of Pocking (population 3000) in Bonn, West Germany, and had a penchant for guns and violence from an early age. Journalist Larry Cross, who visited Pocking shortly after the murders, reported in the *West Australian* that it was no secret in Pocking that Schwab had been an active member of the local criminal gang and was responsible for 20 or 30 automobile thefts and several house breakins.

An informant said that Schwab carried a pistol from the age of 16 and believed that he wouldn't be afraid to use it if the occasion arose. The informant also believed that Schwab had taken off for Australia when he did because it was getting a bit hot for him – referring to Schwab's alleged burglaries and car thefts – in his home country.

The police account of Schwab's movements show that shortly after he arrived in Australia on a tourist's visa on 18 April 1987, he checked into the Atcherley Hotel in Queen Street, Brisbane, and defrauded the ANZ Bank by pretending that his traveller's cheques had been stolen during the flight to Australia. The bank replaced them to the value of $1000.

On 23 April Schwab cashed the supposedly stolen traveller's cheques at two Brisbane banks, went to Fiveways Firearms Store in Woolloongabba, Brisbane and bought a Winchester 12-gauge shotgun and three rifles – a Ruger 223, a Sako .308 and a Bruno .22. He then headed for the Northern Territory in a Toyota 4-Runner he had hired from Avis at Brisbane airport.

On 6 May, Schwab bought petrol from the Shire of Diamantina. On 9 May, he was given a parking ticket at Mt Isa and, after having the front end of the Toyota repaired, he turned up in Darwin on 20 May. On 4 June, Schwab was seen at Carmon Plains, Point Stuart, north-east of Darwin, where he apparently engaged in buffalo shooting as 10 sets of buffalo horns were later found in the back of the Toyota.

On 9 June 1987, Schwab shot and killed 70-year-old Marcus Bullen and his 42-year-old son, Lance, at Timber Creek in the Northern Territory, buried their bodies in shallow graves and set fire to their vehicle. The Bullens, both from Western Australia, were on a camping and fishing trip at the time of their murders. Both were shot in the back.

Almost a week later, on 15 June, Schwab murdered three campers – Julie Anne Warren, 25; her husband, Phillip Charles Walkemeyer, 26; and Terry Kent Bolt – at a picnic spot on the Pentecost River south of Wyndham in north Western Australia. All of the victims were from the Kimberley district.

The body of one of the victims was found in shallow water about three kilometres downstream from their incinerated car. Soon afterwards, another body was found four kilometres further down from the Pentecost River crossing. Another was found on rocks in shallow water nearby. The bodies had been carried along by the strong tide. All had been shot in the back and all were naked. Their clothes had been left in their four-wheel drive, which was set ablaze.

Police had no trouble in connecting the murders to the same killer even though they took place hundreds of kilometres apart. In each case the victims had been shot in the back, stripped, and their vehicle set alight. But police had no idea who the killer was and in which direction he may have headed. What they did know was that he had a 24-hour head start on them, and in that vast expanse of the Kimberley district, he could turn up anywhere and kill at random again. No-one was safe.

On 19 June, local helicopter pilot Peter Leutenegger reported seeing a vehicle camouflaged in the scrub about 10 kilometres west of Fitzroy Crossing. Seven members of the elite police Tactical Response Group (TRG) were flown in to join what was by now the biggest manhunt in West Australian history. They were driven to the sighting and while local police surrounded the area and police aircraft kept an eye on the vehicle from the air, the police marksmen, armed with high-powered rifles and dressed in camouflage clothing, moved in on foot.

As they positioned themselves in the scrub behind tall anthills, about 50 metres from the disguised vehicle, the police aircraft came in low over it in an effort to flush out anyone who might have been inside.

It worked. But it wasn't exactly what the pilot had in mind when a man appeared naked to the waist and in camouflage trousers and started blazing away at the aircraft with a rifle. Fortunately for its occupants, he missed. The leader of the TRG shouted at the gunman: 'Police – stop shooting,' to which he responded by turning the rifle in the direction of the voice and opening up.

'He's shooting at us. Engage him,' ordered the leader and police returned the fire, hitting Schwab on the left thumb and splintering the stock of the high-powered .308 rifle he was firing.

When Schwab disappeared back inside his vehicle police bombarded him with teargas grenades in order to drive him out. The hot grenades sparked off a scrub fire and as Schwab vacated the vehicle and fled into the flames, firing as he went, the ammunition he had left lying on the ground exploded in the heat of the grassfire as it rapidly spread.

Schwab disappeared into the smoke and fire. There was no sign of him until the light aircraft spotted him lying face down in the undergrowth. He was dead from a single bullet wound to the heart. He also had bullet wounds to the left thumb, shoulder and right buttock. In his vehicle police found fishing rods, a tool box, credit cards and bank books belonging to the three people he had killed beside the Pentecost River a few days earlier.

It must be remembered that at this stage police had no idea

who they had killed, only that it was a madman who could have murdered or abducted other tourists in the district. This innocently erroneous headline appeared in the *West Australian* the following morning:

GUNMAN KILLED
Hunt ends in shoot-out with police

KUNUNURRA: Mystery still surrounds the identity of a man shot dead in a gun battle with police near Fitzroy Crossing yesterday.

The police believe he was the Kimberley Killer and said that he was driving a white Toyota 4-Runner which a West German tourist hired in Queensland three weeks ago. The police fear that the tourist, Mr Josef Schwab (23) of Bonn, may have been another of the dead gunman's victims.

The following day, police identified the supposedly missing German tourist Schwab as the gunman responsible for the murders of the five tourists and police were left to ponder over the killer's motives. The most accepted theory for Schwab's actions was robbery. The fact that he took his victim's possessions would indicate that.

Schwab tried to cover his tracks by stripping his victims naked and burning their clothes in their vehicles. He buried his first two victims, and his next three victims were thrown naked into a tidal river, perhaps in the belief that they would be eaten by the huge saltwater crocodiles that infest the area.

Perhaps it appeared to the young German that the vast expanses of northern Australia could just swallow up his victims and his crimes and that civilisation was so far apart that their bodies and his atrocities would not be found until after he was long gone, back in Germany.

Maybe Josef Schwab was insane – a distinct possibility in light of the circumstances. But, since he was gunned down before the prospect of a trial, we shall never know.

Even so, it is of little consolation to the grieving families of his innocent victims. There would have been very few tears, if any, at Josef Schwab's passing.

CHAPTER 22

The Granny Killer

John Wayne Glover
Sydney, 1989–91

Most perpetrators of serial murder very rarely leave a 'calling card', a repetitive clue or injury which suggests that it is the work of the same killer. Some prefer to abduct their victims, have their way with them and then conceal their bodies, as demonstrated in the cases of Catherine and David Birnie, Christopher Worrell and James Miller, and Ivan Milat (each covered in this book). Others, such as Eric Edgar Cooke, used different methods of murder from one killing to the next, while yet others, such as Helen Patricia Moore and Martha Rendell, blatantly went on killing those around them until police finally brought them to justice.

'Calling-card' serial killers murder in an identical fashion again and again until they are caught. Some are never caught. They are also the killers who get the most publicity during their rampage, as the public learns of each murder as it takes place and become aware that there is a maniac on the loose.

As a consequence, these murderers are certainly the best-known serial killers in history. The Boston Strangler, Jack the Ripper, the Yorkshire Ripper, our own William 'the Mutilator' MacDonald, and New York's Son of Sam, who went one step further and taunted police with letters informing them when his next murder would be, were all calling-card serial killers.

So was John Wayne Glover. John Glover was 'the Mosman Monster', 'the Granny Killer', a vicious and calculating serial killer who deep-etched a macabre niche for himself in the history of Australia's most despicable murderers. Glover was the only serial killer who specialised in bashing and murdering little old ladies.

A bully, John Glover forced his defenceless victims into alcoves and alleyways with his superior strength and then set upon them with his fists and his trademark hammer, repeatedly bashing them about the head until they fell to his feet saturated in their own blood. Not content with bashing alone, he would then subject them to the ultimate humiliation and expose their most private parts while he removed their pantyhose and then throttled his victims with them. This final indignity would become John Glover's calling card and detectives knew that the killings were unmistakably the work of the one person.

And because Australian police – and police throughout the world, for that matter – had never experienced such a case, investigators had little or nothing to go on. There were no guidelines to steer those trying to find the elusive murderer. If there had been, Glover might have been brought to justice earlier. In the end it was a combination of police diligence and Glover's almost pathological urge to get caught that brought him to trial.

Towards the end of his reign of terror Glover was leaving clues all over town and, tragically, if this vital information had reached detectives a lot earlier, then perhaps a couple of lives might have been saved.

But John Wayne Glover was the least likely person anyone would suspect to be a serial killer. He was as inconspicuous as he was evil. A big friendly man in his late fifties, he was the type of guy you could leave in charge of your kids or ask to keep an eye on your house while you were away.

Glover was married with two daughters. The middle-class family lived a contented lifestyle in the fashionable suburb of Mosman on Sydney Harbour. But it was mostly in these tranquil surroundings that Glover would bash and kill his victims.

And as if to enhance this tragic deception of normalcy, Glover was a volunteer charity worker with the Senior Citizens Society and listed among his friends a former mayor of Mosman with whom he would often have a drink at his favourite watering hole, the Mosman RSL Club. But Glover's real charity was himself. He would spend the proceeds of his 'earnings' through muggings and murders on gambling and drink.

To add to his image of the regular middle-aged man, Glover held down a job as a sales representative with the Four 'n' Twenty pie company. His warm handshake and jolly smile endeared new acquaintances to him immediately. He was a walking advertisement for his product.

But beneath that jovial exterior lurked one of the most twisted serial killers in the history of Australian crime: a vicious murderer who preyed upon frail old women. If John Glover had been insane, then the grief-stricken relatives of his victims may have found some consolation, however minuscule, in knowing that their loved ones met their cruel demise at the hands of a maniac, someone who was driven to heinous crime by an unbalanced mind. But at his trial, even though John Glover pleaded not guilty on the grounds of diminished responsibility, the jury could not accept this. Nor could they accept that he was even temporarily insane at the time of the killings. Instead, they agreed with a prominent Sydney psychiatrist who studied the case and said: 'He built up a pile of hostility and aggression from childhood against his mother and then his mother-in-law. She was the lightning conductor and when she died he had to take it out on other people. This is a very unusual case because there are very few mass murderers and most of them are mad and have an organic disease of the brain. He is not mad.'

As the Crown prosecutor maintained, John Glover was very much aware of what he was doing. As he killed, he was at the same time planning what to do with the contents of his victims' purses. His killings weren't sexually motivated: John Glover was impotent. The pantyhose wrapped tightly around his victims' necks was to ensure that they were dead. But at the same time it would make the police think that the crime was the work of a sex killer.

Glover knew exactly what he was doing. Only a cool, clear, sane mind would risk the possibility of being caught by lingering for that extra minute or so to remove the pantyhose and strangle his victim with them. But it was worth the chance to throw the police off the scent.

No, insanity or lust was not the cause behind these cowardly murders and muggings. Glover's actual motives were as old as crime itself: revenge and greed. Combined with cowardice, they made the fatal combination that would keep Glover killing until the law finally caught up with him.

Chronically addicted to poker machines, Glover would stand for hours pouring money through the machines at the Mosman RSL Club. And the easiest way for Glover to get more money was to steal it.

As police would reveal later, Glover was a convicted thief and had a record of cowardly attacks on defenceless women. When he migrated to Australia from England in 1956, the 24-year-old Glover already had a criminal record dating back to 1947 for stealing clothing and handbags. Almost immediately after his arrival, he was convicted on two counts of larceny in Victoria and one of theft in New South Wales. And in 1962, he was convicted on two counts of assaulting females in Melbourne, two more of indecent assault, one of assault occasioning actual bodily harm and four counts of larceny.

Incredibly, Glover got off with three years probation. As in the later murders and assaults, the Victorian attacks were extremely savage and on each occasion articles of clothing had been forcibly removed. The victims were violently and repeatedly bashed about the head and body. They were forced to the ground as the attacker frantically ripped off their clothes before their screams alerted local residents who rang the police and came to their aid. Had Glover not been distracted, the assaults could have developed into rape or murder and his killing spree might have started earlier.

Those first on the scene were amazed that the victims were so badly savaged. The second victim, a 25-year-old woman walking home from a meeting at 10.30 at night, was found on the front lawn of a home. Dazed and in shock, she told police that the man had followed her down the dark suburban street and chased her when she tried to run away. She screamed as he knocked her to the ground unconscious. She awoke on the lawn to find herself bleeding profusely and with her undergarments in a state of disarray. The attacker had fled when her screams aroused the neighbourhood.

Residents reported seeing a young man running into a nearby yard and prompt police action saw the apprehension of 29-year-old Glover, then a television rigger with the ABC and living in the quiet, tree-lined Melbourne suburb of Camberwell. Glover said that he had fought with his girlfriend and was emotionally strung out. He was charged, and after spending the night in jail was released on bail the following morning.

As he was leaving the police station, Glover was stopped by two other detectives who had heard of his arrest. They wanted to have a chat with him about a similar assault a couple of weeks earlier. At first Glover denied any knowledge of the incident, but under intense questioning he confessed to the previous assault and was taken back to the station and recharged.

In light of Glover's previous convictions and the ferocity of the attacks, the detectives were astonished when he was let off with a good behaviour bond and three years probation. Retribution finally caught up with John Wayne Glover in 1965 – but only in a small way – when he was convicted on a peeping Tom charge and of being unlawfully on premises. He was sentenced to three months in prison of which he served only six weeks.

Following his release from prison, Glover seemingly changed his ways and, apart from a minor shoplifting charge in 1978, he would not come to police notice again for many years. However, police now agree that it would have been almost impossible for a criminal of Glover's nature to keep his hands to himself for the following 25 years. In fact, some police wonder if Glover could have helped with inquiries into at least five other unsolved murders with similar *modus operandi* committed between 1965 and 1989.

In Melbourne in 1968, Glover married Jacqueline Gail (Gay) Rolls. They had met while Glover was working at a wine and spirits store in inner-city Melbourne. Gay's father, John Rolls, felt that the quiet, handsome young man was a good match for their beloved daughter. At first Essie Rolls, Gay's mother, agreed, but it didn't take her long to figure out that Glover might have something to hide.

Even though she was from a middle-class Sydney background, Gay loved the gentle English migrant who had arrived in Australia in the 1950s with only 30 shillings to his name. Glover came from a very poor working-class family. He told his few friends that he had come to Australia to start a new life and leave behind a traumatic and disruptive family background. With her parents' blessings, Gay and John became engaged, and married shortly after.

In 1970 the happy couple moved to Sydney to live with Gay's parents in their comfortable family home in Mosman. Gay's father was very ill and he had asked the newlyweds if they would move into the house to keep him company. John Glover was delighted. The poor English migrant with a record of theft and violence had done well. To move into a two-storey house near the harbour was more than he could ever have dreamed possible.

Like all of the decisions in their married life, the move was a joint one between John and Gay. It was here that Glover's hatred grew for his mother-in-law, Essie. A separate wing was built on the house so that Gay and John and their two daughters, Kellie (born in 1971) and Marney (born in 1973), could live an almost separate existence from the demanding Essie Rolls.

Glover would say at his trial that he hated Essie, that the atmosphere was always tense, and that the situation worsened when Gay's father died in 1981. Glover told the court that his mother-in-law was a tyrant. Police had no trouble confirming this when they interviewed the staff of the Mosman nursing home where Essie died in 1988.

To add to Glover's domestic woes, in 1982 his mother, Freda, migrated to Australia and turned up on his doorstep. Glover loathed her almost as much as he loathed his mother-in-law. Freda Underwood, as she was now known, had been married four times and had had numerous lovers both during and between her marriages.

When she tried to move in as a temporary companion to Essie Rolls, it was more than Glover could handle. The last thing he wanted was someone in the house who could bring him undone with tales of his unfortunate childhood. This was the type of ammunition that Essie Rolls wanted.

'It was a shock to the system,' Glover would say at his trial. 'Just the thought of having them both under the one roof was more than anyone could stand.' At Glover's instigation, his mother moved to Gosford, 100 kilometres north of Sydney, where she died of breast cancer in 1988. Glover was diagnosed as having the same cancer, which is extremely rare among men.

After a mastectomy, Glover developed a prostate condition and became sexually impotent. In evidence, psychiatrist Dr Bob

Strum said that he believed this to be the time when Glover's life changed. 'It was almost as though his mother was reaching out from the grave and striking him again,' he told the jury.

Despite the family dramas, Gay knew nothing of her husband's dark past and he never did a thing to indicate that he was anything other than an adoring husband and father.

The 'start of it all', as Glover would refer to it later, came on 11 January 1989, when he saw 84-year-old Mrs Margaret Todhunter walking along quiet Hale Road, in Mosman. He parked his car and, after he was satisfied that no-one was looking, he punched the unsuspecting victim in the face with a swinging right hook and relieved her of her handbag, which contained $209. As he fled down the street with her bag, Mrs Todhunter called out, 'You rotten bugger!'

Glover went to the Mosman RSL where he drank and played the poker machines with the stolen money. Investigating police put the incident down to a mugging and suspected that someone saw the elderly woman with the cash and waited for the right moment. In the drug-ravaged suburbs of Sydney, muggings are a daily occurrence and, while the case was investigated thoroughly, little hope was given of recovering the money or finding the perpetrator of such a cowardly act.

Mrs Todhunter survived the ordeal but was badly bruised and shaken. As it turned out, she was also extremely lucky.

Glover's next victim was not so fortunate. On 1 March 1989, after a few drinks at the Mosman RSL in the mid-afternoon, Glover was heading for his car down busy Military Road when he spotted Gwendoline Mitchelhill slowly making her way home from the shops with the aid of her walking stick.

Glover hurriedly took a hammer from his car and tucked it into his belt. He cautiously followed the old woman to the seclusion of the entry foyer of her retirement village. As she turned the key in the lock, he brought the hammer down with a crashing blow to the back of her skull. He bashed her so viciously about the head and body that he broke several ribs in her tiny frame. He fled the scene, taking her wallet, which contained $100. Incredibly, Mrs Mitchelhill was still alive when two schoolboys found her, but she became the Granny Killer's first 'official' murder victim just a few minutes after the police and ambulance arrived. As Mrs Mitchelhill drew her last breath, Glover was sitting in his lounge room wondering out loud to his wife what the sirens in the distance were all about.

Again, the police were baffled. But there was nothing concrete to link the two attacks. There was a theory that they could be the work of the one person, but it was a long shot. Police finally assumed that it was yet another mugging that had gone disastrously wrong.

Ten weeks later, in the late afternoon of 9 May, Glover was heading for the Mosman RSL Club on Military Road when he saw Lady Winifred Ashton walking slowly towards him with the aid of a walking stick. Lady Ashton had been playing bingo at the RSL and was heading towards her home in nearby Raglan Street. Glover pulled on a pair of gloves and followed her into the foyer of her apartment building where he attacked her with his hammer and threw her to the ground in the rubbish-bin alcove.

Even though she was suffering from lymph cancer, the tiny and frail Lady Ashton put up an incredible struggle and Glover later confessed: 'At one stage she almost had me until I fell on top of her and repeatedly bashed her head against the concrete.' Lady Winifred Ashton was 84 years old.

Once Lady Ashton was beaten into unconsciousness, John Glover removed her pantyhose and strangled her with them. Although no sexual act took place, this gruesome ritual would become Glover's signature. And then, as if in respect for the dead woman, Glover laid her walking stick and shoes at her feet before he headed off with her purse, which contained $100.

Glover later commented to the bar staff at the Mosman RSL that he hoped the sirens they could hear just around the corner weren't on account of another mugging. He said this as he calmly fed the contents of Lady Ashton's purse through the poker machines.

Only now did police believe they had a maniacal killer on the loose. There were too many similarities. To date, each of the three victims were wealthy old ladies, all came from the same suburb, all were assaulted or killed in a similar manner, and all were robbed of their handbags. This was no ordinary mugger. Although it was now a strong possibility, the thought of one individual seeking out and murdering defenceless old women was almost beyond comprehension.

But the chinks were starting to show in the maniac's armour. In a bizarre twist of events, Glover started molesting old women confined to their beds in the nursing homes he visited during his rounds as a pie salesman. This was an aspect of the case that detectives and psychiatrists would later find confusing.

Glover maintained that he had no sexual interest in anyone. He never sexually attacked any of his robbery and murder victims. Yet here he was, prowling around nursing homes and assaulting bedridden old women.

Local police investigated, but the alarm bells didn't ring. The molestations were not connected to the murders at the time, though at a later date the incidents would play an important part in identifying Glover.

On his nursing-home rounds, Glover first molested a 77-year-old woman on 6 June 1989 at the Wesley Gardens Retirement Home in Belrose, quite a distance from Mosman. The woman reported the incident and said that the man put his hand under her nightie. She couldn't recall what he looked like.

Then on 24 June, Glover visited the Caroline Chisholm Nursing Home in nearby Lane Cove. He leisurely strolled upstairs, lifted the dress of an elderly woman and fondled her buttocks. Moving to the room next door, he slid his hand down the front of another woman's nightdress and stroked her breasts. The terrified woman cried out and Glover was questioned briefly by staff, but not held, as he made a hurried exit.

The incidents were investigated by local police but were not connected to the murders in Mosman. And it was months before it was thought that this information may be of any use to the Granny Killer task force. By the time the connection was made there had been more attacks, more bashings – and more murders.

On 8 August 1989, Glover bashed elderly Effie Carnie in a quiet street in Lindfield, not far from Mosman, and stole her groceries. On 6 October, he passed himself off as a doctor and ran his hand up the dress of a patient at the Wybenia Nursing Home in Neutral Bay, one suburb south of Mosman. Again he eluded capture when the blind old woman called for help.

It seemed that Glover could walk in and out of hospitals as he pleased. No-one suspected the pastry salesman. Not once through that series of molestations was he ever identified.

That same month, Glover struck again, and this time with a ferocity that would convince police that their worst nightmare was a reality – that the attacks were the work of one man. But in what would later prove to be a cruel irony, this assault would start them looking for the wrong 'type' of offender.

In the mid-afternoon of 18 October, Glover struck up a conversation with 86-year-old Mrs Doris Cox as she slowly made her way home along Spit Road, Mosman. He walked with her into the secluded stairwell of her retirement village then attacked her from behind, using his entire body-weight to smash her face into a brick wall. She collapsed at his feet. After finding nothing that he wanted in her handbag, Glover left her for dead and went home.

Mrs Cox, an Alzheimer's victim, somehow survived the attack. But she was hazy about the description of her perpetrator, even though she had looked at him while he walked with her. In her understandably confused state she thought that her attacker was a younger man and assisted the police as best as she could in preparing an identikit drawing. At last the police believed they had a lead.

To the head of the task force, Detective Inspector Mike Hagan, the new information made sense. He suspected that the killer was a local because of the close proximity of the killings and muggings. As well, police psychological profiles suggested the killer would most likely be a teenager with a grandmother fixation. And Mrs Cox thought that she had been bashed by a young man.

Mike Hagan now concentrated the task force energies in search of a young local who may be acting strangely or had any possible relationship with, or connection to, the victims. Tragically, this theory was correct only to the extent that it suggested the killer was a local. It would almost appear that some unknown force was protecting Glover.

The murder of 85-year-old Mrs Margaret Pahud on 2 November was undoubtedly the work of the Granny Killer. She was savagely bashed on the back of the head by a blunt instrument as she made her way home along a laneway off busy Longueville Road in Lane Cove.

Coronial evidence presented at the trial indicated that the attack was over in seconds and from the force of the blows – indicated by her massively fractured skull – the coroner concluded that it was doubtful that the poor old woman felt a thing.

There were no known witnesses, although Mrs Pahud's body was found within minutes by a passing schoolgirl who at first thought that it was a bundle of clothing dumped in the laneway.

As the police and ambulance sirens wailed their way to the murder scene, Glover examined the contents of Mrs Pahud's purse on the grounds of a nearby golf club where he pocketed $300 and hid the bag in a drain. He then went to the Mosman RSL Club where he drank and gambled with Margaret Pahud's money.

By now police were almost frantic with frustration. This murder was committed about five kilometres from Mosman and their theory about the killer being a local was losing credibility. Now they decided they were looking for a teenager who came from just about anywhere. Baffled and no closer to solving the case than they had been when it had all started 10 months earlier, the police intensified their investigations.

Reinforcements were called in and Australia's biggest-ever task force in the search of one man was formed. Thirty-five of the state's most experienced detectives gathered at police headquarters and were told by task force chief Hagan that they must work day and night and investigate every lead, however minute, until the killer was caught. A $200,000 reward was posted by the NSW Government. Composite pictures of the suspect were left in shops, service stations and newsagents.

Meanwhile, Hagan was becoming a nervous wreck and later said: 'I've had nearly 30 years on the job and I think the worst month of my police experience was November 1989. You get so frustrated with yourself and those around you when you can't get a result and that's very stressful. You'd go home and you're on tenterhooks all night. I wasn't eating or sleeping and this cowardly killer kept murdering frail old ladies.'

For Hagan, the day after Mrs Pahud's death was spent

mostly at the murder scene, yet as the hours passed, he had to face the grim reality that the killer had eluded them once more without leaving so much as a trace. Exhausted by the end of the day, Hagan called into the Pennant Hills police station on his way home to answer an urgent message on his beeper. He dialled task force headquarters. His knees weakened as he was told that they had discovered yet another body – another pantyhose strangling.

He later said: 'I just can't explain my feelings that night. To have just come from a murder and to be told there's another one. It was terrible. We'd had two serial murders within 24 hours. We'd never heard of such a thing before.'

The Granny Killer's fourth victim was 81-one-year-old Miss Olive Cleveland, a resident of the Wesley Gardens Retirement Village at Belrose on the upper north shore. Glover had called there in the early afternoon and, unable to get a pie order out of catering manager Rob Murrell, he eventually left.

On his way through the garden he struck up a conversation with Mrs Cleveland, who was sitting on a bench, reading. When she got up and walked towards the main building Glover seized her from behind and forced her into a secluded side walkway. Here he repeatedly slammed her head against the concrete before he removed her pantyhose and knotted them tightly around her neck. Glover then made off with $60 from her handbag.

No-one connected this murder with the attack on the 77-year-old woman at the Wesley Home only six months earlier. The task force still had no knowledge of the previous offence. If they had, they may have discovered that a portly, middle-aged man with grey hair was in the vicinity on both occasions.

There were no clues, and the seemingly invisible murderer made his escape in the afternoon. Again the task force was baffled. Surely someone must have seen something? They checked and cross-checked witnesses' statements and canvassed retirement villages, joggers, cab and bus drivers, and junk-mail deliverers. They even sent a history of the case to the FBI in the vain hope of a lead. No luck.

Sydney's north shore was now under siege. People stayed off the streets and anyone with elderly neighbours or relatives was checking on them at regular intervals. Old women were being driven to and from the shops. No-one was taking chances. And still police investigations continued. The checking and cross-checking went on. A week after the Olive Cleveland murder, the police got their first break as the agonisingly slow cross-checking paid off and a pattern emerged. In several of the attacks the victims recalled seeing a grey-haired, well-dressed, middle-aged man.

Now the very first victim, Mrs Margaret Todhunter, recalled a man of that description passing her just before she was attacked from behind and robbed of her purse. And Mrs Effie Carnie, who was bashed and robbed of her groceries in August, also described her assailant as a well-built, mature man with grey hair. Both victims described their attacker as an average type of person.

At last police realised that they may have been looking for the wrong man and that their killer could well slip in and out of places unnoticed because he was simply not the noticeable type. Armed with this description, the police still had to find their 'average' man.

On 23 November, another body turned up, the third for the month. While purchasing whisky in Mosman, Glover spotted 92-year-old Muriel Falconer struggling down the street with a load of shopping. He returned to his car, collected his hammer and gloves and followed her to her front door.

As Mrs Falconer was partially deaf and blind, she did not notice Glover slip through the door behind her with his gloves on and his hammer raised. He silenced her by holding his hand over her mouth as he hit her repeatedly about the head and neck. As she fell to the floor he started to remove Mrs Falconer's panty-hose, but she regained consciousness and cried out. Glover struck her again and again with the hammer and only when he was satisfied that she was unconscious did he remove her undergarments and throttle her with them. He closed the front door for privacy. Then he searched her purse and the rest of the house before he left quietly with $100 and his hammer and gloves in a carry bag.

It wasn't until the following afternoon, when a neighbour dropped by, that the body was discovered. Although the murder scene was chaotic, this was the first real chance the police had to obtain clues. This crime had been committed indoors and nothing had been disturbed since.

They found a perfect footprint in blood on the carpet – their first solid clue since the investigation had begun. However, Hagan still needed to get lucky to apprehend this person who seemed to be able to come and go as he pleased without appearing in any way out of place.

The break came on 11 January 1990 when Glover slipped up badly, but it was a further three weeks before the incident reached the ears of the task force. On that January day Glover called at the Greenwich Hospital for an appointment with its administrator, Mr Reg Cadman.

Afterwards, Glover, dressed in his blue-and-white salesman's jacket and carrying a clipboard, walked into a hospital ward where four very old and very sick women lay in their beds. He approached an elderly woman who was suffering from advanced cancer, asking if she was losing any body heat, then pulled up her nightie and began to prod her in an indecent manner.

The woman became alarmed and rang the buzzer beside her bed. A sister at the hospital, Pauline Davis, answered the call and found Glover in the ward. 'Who the hell are you?' she called out, and when Glover ran from the ward she chased him and took down the registration number of his car as he hurriedly drove off.

Sister Davis called the police and later that day two uniformed policewomen from Chatswood police station arrived to investigate. The hospital staff were able to give them Glover's name as he was well known from previous visits on his pastry round. When the police returned a week later with a photo of John Glover, Sister Davis positively identified him and the elderly woman said that it looked 'most like him'.

At last a breakthrough. But for some unaccountable reason another three weeks were to pass before anyone reported the incident to the Granny Killer task force.

Detectives from Chatswood police station confirmed Glover's name with his employers, rang him at home and asked him to drop in at 5 p.m. the following day for a chat about the assault. When Glover hadn't turned up by 6 p.m. the police called his home, where his wife told them that he had attempted suicide and was in Royal North Shore Hospital.

The police went to the hospital, but Glover was too sick to

be interviewed. Staff handed the police a suicide note that included the words 'no more grannies, grannies'. And it still didn't register with police that the middle-aged portly man with the grey hair, who was recovering from attempted suicide after assaulting an elderly patient in a nursing home, may be in some way connected with the murders.

The police returned to interview Glover on 18 January and, with his reluctant approval, picked up a polaroid photo of him to show to Sister Davis and the sexually assaulted woman. After the positive identification, one of the officers told Davis: 'We know who it is. We know all about him.'

Another two weeks would pass before the suicide note and the photo landed on Mike Hagan's desk. As soon as he saw them he knew he had his man. Proving it was a different story.

Head of the detectives in the task force, Detective Sergeant Dennis O'Toole said: 'We still had no evidence. If he had said to us, "I don't want to talk", we couldn't have proved any of the murders'.

Still, the photo matched the numerous descriptions of the mysterious, grey-haired, middle-aged man. And in his job as a sales representative Glover could have been at any of the murder scenes.

Detectives interviewed Glover. He denied everything. They gave him the impression that they were satisfied and left him feeling confident that his luck still held. But John Wayne Glover was under around-the-clock surveillance with six detectives assigned to find out every conceivable thing about him. Even at this stage, the police didn't have a scrap of evidence that would stand up in court. But in their minds there was no question that Glover was their man.

Hagan had to make an agonising choice. Go in now and let the Granny Killer know that they were onto him and take the odds of not finding any solid evidence that would hold up in court? Or sit tight, wait for him to stalk another old woman and catch him in the act? Hagan opted for the latter. Sadly, it was a decision that would cost another life.

The police didn't let him out of their sight, but Glover didn't put a foot wrong. Although he occasionally stopped to look at old women, his behaviour was exemplary.

On 19 March at 10 a.m. Glover called at the home of a lady friend, Joan Sinclair. He spruced himself up in the rear-vision mirror before he was let in at the front door. Police on watch had no reason to believe that it was anything other than a social visit. Besides, the killer had only ever struck in the afternoon and only with elderly women. Still, they kept their eyes on every corner of the house.

At 1 p.m. there was no sign of Glover or of any life from the house. The police surveillance became concerned. At 5 p.m. all remained quiet, and at 6 p.m., deciding that things were not well, they got the okay from Hagan to go in.

Detective Sergeant Miles O'Toole and detectives Paul Mayger and Paul Jacob noticed the pools of blood almost as soon as they crept through the door. With guns drawn, they tiptoed from room to room, covering one another but careful not to be caught in a crossfire should the madman leap out at them with an axe or a shotgun.

They saw a hammer lying in a pool of drying blood on the mat. As they peered further around the doorway they saw a pair of woman's panties and a man's shirt covered in blood. Then a woman's body came into view. Joan Sinclair's battered head was wrapped in a bundle of blood-soaked towels. She was naked from the waist down and pantyhose were tied around her neck. Her genitals were damaged, but Glover would later deny interfering with her sexually.

It was unmistakably the work of the Granny Killer. But where was he? Was he waiting in ambush? Detective Mayger almost breathed a sigh of relief as he found feet sticking out of the end of the bath. An unconscious, naked, grey-haired chubby man was lying in the tub. One wrist was slashed and the air was heavy with the smell of alcohol and vomit. The relieved detectives prayed that he was still alive. Their prayers were answered.

The man in the bath was John Wayne Glover, the Granny Killer. After he had recovered in hospital, Glover told police of the final chapter in the Granny Killer murders. Glover had known Joan Sinclair for some time and they were extremely fond of each other in a platonic relationship.

However, after he entered the house on 19 March, Glover

got his hammer out of his briefcase and bashed Mrs Sinclair about the head with it. He then removed her pantyhose and strangled her with them and with others he found in her bedroom.

This sequence of events completely baffled the police. Murdering Mrs Sinclair was in many ways out of character with the other murders and bashings.

Glover rolled Mrs Sinclair's body over on the mat, wrapped four towels around her massive head wound to stem the flow of blood, and then dragged her body across the room, leaving a trail of blood. He then ran a bath, washed down a handful of Valium with a bottle of Vat 69, slashed his left wrist and lay in the tub to die.

But he didn't die, and the police were glad of that. They felt that if the suicide had been successful, then there would always be speculation as to whether Glover was the right man. Glover further brushed away their concerns by confessing to everything. Nonetheless, he frustrated police and psychiatrists alike with his inability or unwillingness to set out the reasons for his acts.

The question why was repeatedly met with the same answer: 'I don't know. I just see these ladies and it seems to trigger something. I just have to be violent towards them.'

When he was charged with murdering six elderly women, his wife Gay and their two daughters – both in their late teens – were stunned. There had never been the slightest inclination that the man they loved as husband and father was the Granny Killer.

At his trial in November 1991 John Wayne Glover pleaded not guilty to six counts of murder on the grounds of diminished responsibility – in other words, Glover claimed that he was temporarily insane when he carried out the murders. The jury did not agree and it took them just two-and-a-half hours to find that Glover was both guilty and sane.

Justice Wood sentenced Glover to six life terms of imprisonment and said in part: 'The period since January 1989 has been one of intense and serious crime involving extreme violence inflicted on elderly women, accompanied by the theft or robbery of their property. On any view, the prisoner has shown himself to be an exceedingly dangerous person and that view was mirrored by the opinions of the psychiatrists who have given evidence at his trial.

'I have no alternative other than to impose the maximum

available sentence, which means that the prisoner will be required to spend the remainder of his natural life in jail. It is inappropriate to express any date as to release on parole. Having regard to those life sentences, this is not a case where the prisoner may ever be released pursuant to order of this court.'

Just after lunch on 9 September 2005, John Wayne Glover, aged 72, was found hanged in his maximum security cell at Lithgow Prison in rural New South Wales. There were no suspicious circumstances.

INTERVIEW WITH THE GRANNY KILLER
Steve Barrett

The Nine Network's Sydney crime reporter Steve Barrett actively followed the Granny Killer murders and is one of the few journalists who was allowed an interview with the serial killer after he was convicted. This is Steve's exclusive story.

Sydney's Granny Killer had a profound effect on me, both professionally and personally. This vicious serial killer was a horrific criminal phenomenon that forced the sleepy but trendy north shore of Sydney into more than a year of hysteria.

Who was this lunatic who was hammer-bashing and strangling fragile women in their twilight years? They were grannies, for God's sake!

Finally, at the end of John Wayne Glover's killing spree, in which he murdered six elderly women over a 13-month period, my fellow reporter Simon Bouda and I, along with author Larry Writer, wrote a book called *Garden of Evil: The Granny Killer's Reign of Terror.*

As part of that work, in early 1992 after Glover had been found guilty on six counts of murder and sentenced to prison on the recommendation that he is never to be released, Simon and I managed to scoop an interview with him and spent several hours inside Sydney's Long Bay Jail talking to this very troubled man.

In my career with Sydney's Channel 9 as a crime reporter and now a producer with *60 Minutes* I have covered many sensational stories, but the Granny Killer had a more disturbing effect on me than any of the variety of criminals I have encountered.

To put my personal encounter with John Glover into perspective, I need to compare it with some of my other memorable criminal encounters, which included:

- Raymond John Denning, lifer and public enemy number one in Queensland, New South Wales and Victoria, who escaped from jail repeatedly to become an outspoken critic of the prison system, an activist and vocal leader in the criminal world. Denning caused a sensation when he did the unthinkable and turned police informer. In the 'supergrass' section at Sydney's Long Bay Jail I conducted a lengthy television interview with this chilling character, which ran on TCN9 'News' and *A Current Affair*.
- The late Lennie McPherson, the legendary Mr Big of Sydney's underworld. Lennie sobbed during his last interview, not because of anything I asked but because this man with the most fearsome of all reputations maintained he was suffering from Alzheimer's disease. And for a bloke who was supposed to have killed as many as 10 people, it's no wonder his memory was bad.
- Billy Van den Berg, the self-confessed murderer of Sydney socialite Mrs Megan Kalajzich, whom he shot dead as she slept in her waterfront home. Van den Berg became the first prisoner to enter the NSW Witness Protection Jail after pleading guilty and agreeing to dob in the victim's husband, the rich Manly hotelier, Andrew Kalajzich, who organised Van den Berg to kill his wife. Andrew Kalajzich is now serving life behind bars. Four days after I filmed the interview, Van den Berg took his own life.
- The fugitive paedophile Robert 'Dolly' Dunn. In late 1997, with *60 Minutes* presenter Liz Hayes and crew we tracked down and interviewed Dunn in Honduras in Central America, to where he had fled rather than give

evidence to the NSW Police Royal Commission into paedophilia. During an interview in the customs room at Tegucigalpa Airport, Dunn told me he'd rather be referred to as a 'boy lover' than a paedophile.

But for all of these experiences and many, many more, no other encounter with a criminal has had such an effect on me as that of my interview with John Wayne Glover.

Glover was not an underworld figure, a 'boy lover', an institutionalised prisoner-turned-informer or a contract murderer. Glover was a vicious serial killer. Not of young boys, girls or adolescents, but elderly women. For homicide investigators he was unique. His modus operandi had never been seen before in this country. Maybe a long time ago with the Boston Strangler in America, perhaps, but not in Australia.

Glover was, and still is today, the ultimate challenge to forensic psychiatrists. His crimes are now case studies for law enforcement bodies around the world.

I first laid eyes on Glover when the police task force team took him on a 'run-around' of his crime scenes not long after his arrest. I instinctively knew that somehow I would meet him, this portly shaped Father Christmas without the beard who was nudging 60, and probably not far off becoming a 'granny' himself, although his pair of lovely daughters who attended an exclusive north shore girl's school during his reign of terror were only teenagers.

While researching *Garden of Evil* and in the lead-up to actually meeting and speaking with Glover, it was agreed by my co-authors and me that out of courtesy an approach would be made to his wife Gay, informing her of our project.

Although Gay Glover declined to be interviewed for the book, she was very polite and dignified, considering what she had just lived through – the horrific realisation that her husband, the man she slept next to, was in fact Sydney's Granny Killer.

I went to see Gay Glover at her home in Mosman. It was a weird sensation actually sitting in John Glover's lounge room for those 20 or so minutes delicately discussing only minor aspects of the case with her. All the time I kept wondering how close to danger she may have been at any stage. After all, the last woman John Glover killed was an 'on-the-side' acquaintance, someone of Glover's own age who knew and trusted him.

As a working journalist I'd been into a number of prisons, but on the day Simon Bouda and I walked into the Classification Jail at Long Bay in Sydney's south, I was feeling a sense of intense anxiety. My palms were sweaty.

Glover had been in this jail for several months now after being convicted of the six murders. He was still awaiting his classification in the NSW Corrective Services system. What jail would he end up in for his 'never to be released' life term?

In fact, that's exactly how we opened our discussion when we were first introduced. Sporting a green sloppy joe and green prison trousers, John Wayne Glover came into a small office situated in the bowels of the jail complex. Incredibly, for a man who won't be seeing any of the things we may take for granted – such as the Pacific Ocean – for the rest of his life, the incarcerated Glover was in a very jovial mood.

He greeted us with a handshake and a big smile as though we were long-lost acquaintances. In fact, seeing as I'd chased Glover's handiwork around Sydney as a reporter for well over a year, the thought of us being acquaintances without actually meeting wasn't all that obscene. I felt that there wasn't too much I didn't know about him.

But, as I was soon to find out, there was a great deal that I didn't know about the Granny Killer.

I had been well versed on how Long Bay Jail's celebrity inmate enjoyed playing mind games with the homicide case officers, prison psychiatrists and anyone in authority who was allowed to see him. In fact, Glover enjoyed visitors.

But there was something different about Glover's appearance that I didn't pick up on immediately. Then suddenly it hit me. Glover had grown very distinct mutton-chop whiskers. His new fashion style was identical to that of the commander of the Granny Killer police task force, Detective Inspector Mike Hagan, who had led the hunt for Glover.

It was a perverse mind game, to mimic the look of the man who became very publicly known during the hunt for Glover because of the countless media interviews he had given.

To start off, Glover joked about how long it would be before he'd be getting out of 'this place' [jail]. In doing so, he gave me the impression that, despite the despicable and inhumane crimes he'd committed, he still wanted to be liked; he wanted to be considered a fairly intelligent person who knew what was going on around him 24 hours a day.

He obviously picked up on my observation and briefly it caused a tense moment during our interview, and I noticed the many small 'drinker's veins' in his face turn bright red.

I asked him why he had chosen to plead not guilty at his trial on the grounds of diminished responsibility – in other words, he was not mentally fit and could not be held responsible for his actions. He was somewhat embarrassed but basically shrugged off the question by indicating that he really had nothing to lose by this plea.

Glover quickly changed the mood by telling me that he understood that he was being interviewed for the book and not an appearance on television. He then reminded me that he often watched me file reports about him on the Channel 9 6 p.m. news when the police task force was trying to track down the Granny Killer. I quickly changed the mood of the room when I told him: 'John, let's get one thing straight. I have to tell you we're not here to make some sort of star or hero out of you. There's no doubt you're the main character of the book, but that's it. I mean, look at what you've done.'

At that point, both Simon and I sensed a blow to his ego but I had the upper hand, so I continued. We chatted about some of the killings and then I asked him point-blank: 'But John, what was it that pushed you or compelled you to bash little old ladies on the head with a hammer?'

He replied somewhat timidly: 'Well, that's what I can't work out. That's the part that everyone's trying to work out. Maybe you can help me. Half of me is white and half of me is black. Half of me is good and half of me is bad. But I can't understand this grey matter in the middle.'

Again another mind game. Glover quickly changed the subject to how many visitors he was getting a week, but my inner feelings turned to rage when I visualised one of the police forensic photos of an elderly lady naked on the morgue table with her head caved in. As part of the book research I'd seen that heart-breaking photo only the day before.

Glover then gave us a spiel on his daily routine, telling how he worked as a sweeper, but also pointing out that he is protected from mainstream prisoners, some of whom would simply kill him. They, too, have grandmothers.

He was a little proud of the fact that he'd taken under his wing a young man who was also a sweeper and who had been convicted of a number of rapes in the coastal town of Bulli south of Sydney. He was dubbed 'the Bulli Rapist' by the media.

'The Granny Killer and the Bulli Rapist. What a team,' Glover joked.

Towards the end of our interview I asked Glover if he'd received a visit from his wife, Gay. He replied he'd only seen her once, not long after he was first arrested, and indicated that he would never be seeing her again. I told him that I had met her and that the meeting took place at his Mosman home. He remained silent and looked melancholy.

Then came the most tense moment of all. I asked him had his precious daughters been to see him. The tears began to roll down his cheeks. He answered no and became a little agitated.

Simon and I were stunned into silence. John Glover indicated that he didn't want to carry on and then attempted to talk some more, mumbling that he missed his daughters. One had just done the Higher School Certificate and the other had a year of school to go.

This strange and very complex man had basically suckered us into feeling sorry for him ... but not for long. He was feeling very remorseful about what he had put his family through, but on the other hand displayed a degree of cunning in not directly answering the question of why he attacked old ladies.

Simon asked him if he could continue talking and at that point he gestured to turn off our tape reorder. Within a matter of seconds he regained his composure and nonchalantly told us it was time for him to return to his 'garden gate', rhyming slang for his '12-by-8' cell.

Before we left he asked could he get an autographed copy of the book when it came out. We then asked him would he mind if we could obtain his signature on a few copies of the book. 'Not a problem. You know where to find me,' he laughed.

That was the last time I laid eyes on the Granny Killer. As Simon and I were walking out of the jail we both had a sudden and somewhat jolting realisation that we had shaken hands with John Wayne Glover, the infamous Granny Killer.

It was the same hand at which six innocent old ladies had died. And as far as the police are concerned, they believe he's killed more.

The files are still open.

Steve Barrett
Sydney, November 1999

CHAPTER 23

The Backpacker Murders

Ivan Robert Marko Milat
New South Wales, 1989–92

If pure evil had a face, surely it would be that of Australia's worst individual serial killer of the twentieth century, Ivan Robert Marko Milat. From 1989 to 1992, Milat abducted, robbed, sexually molested, tortured and murdered seven young people and concealed their bodies in the Belanglo State Forest south of Sydney.

From the evidence gathered by detectives and the reconstructions of the crimes, it is impossible to imagine the sheer terror that Milat's victims must have gone through until they were eventually put out of their misery.

And although it has never been proved, there is strong evidence indicating that Ivan Milat did not act alone. One of the main arguments in Milat's defence at his trial was that one of the members of Milat's own family could have committed the atrocities and that Ivan Milat had been framed and falsely accused.

Investigators believe that Milat's gruesome tally of seven victims doesn't end there. They have good reason to believe that the 'Backpacker Murderer' may have been involved in at least three more killings. But Ivan Milat isn't saying a word. From his maximum-security cell, where he is under constant surveillance 24 hours a day, he still protests his innocence, even though an appeal against his conviction has been turned down.

The irony of the saga of the backpacker murders is that if it wasn't for a monumental blunder by country police, there was every possibility that Ivan Milat could have been put behind bars very early in the piece, a move which would have saved another five young lives. In the end, Milat was brought to justice by the tireless diligence of a police task force of dedicated investigators who worked around the clock and left no stone unturned, and the perseverance of a young Englishman who wanted to have his story heard of how he was attacked and shot at by Milat after he had accepted a lift with him.

The horrors that would become known as 'the backpacker murders' first came to light on Saturday, 19 September 1992, when a couple of cross-country runners discovered the skeletal remains of two British backpackers, Caroline Clarke and Joanne Walters, both aged 22, in the dense Belanglo State Forest situated off the Hume Highway about an hour-and-a-half drive south of Sydney. The girls had gone missing five months earlier, after they left their backpacker motel in Sydney's Kings Cross to hitchhike towards Melbourne to look for casual seasonal work.

The holes in Joanne Walters's jumper indicated that she had been savagely stabbed in the heart and lungs with a large knife. Caroline Clarke had multiple bullet holes in her skull.

Cigarette butts and empty .22 calibre cartridge cases were recovered from the scene. A thorough search of the area by police revealed no other bodies. But it was clear to them that someone knew and used the area extensively. There was a fireplace built from house bricks just 40 metres from the murder scene.

An autopsy revealed that Joanne Walters had been stabbed a total of 14 times to the chest, neck and back, five of which were savage enough to cut her spine and sever two ribs. From the size of the wounds it looked as though they had been made by a blade the size of a bowie knife.

Joanne's arms and hands indicated no wounds that would have been incurred should she have tried to defend herself. This suggested that she may have been tied up at the time of the attack. The remains of a gag were still tied around her mouth and there was an indication that she had been strangled. Although the zip on Joanne's jeans was undone, the top button was still done up and, due to the decomposition of the body, it was extremely difficult to tell if she had been sexually assaulted.

Caroline Clarke had been stabbed in the upper back once by the same knife used to stab Joanne. She had also been shot in the head 10 times with a .22 calibre firearm. Four complete projectiles were removed from her skull and ballistics experts were confident that they could lead to the identity of the weapon used.

It would be later confirmed that the bullets had been fired from a Ruger .22 rifle.

The bullets in Caroline Clarke's skull had entered from three different angles, yet the 10 fired cases were all found in the one spot. In a later re-enactment at the murder scene, police could only arrive at the one ghastly conclusion: the killer had used Caroline Clarke as target practice, moving her head between shots.

To give police some sort of a profile of the beast(s) they were looking for, they called in leading Australian forensic psychiatrist Dr Rod Milton, who had had over 20 years' experience in profiling mass murderers and serial killers and who had successfully worked with police on such cases as the notorious Granny Killer murders, in which John Wayne Glover strangled six elderly women on Sydney's lower north shore between 1989 and 1990.

While at this stage Dr Milton made no indication that the murders may be the work of a serial killer, he did have a chilling opinion on the possibility that there was more than one killer involved. He believed that if this were the case, they could be brothers with the older one the more dominant over the more submissive, yet equally sadistic, younger brother. They would share a common interest in firearms, and this most likely wouldn't be the first time that they had committed sexually related crimes together.

After a thorough examination of the murder scene, Dr Milton came up with what would turn out to be a remarkably accurate profile of the killer. He believed that the killer would be employed in a semi-skilled job outdoors, be aged in his mid-30s, live on the outskirts of the city in a semi-rural area, be aggressive to authority, be involved in an unsatisfactory relationship and have a history of bisexual activity.

Just over a year later, on Tuesday, 5 October 1993, the first of the remains of what would turn out to be another five young hitchhikers – three women and two men – were found in a nearby area. They were identified as: Deborah Everist and her boyfriend James Gibson, two Victorians who had gone missing on 30 December 1989 while hitchhiking south towards Melbourne; solo German backpacker Simone Schmidl, 21, who vanished after setting out to hitchhike south along the Hume Highway on 20 January 1991; and German backpacking couple Gabor Neugebauer, 21, and Anja Habschied, 20, who were last seen on the same stretch of highway on 26 December 1991.

James Gibson had been stabbed in the spine, the breastbone, both sides of the chest and in the upper back. The zipper fly on his jeans was open but the top button was still done up.

Deborah Everist had been stabbed in the spine, there were several fractures in the skull and there were four slash marks in her forehead. A pair of grey tights and a black bra with a stab wound in one of the cups were found nearby.

Simone Schmidl's body was partially dressed with her shirt and undergarments pushed up around her neck. She had been stabbed in the spine, which would have completely severed her spinal cord and there were numerous stab wounds to the back and front of her body.

Gabor Neugebauer's body was found beneath a log that took three detectives to lift, indicating that it had been put there in the first place by more than one man. The young German had been gagged and there was every indication that he had been strangled. His jaw was broken in several places. There were six bullet entry wounds to his skull, and the zip on his jeans was open with the top button still done up.

The head and first two vertebrae were missing from Anja Habschied's skeleton and her upper-body clothing was bunched up around her neck and shoulders. All other items of clothing had been removed. After closer examination, the medical examiner, Dr Bradhurst, concluded that Anja's head had been severed with a long sharp instrument, most likely a machete or a sword, while she was in a kneeling position as if in some form of ritual decapitation.

It would appear that most of the victims had been first stabbed in the spine with the bowie knife, which had paralysed them while they were still alive before they were sexually assaulted, beaten, stabbed, bludgeoned, tortured, strangled, suffocated, shot, or decapitated.

There were empty cartridge packets strewn throughout the area and police collected more than 90 spent .22 cartridge cases.

There was not the slightest doubt in the minds of the investigating officers that all seven victims were killed by the same serial killer, or killers. It seemed unlikely that a single person could overpower the young German backpacker and his girlfriend and then tie them up single-handedly, and lift a huge log over the body of Gabor Neugebauer. To the experienced investigators, it certainly appeared as if it was the work of more than one person.

In faraway Birmingham, England, a young man named Paul Onions had been following the discovery of the bodies in the Belanglo State Forest outside Sydney, Australia, with more than a passing interest. When the first two bodies – those of the two English backpackers Caroline Clarke and Joanne Walters – had been found in September 1992, it was all over the British newspapers. And when a map of the area was printed in the paper, Paul Onions recognised it instantly as the spot where he had been robbed and almost murdered by a man who had given him a lift.

On 25 January 1990, just three weeks after Caroline Clarke and Joanne Walters had been murdered in the Belanglo State Forest, 24-year-old Paul Onions nearly became the backpacker serial killer's third victim.

The ex-British Navy sailor and Birmingham air-conditioning mechanic had left his job to hitchhike around Australia.

He was approached by a motorist in a silver four-wheel drive as he was waiting for a lift outside a shop on the Hume Highway just on the outskirts of Sydney. His intention was to go to Mildura to work as a fruit-picker.

The friendly motorist, who was of medium height and very solidly built like a body-builder, said his name was Bill. He had a big moustache like the cricketer Merv Hughes. Bill said he was going as far as Canberra and that suited Paul Onions just fine.

After about an hour and a half, after they had passed through the township of Mittagong, Bill's demeanour changed all of sudden and his speech became aggressive. He started complaining bitterly about all the people who live in Australia. He said there were too many immigrants in this country, and he went on about the Asians. Paul Onions was starting to feel a little uneasy.

Then Bill slowed down and kept looking in the rear-vision mirrors. He explained to Onions that he had lost radio reception and that he wanted to play some tapes that were under the driver's seat. Then he pulled over to the side of the road and got out and started messing round with the seat. Onions became nervous and got out of the car on the pretext that he was stretching his legs.

Bill became aggressive and told Onions to get back in the car, which he did. Once inside, Onions found himself staring down the barrel of a big black revolver, the copper heads of the bullets visible in the chambers, with Bill telling him that he was being robbed.

Next thing, Bill produced a coil of rope and the terrified Onions quickly undid his seatbelt, opened the door, jumped out, and ran up the highway against the traffic. Onions heard Bill shout: 'Stop! Get back in here. Stop, or I'll shoot you.' He heard the gun go off but he never looked back. He ran ahead and frantically waved his arms at the oncoming traffic.

But no-one would stop. Instead, the vehicles swerved to miss him and kept going. By now, the much bigger Bill had caught up with Paul Onions, grabbed him by the shirt, and ripped it as he dragged him to a halt and stared down at him. They were in the middle of the road, about 50 metres from Bill's four-wheel drive, and with Bill dragging Onions by the shirt and yelling at him to get back in the car.

Onions broke free and, determined to stop the next car or get hit, he ran in the path of an oncoming vehicle, a family van, and held out both his hands for it to stop. When it came to a screeching halt, he ran around to the side, opened the sliding passenger door, and got in and locked it. There were two women and five children inside; they were all yelling at him to get out and he was yelling back at them: 'He's got a gun! He's got a gun!'

The female driver conferred with the woman next to her and made a hasty decision to help. Bill was making his way back to the car but was still watching the vehicle. The driver then put the van in reverse and drove away from the scene backwards. She turned the vehicle around onto the other side of the road by bouncing across the wide, grassy median strip and headed back in the opposite direction.

As Paul Onions turned around and looked back, he saw that Bill had turned and was just standing there with this strange grin on his face. It was a sight that Paul Onions would never forget for as long as he lives.

The woman who stopped for him was Mrs Joanne Berry, who was heading home to Canberra with her sister Gai and their five children. She was kind enough to drive Onions to the nearest police station at Bowral after they found that the Berrima police station was shut. She was almost as frantic as he was, as she didn't really know what was happening except that someone had a gun and she could see the state her passenger was in.

Mrs Berry took Onions into the Bowral police station and told the female constable on duty that a motorist had just shot at him. The constable, Janet Nicholson, gave him a cup of tea to calm him down and took all of the details.

The police didn't take Paul Onions back to where it happened, they just took a detailed report of the incident and put the description of the four-wheel drive out over the air and told them that the driver was wanted in connection with firearm offences relating to the incident.

A senior police officer took Onions into a quiet room and showed him a bunch of pictures of people who were missing. The officer told him that he was lucky and practically gave him a lecture on the dangers of hitchhiking.

They took a statement from Joanne, who didn't really get a look at Bill, and told her she could go. The police gave Onions $20 because he had lost his rucksack containing his camera, clothing, an air ticket and his passport. They then pointed him in the direction of the railway station and a very jittery Paul Onions walked down to catch the train back to Sydney, still thinking that Bill might pop out from anywhere. He made sure he sat near people on the train.

From the police station, Onions had phoned his friend at the Hereford Lodge in Glebe, Sydney, and booked a room for the night. He got a new passport through the British Embassy, took a job in Sydney and waited for his girlfriend to come out from England to join him for the rest of his holiday.

She arrived in May and they saw the east coast of Australia by public transport. They left Australia to return home on 21 June and never heard another word about the incident.

Almost two years later, in September 1992, Paul Onions was reading about the discovery of the remains of the two English girls who had gone missing during Easter the same year and the map showed that they had been found in the Belanglo State Forest south of Sydney. It was then that he realised his incident could have been related. But then he thought, 'No, it can't be, it's too coincidental,' so he didn't contact anybody. He thought at the time that he'd already given his report and he was pretty sure if it had anything to do with him that they'd contact him. At this stage, Paul Onions had no idea that his report had been lost in paperwork and the incident all but forgotten.

It wasn't until about a year later when the remains of the other five bodies were discovered in the same area that Onions thought that it seemed strange that no-one had contacted him about the man who tried to kill him.

It got big coverage in England and the papers said that they were looking for a serial killer. Then a friend called him from Australia and suggested that he should ring the hotline number and tell them again what happened.

So he went to his local police station in England and sat down with the police and went through it all over again. At the detective's suggestion, Onions phoned the Australian Embassy. He was put in touch with the task force, and he told the whole story to a detective who had no knowledge of the incident.

A few months later, a detective from the task force contacted Paul Onions, who again went over the story, and within two weeks he was on a plane back to Australia.

They unearthed his report and took him down to the scene of the incident. Onions described the man called Bill with the droopy black moustache who had fired at him. He gave them a statement and returned to England.

A few months later, he received another phone call from the task force telling him that somebody was going to be arrested the following day. The next thing he knew, a man was being arrested in connection with the murders and the attempted murder of Paul Onions.

In the meantime, from the time that Paul Onions first read the reports in the papers to when he contacted the Australian police more than a year later, the task force – now known as Task Force Air and headed by one of Australia's most experienced major crime detectives, Commander Clive Small – had been making little progress under the weight of thousands of leads that had been pouring in daily.

By early 1994, police had whittled the list down to 2000 'persons of interest' who may have committed the murders or at least may have some knowledge of who did. There were almost 40 detectives working full-time on the case and every bit of information had to be checked.

Among the folders that were considered to be 'leads' was the report from Paul Onions in England and another report from Joanne Berry, the woman who had picked him up, and who had reported the incident again after the bodies had been discovered nearby. They were just two of the many hundreds of leads that had to be checked out.

Task Force Air needed a lucky break. It would be a few months coming.

One of the 'leads' folders was named 'Milat' and contained three separate reports. One report was that in October 1993, an Alex Milat (Ivan's eldest brother) had volunteered a very detailed statement claiming that he had seen two gagged women being taken into the Belanglo State Forest 18 months earlier.

The second report was from a woman who knew of a man named Ivan Milat who lived near the forest, had lots of guns and drove a four-wheel drive. Detectives called at Ivan Milat's last known place of work, a Readymix work site where he had been employed as a road worker with his brother Richard.

A quick check of their work records revealed that, while Richard was at work on every day that the backpackers went missing, his older brother Ivan wasn't. And while Ivan now drove a red Holden Jackeroo four-wheel drive, at the time of the murders he was driving a silver four-wheel drive. They also learned that Ivan Milat used to wear a big Merv Hughes-type moustache but had shaved it off. He also answered to the nickname of 'Bill'.

All of this information would prove to be extremely relevant when the police got around to interviewing Paul Onions in the months ahead.

The detectives checked out Ivan Milat's criminal record and it came up like a rash across the computer screen. Ivan Robert Marko Milat was the fourth of 10 brothers and four sisters born of Yugoslav parents in Sydney in 1944 and grew up in Sydney's outer south-western suburbs. In 1962, as a 17-year-old, he was put on probation for stealing. Two months later he was back in court for breaking and entering and was sent to an institution for six months. In 1964, he was sentenced to 18 months' imprisonment for two counts of breaking, entering and stealing and shortly after he was released he was sent back to prison for two years for car theft and other charges of larceny. Four months after his release on parole in April 1967, he was sent back to prison for three years with an 18-month non-parole period. In June 1971, a charge was brought against him for robbing a store while armed with a shotgun and three days later he was charged with bank robbery. He fled to New Zealand while on bail, leaving his accomplices, which included his brother Michael, to face long jail terms.

But what intrigued police most in Ivan Milat's long list of crimes was that in April 1971 he was charged with rape after he had picked up two girls who were hitchhiking from Sydney to Melbourne along the Hume Highway, outside of Liverpool. Both the girls alleged that after Milat, who stank of a pungent body odour, had picked them up he pulled into a dirt road, produced a knife and said: 'I'm going to have sex with both of you. If you don't, I'm going to kill you.' The two women negotiated with Milat for almost an hour before he tied them up and said: 'You know what I am going to do? I am going to kill you. You won't scream when I cut your throats, will you?' One of the girls then allegedly asked: 'If I have sex with you, will you . . . will you sort of drop us somewhere and we'll let the whole thing go?'

When Milat returned from his extended holiday in New Zealand and faced the court, the bank robbery charge was dismissed as unproven and he was found not guilty of the rape charge on the basis of consent.

But whether the rape case was proven or not, it was suspiciously familiar to the circumstances surrounding the backpacker murders. Ivan Milat became a prime suspect.

Commander Clive Small assigned a team of five detectives

– David McCloskey, Paul Gordon, Tony Roberts, and Brett Coman, with Detective Royce Gorman as case officer – to gather as much information as they could on Ivan Milat. A surveillance team was allocated to keep an eye on Milat's house at all times and keep track of his every move.

At the same time that Ivan Milat had come under police scrutiny, detectives were also following another line of investigation into the background of a Paul Miller who worked for a company named Boral, a manufacturer of plasterboard. Miller had allegedly boasted to workmates that he knew where some dead German tourists were even before their bodies had been discovered.

When the bodies of Caroline Clarke and Joanne Walters had been found, Miller had told workmates: 'There's more bodies out there. They haven't found the two Germans yet,' and, 'Oh yeah, I know who killed those two Germans.'

Miller was also alleged to have told his workmates: 'Stabbing a woman is like cutting a loaf of bread', and, 'You could pick up anybody on that road and you'd never find them again. You'd never find out who did it, either.'

Secretly, through checking car registration numbers and employment records, police discovered that Paul Miller was, in fact, Richard Milat, Ivan's younger brother, working under an assumed name for reasons known only to himself. Richard Milat was a renowned 'pothead' and drunk who raved mostly gibberish when on marijuana and beer – which was most of the time, even at work.

But while Richard Milat appeared incapable of abduction and murder because he was 'off his face' most of the time, he must have picked up that information somewhere. Their prime suspect, Ivan Milat, was looking better by the day.

By March 1994, Task Force Air had every possible piece of information that could be gathered on the Milat family. But still they had nothing to tie it all together. They believed they had their man, or possibly *men*, but they couldn't prove a thing.

With almost every angle followed up and followed up again, the task force of weary detectives took on the unenviable job of hand-sorting through every report and lead relating to the case. It could take months to check every one but they knew that every stone must be looked under and every possible lead checked and re-checked.

On 13 April, the break police had so desperately been waiting for came when Detective Paul Gordon came across the note saying that a Paul Onions, an English backpacker who had almost been killed while hitchhiking along the Hume Highway in 1990, had rung the hotline from England five months earlier. Detective Gordon read Paul Onions's telephone report to the hotline describing the attack and couldn't believe what he was reading. Here was a credible witness who could link the vehicle, the area and the driver. He took the report immediately to Commander Clive Small, who was furious that such a vital piece of information could be overlooked. He immediately called for the original report that Paul Onions had filed with the Bowral police on the afternoon of 25 January 1990. He was even more furious when he was told that it was lost. Fortunately, Constable Nicholson, who took Onions's original statement, had it all written down in her notebook.

Seeing as Ivan and Richard Milat were very similar in appearance, police checked their work records to find that Richard was at work on the day of the attempted murder on Paul Onions and that Ivan Milat was not.

A week later, a very surprised Paul Onions was on a plane to Sydney to give police a guided tour of what had happened and where it occurred on the day that 'Bill' almost took his life. Police pointed out that Onions had escaped only 2 kilometres from the entrance to the Belanglo State Forest. The next day, Paul Onions positively identified Ivan Milat from a video line-up of 13 photographs of suspects.

At long last Task Force Air had their man and it was time to close in for the kill. They now had sufficient evidence to arrest Ivan Milat for the attempted murder of Paul Onions. Armed with the arrest warrant and a search warrant, they were ready to raid Milat's home at Eaglevale, near Liverpool, just a few short kilometres from the start of the Hume Highway.

And just in case Ivan Milat hadn't acted alone, police would also be paying visits with search warrants to his mother's home; the homes of his brothers, Richard, Walter and Bill; a property that was jointly owned by the brothers near the Belanglo State Forest; and the home of Alex Milat, which was situated at a town called Woombye, a few hours' drive north of Brisbane.

Over 300 police would be involved in the raids. It was so secret that participating police officers would not be given the location of their target until a couple of hours before it was due to take place.

At 6.30 a.m. on 22 May 1994, 50 police officers, which included members of the heavily armed elite State Protection Group, surrounded Ivan Milat's home at Eaglevale. Chief negotiator Detective Wayne Gordon rang Milat on the phone to tell him the situation and that he had better come out quietly. After several attempts, during which Milat hung up thinking that it was a practical joke, Milat eventually appeared at the front door and was taken into custody without a struggle.

At exactly the same time that Ivan Milat was being hand-cuffed and put in a police car to be taken away and charged, the other raids on the Milat family houses had gone just as smoothly and police began the mammoth task of searching every square inch of the properties for anything that could link Ivan Milat or any members of his family with the backpacker murders.

For the relieved detectives, searching Ivan Milat's house was like opening an Aladdin's cave full of incriminating evidence. They found a postcard from New Zealand addressed to a 'Bill'. Milat denied that he was ever known by that name. When asked about a .22 bullet found in one of the bedrooms and if he had any guns in the house, Milat said he had no knowledge of either. In a manhole in the garage, police found the disassembled parts of a Ruger .22 rifle, the type that had been used to murder Caroline Clarke and Gabor Neugebauer. Bullets fired from the rifle would prove to match those found at the murder scenes and taken from the victims' skulls.

Inside Ivan Milat's workbag they found a 12-inch bowie knife. A fully loaded Browning automatic pistol was found concealed in the laundry. Two sleeping bags found in a wardrobe in one of the bedrooms would be positively identified later as belonging to Simone Schmidl and Deborah Everist. A framed photograph of Milat's girlfriend, Chalinder Hughes, showed her wearing a distinctive, striped Benneton top identical to a top that Caroline Clarke owned. They also found Caroline Clarke's camera.

Police found tape, rope, headbands and cable ties identical to those found at the murder scenes. Camping and cooking equipment found in the kitchen would later be positively identified as belonging to Simone Schmidl. A water canteen bore the name 'Simi', some of which had been crudely scratched off.

In the raids on the other Milat households, police found a huge amount of ammunition, an arsenal of weapons that included bows and arrows, shotguns, rifles and an assortment of knives, and camping gear that belonged to the victims.

But the most chilling find of all was that of a long, curved cavalry sword found in a locked cupboard at the house of Ivan's mother, Mrs Margaret Milat. The German backpacker Anja Habschied was believed to have been decapitated with such a sword.

Ivan Robert Marko Milat was charged with the murders of the seven backpackers and the attempted murder of Paul Onions.

At what would be Australia's biggest-ever murder trial, on 26 March 1996, Ivan Milat pleaded not guilty to all eight charges. The prosecution's first witness was Paul Onions, who did not hesitate in identifying Ivan Milat as the man named 'Bill' who had tried to kill him on 25 January 1990.

Then the seemingly endless procession of witnesses had to be heard and over 350 exhibits and photographs were explained to the court and the jury. It was all one-way traffic against Ivan Milat. The court fell silent time and again as the packed gallery and the jury heard details from one expert witness after another of the unbelievable atrocities that had been committed in the Belanglo State Forest.

The trial lasted for almost three months, during which time the jury heard from more than 140 prosecution witnesses. During that time they heard Ivan Milat's defence counsel repeatedly try to incriminate Ivan Milat's own brothers, Richard and Walter, as they cross-examined the witnesses in an attempt to get them to say something that may shift the guilt away from their client.

The defence also said: '. . . it was absolutely irrefutable that whoever has committed these offences must be either within the Milat family or so very closely associated with it, it doesn't much matter. Blind Freddy can see that. There can be absolutely no doubt. The question is, who is it within the Milat family who has committed these eight offences?'

Ivan Milat's own defence was simple. He denied everything. When faced with questions that he could not answer, such as how the gun that killed two of the backpackers came to be in his house along with so many items of their equipment, Milat's answer was: 'Someone's trying to make me look bad.'

But, try as his lawyers would to incriminate other members of the Milat family, Ivan Milat's fate was inevitable. The tireless detectives of Task Force Air had sewn a watertight case and on Saturday, 27 July 1996, almost four months to the day the trial started, and after three days of deliberation, the jury returned a verdict of guilty on all seven counts of murder and one count of attempted murder.

In his summing up, Justice David Hunt said: 'It is sufficient here to record that each of the victims was attacked savagely and cruelly, with force which was unusual and vastly more than was necessary to cause death, and for some form of psychological gratification. Each of two of the victims was shot a number of times in the head. A third was decapitated in circumstances which establish that she would have been alive at the time. The stab wounds to each of the other three would have caused paralysis, two of them having had their spinal cords completely severed. The multiple stab wounds to three of the seven victims would have been likely to have penetrated their hearts. There are signs that two of them were strangled. All but one appear to have been sexually interfered with before or after death.'

Ivan Robert Marko Milat was sentenced to the term of his natural life on seven counts of murder and to six years for the attempted abduction of Paul Onions. Under no circumstances is he to be released.

On 17 May 1997, Milat attempted to escape from Maitland Jail. His accomplice, convicted drug trafficker George Savvas, committed suicide in his cell several hours after the failed attempt. Milat was confined to solitary but was never charged with the attempted escape.

On 26 February 1998, the NSW Court of Criminal Appeal

unanimously rejected Milat's appeal and ordered him to spend the rest of his life behind bars.

No charges have ever been laid against any other member of the Milat family in relation to the backpacker murders.

Police have good reason to believe that Ivan Milat is responsible for more than just the seven backpacker murders. In 1987, an unclothed skeleton believed to be that of a female backpacker who went missing while hitchhiking around Australia was found in bush near Taree in northern New South Wales. At the time of her disappearance it is believed that Ivan Milat was working locally for the Department of Main Roads as part of a resurfacing gang. Milat is also suspected of knowing about other mysterious disappearances in the district.

In January 1988, the body of 18-year-old hitchhiker Peter Letcher, who had gone missing around 14 November 1987, was found in the Jenolan State Forest, 160 kilometres west of Sydney. He had been shot in the head with five .22 bullets and his head was wrapped in material in an identical fashion to that of Caroline Clarke. Letcher had gone missing on the weekend before Milat's road crew was due to start roadwork nearby. Police have little doubt that the teenager was murdered by Milat.

Milat is also suspected to be involved in the disappearance of two hitchhikers, Alan Fox and his fiancée Anneke Adriaansen, between Sydney and the NSW north coast in January 1979.

When asked by Sydney crime reporters Mark Whittaker and Les Kennedy if he thought that he was innocent, Boris Milat said of his younger brother Ivan: 'Everywhere he's worked, people have disappeared. I know where he's been. If Ivan's done these murders, I reckon he's done a hell of a lot more.'

'How many?' Whittaker and Kennedy asked.

'. . . um . . . 28!' Boris Milat replied.

AUTHOR'S NOTE: The full story of the horrors of the backpacker murders can be found in the extensively researched *Sins of the Brother: The Definitive Story of Ivan Milat and the Backpacker Murders* by Sydney crime reporters Mark Whittaker and Les Kennedy.

CHAPTER 24

The Frankston Serial Killer

Paul Charles Denyer
Frankston, Victoria, 1993

Over a seven-week period from June to July 1993, three young women aged 17, 18 and 22 were violently stabbed and slashed to death – one in broad daylight – in and around Frankston in southeastern Victoria. Another 41-year-old woman was brutally assaulted and considered herself lucky to escape with her life.

None of the victims knew each other and there was nothing to connect them in any way, except that they all lived in the Frankston district. After the first two murders and the assault, it became clear to police that there was a serial killer on the loose – a killer who chose his victims at random and murdered for no apparent reason. Tragically, their theory was proved correct when another young woman was stabbed to death three weeks later, on 30 July.

And when he was eventually caught, the serial killer turned out to be a local, Paul Denyer, a 183 centimetre, 120 kilogram, 21-year-old oafish layabout who answered to the nickname of John Candy, after the (now deceased) funnyman of such movies as *Uncle Buck* and *The Blues Brothers*.

But Paul Denyer was no funny man. He was a pudgy, dysfunctional misfit and self-confessed misogynist who, from an early age, indicated that he was always going to be a monster.

As a child, Denyer dissected his sister's teddy bears and at the age of 10 he slit the throat of the family kitten with his brother's pocket knife and hung the carcass from a tree branch in the backyard. He later became obsessed with blood and gore movies which he watched repeatedly. Several months before he embarked on his killing spree, Denyer had disembowelled a friend's cat and cut the throats of its kittens.

When captured, Denyer displayed no emotion whatsoever as he told horrified police how he murdered the three women. He also told arresting officers that he had had the urge to kill since he was 14: 'I've always wanted to kill, waiting for the right time, waiting for that silent alarm to trigger me off.'

The Frankston Serial Killer was born Paul Charles Denyer in Sydney on 14 April 1972, the third of six children – five boys and a girl – to English working-class immigrants Maureen and Anthony Denyer, who came to Australia in 1965 and eventually settled in Campbelltown in Sydney's outer west.

The only significant thing about Paul Denyer's infancy was that, as a baby, he rolled off a bench and knocked his head. This became a family joke for many years and whenever he would say or do anything out of the ordinary it would prompt the comment: 'That's because you fell on your head as a baby.'

When the family relocated to Victoria in 1981 so that Anthony Denyer could take up the position as manager of The Steak Place in Centre Road, South Oakleigh, none of the Denyer children approved of the move. They were happy at Campbelltown, and Paul especially found it extremely hard to make the adjustment. At his new school, Northvale Primary, he was a completely different boy, a loner who found it difficult to make friends and lacked self-confidence and motivation.

To make matters worse, Paul Denyer grew into a big lump of a lad, much taller and a lot fatter than the other kids, and instead of taking up the usual things that would occupy a boy of his age, he grew up fascinated with his collection of knives and clubs and home-made slingshots that fired pebbles or ball bearings.

Just before his thirteenth birthday, Paul Denyer was charged with stealing a car and escaped with a caution. Two months later, he was charged with theft, wilful damage, and making a false report to the fire brigade. At age 15, the bully Denyer forced another boy to masturbate in front of some children and was charged with assault.

In 1992, he entered into a relationship with Sharon Johnson, a girl he had met while working at Safeway supermarket. His job came to an abrupt end when he allegedly knocked down a woman and a child deliberately with a convoy of empty shopping trolleys.

Denyer then applied to join the Victorian Police Force, but was rejected on the grounds that he was unfit due to his massive bulk. Denyer's last place of employment was a marine workshop where he was ultimately fired because he spent more time making crude knives and daggers than completing the tasks assigned to him. It was later alleged that he slaughtered and dismembered two goats in a paddock next door.

Unable to hold down a job owing to a combination of laziness and incompetence, and now nicknamed John Candy because of his 120-kilogram bulk and physical likeness, by the time he was 20 Paul Denyer was a social outcast with a fixation for death, the macabre and horrific murder movies such as *The Stepfather*, *Fear* and *Halloween*, each of which he watched over and over.

In 1992, Denyer moved into a flat on Dandenong Road in Frankston with girlfriend Sharon Johnson. With Denyer unemployed, Sharon held down two telemarketing jobs to support them both and, consequently, she was away from home from very early in the morning until late in the evening. With plenty of idle time on Paul Denyer's hands, it wasn't long before some unusual things started to happen around the block of flats.

One tenant arrived home to find her flat broken into and her clothes and engagement pictures slashed. Another caught a glimpse of someone peeping at her through a window. But the most disturbing incident of all happened to the sister of a woman who lived in the same block of flats as Paul Denyer and Sharon Johnson.

Denyer and Johnson had become quite friendly with their neighbour Tricia and her sister, Donna, who lived with her fiancé, Les, and Donna's tiny baby in a block of flats nearby. On the night of 19 February 1993, Les, Donna and their baby arrived home at about 11 p.m. after working Les's late-night pizza delivery run to be confronted with the most horrific scene. On the lounge room wall next to the television set and written in blood were the words *Dead Don*. Lying on the floor in the middle of the kitchen were the remains of Donna's cat, Buffy, with a picture of a bikini-clad woman strewn over its disembowelled carcase.

The cat's entrails had been dragged through the kitchen and scattered about the walls and the cat's blood was sprayed everywhere. Written in blood in the middle of it all were the words

Donna and Robyn – You're Dead. One of Buffy's eyes was bulging from its socket. The other eye was missing, apparently ripped out of its head and discarded.

In the bathroom they found Buffy's two kittens lying in a baby's bath full of bloodied water with their throats cut. In the laundry, there was blood sprayed all over the walls and over a plastic laundry basket full of baby clothes.

In the main bedroom, the intruder had ransacked every drawer and clothes were ripped and strewn all over the room. Les's collection of centrefold pin-ups had been slashed and stabbed with a sharp instrument. Cupboard doors had been kicked and beaten, leaving splintered gouges in them. The baby's clothing had been slashed and a stabbed photo of a semi-clad model was draped across the baby's crib. The words *Donna and Robyn* had been sprayed in white shaving foam on the dressing-table mirror.

Donna didn't have the faintest idea who the mysterious Robyn was and she never spent another night at the flat, instead staying temporarily with her sister, Tricia, until she found alternative accommodation.

Tricia's neighbour, Paul Denyer, who knew Donna quite well through Tricia, told Donna that she would be safe now and that if the police ever caught the person responsible he would personally take care of him for her.

Four months later, on Saturday, 12 June 1993, the partially clothed body of 18-year-old student Elizabeth Stevens was found in Lloyd Park on Cranbourne Road, Langwarrin, a short drive from Frankston. The teenager had been reported missing the previous evening by her uncle and aunt with whom she had been staying.

Naked from the waist up, Elizabeth Stevens had had her throat cut, there were six deep knife wounds to her chest, four deep cuts running from her breast to her navel and four more running at right angles, forming a macabre criss-cross pattern on her abdomen. Elizabeth Stevens's face had several cuts and abrasions and her nose was swollen, indicating that it had been broken. Her bra was up around her neck. A post-mortem revealed that she hadn't been sexually assaulted.

The killing was as senseless as it was brutal. Elizabeth didn't have an enemy in the world. The attack had to be that of a random killer or perhaps a rape gone wrong.

Police mounted a huge search for her murderer. They used a life-sized mannequin of Elizabeth Stevens at a road block at the bus stop where she was last seen in the hope that someone may recognise her and, hopefully, her attacker.

They knocked on every door in the district and questioned bus drivers, and passengers who were on Elizabeth Stevens's last-known bus ride. They checked out every known library in the vicinity of where she was last known to have been. It all amounted to nothing.

On the evening of Thursday, 8 July 1993, 41-year-old bank clerk Roszsa Toth was making her way home from work after she had alighted from the train at Seaford when she was violently attacked by a man who said he had a gun and tried to drag her into a nearby nature reserve.

Mrs Toth put up an almighty fight for her life during which the man pulled clumps of her hair out of her head and she bit his fingers to the bone several times. She eventually fought the man off and, with torn stockings and trousers and no shoes, she managed to hail down a passing car as her assailant fled into the night. Roszsa Toth had little doubt that had she not resisted so strongly she would have most definitely been murdered. She rang the police who were at the scene of the assault within minutes, but there was no sign of her attacker.

Later that same evening, 22-year-old Debbie Fream, who had given birth to a son, Jake, 12 days earlier, went missing after she drove to her local store at Seaford to pick up a bottle of milk while in the middle of preparing dinner. Four days later, her body was found by a farmer in one of his paddocks at nearby Carrum Downs. Debbie Fream had been stabbed about the neck, head, chest and arms 24 times. She had also been strangled. She had not been sexually assaulted.

The attack of Roszsa Toth, which had before been considered a random purse snatch gone horribly wrong, was now considered to be the work of the same killer of Elizabeth Stevens and Debbie Fream. There was a madman on the loose in the Frankston district.

The women of the Frankston district locked themselves indoors and the streets were noticeably deserted at night. Real estate sales and rental inquiries plummeted. Frankston became known as the place where a serial killer lurked among its residents and everyone was a suspect. Every day the newspapers gave an update and detailed reports of the huge police manhunt that was under way to track down the killer.

Police were relentless in their investigations. Every lead, no matter how small, was followed up and even the slightest clue as to the assailant's identity was looked into immediately. A help centre named Operation Reassurance was set up to advise local women what to do should they be attacked by the Frankston Serial Killer and how to prevent being attacked in the first place.

But it was to no avail. On the afternoon of Friday, 30 July, 17-year-old Natalie Russell went missing while riding her bike home from the John Paul College in Frankston. Eight hours later, her body was found in scrub beside a bike track that ran between the Peninsula and the Long Island Golf clubs. She had been stabbed repeatedly about the face and neck and her throat had been cut. It appeared that the savagery committed to Natalie Russell was much worse than the previous two victims. As was the case with Elizabeth Stevens and Debbie Fream, Natalie had not been sexually assaulted.

But this time the killer had left a damning piece of evidence that would prove him guilty should he be apprehended. A piece of skin, possibly from a finger, was found on the neck of the dead girl. It didn't belong to the victim; the only other possible explanation was that the killer had cut himself as he attacked the student and the sliver of flesh had attached itself – stuck by dried blood – onto her skin.

The other good news was the sighting of a yellow Toyota Corona on a road near the bike track at 3 p.m., the time the coroner estimated that Natalie Russell had been murdered. The observant police officer had written down its number from its registration label because the car had no plates.

Back at the police station, detectives fed the registration number into their computer. It matched up with a report from a postman who had spotted a man slumped in a suspicious position, as if to avoid being seen, in the front seat of a yellow Toyota Corona, though she hadn't written down the registration number because the car had no plates. A quick check through the computer also revealed that the same car had been spotted in the vicinity where Debbie Fream's body had been found. Three sightings of the one vehicle was just too much of a coincidence.

The car was registered to a Paul Charles Denyer, who wasn't home when detectives Mick Hughes and Charlie Bezzina called at his address at 3.40 p.m. They left a card under the door asking him to contact them as soon as he arrived home. At 5.15 p.m. the detectives received a call from a Sharon Johnson and, so as not to frighten Denyer away, she was told that it was merely a 'routine inquiry' and that they were interviewing everyone in the district. Within 10 minutes, a team of detectives, headed by Mick Hughes, Rod Wilson and CIB Detective Darren O'Loughlin, converged at the block of flats at 186 Frankston-Dandenong Road.

Paul Denyer answered the door and commented that he was surprised to see so many detectives for just a routine inquiry, but he cheerily let them in. He explained that while his car had no plates he had a permit to drive it for 28 days while he made necessary repairs to have it registered.

As Denyer explained his whereabouts at the time of the murders, the detectives noticed that his hands were cut in several places. From one cut, the skin was missing and they mentally noted that the missing piece would have resembled that which was found on Natalie Russell's body.

Although he admitted to being in the vicinity of two of the murders at the time they were taking place, Denyer steadfastly denied any knowledge of the killings other than what he had read in the papers. He offered weak excuses for being at the murder scenes, saying that his car had broken down near the place where Natalie Russell was murdered and that he was waiting to pick up his girlfriend from the train on the other occasion. He explained the scratches away by saying that he got his hands caught in the fan while working underneath the bonnet of the car.

But there was no fooling the seasoned detectives. They knew they had their man and that it was only a matter of time before he would crack. Taken to Frankston police station and questioned in an interrogation room while being video-recorded, Denyer maintained his innocence through to the early hours of the following morning. But he knew his number was up when police asked for a blood sample and a sample of his hair and told him that a DNA test would match him up to anything on his victim that came from him.

Denyer asked some questions about how long the DNA results would take and whether or not the police had something with which to compare his DNA. Then he thought for a bit and, out of the blue, volunteered, 'Okay, I killed all three of them', to Detective Darren O'Loughlin.

Just before 4 o'clock on the morning of Sunday, 1 August 1993, Paul Denyer began his confession to the murders of Elizabeth Stevens, Debbie Fream and Natalie Russell, and the attack on Roszsa Toth.

He told them that at around 7 o'clock on the bleak, rainy evening of 11 June 1993, Elizabeth Stevens alighted from the bus in Cranbourne Road, Langwarrin to walk the short distance to her home. Paul Denyer was waiting – not for Elizabeth in particular. Anyone. Just someone to kill. Elizabeth Stevens just happened to be in the wrong place at the wrong time.

Denyer followed the young student along the street in the dense rain and grabbed her from behind, telling her that he had a gun and that if she screamed or tried to run away he would kill her. He told detectives that the 'gun' he held in her back was in fact a piece of aluminium piping with a wooden handle. At 'gunpoint', Denyer marched the terrified girl to nearby Lloyd Park.

Denyer's statement said in part: 'Walked in a bit of bushland beside the main track in Lloyd Park. Sat there, you know, stood in the bushes for a while just – I can't remember, just standing there I suppose. Held the gun to the back of her neck, walked across the track over towards the other small sandhill or something. And on the other side of that hill, she asked me if she could, you know – go to the toilet or, so to speak. So I respected her privacy. So I turned around and everything while she did it and everything. When she finished we just walked down towards where the goal posts are and we turned right and headed towards the area where she was found. Got to that area there and I started choking her with my hands and she passed out after a while. You know, the oxygen got cut off to her head and – and she just stopped. And then I pulled out the knife . . . and stabbed her many times in the throat. And she was still alive. And then she stood up and then we walked around and all that, just walking around a few steps, and then I threw her on the ground and stuck my foot over her neck to finish her off.'

The manner in which Denyer gave his confession chilled the detectives to the bone. It was devoid of emotion or remorse; almost flippant. When the detectives asked questions they were answered in an almost condescending manner, as if Denyer was in complete control of the situation because he was the only one who knew what had actually happened.

Denyer described, matter-of-factly, and demonstrated how he had pushed his thumb into Elizabeth Stevens's throat and strangled her. He made a stabbing motion, showing how he stabbed and slashed her throat. Then, to the astonishment of the detectives, he demonstrated for the video camera how Elizabeth Stevens's body had begun shaking and shuddering as she went through the death rattles before finally dying.

Denyer then told police how he had dragged Elizabeth Stevens's body to the drain and left it, where it was eventually found. He explained that the blade of the home-made knife he had used to stab Elizabeth Stevens to death had bent during the assault and had broken away from the handle and that he dumped all of the bits beside the road as he made his way from the murder scene.

When asked why he had killed Elizabeth Stevens, Denyer replied: 'Just wanted . . . just wanted to kill. Just wanted to take a life because I felt my life had been taken many times.'

After a long and detailed confession to the first murder, Paul Denyer went on to tell of the events of the night of Thursday, 8 July 1993. He told detectives Wilson and O'Loughlin that he approached Mrs Toth from behind after he had seen her walking near the Seaford station. He put a hand over her mouth and held a fake gun to her head with the other hand. Mrs Toth resisted strongly and bit his finger to the bone. The couple wrestled and Mrs Toth escaped from his grasp and ran out into the middle of the road, but none of the passing cars stopped. Denyer chased after her, grabbed Mrs Toth by the hair and said: 'Shut up, or I'll blow your fucking head off', and the woman nodded in agreement but again escaped and this time managed to flag down a passing car while Denyer fled.

When asked what he intended to do to Mrs Toth, Denyer replied coolly: 'I was just gonna drag her in the park and kill her, that's all.' Denyer said that, as well as the fake gun, he was carrying one of his home-made knives with a razor-sharp aluminium blade in his sock.

After the near-miss with Mrs Toth, Denyer went to the nearby railway station and casually boarded the Frankston-bound train. He got off at Kananook, the next station along, and crossed over the rail overpass bridge in search of another victim. Here he saw Debbie Fream get out of her grey Pulsar and go into the milk bar on the corner.

Denyer said that while Debbie Fream was in the milk bar, he opened the rear door of her car, let himself into the back, and closed the door behind him. He crouched in the back seat and listened as her footsteps came back to the car, and she got in and drove away. 'I waited for her to start up the car so no-one would hear her scream or anything,' Denyer said in his confession. 'And she put it into gear and she went to do a U-turn. And I startled her just as she was doing that turn and she kept going into the wall of the milk bar, which caused a dent in the bonnet. I told her to, you know, shut up or I'd blow her head off and all that shit.'

Denyer said that he held the fake gun in her side. The detectives asked Denyer if he had noticed anything in the back and he said that he had seen a baby capsule beside him in the back seat. Denyer must have known that he was about to kill a young mother. Obviously, it made the least scrap of difference to him.

Denyer told Debbie Fream in which direction to drive. It was to an area that he knew well and knew he wouldn't be seen as he murdered her.

'I told her when we got there that if she gave any signals to anyone, I'd blow her head off, I'd decorate the car with her brains,' Denyer told the police.

Denyer told her to stop the car near some trees and get out, and he pulled a length of cord from his pocket. 'I popped it over her eyes real quickly, so she didn't see it . . .'cause I was gonna strangle her. But I didn't want her to see the cord first. I lifted the cord up and I said: "Can you see this?" And she just put her hand up to grab it to feel it and when she did that I just yanked on it real quickly around her neck. And then I was struggling with her for about five minutes.'

Denyer said that he strangled Debbie Fream until she started to pass out. He then drew the knife from his sock and repeatedly stabbed her about the neck and chest. When she fell limp at his feet he set upon her with the knife, stabbing her many times in the neck and once in the stomach.

'She started breathing out of her neck, just like Elizabeth Stevens,' he told the detectives. 'I could just hear bubbling noises.'

When asked if Debbie Fream put up any resistance, Denyer replied: 'Yeah, she put up quite a fight. And her white jumper was pulled off during that time as well. I just felt the same way I did when I killed Elizabeth Stevens.'

The detectives then asked Denyer what happened after he had stabbed her round the chest and throat area. 'I lifted up her top and then ploughed the knife into her gut. I wanted to see how big her boobs were.' He said that when he saw Debbie's bare stomach he 'just lunged at it with the knife'.

Satisfied that Debbie Fream was dead, Denyer dragged her body into a clump of trees and covered it over with a couple of branches he broke from the nearest tree. He then spent about five minutes looking for the murder weapon which he had dropped after the killing, found it and put it in his pocket. He drove off in Debbie Fream's car, dumped it close to where he lived, and walked home in time to ring Sharon at work and pick her up at the Kananook railway station.

The following morning, he brazenly returned to Debbie Fream's car and collected her purse and the two cartons of milk, eggs, chocolate and a packet of cigarettes she had purchased from the milk bar the previous evening, and took them home with him. The only thing of value he found in the purse was a $20 note.

He emptied the milk down the sink, threw out the eggs and burned the carton, as he considered this to be evidence that could be used against him. He then buried the dead woman's purse in the nearby golf course and near the bike track where he would later kill Natalie Russell. Denyer then dismantled his home-made knife and hid the parts in the air vent in the laundry of his apartment.

'Why did you kill her?' the detectives asked him.

'Same reason why I killed Elizabeth Stevens. I just wanted to,' he replied.

As the sun rose on that Sunday morning, 12 hours after they had started questioning Paul Denyer at Frankston police station, the weary detectives began questioning him about the murder of Natalie Russell, 40 hours earlier.

If the detectives were showing any signs of weariness, what they were about to hear would shock them back to attentiveness with a jolt. Denyer's almost unbelievable confession to the murder of Natalie Russell would put him among the most despicable monsters this country has ever known.

Denyer had planned his next murder in advance. His intention was to abduct a young woman, any young woman, as she walked along the bike track that runs alongside the Flora and Fauna Reserve in nearby Langwarrin, drag his victim into the reserve and murder her.

He had gone to his planned abduction spot earlier in the day and, with a pair of pliers, had cut three holes a few metres apart in the cyclone wire fence that ran between the bike track and the reserve. Each hole was cut big enough to fit him and his victim through into the cover of the tree-lined reserve.

At about 2.30 that afternoon, he drove back to the start of the bike track in Skye Road and waited for a victim to enter on foot. His plan was to follow his victim and, as they approached a hole in the fence, he would grab her and take her through it and into the reserve. He was armed with a razor-sharp home-made knife and a leather strap which he intended to use to strangle his victim.

After a wait of about 20 minutes, he saw a girl in a blue school uniform come out of the road where John Paul College was and enter the bike track. He followed.

'I stuck about 10 metres behind her until I got to the second hole,' Denyer told the detectives. 'And just when I got to that hole, I quickly walked up behind her and stuck my left hand around her mouth and held the knife to her throat . . . and that's where that cut happened.' Denyer then indicated the cut on his thumb from which the piece of skin was missing. 'I cut that on my own blade.'

Denyer said that Natalie was struggling at first when he grabbed her but stopped when he told her that if she didn't he would cut her throat. The terrified girl then offered Denyer sex, which disgusted him as he clearly failed to see that Natalie must have realised that she was in the hands of the Frankston Serial Killer and would have done anything, even if it meant having sex with him, to save her life.

'She said, "You can have all my money, have sex with me", and things – just said disgusting things like that, really,' Denyer told the detectives as he shook his head in revulsion at what he obviously interpreted as the schoolgirl's loose morals. Nothing could have been further from the truth.

Upset, Denyer forced Natalie to kneel in front of him and held the point of the knife very closely over her eye. Then he forced her to lie on the ground and he knelt over her, holding her by the throat and still holding the point of the knife over her eye. When she struggled he cut her across the face. She somehow managed to stand up and started to scream.

'And I just said, "Shut up. Shut up. Shut up. Shut up." And, "If you don't shut up, I'll kill you. If you don't do this, I'll kill you, if you don't do that,"' Denyer told the detectives. 'And she said, "What do you want from me?" I said, "All I want you to do is shut up." And so when she was kneeling on the ground, I put the strap around her neck to strangle her and it broke in half. And then she started violently struggling for about a minute until I pushed – got her onto her back again – and pushed her head back like this and cut her throat.'

Denyer then demonstrated how he held Natalie Russell's head back. 'I cut a small cut at first and then she was bleeding. And then I stuck my fingers into her throat . . . and grabbed her cords and I twisted them.'

The detectives could hardly believe what they were

hearing, but somehow managed to contain their abhorrence so that they could prompt him to continue with his confession of horror.

'Why'd you do that?'

'My whole fingers – like, that much of my hand was inside her throat,' Denyer said as he held up his hand, indicating exactly how much of it he had forced into the wound in the schoolgirl's throat.

'Do you know why you did that?' the detective asked again.

'Stop her from breathing . . . And then she slowly stopped. She sort of started to faint and then when she was weak, a bit weaker, I grabbed the opportunity of throwing her head back and one big large cut which sort of cut almost her whole head off. And then she slowly died.'

'Why did you kill her?' the shocked detectives asked, just managing to hold themselves back from being physically ill.

'Just same reason as before, just everything came back through my mind again. I kicked her before I left.'

Denyer then told the stunned detectives that he had kicked Natalie Russell's body to make sure she was dead, slashed her down the side of her face with his knife and left her where she lay. As he walked back the way he had come in, his blood-soaked hands concealed in his pockets, Denyer saw two uniformed officers taking details from the registration sticker on his car, so he turned around and walked home the other way.

At home, he washed his clothes and hid the murder weapon in his backyard. He later picked up Sharon from her work and spent a quiet evening with her at her mother's place.

The only emotion that Denyer had shown through the entire interview was when he was disgusted to think that the schoolgirl Natalie Russell would offer herself to him for sex. Outside of that it was almost as if he were proud of his achievements.

Then Denyer went on to confess to the slaughter of Donna's cats. He said that he had brought a knife that afternoon with the sole purpose of 'cutting Donna's throat' because he 'didn't like her'. When he found no-one at home after he entered through a window he vented his anger on her cats.

Denyer told the detectives that he had been stalking women in the Frankston area 'for years, just waiting for the right time, waiting for that silent alarm to trigger me off. Waiting for the sign.'

'Can you explain why we have women victims?' Detective O'Loughlin asked Denyer.

'I just hate 'em.'

'I beg your pardon?' said O'Loughlin.

'I just hate 'em,' Denyer repeated.

'Those particular girls,' asked O'Loughlin, in reference to Denyer's victims, 'or women in general?'

'General.'

It seemed that the only woman on earth that Denyer didn't hate was his lover Sharon Johnson, who had absolutely no knowledge of her de-facto's murderous activities. 'Sharon's not like anyone else I know. I'd never hurt her. She's a kindred spirit,' Denyer told the detectives.

Paul Charles Denyer was charged with the murders of Elizabeth Stevens, Debbie Fream and Natalie Russell and the attempted murder of Roszsa Toth, which was later changed to the lesser charge of abduction.

At his trial, held on 15 December 1993 before Justice Frank Vincent at the Supreme Court of Victoria, Paul Denyer pleaded guilty to all charges.

The court heard from clinical psychologist Ian Joblin, who had been appointed to examine Denyer in prison while he was awaiting sentence. Mr Joblin told the court that, in his view, Denyer showed no remorse whatever for his crimes. In fact, he revelled in telling of the murders and seemed as if he got pleasure recounting them. Denyer blamed a number of things that had happened in his life for leading him down the path to serial murder. He said that his hard upbringing, the alleged sexual abuse by his elder brother and his habitual unemployment were the major contributing factors that caused him to murder young girls.

But the psychologist did not accept the excuses. He said that thousands of people in the community lived under similar circumstances and none of them had resorted to serial murder. Mr Joblin told the court that of all of the adult offenders he had interviewed over the years – and there had been many – not one was even remotely close to the psychology of Paul Charles Denyer.

Mr Joblin told the hushed court that Paul Denyer was a very rare breed – a killer who murdered at random and without motive –

and this made him the most dangerous type of criminal. He said that Denyer had a cruel and demeaning nature. He had exhibited aggressive behaviour since childhood and he seemed to be amused by the suffering that he had inflicted.

Mr Joblin added that Paul Denyer was a sadist whose pleasure and satisfaction after each murder dissipated quickly so that he would again feel the desire to kill. In closing, he said that there was no effective treatment for Denyer's sadistic personality.

On 20 December 1993, Justice Vincent sentenced Paul Charles Denyer to three terms of life imprisonment with no fixed non-parole period. In other words, the Frankston Serial Killer would spend the rest of his life behind bars without ever the possibility of release. Justice Vincent also gave Denyer an additional eight years for the abduction of Roszsa Toth.

In conclusion, Justice Vincent said: 'The apprehension you have caused to thousands of women in the community will be felt for a long time. For many, you are the fear that quickens their step as they walk home, or causes a parent to look anxiously at the clock when a child is late.'

Paul Denyer appealed to the Full Court of the Supreme Court of Victoria against the severity of his sentence, and on 29 July 1994 he was granted a 30-year non-parole period, the equal-highest non-parole period ever imposed in Victoria. The other recipient was triple murderer Ashley Couston.

The families of Paul Denyer's victims felt cheated by the Supreme Court's decision, as they believed that the only possible sentence for Denyer was jail for life, never to be released. It seems that no-one would argue with that except the Supreme Court judges.

Only time will tell whether the Frankston Serial Killer will ever be allowed back into society.

AUTHOR'S NOTE: The full account of the Frankston serial killings is available in the meticulously researched *The Frankston Murders* by Vikki Petraitis.

CHAPTER 25

Scattered Remains, Splattered Brains

Mark Mala Valera
Wollongong, New South Wales, 1998–2000

The bloody murder scene that greeted police at the Albion Park house of David John O'Hearn on the Saturday morning of 13 June 1998 was shocking, even by crime-scene standards. The battered, decapitated, disembowelled body of the reclusive 59-year-old lying inert on the floor of the lounge room; the deep wounds to the torso; the hammer inserted into the anus; the word 'Satan' and occult symbols scrawled on the wall in the deceased's blood . . . It's little wonder that authorities described what they were confronted with as being 'gruesome in the extreme'.

Leaving the police even more mystified was the fact that the quiet shopkeeper lived alone and wasn't known to have any enemies. There wasn't a sniff of scandal about him that may have led to such a horrific demise. Neither was there any evidence to suggest that he had been involved with any people or groups that had connections with the occult or Satanism. As stories leaked out about what was discovered in the townhouse, the local community – situated 20 kilometres south-west of the coastal city of Wollongong – couldn't believe such a thing could happen in their area. Little did they know there were further horrors ahead.

A post-mortem on O'Hearn's body later indicated that the appalling mutilations had occurred after his death, and that the head had been the first body part to be removed. It also revealed that the skull had been severely fractured and that there were numerous lacerations to the scalp.

The police report told the whole story in detail. O'Hearn's severed left hand had been found on a chair in the lounge room,

not far from the body. His penis had been mutilated, and his head was sitting in the kitchen sink. Sections of intestine lay on the breakfast bar nearby. Near the body's feet rested a tray, silver in colour, upon which sat a section of bowel. Also on the floor were four knives and a variety of other sharp implements, including a corkscrew, razor blade and a small metal saw. Blood stained the carpet around the corpse and was splattered across the furniture and curtains. Covered in blood also, a heavy wine decanter sat on an equally gory lamp table.

Further investigation revealed that the body's abdomen had suffered deep incisions, with wounding evident from above the sternum along to the mid-point. There were also five intersecting and parallel incised wounds on the lower chest across both the left and right sides. Because O'Hearn was lying with his pants and underwear lowered to around his knees, the head of a hammer could be viewed sticking out of his anus, into which it had been inserted. Wounds to his abdomen revealed the hammer's shaft sticking up through the body.

The list of physical violations didn't stop there. The head had been badly battered, with severe injuries evident from the left ear and cheek across the mouth, nose, eyebrow and forehead over to the right side of the forehead and right ear, as well as the back and top of the head. The right side of the head showed a massive Y-shaped laceration, revealing the fractured skull beneath.

The physician who conducted the post-mortem, Dr Cala, found that the left eyeball had been depressed, the result of it being punctured by something sharp. His final verdict was that death had been caused by these numerous head injuries. He also stated that while it would have taken 10 to 12 blows to produce the lacerations observed on the cranium, it was entirely possible that there had been many more that hadn't produced obvious injuries. The force needed to produce the visible head trauma would have had to have been extreme to severe.

As well as all the external head injuries, Dr Cala found gross lacerations to the brain, which he determined were either caused by an implement directly penetrating it, or by pieces of fractured skull, or by the brain itself moving around in a concussive effect during the violent attack.

Adding to the nightmare the murder scene presented was the blood-scrawled writing on the walls, where the word 'Satan' was visible in the lounge room above the same sofa on which the police had found the victim's severed hand. Above that word was a pentagram (the five-pointed geometrical star often used in occult circles and common in the artwork of heavy metal groups), which had also been rendered in blood. Beside the television, an upside-down cross had been drawn in blood, and the word 'Satan' had been written again on a mirror above a table.

Confused and concerned by the intensity and ferocity of the attack, as well as its seemingly random nature, police were still attempting to find a lead among the many dead-ends in the O'Hearn case two weeks later. It was then, on 27 June, that the body of former Independent State Member and one-time Lord Mayor of Wollongong Frank Arkell was discovered in frighteningly similar circumstances at his Wollongong home.

Arkell had been in charge of the city's affairs for 17 years during his tenure as Lord Mayor, and was responsible for the slogan 'Wonderful Wollongong'; he was 68 years old. At the time of his brutal murder, he was living in a weatherboard house that had an adjoining garage, which had been converted into a granny flat. It was in this smaller dwelling that the wealthy local businessman's body was discovered, with its head lying in a dark pool of blood.

But unlike O'Hearn, who was thought to be an unassuming loner on whom no-one would wish harm, Arkell's story was very different indeed. When word spread through the local community that he, too, had been murdered, a common joke was that if the police were short of suspects, all they needed to do was open the phonebook and pick a page. There weren't many people who were fond of the former councilman.

At first though, Arkell had seemed like a picture-perfect Lord Mayor. Although he ruled the city with a population of 200,000 as if it was his and his alone, he went out of his way to attend as many civic functions as he could fit into his diary. Sporting events, weddings, funerals ... if he could press the flesh and make a show of himself by his presence, Arkell was there, smiling. Then, on Thursday nights, he would take himself to the

streets, meeting and greeting as many of his constituents as time allowed. With a photographic memory for names and faces, he portrayed himself as a friend to all, with nothing but a pleasant word to say about anyone he met.

But before too long, the whispers began – whispers that he was a predatory paedophile, preying on the region's young males – and they grew louder until they couldn't be ignored. With the rumours circulating ever wider, Arkell lost the state seat of Wollongong in 1991. Not long after that he was voted out from his position as Lord Mayor.

With his world in a spin, Arkell was linked to the local 'Gang of Four' paedophile ring and was said to be the group's lone surviving member. Others named as being involved in the circle's depravities included another former Wollongong Mayor, Tony Bevan, the alleged ringleader of the group who died of cancer in 1991. Catholic priest Brother Michael Evans was then found dead of carbon monoxide poisoning in his car at Rockhampton, Queensland, in 1994, just as investigators were seeking to question him about child-sex allegations. Another alleged member of the ring, one-time Wollongong councillor Brian William Tobin, 62, also gassed himself in his car, in April 1996.

Arkell had been named as a paedophile in 1994 in the NSW State Parliament by Deirdre Grusovin, MLC. Later, in 1996, while investigating police corruption and whether or not authorities had covered up or failed to investigate allegations of paedophilia, the Wood Royal Commission alleged that Arkell had committed sex acts with a 13-year-old boy in a Wollongong toilet block in the early 1970s; they further stated that he had driven to the encounter in his state-supplied car. On top of this, the commission alleged that Arkell had been supplied with teenage boys for the purpose of sex by Tony Bevan.

The accusations continued and, at the time of his murder, Arkell was on bail while waiting to go to trial for four charges involving the drugging and raping of a pair of teenage boys. The year before, he'd had 25 charges of sex offences dismissed at the committal hearing where the alleged drug charges arose. It's safe to say the former 'man of the people' was no longer popular with the general public. He was spat at in the street, and *W1, you are a wanker* was inked across the front brick fence of his house ('W1' being his code name in the Royal Commission).

Even after his death, he was still being pilloried, the *Daily Telegraph*'s Ray Chesterton devoting a particularly spiteful column to Arkell that concluded: *However violently Frank Arkell might have died on Saturday at the hands of an unknown intruder, it was not enough. Not nearly enough. We can only hope those last fleeting seconds of his putrid life were as psychically painful as the mental and emotional torment he imposed on boys for a long time. Hopefully, as his life ebbed away, Arkell came to realise how depraved and debauched his life had been and suffered a moment of contrition.*

And it wasn't just the big city newspapers that exposed Frank Arkell's crimes. The local *Illawarra Mercury* had already been openly campaigning against Arkell and the other Gang of Four members. With the last surviving member gone, they came out with an eight-page special titled 'The Arkell Murder Edition'. It told of Arkell's plans for the city while Lord Mayor, adding that such civic duties 'pale into insignificance in comparison to the other, dark side of his life'.

The most telling media indictment of the dead paedophile, though, came not from a journalist but from his victims. Taking the opportunity to speak out now that the predator could no longer harm him, one young man told the *Daily Telegraph* of the hell he had endured at the hands of Arkell from the age of seven: the man in question, who had since moved interstate, was repeatedly sexually abused by Arkell, a trusted family friend at the time, in the same room that Arkell would eventually meet his bloody demise. 'It's so fitting and so ironic that he should be killed in the same flat that has given me such horrific memories. I've been so happy all day since hearing about his death,' the victim revealed. 'I'm sure there's countless guys out there cheering with me today. In fact there's a part of me that could have done it [murdered Arkell] and there's a part of me there when it happened.'

Of course that young man was not 'there when it happened'. And police were still looking for clues as to who had been, as well as a link between Arkell and O'Hearn. Not only had both murders occurred in such a short time, but they were both incredibly violent.

The second body had been found clothed in tracksuit pants and a white singlet, and laid on its back with legs stretched out, on the floor beside the bed in the blood-splattered granny flat. Along with the blood covering the walls and sprayed densely across the ceiling, police noted that Arkell's head had suffered severe trauma. A large pool of blood had formed beneath it, and his face was stained heavily with blood.

A leather belt looped partially around his neck, along with the cord of a lamp. Three tie pins had been stuck into his face – one in the corner of the left eye, one through the right eyelid, the last into the left cheek. A splinter of timber was stuck in his neck, presumably from the same bloody wooden stake that lay on the bed. Next to the bed sat a busted-up wooden lamp stand that authorities surmised had been used in the attack, along with a heavy glass ashtray.

Indicating that the attack wasn't limited to the bedroom, there was also a lot of blood on the floor of the tiled bathroom. One of the few clues that the police had to go on was some items of clothing: two yellow Colorado hiking boots, a pair of Nike socks and some black tracksuit pants resting at the foot of the bed on the floor. All were drenched in blood, but as it transpired, none of the clothing belonged to Arkell.

Dr Cala, again performing the post-mortem duties, found 34 separate injuries to Arkell's head region, with lacerations ranging from the chin and left cheek and eyebrow, across the bridge of the nose to the right eyebrow, and up to the forehead. The body's left jugular vein had been punctured, the teeth had been fractured, so too the hyoid bone and sixth rib on the right side. Cala reported that Frank Arkell died from the combined effects of blunt and sharp force trauma to the neck, and ligature strangulation.

Only a dozen people attended Arkell's funeral, and although police checked them all, none could be tied to the case. Over the next few weeks, more young men came forward with sad stories of being abused by Arkell, but still the police had nothing definite to go on. Then, three months after the bloody scene at the former Lord Mayor's house had been discovered, 19-year-old

Mark Mala Valera walked into Wollongong Police Station out of the blue and confessed to the murders of both men. The former Planet Hollywood nightclub dishwasher said he was turning himself in because it 'seemed like the right thing to do'.

Stunned police officers listened as Valera told them he had never met David O'Hearn before the day of the first murder, and had only attacked him because he 'just wanted someone to kill'. He explained that his visit to O'Hearn's house was 'just random' (a term he would use several times when telling his story), without any forward planning, and that he had felt angry. Quite simply, Valera said, he had felt as if he could kill someone.

According to the statement Mark Valera made at the time, he gained access to the shopkeeper's residence by pretending he was looking for somewhere to live. 'I stayed at the door and asked if there was any, like . . . accommodation around,' he told the authorities. 'And the bloke said, "Come in and we'll talk about it."'

When it came time to talk about the slaying, Valera admitted that he had used the blood-smeared wine decanter found at the scene to beat O'Hearn about the head, counting the number of blows as he went. He hit the victim 10 times, checked his pulse, and reasoned that the man was obviously dead.

Valera then went upstairs to search for valuables before gathering the implements needed to dissect and mutilate the body. After he had used the various devices – the knives, saw and corkscrew found next to the body; the hammer found inside it – he used the severed hand to draw the Satanic symbol on the wall.

As the questioning continued, Valera maintained that he murdered David O'Hearn for no reason other than he felt angry enough to kill someone, but when it came to talking about the second victim, he changed his tune, explaining that he knew Frank Arkell's reputation as a paedophile. He called him a 'very, very horrible man'. After deciding he wanted to kill again, Valera told police, he chose Arkell as his victim. He then telephoned the older man and, pretending that he was gay, invited himself over to Arkell's house. Valera explained to the police several times that he went to the house with the sole intention of killing him, and he only spoke to Arkell for a few minutes after arriving at the granny flat before he attacked him, picking up the lamp and beating him on the head with it some 40 times. Arkell attempted to escape, crawling for his life across the floor, but Valera used the lamp's power cord to violently strangle the life out of the 68-year-old.

According to what he told the police, once he thought Arkell was dead, he kicked him in the face several times, before inserting the tie pins into his face. That done, Valera pushed a garden fork into the dead man's neck, but the wooden handle broke. Realising that his clothes were now covered in his victim's blood, Valera then removed them and found a pair of Arkell's tracksuit pants to wear home.

After providing these descriptions of the two murders, Valera repeated his claim that his reason for disliking the former Wollongong Lord Mayor was 'all the nasty things he has done to kids'. He'd heard all about Arkell, he admitted, from the reports in the press: 'I knew of him, I knew he was a paedophile. I knew it wasn't for me to take it into my hands but . . . I felt someone should've killed him [for] all the nasty things he's done to those kids.'

The police then went to Valera's flat in Wollongong, where they found a copy of the book *The A–Z Encyclopedia of Serial Killers*. Inside, the words 'Who will be my number three?' and 'The first one is always the best' were handwritten. Beneath the words were the names of Arkell and O'Hearn. Scarily, Valera asked for 'volunteers' to be his third victim. During the search of the unit, police also uncovered a disturbing, handwritten poem called 'Scattered Remains, Splattered Brains'. It was about a 'psychotic coroner' who cut out people's eyes after slicing up their bodies.

Charged with killing Frank Arkell and David O'Hearn, Mark Mala Valera was committed for trial in May 1999. Prosecutor Mr Ray Willis then went to some lengths to address the media to ensure it was clear that O'Hearn was in no way connected with Arkell or the paedophile's sexual preferences. He stated: 'The selection of David O'Hearn was an entirely random thing. [His] murder was not motivated by any sexual orientation he may have had, and indeed the defendant denied any knowledge of any sexual orientation. Apart from the fact that the prosecution alleges the defendant killed both men, there is no evidence that there was any connection between the murders, nor that there was any connection between the two deceased.'

Beginning on 12 July 2000, the trial was held in the NSW Supreme Court in Wollongong with Justice Timothy Studdart presiding. Valera, who was also known as Mark Van Krevel, pleaded not guilty to the two murders, but guilty to lesser charges of two counts of manslaughter. His mother, Elizabeth Carroll, attended the sessions every day.

Valera's defence counsel, Mr John Nicholson, contended that his client had suffered post-traumatic stress caused by years of physical, mental and alleged sexual abuse by his father, Jack Van Krevel. Nicholson added that when Valera killed his victims he was confused, believing he was murdering his abusive father. According to Nicholson, his client was suffering from a 'substantial impairment' and lost control when each of the victims asked him to become an active partner in anal sex. The defence went on to assert that three separate forces were at play with Valera when he killed his victims: the anger and frustration he felt in dealing with homosexuality; loathing for his father, who he alleged physically and sexually abused him from the age of seven; and the impact and interest he had in 'things Satanic'.

It came out during the trial that Valera had been born Mark Van Krevel on 24 April 1979. His mother left the family two or three years later, and Valera's earliest memory was of his father throwing him into a toy box at the age of six or seven. Another memory he had was of Jack Van Krevel threatening to shoot him and holding a loaded rifle to his head. Valera is said to have wet his pants on that and other occasions, out of the fear of what his father could do. According to Nicholson, Valera was kicked and punched by Van Krevel a few times a week until the accused turned 15. At that point the alleged violence diminished but didn't stop completely until Valera turned 17. The final incident saw Valera having to attend hospital after being punched in the face by his father.

Besides the physical abuse, the court also heard that Van Krevel allegedly began sexually abusing his son when the boy was seven, with the first incidents involving the father fondling his

son's penis and digitally penetrating him. Later, the abuse escalated to include mutual oral sex and Valera being forced to
masturbate Van Krevel. From there, Nicholson alleged, Valera
was regularly sexually assaulted by Van Krevel, with the incidents
now including the father forcing him to submit to anal sex at least
20 times in four years, as well as masturbate him and perform oral
sex. When Valera was 12 he was allegedly made to perform anal
sex on Van Krevel.

When Valera turned 18, he left home in an effort to distance
himself from the abuse, and moved in with a mate from school
named Keith Schreiber. It was at this point that he changed his
name by deed poll from Van Krevel to Valera.

When it came time for Mark Valera to step up to the witness
box he admitted that he had lied in his police statement: he had
met Arkell before the murder. Indeed, he had been a casual sexual partner of the older man for more than 12 months. According
to what he told the court, Valera was 'put on the spot' by Arkell
the night he murdered him. Arkell's request for Valera to be the
active member of their sexual relationship reminded Valera of the
abuse, both physical and sexual, that his father had meted out.

Again contradicting his earlier statements to the police,
Valera then admitted to previously knowing David O'Hearn also,
and said that he had been at the quiet shop-owner's Dapto store
on 12 June 1998. He also alleged that O'Hearn had masturbated
him in a closet there at the time and invited him to his home that
night. He said that the reason he killed O'Hearn, too, was
because he had put him 'on the spot'.

Valera told the jury that he had arrived at O'Hearn's house at
around 6 p.m. on the night of the murder. They proceeded to watch
a pornographic film together, but after about a quarter of an hour
O'Hearn moved to the floor and asked Valera to have sex with him.
Valera continued: 'That's when I grabbed the wine decanter and
whacked him over the head with it. I felt like I was put right on the
spot and I was there and there was no way out of it.'

Next to take the stand after Valera's testimony was his
father, Jack Van Krevel. Despite rigorous questioning, he strongly
denied ever having sexually assaulted his son. He did, however,
admit that he was a violent man with a short temper. A carpenter

by trade, Van Krevel said that his wife's desertion was one result of his physical attacks upon his son, whom he admitted to hitting, punching and kicking, as well as throwing a spanner at on one occasion. On top of all this, he had verbally abused Valera and teased him openly about his slow speech habits.

Following his father, Valera's sister Belinda Van Krevel took the stand. Some 18 months older than the accused, Belinda said she had never witnessed her father actually physically abusing her brother. She did, however, tell the court that Van Krevel would often read her bedtime stories from the age of 13 onwards while wearing nothing but his dressing gown, and that he would then go down to her brother Mark's room and close the door behind him.

Speaking for the prosecution, Mr Paul Conlon told of a conversation between a Crown witness and Mark Valera after the murders of O'Hearn and Arkell, in which Valera allegedly talked about plans to make his father his third murder victim and added, 'I haven't finished my journey yet.'

The trial drew to a close on 8 August 2000, when Mark Mala Valera was found guilty of the murders of Frank Arkell and David O'Hearn, though his sentence wasn't scheduled to be handed down until some four months later.

Elizabeth Carroll had an emotional outburst as Valera was led away, breaking down and crying: 'That's my son. I gave birth to him. It's not fair – his father did this to him.' Trying to comfort her, Valera replied, 'Don't worry about it. Paedophiles always get away with it.'

This, however, was not the end of the story. Just 10 days after Mark Valera was found guilty of double murder, Jack Van Krevel was found dead, his body butchered and mutilated until it was almost unrecognisable. Hacked at with an axe and stabbed from top to toe, blood splattered the room of his home where his body lay. His daughter, Belinda Van Krevel, arrived at the police station at 3 a.m. on 18 August, explaining that she had found her father's dead body.

Thankfully, the authorities didn't have to spend long investigating the third murder, as later that day Valera's friend and flatmate Keith Andrew Schreiber turned himself in, openly confessing to the crime.

Schreiber was already known by police and mental health workers. With a history of low self-esteem, the result of a lifetime of being bullied and neglected, the 21-year-old already had a juvenile record, having held up the Albion Park railway service station with a samurai sword. A year earlier, a local mental health crisis team had interviewed him after he admitted to thinking about killing himself and others. It was also known that Schreiber had a keen interest in the dark side having been named as an occultist in Valera's trial.

Although he had allegedly said in a tendered police record of interview that he had killed Van Krevel as revenge for Valera and Belinda Van Krevel, Schreiber pleaded not guilty to murder at his committal hearing on 28 November 2000. One of the biggest shocks of the trial, however, was the news that just four days before his murder, Jack Van Krevel was tipped off about an allegation that his daughter had taken a contract out on his life. According to a police brief of evidence, Van Krevel was supposedly told the news by his ex-wife, who said Belinda was saving her unemployment benefits for the contract, and when she had $32,000 put away, Schreiber would carry out the murder.

The court was then told that Schreiber attacked the sleeping Van Krevel with a tomahawk and a knife. He also attempted to cut his friend's father's heart out before beating him over and over again with a fire stoker until he heard the older man's backbone snap. As a result of the evidence, Keith Schreiber was committed for trial on murder.

Less than a month later, on 21 December 2000, Valera fronted up for sentencing at the NSW Supreme Court in front of Justice Timothy Studdart. He received two terms of life in jail without the possibility of parole, giving him the dubious distinction of becoming the third youngest prisoner in Australia to be incarcerated for life, never to be released. In summation, Justice Studdart told the court: 'David O'Hearn was subjected to the most savage attack, and I am satisfied beyond reasonable doubt that the prisoner acted in such attack with intent to kill and that it was a random and utterly senseless killing. The way in which the prisoner mutilated the body of this victim showed his utter contempt for his victim and so too did his use of the severed hand

and his writings on the wall and on the mirror. Indeed, this first crime scene exuded evil of the prisoner's making. Francis Arkell was likewise subjected to the most brutal attack, and again I am satisfied beyond reasonable doubt that the prisoner conducted the attack with intent to kill. The prisoner sought to explain, and indeed to justify, his attack upon an adverse judgment he had formed of his second victim.'

Schreiber's trial commenced on 1 March 2001. He pleaded guilty to the murder of Jack Van Krevel, explaining that he had entered the house through a window that had been purposely left open for him by Belinda Van Krevel, who it was revealed was his lover. Schreiber then said that his victim woke during the attack and recognised him, calling out 'Keith!' as Schreiber stabbed him more than 50 times in the head, neck and body. Schreiber claimed he was there to 'deliver' Van Krevel and 'assist his destiny'.

'I just wanted it to be quick,' he told the court. '[I said], "Die you fucker, hurry up and fucking die." He rolled off and was going, "Hey, hey, hey . . ." I got him a few more times . . . the fucking prick wouldn't die . . . resilient bastard. I said to him, "This is from Mark, you fucking paedophile bastard. You'll never molest kids again."'

Schreiber then told the court that he first met Valera (then known as Mark Van Krevel, of course) while the pair were still at school, bonding over their mutual interests in the devil and dismemberment. They eventually moved in together, and spent most of their time discussing death.

Having been found guilty of the brutal slaying, Schreiber's sentencing hearing began on 11 May. The court was told that Belinda Van Krevel may have solicited her boyfriend into murdering her father. The story went that the day prior to the killing the pair spent time together shopping for the black leather gloves Schreiber wore during the frenzied attack.

With that evidence, on 1 June 2001, Belinda was charged with the murder of her father. She was 20 years old at the time. Her committal hearing took place at Wollongong Local Court, where it was claimed Belinda was a single mother who had a $1000-a-week drug habit. A police statement said she had gone to 'extreme lengths' to interfere in the investigation into her father's murder, including death threats and soliciting people to kill witnesses. The authorities alleged that Belinda Van Krevel hated her father with a passion and had asked more than one person to kill him. They also said that Belinda waited in her room while Schreiber killed Jack Van Krevel. Once the sounds of the struggle abated, a blood-covered Schreiber opened her door and said, 'Hey babe, it's finished.'

The police also presented electronic surveillance and witness statements identifying Belinda as she offered $2000 and a car to have witnesses in the case – including her own mother – killed or injured to keep her own involvement in her father's death secret. Belinda was eventually committed for trial for murder and soliciting Schreiber into the slaying.

Keith Schreiber's sentencing took place at the NSW Supreme Court on 19 December 2001. Presiding over the case was Justice Peter Hidden, who explained that Schreiber had been sexually assaulted by a teacher while still in primary school. Schreiber blamed himself for the divorce of his parents when he was 12, and both of his parents' new partners are said to have made the boy feel unwelcome. As a result, Schreiber grew increasingly dependent on the friendship of Mark Valera, as well as his relationship with Belinda Van Krevel, who Justice Hidden described as 'a malign influence'.

Justice Hidden continued: 'Whatever her role might have been, I am satisfied that to a significant degree the offender's actions were the result of her influence.' Schreiber was then sentenced to 16 years in jail with a 12-year non-parole period – meaning he can apply for probation in August 2012.

Belinda Van Krevel pleaded not guilty to the charges of murder and soliciting when she faced the Sydney Supreme Court on 23 July 2002. She said that she and her three-year-old daughter awoke on the night of the slaughter to the sound of someone repeatedly striking Krevel about the head and neck with a tomahawk. She heard him moaning and her young daughter questioned her about the sounds.

The court also heard that after the noises finally finished, Keith Schreiber entered her room to tell Belinda her father was dead, leaving a bloody handprint on the door. Schreiber, Belinda and her daughter then allegedly watched television and snacked on Vegemite sandwiches before Belinda went to the police station to report the murder, telling them she believed an intruder had been responsible for the killing.

With too much strong evidence against her, Belinda Van Krevel eventually pleaded guilty to the lesser charge of soliciting the murder of her father. On 4 April 2003, she was sentenced to six years in prison. She is now eligible for parole.

For perpetrating two of the most evil murders in Australia's history, Mark Mala Valera will die in jail. And although he was never charged in connection with the death of his father there is little doubt that from his jail cell he instigated his friend to commit another murder equally as horrific.

AUTHOR'S NOTE: It could be said that Mark Valera's two murders don't qualify him for inclusion in this book on serial killers, given that the accepted criterion is a minimum of three killings (see Introduction). But, as is the case of two other chapters here – those on Barry Gordon Hadlow and Peter Norris Dupas – I believe that there are exceptions to the rule. To my mind Valera's terrible crimes and the fact that he was also a major instigator in the murder of his own father in an almost identical fashion more than qualify him as a serial killer.

CHAPTER 26

The Wagga Serial Killer

Matthew James Harris
Wagga Wagga, New South Wales, 1998

There were emotional scenes in the Wagga Wagga Local Court in rural New South Wales when, on 7 December 1998, the man accused of murdering three local residents appeared in the dock. A relative of one of the victims drew his finger across his throat in a grim warning to the 30-year-old accused, local bus driver Matthew James Harris. Police officers were strategically positioned about the packed courtroom in the event of trouble. Emotions were running high. Serial murder had come to Wagga and the locals didn't like it one bit.

The accused, dressed in a white shirt and dark pants, sat quietly while a distraught female friend tried to catch his eye as she mouthed the words 'I love you' to him in the dock. But the prisoner's head was down and he only looked up when the police prosecutor told the magistrate that the prisoner had admitted to the three murders.

Harris, a regular heroin user, had confessed to the strangling murders of his 62-year-old neighbour, Peter Wennerbom, on 4 October 1998; a 30-year-old bus passenger, Yvonne Ford, on 17 October; and another neighbour, Ronald Edward Galvin, who went missing on Melbourne Cup Day. All of the victims were disabled pensioners.

The court heard that Yvonne Ford's body was found in the bath of her premises. Mr Galvin's badly decomposed body was found in bushland by a man walking his dog on the day that Harris was arrested, and Mr Wennerbom's remains were found in his home, just a few hundred metres from where Harris lived. All of the victims were known to Harris as passengers through his job driving for the Wagga Wagga Community

Transport Service for incapacitated and disabled local residents.

Harris was arrested in Sydney after he made a phone call to a local Wagga resident and confessed to her that he had murdered the three victims and robbed them for money to buy drugs. Harris was arrested at 4.35 a.m. on 1 December 1998 in Sydney's notorious Kings Cross after the woman he had confessed to went to the police; the Wagga police then notified Sydney detectives, who picked Harris up as soon as he was located.

Harris was remanded at the Wagga Local Court to stand trial in the NSW Supreme Court. At the trial, held in March 2000, Harris pleaded guilty to three counts of murder and was bound over for sentencing. On the eve of his sentencing, the local WIN Television network broadcast a taped police interview with Harris that provided a chilling insight into the motive for the killings.

'To me, I think of it as an achievement, because I have achieved absolutely nothing in my lifetime,' Harris said. 'And to murder, and to keep murdering and to get away with it, was an achievement. But at the point of killing these people I didn't care. I just thought I'd keep going and going, and obviously I was going to get caught – and I was caught – but I just kept going.

'The first one was like just a one-off. It wasn't an accident . . . I just wanted to kill somebody, basically. I just wanted to kill someone. And I got away with it and I thought, Well, why not go again? And I go again and I got away with that one. And I went again and I got away with that one . . . I'd still be going if I hadn't been caught.'

WIN Television also reported that police raids on Harris's home uncovered a number of books about serial killers, including one on Australia's most notorious serial killer, Ivan Milat. During the taped police interview Harris said: 'The Ivan Milat book was an all right book. I don't know . . . if I had to say one book, I'd say Ivan Milat's book wasn't an influence but it was a good read and it sort of sparked something off in me.'

In her summing up prior to sentencing Harris in the NSW Supreme Court, on 7 April 2000, Justice Virginia Bell told the court that Harris had experienced a 'significant level' of emotional deprivation and rejection, and that his 'unfortunate background was causative in the commission of these offences'.

Justice Bell told the court that Harris believed his adoptive parents treated him differently from their natural children and he left home at age 14 to live on the streets, prostituted himself and became a heroin user. She said that his lifestyle led to feelings of debasement and worthlessness.

When Harris was later reunited with his natural mother, the meeting lasted less than four minutes, with her saying she had given him up at birth and wanted nothing to do with him. Around the time of his 30th birthday, Harris became overwhelmed by feelings of depression because he had achieved nothing with his life.

Justice Bell said that Harris had participated in an armed robbery with another man, forcing their way into a woman's unit and holding a knife to her throat as her children looked on. 'This ugly crime seemed to mark [Harris's] degeneration,' Justice Bell continued. 'In six weeks he strangled three people in separate incidents. Emboldened by the armed robbery Harris went to the unit of Mr Wennerbom, whom he knew was ill and affected by a stroke, with the intention of robbing him, but then strangled him to avoid detection.

'After getting away with Mr Wennerbom's murder Harris continued carrying out "opportunistic killings",' Justice Bell said. 'He strangled Ms Ford, who had a mild intellectual disability, after convincing her to get into her bath, and got in with her saying he would rub her neck. Harris told police he strangled Ms Ford because he believed she would be easy to kill.

'Harris then strangled his immediate neighbour in the unit block he lived in, Ron Galvin, who was physically disabled. After Mr Galvin's "senseless killing", Harris attempted to kill himself twice with heroin overdoses. Harris admitted to police [that he'd] murdering the three after confessing to a friend, Mr Wennerbom's sister, that he had strangled Mr Galvin,' Justice Bell concluded.

In sentencing Harris to a minimum of 25 years' imprisonment, Justice Bell said that the prisoner's admissions were significant and he was not entirely without hope of rehabilitation. But the locals were far from impressed with the judge's decision. It only worked out at 8.3 years for a human life, and that wasn't enough. Along with the families of the victims, the citizens of

Wagga campaigned long and hard to have Justice Bell's sentence overthrown and a longer sentence imposed. They wanted the maximum – life without parole.

The Crown agreed and appealed the leniency of the sentence. Three days before Christmas in 2000, the NSW Court of Criminal Appeal, consisting of Justice Roger Giles, Justice James Wood and Justice Bruce James, unanimously agreed that Justice Bell had failed to give due recognition to the degree of heinousness involved in the murders, and sentenced Matthew James Harris to life imprisonment.

And in New South Wales, life means life. There is no possibility of parole. The Wagga Serial Killer will die in jail. And given the nature of his despicable crimes against three of their less fortunate citizens, the residents of Wagga agree that that is fair justice.

CHAPTER 27

Lennie the Loon

Leonard John Fraser
Rockhampton, Queensland, 1998–99

There were no obvious indicators in the early childhood of Lennie Fraser to suggest he would grow up to become one of this country's most vicious rapists and serial killers. Nor that he would be involved in one of Australia's most high-profile missing persons cases after Natasha Ryan, a Queensland teenager whom he had boasted of murdering, turned up alive during his subsequent murder trial. Missing for four-and-a-half years and presumed dead, it turned out that Natasha, by then 18, had been hiding out with her boyfriend, and that Fraser had been lying about murdering her. Unfortunately, that wasn't the case of at least three other female victims.

The second youngest of four children, Leonard John Fraser was born on 27 June 1951 in Ingham, a north Queensland sugar-growing community. When he was six years old the family moved to Mount Druitt, an outer-west suburb of Sydney. A slow learner, Fraser didn't exactly excel at studies, and he dropped out in his second year of high school at the age of 14. He could only read a bit by then and he even had difficulty writing his own name.

Fraser was incarcerated for the first time at the age of 15, when he was sent to Gosford Boys Home for a year for stealing. It was far from the last time he would find himself locked up. By the time he was eventually sent to prison for life on 7 September 2000 for abducting, raping and murdering a nine-year-old girl, Fraser had spent almost 20 of the previous 22 years in prison.

Fresh from his release from the boys home, he was quick to return to a life of violence and crime, receiving a two-year bond for assaulting a railway guard. Before long he found himself serving 12 months' hard labour for offensive behaviour as well as stealing cars and driving without a licence. After that stretch, Fraser had been out of prison for just six months when he was found guilty of transporting stolen goods into Queensland, a crime for which he received another two years' probation. And it was only five weeks later that he found himself in a Townsville jail for two weeks on stealing offences.

Moving to Sydney after his release, he was fined $100 in 1972 for living off the earnings of prostitution. A series of robberies later that year saw him receive five years' hard labour in Long Bay Jail. But two months before that stint, Fraser had committed the first of what would become a long run of violent rapes, assaulting a 37-year-old French tourist in Sydney's Botanical Gardens in broad daylight. Police, however, would not learn of this crime until Fraser confessed to it sometime later. By then, Fraser had become a serial rapist.

Three weeks after he was released from Long Bay, he attacked a young married woman from behind as she made her way along a street in the suburb of St Marys in Sydney's outer west. It was 10 a.m. on 11 July 1974 when Fraser twisted the woman's arm up behind her back (this would become a recurring signature in his attacks) and dragged her down an embankment before sexually abusing her. Disturbingly, Fraser seemed to be under the misapprehension that the woman had enjoyed the experience and he held her hand as if they were lovers while walking her back up to the road before making his escape.

Fraser only waited six days before attempting to rape another woman. This victim was a 20-year-old who was working alone in a dry-cleaners at Mount Druitt. When she went to look for clothes that Fraser claimed he was there to pick up, he followed her behind the shop's counter and twisted her hand up behind her back. Luckily for the young woman, some other customers entered the shop at that time, and Fraser made a hasty retreat.

Just three days later Fraser tried to force himself on a woman again, this time in nearby Rooty Hill, where he spoke to a young lady for a short time while she was walking along a quiet street. Fraser then punched her in the face before twisting her hand up behind her back. As he forced her towards a small creek, the woman bravely pretended that she was actually feeling like having sex and said she would willingly make love to Fraser if they instead went to his house and did it in bed. No doubt excited, Fraser held hands with the woman as they walked back up to the road – where she managed to escape by running to the nearest house for help.

The authorities had little trouble finding Leonard Fraser, as he had left his wallet containing his birth certificate at his last attack. He was soon taken into custody, where he admitted to the rape and two attempted attacks, although he held the deluded belief that the woman in the dry-cleaners would have been willing to submit to his advances had they not been interrupted by the other customers. 'I would not have had to force her,' he told the police. 'She was just about to come across.'

Then, to the detectives' surprise, and without any prompting, Fraser confessed in detail about raping his first victim, two years earlier. 'I don't know what came over me ... I have always regretted it,' he said, filling in the details of the attack on the French woman who had been visiting Sydney with her husband and two baby daughters.

The woman had been walking alone through the Botanical Gardens at 10 a.m. when Fraser stepped out from behind a group of banana trees and placed his arm around her neck from behind. He then proceeded to punch her in the face several times before dragging her back behind the trees and sexually abusing her. It was only after a person walking by interrupted him that Fraser ran off with the woman's handbag. His distraught victim was left semi-conscious and suffering from multiple fractures to her face as well as severe shock.

When later interviewed by a psychiatrist, Fraser explained that at the time he raped the French tourist, he had been living off the proceeds of a number of Kings Cross prostitutes, and he claimed he handed the majority of the money over to a 'minder'. He added that he had not engaged in sexual relations with any of the prostitutes, although he'd had several homosexual relationships. He also told the psychiatrist that his biggest ambition in life was to become a member of the Hell's Angels motorcycle club, and that he hated his parents and didn't want to ever see his brothers or sisters again.

Fraser pleaded guilty to two counts of attempted rape and two counts of rape at the Sydney District Court in December of 1974. According to the court psychiatrist, there was no way to help the violent rapist. The expert explained: 'He has no conscience at all. He will use anyone and anything to his advantage without giving a lot of thought to other people's feelings. He has little or no impulse control. Apart from this, there is no real psychiatric disability – there is no known treatment for this type of psychopathic state.'

The judge then sentenced Fraser to the maximum of 22 years in jail with a non-parole period of seven, adding, 'I wish to make it clear in doing so that I am not in any way suggesting that you should be released at the end of the period.'

Fraser's mother was in the room when the sentence was read out. She later told the *Sydney Morning Herald* newspaper: 'I have abandoned him as my son. I know it is a terrible thing to say, but I can rest when he is inside. I go to bed at night and when I hear news of an assault or robbery, I know it will not be Lennie.'

Despite the judge's reservations, Fraser was released from jail in 1981 having served the minimum time of seven years. He then moved north to Mackay in Queensland, where he found work as a labourer. The next year he again attacked a woman, entering her house by feigning interest in a car she had for sale. Once inside the house, Fraser grabbed her from behind, employing his signature move by twisting her arm up behind her back. Bizarrely though, the woman convinced Fraser to let her call her husband during the attack. While the man was on the line, Fraser grabbed the phone from his victim and told her spouse: 'I hope you're not going to kill me. I just wanted to prove a point that somebody could break in and rape your missus.' The incident led to Fraser receiving a two-month jail sentence for aggravated assault.

Settling back in Mackay after his release, Fraser began living with a woman and her son in a house converted into flats. He had a daughter with the woman and kept his job as a labourer for two-and-a-half years before his violent, antisocial urges resurfaced in late 1985.

Fraser stalked his next victim, a 21-year-old woman, for a

number of days while she took walks at a quiet beach at Shoal Point, to the north of Mackay. He eventually committed a savage rape on her in broad daylight using his regular method – attacking her from behind and forcing her arm up behind her back. Police had little trouble identifying Fraser as the attacker and he was soon sentenced to 12 years in prison. Critical of Fraser's belief that his female victims wanted or even enjoyed his violent advances, Justice Derrington said that he believed Fraser to be a danger to society, stating: 'They [the victims] would regard you as being the equivalent of a filthy animal. It [rape] is one of the worst forms of degradation on another human being you can think of and it deserves no sympathy whatever.'

Fraser served his time at Etna Creek Prison in Rockhampton, Queensland, earning the nickname 'Lennie the Loon' because of an erratic and unpredictable nature that would see him erupt into violence for no reason. As a result, other inmates steered well clear of him.

Once he had served the entire 12 years, Fraser moved to the coastal town of Yeppoon near Mackay and, in January 1997, he settled with a terminally ill woman with whom he had corresponded while in prison and who had regularly visited him. The relationship became sexual and Fraser grew more aggressive as time went on. At one point the woman had to go to Brisbane for cancer treatment, and Fraser followed her; when the woman refused to return to Yeppoon with him, he allegedly raped her. She died just six months later and Fraser moved to Mount Morgan, a small mining town (population 3500 at the time) near Rockhampton.

It wasn't long before Fraser again came to the attention of the local authorities, with an intellectually disabled woman complaining to police that he had bothered her on a bus. Disturbingly, Fraser could also often be found waiting at the gate of the local school, trying to talk to any female no matter how young or old they were. He also looked for women at employment agencies that dealt with intellectually handicapped clients, and earned spare money mowing lawns and driving children to school.

He moved to the larger town of Rockhampton in late 1998 and settled into a flat with an intellectually handicapped 19-year-old named Cristine Wraight. A woman with an 11-year-old daughter joined them in the flat to ease costs in April 1999 but soon moved out, accusing Fraser of interfering with the child. Fraser himself was asked to move out of the building when the landlady later saw him in the backyard having sex with Wraight's blue heeler cattle dog. Some weeks after that, the dog was found dead. It had ingested rat poison. Fraser's career of violence was also about to escalate.

Keyra Steinhardt was just nine years old when she disappeared on the way home from school on 22 April 1999. She was taking a shortcut through a vacant lot at the time. Lynette Kiernan lived opposite the lot and later told authorities that she had seen a man approach the child from behind and hit her. When the young girl fell into some long grass, Lynette lost sight of her, though she saw the man lower himself to the ground and move his body as if he were committing a rape.

The man then ran away but soon returned with a car. He picked up the nine-year-old, placed her in the boot of the automobile and drove off. Unfortunately, a frightened Lynette waited 20 minutes before reporting the attack to the authorities via an anonymous phone call. By that time young Keyra was dead, her small body already disposed of.

Fraser was picked up by police the next day. They found him through Lynette's description of his red Mazda 626. It took two weeks, however, before he would confess to the murder and lead detectives to where he had dumped Keyra's naked body near the local Rockhampton horse-racing track. The young girl's throat was cut and her green school jumper was placed over her body.

Police questioned Cristine Wraight, who told them she had gone on a drive with Fraser on the day Keyra had gone missing. While heading down a bush track near the racecourse, Fraser stopped the car, got out and told her not to look at what he was doing. She then saw him take out of the car's boot what appeared to be a blonde doll in a green uniform. When Fraser noticed that she had been looking at his actions, he dropped his bundle and ran over to punch the intellectually handicapped woman though the car window; he then went back about his business while Cristine stared straight ahead. Back at home that night, Fraser went to great lengths to clean out the boot of his car.

Still, the police managed to retrieve blood and hair samples from the Mazda, and DNA tests proved they belonged to Keyra. They also found the blood of another female on the hinge of the boot and a cigarette paper in the glovebox.

Leonard Fraser was officially charged with raping and murdering Keyra Steinhardt in September 2000. He pleaded not guilty. Prosecutor Paul Rutledge told Brisbane Supreme Court that Fraser attacked the schoolgirl for his own sexual pleasure and nothing else. 'Why did he follow a nine-year-old into the allotment and hit her so hard she dropped to the ground? Why did he strip her naked?' the prosecutor asked rhetorically.

Lynette Kiernan testified that she had also seen Fraser standing next to Keyra at a set of traffic lights the day before she was murdered.

The court then heard the horrible details of Fraser's attack, and how the rapist had hidden the young child's naked body behind a tree and thrown away her school bag once he had finished violating her. It was also said that because her body had badly decomposed in the two weeks between the murder and its discovery, it wasn't possible to prove the cause of death or even that she had definitely been sexually assaulted. Still, the authorities had a recent tape recording of Fraser talking to another prisoner while incarcerated at Rockhampton. On the tape he could be heard asking the other man if he could get rid of a knife stashed at his apartment. The prosecutor explained that the knife in question was the one that Fraser had used to stab into the neck and upper body of Keyra Steinhardt.

For his part, Fraser remained silent during the trial, except to strongly deny any involvement with the young girl or that he was even near the vacant lot on the day she disappeared. This, however, went against what he had told police on the day he'd originally been charged. Back then he had offered an apology of sorts to the child's parents, saying: 'I'd like to say to her mother and father, and I know a lot of people won't believe me but, if you check my background, it's not my go to harm a child. I'm just sorry this is happening and I don't know what made me do it; at least I can try to . . . I'm going to try and get help after I get sentenced and all, so that's a good step.'

With so much evidence against him, it was unsurprising that Fraser was found guilty of abducting and killing Keyra Steinhardt. At his sentencing, on 9 November 2000, the judge spoke out against the crime and the man who committed the horrible act. 'Lone females in a public place, as is present in this case, were compelled by force and threats to go to a place where the risk of disturbance was less,' Justice Ken Mackenzie said. 'The offence involved severe, indeed extreme, violence on a child. Fraser's story is that of a sexual predator of the worst kind.'

Seeing no reason to believe a habitual re-offender like Fraser could ever be rehabilitated, the judge proceeded to sentence him to an indefinite life sentence, effectively meaning he will remain locked up for the rest of his days. Also, now that the authorities had Fraser behind bars, they could question him about other cases they believed him to be involved with – namely the murders of schoolgirl Natasha Ryan and three other women who had all gone missing in or around Rockhampton between September 1998 and April 1999.

Natasha Ryan disappeared in the same area where Keyra Steinhardt had been murdered. She had been on her way to a north Rockhampton school on 2 September 1998. Of the missing women, the first, 39-year-old Julie Dawn Turner, had briefly worked with Fraser at the local abattoir. She had left a Rockhampton nightclub in the early hours of the morning of 28 December; believed to be drunk and broke, she reportedly asked several people for a cab fare but ended up walking home. She was never seen again. Before she disappeared, however, she had told associates she intended to move in with a man named Lennie.

The second of the missing women, 36-year-old Beverly Doreen Leggo, met Fraser at a hostel in Mount Morgan where he had been staying back in 1997. Her last reported sighting had been at a bank near Rockhampton's East Street Mall on 1 March 1999.

The final missing woman that police believed Fraser had been involved with was 19-year-old Sylvia Maria Benedetti, who disappeared on 17 April that year. It was six days after that, while they were looking for the body of young Keyra Steinhardt, that police were tipped off to the gruesome discovery a group of wreckers had made at the derelict Queensland Hotel. In room 13 of the ramshackle building they found blood sprayed across the floor, walls and ceiling. Bone fragments littered the carpet, and a pair of shoes sat in filthy water in a downstairs freezer.

When forensics tests revealed the blood to be human, police suspected it was Sylvia Benedetti's. They also believed they had a serial killer on their hands. The attack on the teenager had been so severe that she'd lost around 4 litres of blood, a lot of which was trapped in the room's soggy carpet. Four litres would have been about all the blood a body the size of Sylvia's could hold. It was thought the victim was known to Fraser, and she had been seen with him the night prior to her disappearance. Through DNA testing, police were also able to match the blood found in the hotel's dingy room with samples found in Fraser's boot.

Still, even though the authorities were convinced Leonard Fraser was responsible for four more murders, without the bodies or a confession there was nothing anyone could do. Then they got the break they so desperately needed – when Fraser began to talk to his cell-mate Allan Quinn, telling him openly about the horrifically violent crimes. Quinn, a fraudster, was appalled at what he heard and went to the police.

'What I have gone through has caused me to kill these people,' Fraser allegedly told Quinn. 'All the hate over the years came to the fore and ended with the murder of the people.'

Police later confronted Fraser about the supposed confessions and he offered to lead detectives to the hidden bodies. An elaborate and secret operation was set up in December 2000 whereby Fraser was taken in the Queensland Premier's private jet to Rockhampton, where he was covertly taped leading investigators to the remains of Beverly Leggo and Julie Turner. The partial remains of Sylvia Benedetti had already been discovered in an area of bushland near Sandy Point Beach, but Fraser claimed he wasn't able to direct them to the rest of her body. Despite this, police believed they had enough evidence on hand to charge the rapist and murderer with the further offences.

Come April 2003, Fraser found himself facing Mr Justice Brian Ambrose in Brisbane Supreme Court, where he pleaded not guilty to the murders of Natasha Ryan, Julie Turner, Beverly

Leggo and Sylvia Benedetti. Prosecutor Paul Rutledge then told the jury about Fraser's boast to cell-mate Allan Quinn that he had murdered young Natasha Ryan because she was pregnant by him, knifing her and dumping her body in a grave on a property near Rockhampton. He told Quinn that after he'd killed Benedetti he 'bled her like an animal' in the derelict hotel before making a bloody mark with his hand on the wall and smearing it. As for Turner, Fraser claimed to have met her at a shopping mall. While giving her a lift home he allegedly put a hand on her leg; when she slapped him he said he 'flogged into her'.

While listening to the tape made secretly on the day Fraser showed authorities to the bodies of his victims, the court heard that when he was leading them to the body of Beverly Leggo at Nankin Creek, 20 kilometres out of Rockhampton, he said that he didn't remember which body he was leading them to because his brain had become 'scrambled'. Not that it mattered – he had already resigned himself to spending the rest of his life in prison.

The court later heard that it was indeed Benedetti's blood in the room at the derelict Queensland Hotel, and that she had last been seen sitting with Fraser in Rockhampton City Mall on 18 April 1999. Called to give evidence, a man who owned a shop across from the hotel told the court he had spoken to Fraser on 21 April and told him the building was set to be torn down. This had made Fraser visibly angry. With a red face he had clenched his fists and said, 'They can't do that.' The conversation took place just two days before the wreckers made their horrific discovery and told the police about the blood-splattered room 13.

With the evidence mounting up against Fraser, the case made headlines around the nation on 10 April 2003. Acting on a tip-off that came as a result of the trial's publicity, detectives found Natasha Ryan hiding in a cupboard at the home of her 26-year-old boyfriend, Scott Black. The house was just a kilometre away from her mother's.

Despite the flurry of press about the girl's reappearance, Natasha refused to talk to the media. Her story was to be sold to the highest bidder and she kept a low profile at her mother's residence while a deal was worked out. It is believed she eventually received $250,000 for her tale. Her father, Robert Ryan, by this time separated from Natasha's mother, told local media he had long believed his daughter to have been dead. 'I couldn't stop cuddling her,' he said after seeing her alive and well. 'It was like I saw a ghost.'

As a result of the shocking news, the court did the only thing it could and immediately declared Fraser not guilty of Ryan's murder. His lawyers asked to have the whole trial cancelled, and the hearing was adjourned while all parties tried to work out the best way to approach this suddenly controversial situation. It took Justice Ambrose four days to rule that the trial would continue unabated on the remaining charges. The parents of all the victims were greatly relieved by his decision and the trial continued on 15 April, with Allan Quinn taking the stand to tell the jury of how Fraser liked to talk himself up to other inmates, boasting that, 'They're trying to get me on these murders . . . but they won't be able to pin them on me.'

Regarding the Natasha Ryan situation, Quinn explained that Fraser had falsely confessed to the teen's murder, indicating that the knife he used as a murder weapon would never be found. Fraser allegedly told Quinn he had been giving Natasha a lift to the town of Yeppoon when she fell asleep leaning on his shoulder as he drove. He then claimed to have knocked her out and placed her body underneath a mango tree. Fraser also claimed that an accomplice by the name of Casper later moved the body to the coastal New South Wales town of Yamba. But this was just one of several lies Fraser had fed Quinn, not knowing that the big man was relaying everything back to the authorities, who then investigated every sick claim.

Another untruth that Fraser told Quinn involved him murdering a woman backpacker and dumping her body in a crocodile pond north of Rockhampton. Police conducted a thorough search of the area but no body was found, and they concluded that Fraser had simply been lying.

Using a concealed surveillance device, Quinn had managed to tape Fraser speaking about the murder of Beverly Leggo, the woman he'd met in Mount Morgan. Fraser described how he had taken the woman for a swim at Nankin Creek, near Rockhampton. He then told Quinn what he did in explicit detail, claiming:

'I smashed her across the jaw . . . she was semi-conscious. I pulled the rope that is used for a swing . . . over and put it around her neck twice and tucked the end through the loops and pulled it tight.' Laughing callously, Fraser added: 'You should have seen her kick when I let the rope go . . . I heard her neck break . . . and then she stopped kicking and her legs dangled in the water. It didn't take much to kill her . . . because she was really skinny. I took the rope off her and dragged her through the waterhole into the long grass, where I put her on that ditch. I made sure that I pulled the tall grass back up as I went . . . so there was no trail left behind in the grass. To make sure she was dead . . . I placed her black sporting briefs around her neck and pulled them tight . . . so if she woke up she wouldn't breathe, she would die.'

Speaking about the Sylvia Benedetti murder, Quinn taped Fraser telling him that it was 18 April 1999 when he met the nineteen-year-old at Rockhampton City Mall. At the time she was going through a rough patch, arguing with her boyfriend and unhappy with the place she was living. Fraser then revealed that: 'I took Benedetti to a disused hotel . . . to room 13 . . . I told her that I had drugs stored there . . . I tried to kiss her . . . she didn't like it. I hit her and knocked her out. I went downstairs to check if anyone had heard her scream. I went back upstairs and she was just lying there staring at me. When they are unconscious they always stare at you. I knew I was going to be in trouble. So I picked up a block of wood. I thought that it was a block of wood. It could have been a window counterweight, I don't know . . . but it had serrated edges.'

Compared with the excitement caused when she turned up alive after four-and-a-half years, Natasha Ryan's much-hyped appearance at the trial was relatively low key. Having sold her story to *60 Minutes* and *Woman's Day*, she told the crowded court that she had never laid eyes on Leonard Fraser in her young life. Explaining the circumstances behind her disappearance, she said her mother had taken her to school on the morning of 31 August 1998 but she had then found herself in trouble with a teacher and decided to run away to her boyfriend's house. She had been with him ever since.

With the trial now drawing to a close, it came out that Fraser had attempted to shake the authorities off his trail by sending police a press release from a man dubbed 'Mr Squeaky'. The document – which Fraser put together in prison on 18 January 2001, just three weeks after he had shown police to the remains of his victims – read: *I want you to understand that I am responsible for all the murders in the Rockhampton area. You will never know my real name, you can refer to me as Squeaky.*

Fraser had no idea that his conversations with Quinn were being recorded in jail, and the Mr Squeaky plan failed primarily because the press release contained information only the killer could know. The prosecution were quick to point out that all it did was further incriminate Fraser.

Among the details provided in the release was how Ms Leggo had been strangled with her black underwear and a bra. This came out three days before forensics experts told the court the same news. What was disturbing about the phony press release, however, was that Mr Squeaky had admitted to other crimes in the Rockhampton area, including several unreported rapes.

When the time came to decide Fraser's fate, the members of the jury deliberated for little more than a day before, on 9 May 2003, finding him guilty of murdering Sylvia Benedetti and Beverly Doreen Leggo. A verdict of manslaughter was handed down in Julie Dawn Turner's death because the jury held the belief that he hadn't actually intended to kill her.

A red-faced Fraser merely yawned and stretched his hands behind his head as the verdicts were read out. On 13 June, Justice Brian Ambrose sentenced him to three indefinite jail terms, in the process describing Fraser as 'an untreatable psychopath' whose motivation to kill came from his 'unusual sexual desire'. Justice Ambrose added that Lennie Fraser wouldn't become eligible for parole until he was 81 years of age, and given the circumstances it would seem that he would die behind bars.

As there was no reward posted by Rockhampton police for information about the missing women, Allan Quinn, who was serving a short sentence for fraud, received no monetary compensation for his efforts. Neither did he receive a reduction in his jail sentence.

Leonard Fraser died in custody of a heart attack on 1 January, 2007 aged 55.

CHAPTER 28
'How Did You Come to Be as You Are?'

Peter Norris Dupas
Melbourne 1997–99

When caught by the police during the early stages of his career as a serial rapist, the only explanation predatory sex offender Peter Dupas could offer for his antisocial acts was that he 'got the urge'. He added: 'I just find it hard to mix with people and I haven't many friends. I just don't know what to say.' Soon enough, his urges and inability to mix with others would see him graduate to serial murder.

The youngest of three children, Peter Norris Dupas was born into a loving and caring family environment on 6 July 1953. While he was still a baby, the family moved from Sydney to Melbourne and the spoilt child grew up in the Frankston and Mount Waverley areas. Because his siblings were some years older, young Peter was treated like an only child by an overprotective mother and a father who accepted nothing less than perfection. Both were old enough to be his grandparents.

By the time he was regularly attacking innocent women, Dupas had grown into an inconspicuous man, the sort who got lost in crowds because he didn't stand out in any way. When told about the sexual abuse he was capable of, most people found it hard to believe that the unassuming figure before them could be capable of such horrendous acts. But he was, and more. A habitual offender, Dupas would be back to his old tricks as soon as he was released from each stint in prison, leaving any of his victims who survived the ordeal severely traumatised for the rest of their lives.

Despite having supportive parents, Peter Dupas was a slow learner, with a weight problem. His nickname was 'Pugsley', taken from the rotund young character in the US television show *The Addams Family*. He was the class dunce and was made to repeat first form. By the age of 15 he had started his criminal career by attacking his neighbour with a knife. The only major difference between this first attack and later ones was that he would eventually add a balaclava to his modus operandi.

When Dupas went to the house next door on 3 October 1968, however, he was wearing his school uniform. His 27-year-old neighbour was looking after her five-week-old baby when she answered her door to find the round-faced youngster on her step asking to borrow a sharp knife to peel potatoes with. After handing one over, the woman told Dupas how good it was that he was helping his mother with the meal when he suddenly stabbed her in the stomach with her own knife. Dupas didn't say a word for most of the attack, and his victim later told detectives: 'He knocked me down onto the floor and fell on top of me. He kept on stabbing me with the knife and I kept trying to ward him off. I felt the knife cut into my hands, mainly my right hand, my face and my neck. I was holding on to the knife at one stage, trying to break the blade. I was lying on my back and he was sitting on top of me. He said, "It's too late, I can't stop now, they'll lock me up."'

The teenager then covered the woman's mouth with his hand and bashed her head on the floor time and time again until he called his frenzied attack to a halt as suddenly as it had begun. When later questioned by the police about his motive, he explained that he had no idea why he had viciously assaulted the woman, adding that he would never hurt anyone on purpose. 'I can remember having the knife in my hand,' he said. 'I must have been trying to kill her or something.'

Dupas received psychiatric assessment at Larundel Hospital. When he later appeared in court to answer for the assault, it was said that he was 'caught in an emotional conflict between the need to conform to the expectations of his parents and the unconscious urges to express his aggression and his developing masculinity'.

The 15-year-old was told to submit to psychiatric treatment and placed on 18 months' probation. He eventually left school during his fifth year of high school and started an apprenticeship as a fitter and turner at the General Electric plant at Notting Hill, not far from his home. While doing the apprenticeship he applied to join the Victorian Police Force, but was rejected because he was 1 centimetre shorter than the minimum height requirement. He would soon become familiar with police techniques from the other side of the law.

When Dupas was 19, a man spotted him staring through a bathroom window at his showering wife. The man chased the peeping tom and caught him. More than a year later, on 15 November 1973, the authorities spoke to Dupas after a man driving a car reported him for repeatedly motoring alongside his vehicle and staring and smiling at his 12-year-old daughter. Then, just two weeks after this, Dupas was arrested and charged with having raped a married woman on 5 November that year. It was said that Dupas claimed his car had broken down outside her Nunawading home, and while she looked for a screwdriver, he hid in the house; he then threatened the woman and her young baby with a knife before raping her.

Police alleged that it wasn't the first time Dupas had tried this method. In the fortnight before that attack, they claimed, he had tricked his way into two other homes, but had stopped short of sexual assault on both occasions. At the first house he had only stolen a sum of money, and he ran away from the second when the woman told him her husband was due to arrive home at any moment.

The man in charge of the police investigation, Senior Sergeant Ian Armstrong, was quick to see that Peter Norris Dupas had the potential to grow into a far greater danger to society. Armstrong went on to describe Dupas as 'an evil, cold, baby-faced liar who would possibly cause the death of one of his victims if he wasn't straightened out'.

Making the investigation difficult were Dupas' continual lies, despite the strength of the damning evidence against him. When confronted with the proof of his evil deeds, he would merely deny everything. Even when he looked to be about to break down and admit to his violent wrongdoings, he would reassess the situation and deny everything again, forcing investigating officers to start the whole process anew.

One thing the detectives found during their time with Dupas, though, was that unlike more common rapists, who mostly pick victims at random, he went about matters with a calculated coldness, choosing his victims in advance and planning the attacks down to minute detail. Talking to reporters, Senior Sergeant Armstrong later called Dupas a 'cool, cunning liar' and observed: 'You'd look at him and think, Could he be this callous, this dangerous? But I knew this guy would be a danger . . . you could smell it.'

Released on bail after being charged with the Nunawading rape, Dupas found himself on remand at Mont Park Psychiatric Hospital, where, despite the seriousness of his crimes, he could come and go freely. During his stay there he was again arrested, for a string of misdemeanours at the Rosebud Beach foreshore, not far from the facility. Among the incidents were at least three occasions when he was viewed entering a women's toilet and shower block where he watched females shower. A police stake-out later caught him and he was returned to Mont Park, where he was admitted as a voluntary patient. He remained there for a month and a half, until 22 February 1974.

When he fronted up to court, to answer charges of loitering with intent and offensive behaviour in relation to the Rosebud allegations, psychiatrists from Mont Park said they were unable to find any specific psychiatric disorder with the 21-year-old. They admitted, however, that there was the possibility he would develop personality problems in the future. Dupas was fined $140 and sent on his way.

His luck didn't hold out, though, and six months later, on 5 November, County Court Judge John Leckie sentenced him to nine years in prison, with a non-parole period of five years, for the rape of the married woman in Nunawading. Leckie was incensed and told Dupas exactly how he felt about the shocking violation: 'You raped a young married woman who was previously unknown to you in her own home and on her own bed. You invaded the sanctity of her home by a false story about your car breaking down. You threatened her with a knife, you tied her up with a cord, you struck her when she tried to resist and, worst of all, you threatened to harm her baby when she tried to resist. Whilst accepting that you are psychologically disturbed, I believe you were fully responsible for your actions.'

After examining Dupas, Dr Allen Bartholomew, one of Australia's most experienced forensic psychiatrists, offered his valued opinion. 'I am reasonably certain that this youth has a serious psycho-sexual problem,' he said, 'that he is using the technique of denial as a coping device, and he is to be seen as potentially dangerous.'

Unfortunately, prison and attempts at rehabilitation had little to no effect on the serial offender. Released from jail on 4 September 1979, Dupas violently attacked four women in just 10 days. By now he was using his trademark knife and balaclava in the attacks.

His first victim was raped in a public toilet facility in Frankston. Thankfully, his next three victims managed to escape his clutches before he could physically violate them. One of the women, though, an elderly lady, was stabbed in the chest as she tried to fend off his attack and escape. Having been denied his chance to rape her, Dupas fled the scene. It was only after the victim had got to her feet and noticed the blood pouring freely from her chest that it dawned on her that she had been stabbed.

Dupas was picked up by the law not long after these attacks and confessed to having taken part in all of the incidents. It was then that he offered his excuse of simply responding to 'the urge'. 'It just comes over me,' he said during the police interview. 'I can't help myself. I have had this problem for about six years. It all started again about a year ago. I don't know if it was because me girlfriend left me or what it is.'

Dupas was soon facing charges of rape, three counts of assault with intent to rape, and charges of malicious wounding, indecent assault, and assault with intent to rob. But despite the fact that this was the second time he had been charged with rape, Judge Leo Lazarus handed down a seemingly light six-and-a-half-year sentence with a five-year non-parole period.

Now aged 41, Peter Dupas was free once again on 27 February 1985 after serving just five years and three months. Four days later he raped a 21-year-old receptionist while she relaxed and soaked up the sunshine at Blairgowrie back-beach. The woman managed to ask two men for help after the attack, and they caught Dupas as he made his way along a road from the beach after losing his car. Asked to explain his brutal actions, Dupas could only say that he had been enjoying himself and 'laying back' on the beach when he saw the woman and was again overcome by a violent sexual urge. He added that he felt sorry about the attack but he had been told by medical professionals that he was better. All he wanted, he said, was to live a regular life.

Despite obvious similarities with the rape he had just committed, Dupas said he couldn't help the authorities with their investigation into the murder of sunbather and mother-of-four Helen McMahon, who had been beaten to death 16 days earlier in the sand dunes at Rye back-beach, just 4 kilometres away from Blairgowrie. Dupas had been on temporary leave from prison at the time.

Facing Judge John Leckie for rape once again – the same judge who had earlier berated him for the violence he'd shown towards his female victims – Dupas was sentenced to 12 years in prison with a non-parole period of 10 years. Leckie branded the lenient sentence handed down by Judge Lazarus five years earlier as 'inadequate' and claimed that Lazarus's efforts to rehabilitate Dupas had 'failed miserably'. The offender, Judge Leckie declared, was 'walking around with a loaded time bomb in his pocket'.

Now back behind bars, Dupas received medical treatment to lower his sex drive. It was thought he had put his violent past behind him when, while still incarcerated in Castlemaine Jail, he married a nurse 16 years older than him, whom he had met while she was working at the facility. A psychiatrist from Mont Park even later offered the opinion that Dupas 'believes all of that [his sex attacks] is behind him, since he understands himself better and has become more assertive'.

He walked out of prison a free man on 3 March 1992 after serving a mere seven years. It is believed that a whole 18 months went by before he again attacked a female. This time it was a 15-year-old out horse riding at Kyneton, on 23 September 1993. The girl escaped unharmed by jockeying the horse between herself and her attacker. Dupas managed to escape unidentified.

A few months later, at 11.30 a.m. on 3 January 1994, Dupas was up to his old tricks yet again when he assaulted a 26-year-old bank teller holidaying with her fiancé and three friends near Lake Eppalock in north-western Victoria. She was sitting in a public toilet block when Dupas forced his way into her cubicle, holding a knife to her face while clad in a hood with eye-holes. He repeatedly yelled for the woman to face the wall but she refused to, and she received bad cuts on her hands attempting to fight off the intruder. Realising he was getting nowhere, Dupas suddenly halted the attack and walked back to his car.

The young woman's fiancé was an off-duty federal police officer, however, and he and some of the couple's friends chased Dupas' vehicle for 15 kilometres before it ran into the bush on a dirt road. The men overpowered the assailant and police later arrived at the scene. In Dupas' pockets they found metal handcuffs and a roll of insulation tape. His station wagon held an even more frightening array of rape weapons: knives, condoms, his trademark balaclava, and a sheet of plastic and a shovel.

The case soon went to court, but even though the authorities believed that the various items found pointed to the probability that the serial offender had planned to rape, murder and hide the body of his victim, the prosecutors told the judge presiding, Leo Hart, that the evidence wasn't enough to sustain a charge of attempted rape. They had to settle for false imprisonment. As a result, Dupas pleaded guilty to the lesser charge and was sentenced to just three years and nine months' jail, with a minimum of two years and nine months. This was despite the fact that the court had been told that the woman he had attacked was now too frightened to walk from her bedroom to the toilet at night.

After serving the whole minimum term, Peter Dupas was a free man come 29 September 1996. His wife had by now left him, but he found a job in a factory and soon moved in with a woman who was unaware of his violent background. The couple settled in Coanne Street, Pascoe Vale, near Cumberland Road's busy shopping district. The area was about to come under a murderous siege.

Local prostitute and recovering heroin addict Margaret Maher often did her shopping in Pascoe Vale. On 4 October 1997 she was abducted and brutally murdered. Her body was later found on industrial land: she had been stabbed repeatedly and her breasts were mutilated. But the horrors continued . . .

Just a month later, on 1 November, Mersina Halvagis, 25, was stabbed over and over again and left to die in nearby Fawkner Cemetery, where she had been placing flowers on her dead grandmother's grave. The grave of Dupas' grandfather was just 100 metres away and the disturbed rapist had been seen there often in the weeks before the murder.

It was at 6.30 a.m. on 31 December 1997, New Year's Eve, that the next local woman was murdered. A weak, 95-year-old great-grandmother of nine, Kathleen Downes used a walking frame to get around, having suffered two strokes. She was found stabbed to death in the room of the nursing home where she had lived quietly for the previous eight years. A check of her telephone records revealed that calls had been made to Kathleen's room from the Pascoe Vale home of Dupas, but, fortunately for him, there was no way to establish a link between the two addresses or an explanation for the calls.

The next body wasn't found until around 6 p.m. on 19 April 1999, when Rena Hoffman visited her 28-year-old friend Nicole Patterson at the latter's Westgarth home. No-one replied to her knocking, so Rena walked into the house, where Nicole also worked as a consulting psychotherapist. She found the slain body of Nicole Patterson there on the floor of her consulting room. The victim's clothes had been ripped at and cut up, and she was naked from the waist down. In a statement to the police, Rena Hoffman said: 'I saw Nicky arranged naked and there was blood near her, not actually on her. She seemed [to have been] cleaned up or something.'

The autopsy results later showed that the woman had died that morning, having been stabbed 27 times, including several defensive wounds to the hands. Both her breasts had been sliced off and were no longer at the murder scene, but there was no way to tell whether she had been raped.

One of Nicole Patterson's neighbours reported hearing a

woman scream at around 9.30 a.m. on the morning of her death. A separate witness claimed to have heard 'a scream of pain, not fear'. Ten minutes later, the witness said, they saw a man walking away from the Patterson house with 'a sort of intentness' about him.

Nicole Patterson's killer took the time to clean the crime scene after the attack, ensuring there were no prints of any kind to be found. The house had been thoroughly wiped down, but the most incriminating piece of evidence was overlooked – Nicole's business appointment book, which was found under a couch. Inside the book, police found an appointment under the name of 'Malcolm' for 9 a.m. on the morning of the murder, with a mobile phone number written beside the name.

The Malcolm in question turned out to a be a student, and he had no idea who this Nicole Patterson was, or why she would have his name and number. The detectives asked if he had given out his contact details to anyone lately. The list he gave them included the name of Peter Dupas, for whom the student was doing some general handiwork. When police entered the name into their computers, warning bells rang. They knew where to focus the investigation.

Putting together likely scenarios, the authorities realised that Nicole advertised her business in the local newspapers. Dupas, who lived less than 30 minutes away from the victim, had simply made an appointment using his young handyman's name and number. Police officers raided Dupas' residence three days after the attack. The suspect had a fingernail scratch to his face, and a bloodstained green jacket was found. According to DNA tests, there was a less than one in 6.5 billion chance that the blood in 13 of the 14 drops on the jacket did not belong to Nicole Patterson. The other drop of blood was a mix of hers and Dupas'.

Police also found a black balaclava, along with a newspaper report about the murder that included a photo of the deceased. The picture had been slashed. In a rubbish bin, some torn-up pieces of newspaper were soon found to make up a handwritten note, on which *nine o'clock Nicci* and *Malcolm* appeared. With their case against Peter Dupas building, police then uncovered video footage of him buying petrol near Nicole's home on the day of the slaying.

Still Dupas ignored the mounting circumstantial evidence against him and maintained his innocence. He claimed that the authorities had planted the evidence in order to convict him. Nonetheless, he was charged with murder and remanded in custody awaiting trial while the police further pieced together what had gone on.

It transpired that Dupas, using the alias Malcolm, made the first of 15 phone calls to Nicole Patterson on 3 March. Claiming to have a chronic gambling problem, he finally made an early-morning appointment for Monday, 19 April. The belief was that he arrived on time and was shown to the consulting room, where he set upon Nicole as she made coffee for them both, stabbing her with a knife he had brought along for the purpose. The witness reports of screams seemed to indicate that the victim put up firm resistance, a supposition that was backed up by the cuts to her hands. After the killing was complete, Dupas cleaned up the crime scene and collected for himself some souvenirs, including body parts and his victim's purse.

Peter Dupas faced Justice Frank Vincent at the Supreme Court of Victoria in August 2000. The accused said he was a part-time furniture maker, and repeated that he believed the evidence, including the blood found on his jacket, had been planted by the police. Although he admitted to having spoken to Nicole Patterson, Dupas had never been to her home, he claimed, and had had no involvement with her after 12 April 1999, when he cancelled an appointment to discuss his gambling problem. He further stressed that he had not contacted the deceased on the day of her death or gone anywhere near her residence. The only time he'd left his own house that day, he said, was to buy milk and petrol, grab some shopping and pick up his de facto partner. Apart from that, his story went, he'd spent the day in question washing clothes, preparing for an upcoming camping trip and working in his shed.

Once all the evidence had been heard, the jury took just two-and-a-half hours to find Peter Norris Dupas guilty of murder. He was sentenced on 23 August 2000, with Justice Vincent providing the following stinging rebuke: 'I note that you have an appalling criminality history, involving repeated acts of sexual violence, and which extends over approximately 30 years. You have admitted 16 prior convictions involving six court appearances between 27 March 1972 and 11 November 1994. All of the offences were sexually related or motivated. A number of them involved physical violence and the use of a knife. On three separate occasions you were sentenced to terms of imprisonment for the commission of rape, aggravated assault or assault with intent to rape.

'On the second and third of these occasions, you committed your offences within a very short time of your release from custody. It appears that the only periods during which you were at large in the community without committing offences were two periods of approximately 12 months each during which you were subject to strict parole conditions following your release from prison in 1992 and 1996. However it was not long after that form of control was lifted by the expiration of the sentence to which it was related that you reverted to your usual type of criminal behaviour.

'You regarded Nicole Patterson as nothing more than prey to be entrapped and killed. Her life, youth and personal qualities assumed importance in your mind only by reason of the sense of satisfaction and power you experienced in taking them from her. At a fundamental level, as human beings, you present for us the awful, threatening and unanswerable question – how did you come to be as you are?'

Justice Vincent then sentenced the accused to life in prison without the possibility of parole, but the story still wasn't over.

On 16 August 2004, Dupas was sentenced to another term of life imprisonment without the possibility of parole after he was found guilty in the Victorian Supreme Court of the murder of prostitute Margaret Maher, whose near-naked body was found dumped in long grass at the side of the road in Somerton on 4 October 1997. One of her breasts had been severed.

In passing sentence, Justice Stephen Kaye said that Dupas left Ms Maher's mutilated body at a desolate place in a disgusting display of loathing for her and contempt for her dignity. 'These actions are, I consider, an eloquent insight into the unmitigated evil which actuated you to kill Margaret Maher and to behave as you did,' Justice Kaye said.

Peter Dupas has since been questioned about the unsolved

murders of Helen McMahon, Renita Brunton, Mersina Halvagis and Kathleen Downes. He has denied any knowledge of the killings, but the facts are damning:

- Dupas was temporarily on leave from prison at the time of Helen McMahon's murder in February 1985, and would commit rape just over a fortnight later, by which time he had been released from jail. The crimes took place just 4 kilometres apart, both on back-beaches along the Mornington Peninsula, south of Melbourne.
- Renita Brunton was stabbed to death in her used-clothing shop in Sunbury in November 1993. At the time, Dupas lived near her shop and drove past it almost on a daily basis.
- At the 2005–06 Coronial Inquest into Mersina Halvagis' murder, the Coroner was told that Dupas was a frequent visitor and stalker of women in Fawkner Cemetery, where Mersina was brutally stabbed to death and mutilated on All Saints' Day in November 1997 as she tended her grandmother's grave. Dupas' grandfather's grave was only 100 metres away from the murder scene. The Coroner heard from nine witnesses who all said they saw Dupas in the cemetery before the murder, and mourners claimed that Dupas was within 20 metres of the murder scene at the time of the attack. A woman told the inquest that she believed she was to have been Dupas' original target on the day of the murder, but fled the cemetery after he stalked her. A profiler told the inquest that the murder of Ms Halvagis had all the hallmarks of crimes previously committed by Dupas, while police detectives said Dupas lied about how he had received a facial injury at the time of the murder and that he had attempted to change his appearance after the attack. Task force detectives also stated that it was their belief that Dupas had almost certainly described intimate details of one of his killings to a prostitute.
- Detectives established that phone calls were made from Dupas' Pascoe Vale residence to the Brunswick nursing home in the weeks before 95-year-old Kathleen Downes' stabbing murder in December 1997.

The McMahon, Brunton, Halvagis and Downes cases are still open, and detectives are actively working them. They believe it is only a matter of time before they get at least one other conviction against Peter Norris Dupas.

AUTHOR'S NOTE: As defined in the Introduction to this book, the 'qualification' for the status of serial killer is that the offender has a minimum of three or more murders to their name, and the reader will be aware that, officially at least, Peter Dupas does not fit this criterion. However, given the circumstances of the unsolved McMahon, Brunton, Halvagis and Downes murders as outlined above, it is extremely difficult to accept that Dupas has killed only two victims.

The murder techniques were similar in each case and all of the killings were committed in and around areas that Dupas frequented. But more than these factors, the odds of the twice-convicted murderer having not killed at least one of the four women run into the billions. It is for this reason that Peter Norris Dupas has been included in *Australia's Serial Killers*.

AUTHOR'S NOTE 2011: Peter Dupas legitimately qualified as an Australian serial killer when, in August, 2007, he was found guilty of the murder of Mersina Halvagis at Melbourne's Faulkner Cemetery in 1997. Dupas' conviction came about mainly due to evidence from his cellmate, convicted drug trafficking lawyer Andrew Fraser, to whom Dupas confessed details of the murder that only the killer would know. A subsequent appeal trial failed and in November 2010, Peter Dupas was sentenced to his third term of life imprisonment without the possibility of parole.

CHAPTER 29

Snowtown: The 'Bodies in the Barrels' Serial Murders

John Justin Bunting, Robert Joe Wagner and
James Spyridon Vlassakis
Adelaide, 1992–99

AUTHOR'S NOTE: Ever since the first edition of *Australia's Serial Killers* went on sale in 2000, it has concerned me that one of the nation's most terrible cases of serial murder wasn't in it. The name of the case is the Family Murders and the reason for its omission is, given that *Australia's Serial Killers* is about the perpetrators as much as the crimes, that no-one was ever convicted of all of the killings, so subsequently there was no serial killer as such to write about in the context of this book.

But a man was convicted of one of the killings, and if it wasn't for the disallowance of crucial evidence in further court proceedings against him, it is most likely he would have been found guilty of more of the murders. As it was, he was sentenced to what was the longest non-parole period in South Australia's history at the time.

Now, however, with the more recent horrors of the Snowtown murders, I believe that I have the catalyst to include the story of the Family Murders in this book. Not as an individual case, but as one of the many examples of the atrocities that have taken place in South Australia over the years in a prelude to this chapter's discussion of the events behind the Snowtown killings.

In defence of the beleaguered state, it is only fair to note that more recently South Australia played a big part in bringing to justice Bradley Murdoch, who was convicted of the highly publicised murder of English tourist Peter Falconio after the latter's girlfriend, Joanne Lees, escaped to raise the alarm.

337

There is no logical explanation as to why laid-back Adelaide, the capital of South Australia, should be the home for so many horrible murders and abductions. Its population stands at around 1 million, which is small in comparison to most of the other state capitals, yet the fact remains that by the early 1990s the city and its environs had earned themselves the unenviable title of 'the Murder Capital of Australia'.

Rich in culture and beauty, Adelaide and the surrounding districts are responsible for some of the finest wines in Australia. Throughout the city, seemingly on every corner, are houses of worship of all denominations. For this reason, Adelaide is referred to as 'the City of Churches' – an altogether more palatable moniker to the locals, no doubt, than the homicide-related one. And they have never had to canvass for business in the city's churches, for South Australians are notoriously reverent.

But not all of them, it seems, as there is an inexplicable dark side to Adelaide. In the annals of Australia's most horrific crimes, Adelaide's sinister past (and present) makes other cities look like Camelot. The following is just a portion of Adelaide's appalling track record of carnage in modern times.

- **1958:** Rupert Max Stuart rapes and murders nine-year-old Mary Olive Hattam at Thevenard.
- **1966:** The three Beaumont children – aged four, seven and nine – are abducted from Glenelg Beach and never seen again.
- **1971:** In South Australia's worst mass murders, 10 people, comprising seven children and their mother from the Bartholomew family and two family friends, are shot dead by a man at Hope Forest.
- **1972:** Homosexual Adelaide University law lecturer Dr George Duncan is thrown into the Torrens River and drowns. Two Adelaide Vice Squad detectives are eventually charged with the death.
- **1973:** Schoolgirls Joanne Ratcliffe, 11, and Kirsty Gordon, aged four, disappear from Adelaide Oval while attending a football match and are never seen again.
- **1976–77:** In what were Australia's worst serial murders at the time, seven women aged 15 to 26 go missing in and around

Adelaide over a 51-day period from Christmas 1976. Their skeletal remains are discovered in the Adelaide foothills several years later, in what become known as 'the Mass Murders of Truro' (as discussed in chapter 17).

- **1979:** David Szach murders his lover, lawyer Derrance Stevenson, and conceals the body in a freezer in Parkside.
- **1979–83:** Between 1979 and 1983, in what are later dubbed 'the Family Murders', five men are abducted, drugged, held captive, sexually assaulted, grotesquely mutilated and murdered.
- **1984:** Sexual sadist Bevan Von Einem is tried for the horrific torture and murder of one of the Family Murders victims, a 15-year-old youth. He is found guilty and sent to prison for life, with a non-parole period of 36 years.
- **1994:** A letter bomb kills Sergeant Geoff Bowen at the Adelaide offices of the National Crime Authority.
- **1999:** Six bodies are found in casks filled with acid in a bank vault in rural Snowtown, leading police to the discovery of another five bodies buried in and around Adelaide. Four men are charged with murder.

The Family Murders gave Adelaide the reputation of having a network of people in high places who carried out their disgusting sexual practices on children without fear of retribution. Over the years since, that reputation has been hard to shake.

It all began at around midnight on a chilly autumn night in May 1972 on the banks of the Torrens River, which flows through the heart of Adelaide. The area is a notorious pick-up spot frequented at night by homosexuals, which was where university lecturer Dr George Duncan and Roger James were attacked by four men, bashed, and thrown in the river and left for dead.

Duncan, a frail man with just one lung as a result of juvenile tuberculosis, was drowned. Severe bruising beneath his armpits indicated that he had been manhandled and thrown into the freezing river by a number of people.

Roger James escaped with a broken ankle after being saved by a tall blond man in his mid-twenties who just happened to be passing by at the time. The young man was Bevan Spencer Von Einem, a name that would be of enormous significance in years to come.

Dr George Duncan's death was treated as murder, and within days the spotlight fell on three senior Vice Squad detectives who were alleged to have gone to the Torrens River that night in search of 'poofters' to bash after they had attended a drunken send-off for one of their comrades. Witnesses said that the detectives were accompanied by a tall civilian, whose name never came to light.

All three detectives were called upon to give evidence at the Coronial Inquest into Dr Duncan's death, but all refused to answer any of the incriminating questions put to them and were immediately suspended from duty. A subsequent police inquiry failed to find sufficient evidence to recommend a prosecution of the three police officers. The public were outraged, and while the whole matter stank of a cover-up, there was little that could be done and the incident was soon forgotten, for the time being.

In June 1979, while the God-fearing citizens of Adelaide were trying to come to terms with the murders of seven young women in the Truro Serial Murders, the hideously mutilated body of 17-year-old Alan Barnes was found on the banks of the South Para Reservoir, north-east of Adelaide, after he had been reported missing seven days earlier. The 'fresh' corpse indicated that Alan had died the day before he was discovered, while a post-mortem revealed that he had died of massive blood loss from ghastly injuries inflicted upon his anus by a large blunt instrument while he was still alive.

Two months later, the police were called to investigate what looked like human body parts found in plastic bags that had floated to rest on the banks of the Port River at Port Adelaide. They turned out to be the dissected remains of 25-year-old Neil Muir, neatly cut into many pieces, placed in the garbage bags and thrown into the river.

On 27 February 1982, 18-year-old Mark Langley disappeared while walking near the Torrens River. Nine days later his mutilated body was found in scrub in the Adelaide foothills. Among the mutilations was a wound that extended from his navel to the pubic region and appeared to have been cut with a surgical instrument. The hair around the area had been shaved as it would have been in an operation in a hospital. Part of his small bowel was missing. The post-mortem revealed that Mark had died from a massive loss of blood from gross injuries to his anus.

Then, in June 1982 the skeletal remains of 14-year-old Peter Stogneff, who had gone missing 10 months earlier, were found at Middle Beach, north of Adelaide, cut into three pieces as if by a surgical saw.

By now the zealous press were convinced that the murders were the work of a group of surreptitious Adelaide homosexuals in very high places throughout the community; politicians, judges, religious leaders and the like, who paid handsomely for kidnapped young men, whom they drugged and kept alive for their pleasure. When the victim was no longer of any use to them, the procurers disposed of the body. The press christened this unconfirmed clandestine group 'the Family', and from then on the case was referred to in the national press as 'the Adelaide Family Murders'.

Working on the now obvious assumption that the murders were the work of the same individual(s), and that the person(s) they wished to talk to most of all was a homosexual, SA Police Major Crime Squad detectives infiltrated the vast South Australian homosexual network. Through their secret contacts, the investigators eventually came up with a short-list of possible suspects, consisting of known deviants and 'closet' kinks known only in the homosexual subculture.

One such person of interest was a tall, blond, well-groomed 37-year-old accountant named Bevan Spencer Von Einem. Openly homosexual, Von Einem was well known to the police as a frequenter of homosexual pick-up spots, or 'beats' as they were more commonly known. He also had a reputation of being particularly fond of young boys, a pastime scorned by the homosexual community.

Von Einem was brought in and questioned at length about the Barnes and Langley killings. He vigorously denied any knowledge of the murders, other than what he had read in the papers, and the rumours that were circulating about the specific injuries to the victims. The police had no choice but to let him go.

On 23 July 1983, a fifth victim turned up. Seven weeks beforehand, 15-year-old Richard Kelvin was abducted a short distance from his North Adelaide home; now his body had been found by an amateur geologist off a track near One Tree Hill in the Adelaide foothills. The boy was wearing a Channel 9 T-shirt, jeans and sneakers – the clothes he had on when he left his parents' home on 5 June. He had gone to a bus stop only 200 metres from his home that afternoon to catch a bus to farewell a friend. Several neighbours reported hearing calls for help at about that time and police were convinced he had been kidnapped.

No real attempt had been made to conceal the body. Detectives weren't surprised that the post-mortem revealed that the lad had similar grotesque wounds to the anus as the other victims. The examination also revealed that the victim had been heavily drugged and had been kept alive for up to five weeks before he was murdered. Richard's body was found to contain traces of four different drugs.

Police rounded up the usual suspects once again, and this time Bevan Von Einem aroused their suspicions by not protesting as vehemently to their questioning as he had previously. Task force detectives decided to search Von Einem's house and give him and his clothing a thorough scientific once-over. It paid off in spades. In Von Einem's possession they found three of the drugs taken from the dead boy's body; while Von Einem's hair was a match for the hair found in the deceased's clothing.

Bevan Von Einem was charged with the murder of Richard Kelvin. At his trial Von Einem pleaded not guilty, and even though he was faced with undeniable evidence that he had been in Richard's company, he denied ever having known the boy. Then, in a complete turnaround, Von Einem said that he had picked Kelvin up one time when he was hitchhiking and dropped him off near his home.

The jury was obviously unimpressed and found him guilty of murder. Bevan Spencer Von Einem was sentenced to life imprisonment with a non-parole period of 24 years, which was later increased to 36 years on appeal by the Crown, a record for South Australia.

But that was not to be the end of it. Not by a long shot.

The detectives who had worked on the Kelvin case were absolutely convinced that Von Einem – perhaps alone, but most likely with others – was responsible for the deaths of the other youths, or at the very least knew who was. Apart from the fact that most of the other victims had suffered identical anal injuries and had died in similar circumstances, the investigators' informants told them that it was common knowledge that Von Einem regularly picked up young hitchhikers, drugged them and then sexually abused them.

The detectives worked tirelessly on new leads and new witnesses. After four years, they visited Von Einem in Adelaide's Yatala Prison, in the protective custody division (where he was being held for his own safety), and charged him with the murders of Alan Barnes and Mark Langley.

At Von Einem's committal hearing held in 1990, the Crown chose to pursue a committal for Von Einem on the lines that 'similar fact evidence' was admissible, and alleged that if he was guilty of the Kelvin murder, then he must also be guilty of the murders of Barnes and Langley as they were identical in every fashion. And furthermore, the Crown alleged, it had circumstantial evidence that could back this up. Magistrate David Gurry allowed Crown prosecutor Brian Murray, Queen's Counsel, to proceed along these lines. It would ultimately prove to be a disastrous ploy.

And if the packed public gallery thought they had heard stories of unbelievable horror as the evidence unfolded of how the boys had died, then they must have thought that the Crown had saved the most shocking allegations for last. If what they were about to hear was true, Bevan Spencer Von Einem would go down in history as one of the most sadistic monsters the world had ever known.

The Crown prosecutor called 22 witnesses, including former hitchhikers and associates of Von Einem. The police had really done their homework and had left no stone unturned in their efforts to nail what they believed was the most heinous killer in Australian history.

The first prosecution witness would only give testimony under an alias of 'Mr B', for his own protection, and his name was withheld from publication by court order. Mr B claimed that Von Einem had killed 10 young people, including five children who had disappeared 24 years earlier.

Mr B denied that he was a 'perpetual liar' or that a reward over the unsolved murders of several Adelaide teenagers (which stood at $250,000) had anything to do with his giving information to police. In an angry outburst, Mr B claimed that the reason he was telling what he knew of Von Einem's activities was out of concern and respect for the murdered boys' families. 'I have given a lot of consideration to the relatives of the kids,' he told the court. 'They deserve to know what's really happened.'

Mr B was a former friend of Von Einem's and a homosexual. He said he had evidence that linked Von Einem to the five Family murders and also to the disappearances of the three Beaumont children back in 1966, as well as the 1973 disappearance of schoolgirls Joanne Ratcliffe and Kirsty Gordon from Adelaide Oval. The courtroom was stunned. No-one could believe what they were hearing.

For four days Mr B testified how he and Von Einem picked up young boys who were hitchhiking and drugged them and raped them. On the night that Alan Barnes died, he and Von Einem went looking for hitchhikers after meeting on the banks of the Torrens River.

He said that they gave Alan Barnes a lift and gave him alcoholic drinks containing a very strong sedative called Rohypnol, which they knew that when mixed with alcohol would induce unconsciousness. They all then went into a café, where Barnes was obviously affected by the drug and was showing signs of passing out. Von Einem went away and made a phone call, and when he came back, he said that he'd rung a friend and arranged to meet him back at the Torrens River. They met up with a man known only as 'Mr R'. Von Einem went for a walk with Mr R and came back 10 minutes later and asked if Mr B would like to go with them while they 'performed some surgery' on the now unconscious Barnes.

Von Einem went on to say that they also intended to take videos of what happened, before killing the boy and throwing his body from a bridge. Mr B told the hushed courtroom that he had declined the offer, and Von Einem, Mr R and the unconscious teenager had driven off.

Mr B saw Von Einem a few days later, he continued, and was

told that the youth had died and that Mr R was concerned about what Mr B knew of what had happened. Von Einem then warned him that if he said anything to anyone about what he had seen, he would be implicated in the murder as well. Mr B explained to the court that since that night his life had been a mess and he lived with constant threats from an 'Adelaide businessman'.

Mr B stated that Von Einem had also told him he had picked up the Beaumont children at Glenelg Beach on 26 January 1966. Von Einem had said that he went to the beach regularly to have a perve on people in the showers and had picked up the three children and performed some 'brilliant surgery on them'; he told Mr B he had 'connected them up' and one had died. Von Einem then allegedly dumped the children's bodies at Moana or Myponga, south of Adelaide.

Von Einem also told him that he had picked up two children at a football match and killed them, Mr B claimed, and even though Von Einem didn't mention any names, it seemed apparent that he was talking about Joanne Ratcliffe and Kirsty Gordon, who had gone missing from the Adelaide Oval in 1973. Mr B said that Von Einem didn't elaborate any further.

Mr B alleged that an Adelaide trader who could have helped kill Alan Barnes was there in the courtroom while he was giving his evidence. 'You've got no idea what I've had to go through . . . coming here . . . facing crap like [the Adelaide trader] sitting in the body of the court,' he said.

The magistrate, Mr David Gurry, immediately suppressed the name of the trader Mr B had just identified. The man's counsel said the trader categorically denied being with Von Einem and Alan Barnes the night the boy was last seen alive.

The trader was not called as a Crown witness. The trader's counsel said that the man's business of 20 years would be ruined if he was identified, and also challenged Mr B's claim that the trader was in the public gallery listening to evidence.

Another witness, an insurance worker in his thirties named Garry Wayne Place, said that he'd come forward to the authorities late the year before because he had 'had enough', having put up with 11 years of telephone threats to his life if he talked. Mr Place said that the last anonymous call was about a week earlier and the caller had told him to 'keep your mouth shut or you and your wife will get it'.

Place told the court that Alan Barnes had introduced Von Einem to him one Saturday at an Adelaide hotel about a week before the murder. Barnes had also introduced three other people with Von Einem: a doctor whose name sounded like Goodard, a man called Mario, and a woman. There had been talk about a party that night where there would be 'women, drugs, booze – anything you like'. Later that week, Place and Barnes had gone to a hotel where Von Einem had told Place that if he provided sex, he would get 'drugs, women, anything' and the same things would be provided if he brought along some young lads.

The first threatening telephone call Place received came the night he learnt that Alan Barnes had been murdered. A muffled male voice had said something like: 'Keep your mouth shut or you're going to get it', and there had been about 20 other calls that night.

If the parents of the missing kids were holding their breath in the hope that Bevan Von Einem was going to confess and tell the police where the remains were, then they were sadly mistaken. Von Einem vigorously denied any involvement in the abductions of the children and lashed out at Mr B, claiming that the witness was merely out for a portion of the $250,000 reward on offer.

But the circumstantial evidence against him appeared to be overwhelming. After two months of hearings, on 11 May 1990, Bevan Spencer Von Einem was committed to stand trial in the South Australian Supreme Court on charges of having murdered Alan Barnes and Mark Langley.

Immediately Von Einem's defence counsel lodged an interjection to have the trial put on permanent stay of proceedings due to the fact that no matter what, their client could not possibly get a fair hearing due to the amount of public animosity towards him and the over-exposure of the committal hearing in the newspapers. It didn't work. The trial judge, Justice Duggan, chose to throw it out. But there were other matters about the forthcoming trial that worried His Honour. At a pre-trial hearing, Justice Duggan ruled the similar fact evidence, so successfully used in the committal hearing by the Crown prosecutor, as inadmissible. This ruled the evidence presented at the committal all but useless.

The Crown tried different tactics. It would present two separate trials for the murders of Barnes and Langley. But a couple of days later, the Crown withdrew the Langley murder charge, believing that it could build a stronger case by trying Von Einem on the Barnes murder alone, the case for which the prosecution had the strongest evidence.

Then came the killer blow. After lengthy consideration, Justice Duggan ruled that evidence from the Von Einem trial and conviction for the murder of Richard Kelvin was disallowed. Justice Duggan also ruled inadmissible any evidence about Bevan Von Einem's alleged involvement with hitchhikers and his purported associates.

The Crown case was in tatters and if it went to court without their evidence, the Crown didn't have a prayer of gaining a conviction. To their disgust, on 1 February 1991, the Crown had no choice but enter a nolle prosequi (unwilling to pursue) on the second charge of the murder of Alan Barnes.

To the detectives who had worked tirelessly on the case for years, it was a bitter pill to swallow. To the parents of Alan Barnes and the other young men who were so inhumanely violated and died such ghastly deaths, it meant that their nightmare of wondering would go on.

And to many Australians, there is little doubt in their minds that 'the Family' of depraved and murderous paedophiles did, and possibly still does, exist in South Australia. They also believe that there are more victims as yet unaccounted for. Transient hitchhikers from other states and young tourists perhaps. And those same believers are also convinced that the tall, blond, well-groomed accountant with the aristocratic name, Bevan Spencer Von Einem, knows all the answers to where the bodies are buried and who the guilty parties are. But while he rots in Yatala Prison, Von Einem is keeping his dark secrets to himself.

As for the citizens of Adelaide, after the Truro murders and then the Family Murders they must have thought they'd had more than their share of horror for a good while to come. But that was not to be the case. By the end of the decade, they would be confronted with the most prolific case of serial murder Australia has ever known.

The Snowtown Serial Murders

Never before in the grim history of serial murder in Australia, perhaps the world for that matter, has there been a convicted gang of serial killers. Couples, yes, but never a larger group killing in harmony. Never, that is, until the Snowtown Serial Murders – otherwise known as 'the Bodies in the Barrels Murders' – which would prove to be Australia's most prolific set of serial killings. And as if to add further heinousness to their already despicable crimes, the murder gang went on cashing their victims' welfare cheques to supplement their income, as well as grabbing the deceased's furniture, stereo systems and cars for their own use.

Before Thursday, 20 May 1999, Snowtown, situated 150 kilometres north of Adelaide, was best known as a sleepy rural hamlet with a nostalgic feel, in that it was ideal country for sheep grazing and wheat growing. But Snowtown's image changed forever that afternoon. For there, stored in the vault of a disused branch of the State Bank of South Australia, the authorities discovered the decomposing remains of eight victims, floating head-first in hydrochloric acid, inside six black 44-gallon plastic barrels. On further investigation, the police would connect 12 bodies to the case, and juries would determine that at least 11 of those had been the victims of homicide.

Inside the bank vault, detectives found what prosecutors would later call 'the paraphernalia of murder and torture'. There were knives sitting on top of the barrels, while elsewhere in the building was a variac machine (usually used for nickel plating) capable of delivering electric shocks. Officers wearing breathing apparatus opened the barrels and looked inside, and to their horror discovered clothing and random body parts, including severed hands and 15 human feet. Detective Steve McCoy was the first to see the barrels, after he'd opened a plastic sheet covering the entrance to the vault. 'The stench was unbearable,' he remembered, four years afterwards. 'It was the stench of what I would say was rotting flesh, rotting bodies, human bodies. It was putrid.

It permeated your hair, your clothing – anything you had on, the stench got into. It was horrific.'

Speaking for the prosecution in the eventual court case, Wendy Abraham, QC, described how rubber gloves, handcuffs, rope and tape used in the torture killings were found strewn throughout the bank, saying: 'A number of [the victims] had been dismembered, with legs and feet removed from their bodies, or they had been cut. One of his hands handcuffed behind his back and his legs tied together. More than one of the bodies had marks consistent with burn marks.'

There was no doubting the brutality of what had gone on; there were bodies with ropes around their necks, and heads still stuffed with gags. 'It was a scene from the worst nightmare you've ever had,' said another police officer who attended the scene. 'I don't think any of us was prepared for what we saw.'

An examination by a leading pathologist would later conclude that prolonged torture had taken place, using common everyday tools such as pliers, pincers and clamps, some of which were found in the bank. After the victims were tortured, they were strangled or asphyxiated.

Information received by the authorities suggested that the remains had been in storage behind the vault's 10-centimetre-thick metal door for up to four months, but the roots of the Bodies in the Barrels case went back a lot further than that, back to a man called John Justin Bunting.

Bunting was born in the Brisbane suburb of Inala in December 1966. He grew up in the area before travelling west with a group of young people seeking a new life in Western Australia. He was 20. When the car he was in developed engine trouble, he ended up staying in Adelaide, finding his place in the troubled northern suburbs of the city.

By the time the barrels were discovered, John Bunting was 32. In the interim, he had met and befriended Mark Ray Haydon, his closest friend, Veronika Tripp, the woman who would become his wife, and Robert Joe Wagner, the man who would be his main accomplice in the string of murders. The biggest single character trait displayed by Bunting was an unquenchable hatred for homosexuals and paedophiles, whom he called 'dirties'. Bunting told a number of people – some of whom were later witnesses at his trial – that he had been sexually abused as a child, referring to the incident as his 'accident'.

Indeed, observers of his trial would soon conclude that the heart of the case itself seemed to rest within John Bunting's seething hatred. It appeared that he had made it his life's work to seek revenge on and punish people he suspected to be homosexuals and paedophiles, not distinguishing between the two groups.

Bunting met Mark Haydon at a TAFE course on welding in Adelaide's northern suburbs, but it was the pair's love of cars that made the friendship. They would talk about cars and spend time restoring them at Haydon's home. Bunting met Veronika Tripp, an intellectually disabled woman, and eventually married her, before the couple moved to a new Housing Trust home at 203 Waterloo Corner Road, Salisbury North, about 30 minutes' drive from the Adelaide CBD.

On their first day in their new house they met Robert Wagner, then in his early twenties, and his housemate Barry Lane. Wagner, described by neighbours as 'brooding' and 'illiterate', had been sexually abused at a young age and had never fitted in at school. When he was in his early teens he had met the much older Lane – a convicted paedophile and transvestite who also went by the name of Vanessa; they were at a party, and Lane had asked the youth for oral sex. Despite Wagner's mother's best attempts, the teenager would remain with Lane, drawn in by a web of 'boy toys', like motorised cars and computer games. Suddenly, when Wagner was 14, he vanished along with Lane. His mother would not see him for four years, during which time Lane and Wagner lived in a variety of states before heading to Adelaide and a new home at 1 Bingham Road, Salisbury North, a few hundred metres from Bunting. Wagner was angry and resentful of Lane, a fact not lost on Bunting.

The Queenslander began to befriend Robert Wagner, sharing his hatred of paedophiles with the young man, while simultaneously using Barry Lane as an informant on the whereabouts and activities of suspected paedophiles. In fact, it was one of Lane's former lovers, a young man by the name of Clinton Douglas Trezise, who would become John Bunting's first victim.

Trezise was murdered in the lounge room of 203 Waterloo Corner Road in August 1992, bludgeoned to death by Bunting. His body was quickly driven to the country and dumped in a shallow grave at Lower Light, 50 kilometres north of Adelaide. Trezise's skeletal remains were not found until nearly two years later, and he was not identified until 1999. But when the television program *Australia's Most Wanted* reported on the mystery of the body's identity, Bunting allegedly told James Vlassakis, a youth who would become involved in later murders, 'That's my handiwork.'

Like Wagner and Bunting (allegedly), James Spyridon Vlassakis had been the victim of sexual abuse. When he was at his lowest ebb, filled with self-loathing and being molested by his half-brother Troy Youde, he would come into contact with Bunting through his own vulnerable mother, Elizabeth Harvey. Vlassakis was tormented by his hatred, and by what he felt was his inability to save himself and his siblings from the unwanted attentions of family friend and paedophile Jeffrey Payne. Bunting set about drawing the distressed teenager out of his shell, as he had done with Wagner. The older man took the youth riding on his motorcycle and soon became something of a father figure to Vlassakis.

Before long, John Bunting became the first person Vlassakis trusted enough to tell about his abuse. Feeling guilty, Vlassakis then moved away from his family home to live with Bunting, who set about grooming the youngster for violence. Bunting became so obsessed by what he perceived as his mission against those he saw as dirty that he created what came to be known as 'the Spider Wall' (a reference to 'rock spiders', the colloquial term for paedophiles). Pinned to the wall in a small bedroom at the house at Waterloo Corner Road, the Spider Wall was a detailed diagram that had names and contact details for people he believed were paedophiles and homosexuals. The diagram was covered in Post-it notes and cross-referenced by links of coloured wool. According to one witness who visited the house: 'On a few occasions the Friday night thing was to go into the room, where [Bunting would] close his eyes and walk up to the wall, and whichever card he'd touch he would take down and ring the person and abuse them over the phone.'

Also stuck on the wall was a chart that had been drawn up on the back of an anti-paedophile leaflet. In the centre of the chart was written a single name, *Barry* – Barry Lane, the transsexual and paedophile who had forced Wagner into a homosexual relationship as a teenager. From Lane's name spread a twisting maze of lines connecting him to dozens of other people Bunting considered to be paedophiles.

In John Bunting's eyes, Lane was a pivotal figure in his self-proposed mission because of the abuse he had committed on Wagner. Bunting and Wagner also gathered information on other paedophiles from Lane. It was Bunting's friendship with Wagner that loosened Lane's psychological grip on him. Lane was known for his flamboyant dress sense – he often wore bright pink hot-pants and had dyed his hair blonde before renaming himself Vanessa. He even got a driver's licence in the name of Vanessa Lane.

Neighbours described him as 'outgoing', but he was sometimes persecuted by the local community because of his paedophilia convictions. The abuse was mainly verbal, although there were times when Lane and Wagner's house was pelted with eggs. The pair – both of whom received disability benefits – eventually built a 2-metre-high fence around the house, and they also kept four Doberman dogs on the property.

It was three years after Trezise's death that the killings resumed. Ray Davies was a friend of Lane's, the pair often spending time hanging around homosexual beats in Salisbury. He was a sexually disturbed young man, who reportedly used to expose himself to children walking home from school in Salisbury. Davies and his family came from Port Pirie, 250 kilometres west of Adelaide, but by the mid-1990s he was living in a caravan at the back of a house at Ghent Street, Salisbury North. The Housing Trust home was the residence of a woman called Suzanne Allen, who had had a failed relationship with the troubled Davies.

Allen was a woman who fancied herself in love with many men. Unfortunately for her, most of these men quickly tired of her and left her feeling hurt. Even more unfortunately for her, one of the men she fell for was the bloke who lived only a few hundred metres away from her in Salisbury North – John Justin Bunting.

On Boxing Day 1995, one of Allen's grandchildren went to her daughter, Annette Cannon, accusing Davies of sexual abuse. The story devastated both Cannon – who had never liked Davies – and Allen, and led them to go straight out to a local police station to lodge an official complaint. Somehow news of the allegation made its way to Bunting, and this would prove fatal for Davies. By the time Allen and Cannon got back to Ghent Street later in the afternoon, Ray Davies was nowhere to be found, although his belongings were still in the caravan where they had been when they went out.

While they were out, Bunting and Wagner had turned up at Allen's house and seized Davies. They dumped him in the back of a car and drove him up to a Riverland farmhouse, two-and-a-half hours' drive north-east of Adelaide, with Wagner beating Davies in the back seat to keep him quiet as they travelled. When they got to the farmhouse they dragged him into the bathroom, put him in the bath and beat him mercilessly in the genitals – as a symbolic punishment for what he was alleged to have done. After torturing the terrified man for some time, they put him in the car again and drove him back to Waterloo Corner Road.

James Vlassakis' mother, Elizabeth Harvey, was by this point having a relationship of sorts with Bunting, and she was around when they arrived at Waterloo Corner Road. Veronika Tripp had left for a while to spend time with her parents, leaving the house to Bunting and his plans. Just like Wagner and Vlassakis, Harvey had been abused as a child, and the trauma of her sons' abuse was still fresh in her mind. Bunting drew her into the murder, letting her know what Davies was alleged to have done, harnessing Harvey's anger. She stabbed Davies in the leg with a tool she used in her ceramics class, but it was not enough to kill him. In the end, she and Robert Wagner strangled Davies, while Bunting watched on. They then dumped his body in a hole in the backyard of the house at Waterloo Corner Road.

A year later, Suzanne Allen was proving to be a pain for John Bunting and his gang. Although never proven conclusively, Allen was the most likely person to have told Bunting what Davies was supposed to have done, and so she would at least have suspected what had happened, thus making her a potential threat. Bunting was also getting tired of Allen's crush on him. She had gone to see him in the Riverland at Bakara – the same place Davies had been tortured, where Bunting lived for a time – and her daughter believed Allen had stayed the night in Bunting's room.

Allen disappeared in late 1996, having appeared to be quite depressed in the weeks beforehand. She had learnt that her daughter had become pregnant to a man she herself had been going out with for a while, and she felt betrayed. Bunting would tell James Vlassakis that he had gone around to Allen's home and found her in her bathroom, dead from a heart attack. Even if this was true, Bunting had sensed an opportunity to make some money, and together with Wagner, he had embarked on what he called a 'slice and dice' – the systematic dismemberment of Allen's body.

Suzanne Allen's body would eventually be found in 1999, buried beneath the backyard of 203 Waterloo Corner Road, her dismembered remains stuffed in 11 plastic garbage bags. Pathologists would determine that Allen had had her limbs severed, her head cut off, and her breasts and genitalia mutilated, among other vile treatment. It seemed a lot of work simply to dispose of a body and allow the murder gang to pick up her social security benefits. In the end, Suzanne Allen was the only murder count that juries could not agree on, finding there was enough reasonable doubt as to whether she had been cut up after a heart attack or after her killing.

Bunting referred to the next victim, Michael Gardiner, as 'the biggest homo'. Gardiner was an effeminate young gay man who was an obvious candidate for Bunting's hatred because of his lifestyle. In September 1997, Gardiner disappeared from the property he was housesitting in the northern suburbs of Adelaide. He had been due to move in with his aunt when the woman who normally lived at the house he was staying at returned from holiday. In fact, Bunting and Wagner had seized Gardiner from the house and taken him up to Murray Bridge, a town 80 kilometres to the east. They had gone to a Housing Trust property at 3 Burdekin Avenue, which was where Bunting was now living, with Vlassakis' mother, Elizabeth Harvey.

Bunting and Wagner had taken Gardiner to the shed at the

back of the house and gotten a laugh out of the young man's struggles as they strangled him. Michael Gardiner had the unfortunate distinction of becoming the first victim whose body ended up in a barrel.

Very soon after this murder, Bunting and Wagner struck again, and it was not very surprising that this time the target was none other than Barry Lane. Both men had been harbouring a seething hatred of Lane for some time. Bunting had been biding his time ever since he'd heard from Veronika Tripp that Lane had told her of his part in the disposal of Clinton Trezise's body at Lower Light, and of Bunting's role in the murder of the young man. Although Tripp hadn't believed Lane, she later told a court that John Bunting had eventually admitted to the murder, while ordering the intellectually disabled woman never to tell anyone else of his secret. He also told her that Barry Lane had a 'big mouth' – a virtual death sentence for the man Bunting had always viewed as a sexual freak.

Lane had finally left Bingham Road in 1996 – a furious Wagner having kicked him out when the house was firebombed after allegations that the older man had interfered with a local boy. Lane then moved to the other side of Adelaide, settling in a Housing Trust home in the eastern suburb of Hectorville. He met a young mother called Michelle Bihet, and appeared to be turning over a new leaf. He even got engaged to Bihet, until his past history emerged and the authorities stepped in to ensure that he was not allowed to be alone with her children. The engagement was called off, although they still saw each other. Even as this was going on, however, Lane was falling into old patterns, meeting a young schizophrenic man by the name of Thomas Trevilyan, with whom he started a relationship.

Barry Lane disappeared in October 1997. Weeks later Trevilyan told his disbelieving cousin Lenore Penner that he had been involved in Lane's murder. Lane had been beaten and tortured before he died; his toes were squeezed between pliers, among other indignities. According to James Vlassakis, talking about Lane's murder had no real effect on Bunting and Wagner. 'It's like, you know, when you go to a shop with a young kid and you buy them a toy and the kid gets really excited, it [their reaction] was like that,'

Vlassakis later explained. 'When they squeezed the toenail, Barry screamed more, which obviously hurt more.'

Wagner finally strangled Lane, putting him out of his misery. In Bunting's words, according to Vlassakis, Lane had finally been 'made good'. His body was put in a barrel in the shed at Burdekin Avenue.

Whether or not Thomas Trevilyan was part of the murder will never be known for sure, because he soon became the next victim of the killing spree. After Lane's death, Trevilyan moved in with Wagner and a woman he was having a relationship with, Vicki Mills, into a house at Elizabeth Grove, in Adelaide's north. On Melbourne Cup Day, Mills told Wagner and Bunting that Trevilyan had to go, after he had allegedly chased her daughter with a knife. Trevilyan went for a drive with Bunting and Wagner and was never seen alive again. His body was found the following day, hanging from a tree at Kersbrook in the Adelaide Hills.

The next victim was Gavin Porter, a drug-addicted drifter. Porter was Vlassakis' best friend – the pair had even received treatment together at the same methadone program. In late 1997, the two men moved to Murray Bridge to live with John Bunting, Elizabeth Harvey and others.

Bunting and Wagner tried to strangle Porter at Burdekin Avenue in April 1998. Their initial attempt failed, when the rope got caught around the helpless victim's nose. They eventually succeeded, however, and stashed the body in the shed at the Murray Bridge house. It was in this shed, confronted by the body of Gavin Porter on the floor, plus the decomposing remains of Lane and Gardiner in a barrel, that James Vlassakis finally realised that the stories his father figure had told him of murder were true.

Vlassakis' half-brother Troy Youde was the next to die, and the first victim in whose murder Vlassakis played an active role. The troubled teenager had a love–hate relationship with Youde, who had sexually abused him years before. In August of 1998, at the Burdekin Avenue house, Vlassakis was woken by Bunting, Wagner and Mark Haydon; they went to Youde's room, armed with jackhandles, and surrounded the sleeping man before beginning a lethal assault at Bunting's signal.

They handcuffed, beat and tortured Youde in the bathroom. Vlassakis tried to put Youde out of his misery by strangling him, because he couldn't handle seeing his brother slowly and agonisingly slaughtered. The rope broke, but eventually Robert Wagner finished him off. Vlassakis later testified: 'John said, "We better make sure Troy's dead." So Robert stood on Troy's chest, and the air from Troy's lungs came out of his nose and it made a grunting noise. John and Robert laughed and Robert kept pushing on Troy's chest.' Youde's body would end up in a barrel in the bank vault, after being stored at Murray Bridge and other places.

The death toll continued to rise. Fred Brooks, the nephew of Elizabeth Haydon (Mark's wife and a later victim), disappeared in September 1998. Despised by Bunting, he was tortured horrifically over an extended period before finally being killed after an ordeal lasting a number of hours. With Vlassakis again taking part, Brooks was handcuffed and thumbcuffed. He had a 'smiley face' burnt into his forehead with a lighter, had lit cigarettes put in his nose and ear, and received electric shocks to the genitals from the variac machine. Water was injected into his testicles by syringe, and sparklers were inserted into the eye of his penis and left to burn down.

The next man to die, Gary O'Dwyer, lived near Bunting in Murray Bridge. Bunting took a set against the intellectually and physically disabled man, who had the misfortune to look very similar to the recently deceased Troy Youde. Bunting got Vlassakis to persuade O'Dwyer to invite the two of them and Wagner over for drinks. Wagner eventually grabbed O'Dwyer, who was then beaten by all three men before being killed. His bank account was accessed and, like a number of other victims, a voice recording was made on the night of his death. Some of these recordings were later played down the phone to the deceased's family and friends to convince them the victims were still alive.

These voices from the dead would also be played in court during the main trial. It is obvious that O'Dwyer is in pain when he is made to say: 'I'm Gary O'Dwyer, I'm a paedophile. Now I'm really happy, I've had treatment.' A voice identified as John Bunting's then asks, 'Did you like the treatment you got?' To which O'Dwyer responds, 'No.'

After admitting that the treatment hurt, O'Dwyer is asked, 'Are you ever going to fuck another little girl or boy?' He answers: 'No, I'm not. I know I will get hurt if I hurt someone else.'

The next victim was Elizabeth Haydon, a woman Bunting is alleged to have referred to as 'Scabs 'n' Pus'. Shortly before her disappearance, Mark Haydon told Bunting that he had revealed to his wife the story of the murder and disposal of the body of Clinton Trezise. Bunting said nothing, but later told Vlassakis that this was 'a problem'.

On a Saturday night in November 1998, Bunting and Wagner organised to get Elizabeth's sister, Jodie Elliott (the mother of previous victim Fred Brooks), to take Mark out of the house the couple lived in at Smithfield Plains, in Adelaide's north. The story given to Elliott was that they needed to get Haydon out so that his birthday present could be delivered to the house.

While they were gone, Bunting and Wagner murdered Elizabeth in her bathroom. When Elliott and Haydon returned, Bunting spun a tale about her making a sexual pass at him, then stomping off in a huff. By the Monday morning, Elizabeth Haydon's children sensed something was wrong and wagged school to visit their uncle and aunt, who lodged a missing persons report a couple of days later. This brought the police into play, and their extensive investigations into the Haydon household – which led them to speak to Bunting and Wagner as well – freaked out the murder gang.

The presence of the authorities had a double effect. Firstly, Bunting and Wagner quickly shifted the dead bodies, which had been held at Murray Bridge and then in the shed at Mark Haydon's home at Smithfield Plains, to a country property owned by (innocent) friends of the killers. The other effect was to stall any further attempted murders for the time being, to allow time for the trail to go cold.

The friends at the country property were upset by the smell of the barrels, which Bunting had claimed contained 'happy roos', or kangaroo carcasses. Bunting never managed to find another home for them, so when the family moved from the property to Snowtown in January 1999, the barrels went with them, packed in Haydon's four-wheel drive. Eventually, the friends' protests forced Bunting and co to move the barrels. As a result, Bunting and Haydon leased the former State Bank building at Snowtown, and they moved the barrels into the vault in late January.

The final victim was James Vlassakis' 21-year-old step-brother, David Johnson. The murder occurred on Mother's Day, 9 May 1999, after Bunting had instructed Vlassakis to lure Johnson up to Snowtown with a ruse that there was a computer going cheap somewhere north of Adelaide. Vlassakis then drove up in a car with Johnson, knowing every step of the way that his step-brother was heading to his slaughter.

The pair arrived in Snowtown and entered the bank, at which point Wagner seized Johnson from behind as Bunting handcuffed him. Johnson was beaten and tortured, and another 'voices from the dead' tape was made. The victim's keycard and personal identification number were stolen, and Bunting told his two accomplices to access the account at a roadhouse half an hour from Snowtown.

Wagner and Vlassakis were unsuccessful in their attempts to withdraw any money, and when they returned, David Johnson lay dead on the floor of the bank. Bunting claimed Johnson had grabbed a Stanley knife and fought for his life until Bunting strangled him. Vlassakis and Wagner then cut up Johnson's body so it could fit into a barrel in the vault.

That night, Wagner cut a slice of flesh from the body and kept it to one side. When the trio later went to another address in Snowtown, Wagner fried the piece in a pan, and he and Bunting allegedly ate it.

Authorities got their first real break through the Barry Lane missing persons case, when they checked Lane's bank account and found it had been accessed, after his disappearance, at a service station in the north of Adelaide. After setting up extra cameras there, they got footage of Robert Wagner accessing the account again. Bunting's name came up as an associate.

The Elizabeth Haydon missing persons case saw police close in on the killers. They made Mark Haydon's four-wheel drive a 'vehicle of interest', and it was the spotting of this vehicle in the driveway of a Snowtown house in May 1999 that led them to speak with a man who pointed them to the old bank building. There, they made their grim discovery.

Thanks to information already gathered in relation to the

missing persons cases, the police were able to swoop in the very next day, when arrest teams raided the homes of Bunting, Wagner and Haydon. The three men were taken into custody and charged with one count of murder of a person unknown between 1 August 1993 and 20 May 1999.

People wouldn't know the full extent of what had happened to the Snowtown victims until the arrest of Vlassakis, then aged 19, on 2 June. James Spyridon Vlassakis would go on to plead guilty in 2001 to four killings and turn star witness for the Crown, an action that saw his eventual sentence reduced from 42 years non-parole to 26 years non-parole. The other result of Vlassakis' co-operation with the authorities was that it brought to light some of the most shocking tales of torture ever heard in an Australian court. The young man spilled information on everything from the location of further bodies (at 203 Waterloo Corner Road) to the stench of death in the barrels, to the sounds of the victims' screams.

Those responsible for the killings and their concealment after the fact – Bunting, Wagner, Vlassakis and Haydon – would later be described by police investigators as a group that 'preyed on itself'. The men also seemed to live in their own world, a world in which the shocking was commonplace and vulnerable people were routinely singled out for brutal slaying. The victims were restrained and beaten, forced in many cases to address their attackers by names such as 'Lord Sir', 'God' and 'Master', before being tortured to the brink of death. During the ordeals, the murder gang celebrated their power over their captives by playing a song by the band Live, 'Selling the Drama', which has the chorus: 'Hey, now, we won't be raped, we won't be scarred like that.'

After the murders, the men would impersonate their victims in Centrelink interviews and continually withdraw funds from their bank accounts, stealing nearly $100,000 in social security benefits from eight of their victims before being caught. Prosecutors would later say that by 1998, Bunting and the rest of the murder gang were 'in the business of killing'.

On 3 July 1999, Wagner, Bunting and Haydon were jointly charged with 10 counts of murder. This number was raised to 12 after James Vlassakis agreed to turn star witness. John Justin Bunting and Robert Joe Wagner were tried together, in 2002:

Bunting was found guilty of 11 murders; Wagner, who had pleaded guilty to three of the murders pre-trial, was found guilty of another seven. They each received mandatory life sentences under South Australian law, without any parole period.

Neither Bunting nor Wagner showed any emotion as the judge handed down the court's ruling. Marcus Johnson, the father of the final victim, told reporters outside the court, 'I feel there's no remorse there, none at all.' Although the judge was not allowed by law to mark their files 'never to be released', both men are almost certain to die in jail.

At Mark Haydon's trial, which began in December 2004, he faced eight charges, relating to the bodies found inside the barrels in the bank vault, since his signature was on the rental lease. The jury unanimously convicted him of five separate counts of assisting Bunting, Wagner and/or Vlassakis in five of the murders; they failed to reach a verdict on a sixth count of assisting offenders in another murder. Despite five days' deliberation, the jury could not agree on whether Haydon was actually a killer. They could not reach a verdict over two counts of murder relating to the 1998 deaths of his wife Elizabeth and Troy Youde.

The Office of the Director of Public Prosecutions eventually dropped these murder charges without a retrial, and Haydon pleaded guilty to two more charges of assisting offenders, relating to the deaths of his wife and Youde. On 24 February 2006, more than six-and-a-half years after the initial discoveries and arrests, Mark Ray Haydon was sentenced by Justice John Sulan to 25 years' jail, with a non-parole period of 18 years. Backdated to the time of his arrest, the sentence means that Haydon will be eligible for parole in May 2017.

City of Churches or not, it seems, Adelaide and its surroundings remained the Murder Capital of Australia.

AUTHOR'S NOTE: The whole story of this case can be found in *The Snowtown Murders* by Andrew McGarry, the award-winning journalist who covered the case for *The Australian* from the day the story broke.

CHAPTER 30

Mummy Dearest

Kathleen Megan Folbigg
Newcastle, New South Wales, 1989–99

Statistics tell us that there are far fewer female serial killers than there are male ones. Throughout the world the average is about 93 per cent males, 5 per cent females, the other 2 per cent being married couples or the like. Yet of the 30 cases of serial murder in Australia since 1822, there have been 28 male offenders and nine females – an average of almost 30 per cent, which is a good 25 per cent above the world average.

Why? There is no logical reason, other than perhaps that they *could* commit murder so they did. And given that the known cases of Australian female serial killers are so widely spread apart over the course of the 185 years since 1822 and so diversified in their manner, there never will be a generic explanation.

Which makes it all the more difficult to understand the crimes of Kathleen Megan Folbigg. Like the previous recorded case of serial murder by a female in Australia – Helen Patricia Moore in 1979–80 – Kathleen Folbigg murdered children. But unlike Helen Moore, the children were Folbigg's own.

To find another case of serial maternal filicide (the murder of her own child or children by the mother) in Australian history, we have to go back 100 years or so to the case of Martha Needle, who between 1885 and 1894 murdered her husband and their three children for the insurance money. At least Needle had a reason to kill her family – a terrible one, but a reason just the same. Tragically, it seems as though Kathleen Folbigg didn't have a reason on earth to kill her little children.

Even in the early days of his inquiries, Detective Inspector Bernie Ryan had his suspicions that the circumstances surrounding the deaths of Folbigg's four infant children over a 10-year period would become a major investigation. But, as he has said, 'Not in my wildest dreams did I imagine how it would turn out.' So he could never have imagined that Kathleen Folbigg would become one of the most despised of all Australian serial killers.

Born Kathleen Megan Marlborough, the woman whose unspeakable crimes numbed the nation was just 18 months old on the December evening in 1969 when her father fatally stabbed her mother 24 times in the street outside their home in the Sydney suburb of Annandale. When her father was sent to prison, Kathleen was placed in an orphanage, where she remained until she was fostered out at the age of three to a family who lived in the Newcastle suburb of Kotara.

Kathleen didn't find out the truth about her parents until later in life. She went on to write the following in her diary: *So many things point to the fact that I'm not meant to be. Unwanted at birth. Shuffled about for whatever reason.* Another passage reads, *Obviously I am my father's daughter.* It would be the diary entries that eventually led to Kathleen's arrest, in April 2001.

According to her foster sister, Lea Bown, 'When Kathy found out about her birth mother, I don't think any of us realised what emotion or what feelings Kathy had, because Kathy is very good at keeping things so deep inside her.' Lea was 17 when Kathleen joined her family. 'She was this little girl with blonde curly hair, and the biggest smile,' she says. 'Just a really happy little girl who craved love.'

Having always wanted a sister, Lea – who had only recently got married – was thrilled to have little Kathleen around. So too, it seemed, were her parents. But that all changed once Lea had her first child, a son. 'He became the centre of Mum and Dad's world,' she admits, 'and Kath was virtually pushed aside . . . There were big changes in Kathy from then on.' Lea distanced herself from her mother because she felt her mother's treatment of young Kathleen was 'unfair'.

Kathleen left school in 1982, when she was just 15. With limited education, she moved from one minimum-wage job to another before marrying 25-year-old steel worker Craig Folbigg at the age of 20. The couple settled in the Newcastle suburb of Mayfield and Kathleen fell pregnant within a year. Her first child, a son named Caleb, was born in February 1989. The child was dead just 20 days later.

Craig woke up at 3.30 a.m. on 20 February to the sound of his wife screaming: 'My baby! Something is wrong with my baby!' The official cause of death was listed as Sudden Infant Death Syndrome (SIDS).

Kathleen fell pregnant again just seven months later, and gave birth to another son in June 1990. An entry in her diary reads: *This was the day Patrick Allan David Folbigg was born. I had mixed feelings this day – whether or not I was gonna cope as a mother or whether I was gonna get stressed out like I did last time.*

Despite these doubts, life seemed good for Kathleen and her family. But just four months later, at 3.30 a.m. on 19 October 1990, Craig again woke to the sound of his wife screaming. Rushing into the infant's room to find his wife standing over Patrick's cot, Craig noticed that the small child was still breathing, albeit faintly. The distressed father administered CPR until an ambulance arrived. According to a police statement, the four-month-old did regain consciousness, but was later found to have epilepsy and to be blind.

The infant lived for another four months. On the morning of 13 February 1991, Craig received a call at work from Kathleen, telling him, 'It's happened again.' He rushed home, arriving at the same time as the ambulances. Young Patrick was taken to hospital but was dead on arrival. According to an autopsy, an epileptic fit resulted in death by an 'acute asphyxiating event'.

Soon after the loss of their second child, the Folbiggs moved to the town of Thornton, north-west of Newcastle, and decided to have another baby. A daughter named Sarah was born in October 1992. According to everyone involved, Sarah was healthy and happy for the first 11 months of her life. Then, as Detective Ryan would later explain, 'Kathleen says she got up in the middle of the night to go to the toilet, and she discovered her daughter in the bed, deceased.' The official cause of death was once again put down to SIDS, although the chairman of the world SIDS organisation, who conducted the post-mortem, noticed small abrasions on Sarah's chin, as well as 'something unusual' about her throat.

Kathleen and Craig soon decided to move again, to Singleton

in the Hunter Valley, north of Newcastle. Two years later they were expecting their fourth child. Their second daughter, Laura, was born in August 1997 and, having been declared healthy by medical authorities, was bought home after three days. According to Lea Bown, 'Kathy idolised Laura. She really was a fantastic kid. Kathy and Laura bonded, as far as I was concerned – bonded really well.'

But 19 months later, Laura caught a cold. At 12.05 p.m. on 1 March 1999 Kathleen called an ambulance after Laura had allegedly stopped breathing. The medical team arrived to find Kathleen performing CPR on her young daughter, but when they examined Laura they realised that she wasn't breathing and had no pulse.

An autopsy found that the child was too old to have died from SIDS. The cause of death was recorded as 'undetermined' and a police investigation was ordered. Detective Sergeant Bernie Ryan was assigned to lead the case. When he learnt that Laura was the fourth Folbigg child to die in similar circumstances, alarm bells rang, naturally. But the investigation would still be an uphill battle, because, as Ryan himself observed, 'it's very, very hard to believe that a mother can kill her children.'

By this time Kathleen had just left Craig; she moved out with only a few of her possessions. In a letter to Lea dated 15 April 1999, Kathleen wrote: *No one knew about the rough time that Craig and I were having holding it together . . . Us as a married couple has run its course. There's too much pressure, sadness, depression, etc, for a relationship to bear.*

When Craig Folbigg found his wife's diaries in a bedside drawer, the case finally took a major turn. He called the authorities and informed them that he wanted to talk. 'Craig had told us that Kathleen continually became stressed with the children,' says Detective Ryan. 'The morning of Laura's death, Kathleen had screamed at Laura and held her fists up to her head – so loudly and violently that it caused Laura to be scared to go near her . . . And then finally he said, "I've found my wife keeps a diary, and there's suspicious entries in that."'

Indeed, many of the entries were of concern. *With Sarah, all I wanted was her to shut up. And one day, she did*, Kathleen had written, as well as noting her own mood swings with the comment *I don't know, how do I conquer this? Help is what I want.* Another entry states, *I feel like the worst mother on this earth.* To use Bernie Ryan's words: 'Her diaries have been written for her only. They are the deepest look into her soul that you could get.'

The pages were filled with Kathleen's doubts about her skills as a mother and concerns about her inability to breastfeed, despite repeated attempts with all four children. She also detailed her fears that her husband would leave her, based on his teasing about her weight and what she called his 'roving eye'. One entry reads: *Must lose extra weight or he will be even less in love with me than he is now. I know that physical appearance means everything to him.*

When pregnant with Laura, Kathleen wrote: *On a good note, Craig said last night he accepts that I'm not going to be skinny again. That's wonderful, but I know deep in my heart he wants his skinny wife back.* More worrying were the stories of how stress made her 'do terrible things', and that she felt 'flashes of rage, resentment and hatred' towards her children.

Once the authorities saw the diaries, they decided they did indeed have a murder case on their hands. Still, it wouldn't be an easy one to prove. Detective Ryan took two years to pull together an argument that he believed would provide a conviction. On 19 April 2001, Kathleen Megan Folbigg was arrested and charged with murdering her four children.

At the two-month trial, at Sydney's Darlinghurst Supreme Court, the prosecution portrayed Kathleen as a woman 'preoccupied with her own life and looks, more interested in going to the gym and nightclubs than in looking after her own children'. Lea Brown has backed up this statement, commenting that, as much as Kathleen had wanted to have these children, 'Kathy likes to sleep in, Kathy likes to go out and party. That was her thing that she did nearly every Friday night, and the children simply got in her way.'

In short, the prosecution asserted that Folbigg murdered her four infant children by smothering them because she couldn't deal with her parental responsibilities.

Lea told the court about Kathleen's behaviour at Laura's funeral, saying her foster sister had changed quite suddenly that day – 'from crying to being a totally different person. She was happy, laughing, enjoying a party.' The court also heard how the accused had once pinned Laura to her highchair and tried to force-feed her, before dumping the infant on the floor with the words 'Go to your fucking father!'

It took the jury just under eight hours to find Kathleen Megan Folbigg guilty of murdering three of her four children and the manslaughter of the other. She was taken to Mulawa Women's Detention Centre and placed in protective isolation.

In August 2002 she returned to court and was sentenced to 40 years in prison with a non-parole period of 30 years. But on 17 February 2005, in the NSW Court of Criminal Appeal, Justice Brian Sully reduced Folbigg's maximum sentence by 10 years and her non-parole period by five. Her minimum sentence became 25 years and she will be due for parole in 2028. Justice Sully said in the judgment that the original sentence was too high when compared with similar cases: 'I am of the opinion that the overall results of a head sentence of 40 years and a non-parole period of 30 years are so crushing as to manifest cover error.'

Given that Kathleen Folbigg was found sane at her trial, it wasn't madness that drove her to kill her children. If she had been mad, then perhaps she could be forgiven. But she committed crimes that to any parent (especially a mother) are unimaginable. And for that she will spend the best part of her adult life in protective custody – a 'rock spider', as they call child-killers in jail – with a price on her head.

Acknowledgements

from the first edition of *Australia's Serial Killers*

Special thanks to:
Amanda Hemmings, who acquired the project for Pan Macmillan
Beth Martin of the Albany Historical Society
Bob Stapleton, NSW Corrective Services
Dr Rod Milton, forensic psychiatrist and serial-killer profiler
Julie Nekich, editor, Pan Macmillan
Professor Paul Wilson, Dean of the Bond University, Queensland
Tom Gilliatt, publisher, Pan Macmillan

Allan Sharpe, Australian Historian
Alona Wooley, research for Alexander Pearce
Ariette Taylor, producer, *The Eye of Martha Needle*, *La Mama*
Ben Kidd, editorial assistant
Betty Terwindt and Noel Inglis, Albany Historical Society
Bill Bullock, Karrakatta Cemetary, Western Australia
Bill Power, SA Corrective Services
Charles Wooley, *60 Minutes*, Nine Network
Department of Public Prosecutions of NSW
Diane and Steve Meads, editorial assistants
Doreen Peace, Berrima Court House
Dr Graham George, psychiatrist
Dr Judith Cockram, criminologist, Edith Cowan University, WA
Elena Lonergan, *Sydney Morning Herald*, research
Estelle Blackburn, author of *Broken Lives*
Georgia Gowing, SA Courts Administration Authority
Irene Tritton, Fremantle Cemetery, Western Australia
Jennifer Greene, researcher and editorial assistant
Jenny Mouzos, Australian Institute of Criminology
Joseph Morris Snr, deceased legendary *Daily Mirror* crime reporter
Karen Collier, Library, Australian Institute of Criminology
Leanne Hardyman, NSW Corrective Services
Luke Morfese, West Australian Newspapers
Mark Llewellyn, *60 Minutes*, Nine Network
Maureen Doughty, *Sydney Morning Herald*, research
Robyn Fisher, editorial assistant

Roger Carstens, Queensland Corrective Services
Steve Barrett, *60 Minutes* producer, Nine Network
Steve Warnock, freelance crime writer
Tim Hickie, Governor, Long Bay Prison Hospital
Victoria Hayes, Channel 7, Sydney
Vikki Petraitis, author of *The Frankston Murders*

Bibliography

Blackburn, Estelle, *Broken Lives*, Stellar, Perth, 1998.

Blundell, Nigel, *Encyclopedia of Serial Killers*, PRC, London, 1996.

Bouda, Simon, *Crimes that Shocked Australia*, Bantam, Sydney, 1991.

Connelly, Michael, *Concrete Blond*, Brilliance, London, 1994.

Douglas, John, and Olshaker, Mark, *Journey into Darkness*, Arrow, London, 1998.

Douglas, John, and Olshaker, Mark, *Mindhunter*, Mandarin, London, 1996.

Douglas, John, and Olshaker, Mark, *Obsession*, Pocket, New York, 1998.

Encel, Vivien, and Sharpe, Alan, *Murder!*, Kingsclear, Sydney, 1997.

Harris, Thomas, *Hannibal*, Heinemann, London, 1999.

Harris, Thomas, *Red Dragon*, Bantam, New York, 1981.

Harris, Thomas, *The Silence of the Lambs*, Mandarin, London, 1989.

Hickey, E.W., *Serial Murderers and their Victims*, 2nd edn, Belmont University, California, 1997.

Holledge, James, *Australia's Wicked Women*, Horwitz, Sydney, 1963.

Jones, Richard Glyn (ed.), *Killer Women*, Robinson, London, 1993.

Kelleher, Michael D., and Kelleher, C.L., *Murder Most Rare*, Dell, New York, 1998.

Kidd, Paul B., *Never to be Released*, Pan Macmillan, Sydney, 1993.

Kidd, Paul B., *Never to be Released Volume 2*, HarperCollins, Sydney, 1999.

Lane, Brian, and Gregg, Wilfred, *The Encyclopedia of Serial Killers*, Headline, London, 1992.

Lucas, Norman, *The Sex Killers*, Virgin, London, 1997.

Martin, Beth, *Albany's Brush with a Mass Murderer*, Albany Historical Society, Albany, 1998.

Mercer, Neil, *Fate – Inside the Backpacker Murders*, Random House, Sydney, 1997.

Miller, James, *Don't Call Me Killer*, Victoria, Melbourne, 1984.

Mykyta, Anne-Marie, *It's a Long Way to Truro*, McPhee Gribble, Melbourne, 1981.

Newton, Michael, *The Encyclopedia of Serial Killers*, Facts on File, New York, 1999.

Norris, Joel, *Serial Killers*, Anchor, London, 1989.

Patterson, James, *Cat and Mouse*, Headline, London, 1997.

Petraitis, Vikki, *The Frankston Murders*, Nivar, Melbourne, 1995.

Phillips, Conrad, *The Cry of the Dingo*, A. Barker, Sydney, 1956.

The Problems with Defining Serial Murder, uncredited university paper

Ressler, Robert K., and Shachtman, T., *I Have Lived in the Monster*, Pocket, London, 1998.

Ressler, Robert K., and Shachtman, T., *Whoever Fights Monsters*, Simon & Schuster, London, 1993.

Ritchie, Jean, *Myra Hindley*, Angus & Robertson, London, 1998.

Russell, Sue, *Damsel of Death*, Virgin, London, 1992.

Segrave, Kerry, *Women Serial and Mass Murderers*, McFarland, Jefferson, North Carolina, 1992.

Sharpe, Alan, *Crime and Punishment*, Kingsclear, Sydney, 1997.

Sharpe, Allan, *Crimes that Shocked Australia*, Currawong, Sydney, 1982.

Shears, Richard, *Highway to Nowhere*, HarperCollins, Sydney, 1996.

Simpson, Lindsay, and Harvey, Sandra, *Killer Next Door*, Random House, Sydney, 1994.

Small, W.G., *Reminiscences of Jail Life in Berrima*, A.K. Murray, Sydney, 1923.

Sprod, Daniel, *Alexander Pearce of Macquarie Harbour*, Cat and Fiddle, Hobart, 1977.

Therry, Roger, *Reminiscences of Thirty Years Residence in New South Wales and Victoria*, Sydney University Press, Sydney, 1974.

Whittaker, Mark, and Kennedy, Les, *Sins of the Brother*, Pan Macmillan, Sydney, 1998.

Wilson, Colin, and Seaman, Donald, *The Serial Killers*, Virgin, London, 1992.

Wilson, Prof. Paul, *Murder of the Innocents – Child Killers and their Victims*, Rigby, Adelaide, 1985.

Writer, Larry, Barrett, Steve, and Bouda, Simon, *The Garden of Evil*, Ironbark, Sydney, 1992.

OTHER SOURCES

Adelaide Advertiser, 1892

Australian Advertiser, 1892

Australian, 1842

Colonial Observer, 1842

Daily Mirror, Sydney

Daily Telegraph, Sydney

Hobart Town Gazette, 1824

Melbourne Age

Sunday Age, Melbourne

Sydney Gazette, 1842

Tasmanian State Library

Nine Network, *60 Minutes* Milat family interview by Richard
Carlton, and Paul Onions interview by Charles Wooley
West Australian
Channel 7, *Witness* story on Archibald Beattie McCafferty
Weekend News, Western Australia, 1963
Mitchell Library, Sydney

The Crisford family and staff at Dr What's Video
Emporium in Bondi Junction, Sydney, which carries
Australia's largest range of serial-killer movies and
documentaries, was the source of all video research used
in this book unless otherwise stated.